The Dog Who Ate the Truffle

The Dog Who Ate the Truffle

A MEMOIR OF STORIES AND RECIPES FROM UMBRIA

SUZANNE CARREIRO

THOMAS DUNNE BOOKS
ST. MARTIN'S PRESS 🏲 NEW YORK

THOMAS DUNNE BOOKS.
An imprint of St. Martin's Press.

www.thomasdunnebooks.com
www.stmartins.com

Maps by Adriano Bottaccioli
Photographs by the author. Captions appear on page 357.
Designed by Jessica Shatan Heslin / Studio Shatan, Inc.

Library of Congress Cataloging-in-Publication Data

Carreiro, Suzanne.
   The dog who ate the truffle : a memoir of stories and recipes from Umbria / Suzanne Carreiro.—1st ed.
      p. cm.
   Includes bibliographical references and index.
   ISBN 978-0-312-57140-5 (alk. paper)
 1. Cookery, Italian.   2. Umbria (Italy)—Social life and customs.   I. Title.
   TX723.C2966 2010
   641.5945—dc22

                                                          2010013057

First Edition: August 2010

10   9   8   7   6   5   4   3   2   1

In memory of my mother, Virginia Carreiro

To my son, Jacob Fenston,
my "adopted" Umbrian son, Mario Ramaccioni,
his partner, Michela,
and Mario's mother, Paola,
and his aunt Silvia

CONTENTS

ACKNOWLEDGMENTS

To write this book I relied on the help and encouragement of my family and several dozen friends—both in the States and in Umbria. The book might have been just a cookbook if I hadn't been so fortunate as to land in the lap of the Ramaccioni family. This generous clan who "adopted" me added richness to my experiences and gave life to the book. Mario Ramaccioni taught me Italian—and he and his partner, Michela, were the best neighbors I've ever had. Mario's mother, Paola, and his aunt Silvia shared family traditions and recipes. Silvia provided the roof over my head.

Thanks to my agent, Nancy Crossman, for believing in me and in my idea—and for placing the book. And *mille grazie* to my editor, Katie Gilligan, at Thomas Dunne Books for falling in love with the book and making its publication a reality.

Thanks to Umbrian food historian and artist Adriano Bottacioli, who donated the book's two beautiful Umbrian maps. Both Adriano and cookbook author Rita Boini generously shared their knowledge of the food history and Umbrian cuisine with me. Thanks to all of the Umbrian friends, cooks, winemakers, farmers, and artisans who welcomed me into their lives, homes, and businesses. And thanks to the rest of you in Umbria—my doctor, techie, photographer—who came to my rescue when I needed you.

Thanks to my son, Jacob, who encouraged me to spend a year in Umbria to work on the book. *Grazie* to my friend Ann Hogue, who helped me finish my book proposal, and to Vicki Roberts Russell, who helped me pack up to move to Umbria. Thanks to Paige Dotson and Michelle Wing for taking care of my house and cats while I was in Umbria, and to Rita Held for handling my mail. And to Kim Farmer, who did my banking and kept my car running.

And thanks to Maria Cianci for letting me tag along with her on my first trip to Italy. She introduced me to her Italian relatives, including her Tuscan cousin Liana, who changed the way I cook.

I am honored to write the foreword for Suzanne's Umbrian cookbook for several reasons. First, I recognize the value of the great work she has produced. Also, it makes me happy to contribute to the understanding and appreciation of Italy's cultural variety. I believe this fine book will help do that. And I appreciate Suzanne as a person. We met through the agency that represents our wines in the United States.

I live in Tuscany and operate my family's winery, Badia a Coltibuono, and our cooking school at the winery in Chianti, started by my mother, Lorenza de' Medici. Since I live in Tuscany, one might think I would not be happy with the book's attention to Umbria. But in Italy we are all about differences. Each region has a strong local culture, and I believe this diversity has an important role in shaping the Italian image. Indeed Umbria is coming out of Tuscany's shadow. Today Umbria is not so much perceived as Tuscany's lesser-known cousin. Tuscany will always be beloved by people from around the world, but I am sure there is enough room in people's hearts to include many other beautiful places. Among these places certainly Umbria should become a favorite.

The Dog Who Ate the Truffle has a lot to say to anyone who would like to travel to Umbria and to all of those who have been there already. The book has many aspects that make it extremely accurate and passionate. Before undertaking this endeavor, Suzanne spent a great deal of time learning to speak Italian like an Umbrian. This is not a secondary detail, since she spent months living in Umbertide, studying several hours a day with a private tutor, fully immersing herself in Umbrian culture. She returned to Umbertide for a year to learn recipes directly from Umbria's home and professional cooks, traveling to their own kitchens in villages and towns around the region. She studied with many different people in order to provide a vast culinary perspective and to better appreciate the cuisine's nuances. Suzanne tested and retested the recipes, using both American and Umbrian ingredients when there might be a difference in outcome. *The Dog Who Ate the Truffle* will appeal to both the novice and the serious cook and has much to offer to all those who appreciate regional authenticity and culinary tradition.

Not only did Suzanne live as part of an Umbrian family, but she also befriended young and old cooks, artisan butchers, hunters, farmers, winemakers, and many others. She therefore has been able to write an up-close, richly detailed memoir. The personal stories she tells are as much a part of the cuisine's essence as are the crops the locals grow and the family dishes they prepare. Suzanne illustrates Umbrian life in words and images that render its splendor and uniqueness.

I am always very touched by anyone's immense love for Italy. Suzanne's book conveys that affection and is a welcome contribution that will help strengthen, deepen, preserve, and disseminate an understanding of Italian culture. We appreciate this love and support.

—EMANUELA STUCCHI PRINETTI

Umbria

CITTÀ DI CASTELLO

UMBERTIDE

Romeggio

GUBBIO

GUALDO TADINO

LAKE TRASIMENO

PERUGIA

MAGIONE

ASSISI

COLFIORITO

Città d. Pieve

Torgiano

Deruta

FOLIGNO

MONTEFALCO

TREVI

CASTELLUCCIO

ORVIETO

TODI

NORCIA

SPOLETO

CASCIA

TERNI

ADRIANO BOTTACCIOLI 2009

North Umbria

South Umbria

ADRIANO BOTTACCIOLI 2009

Everyone wonders how I came to write a book about Umbria. When I started my research the region was relatively unknown to Americans—and to me! I had breezed through Assisi (in Umbria) on my first trip to Italy in 1994 with my friend Maria's cousins, but we spent more time in Tuscany with her cousin Liana. Watching Liana cook for a few days transformed the way I cooked when I got home. I watched her turn a simple zucchini into a delicious sauce for pasta. I was amazed that to her "a little extra virgin olive oil" meant an inch-deep layer in the pan. Everything Liana cooked was simple but delicious.

During my long culinary career, I had always wanted to publish a cookbook.

I had written for newspapers and magazines, but my life as a single mother kept me too busy to write a book. Finally, with my son off to college, I decided to get away. My teenage dream of becoming fluent in another language and of immersing myself in a foreign culture was still with me. I had already started studying Italian, so I decided on Italy.

I knew Liana and her family, and I had worked with folks in a Tuscan winery, so Toscana was a natural choice. But rental prices were too high in the region, so I took the advice of my Tuscan winemaker friend, who told me to go to Umbria. Rentals would be cheaper and Umbrian wines were gaining renown, he said. I perused the cookbook section of my favorite bookstores. There were no Umbrian cookbooks. Next I found *un appartamento* on the outskirts of Umbertide in Umbria's Upper Tiber River valley.

When I settled into my country apartment in Umbertide, things fell into place. My next door neighbor Mario agreed to tutor me in Italian—and soon I was good friends with his entire family. Paola, Mario's mother, and her sister Silvia became my best friends. When I wasn't studying, I was visiting wineries and searching for good cooks. I ended up staying in Umbertide for five months. By then I loved Mario like a son, and I was infatuated with Umbria.

When I returned to Umbertide a few years later to stay for a year, Mario, his partner, Michela, and his family welcomed me like a lost *parente* (relative). During those twelve months of living as part of Mario's family, I cooked with dozens of people and finished collecting recipes for my book.

I introduce you to Mario and his family in the first two chapters of the book. And then you'll bump into them again in later chapters. You'll meet the rest of the cooks—young and old, home cooks and professionals. And you'll meet a few friends—Il Simba, the legendary truffle hunter, and his dog Sara, who ate the truffle, are among them. I so loved my time in Umbertide—the language, culture, traditions, and cuisine—that what I had originally envisioned as a cookbook turned into a story-filled book with authentic recipes. While the book is a fairly comprehensive look at Umbrian cuisine, it would take a lifetime—and several volumes—to catalog all the culinary nuances and recipes of this region, which is about half the size of the San Francisco Bay Area! I invite you to share my culinary journey. Read on. *Buon appetito!*

How Umbrians Eat

If you enjoy spending time at the table savoring good food and wine, you'll be happy in Umbria. Everyone is passionate about good food—and eating well.

Lunch and dinner are important times of the day, but breakfast is often rushed, as families head out the door for work and school. Even on weekends, *la prima colazione* (breakfast) is light and usually sweet—*un cornetto* (an Italian croissant) or cookies dunked into caffè latte or cappuccino. A mid-morning snack is common—a sweet roll or *panino* (roll) filled with prosciutto.

By custom lunch is the main meal, served around one o'clock. Whenever possible, people return home from work or school for a multicourse meal. But the number of workers with long commutes is on the increase—those unhappy folks have a sandwich or plate of pasta near work. Dinner is usually served between eight and eight thirty. If lunch was the main meal, dinner is light—soup or pasta or hearty salads, pizza or bread with cold cuts and cheese, or a combination of plates.

Many families still hold sacred the traditional Sunday *pranzo* (lunch). Everyone in the immediate family is expected to come. A classic *pranzo* has several courses, and each dish is equally important—there is no main dish. A celebratory lunch can last for hours and feature many courses. Since you (as a guest) never know how many dishes will come to the table, it is hard to know how much to eat!

In homes, meals are served family-style. Sliced salt-free bread and bottles of mineral water and wine (often homemade), and sometimes soda pop, are available on the table. The meal starts with an antipasto (literally "before meal"), typically crostini (sliced bread topped with something savory). Next up is the *primo piatto* (first plate)—pasta, soup, polenta, risotto, or gnocchi. Grilled (preferred), roasted, or braised meat, sausage, or poultry usually makes up the *secondo piatto* (second plate). Meat servings tend to be smaller than American portions. *Contorni* (side dishes)—vegetables and potatoes—are served along with the *secondo piatto*. Salad is served with the side dishes or after the *secondo piatto*. A bowl of fruit usually signals the end of the meal, but sometimes cheese and dessert follow the fruit course. Especially when there are guests, dessert wine—*passito* or *vinsanto*—is often paired with the cheese and/or the dessert. Liqueurs are served to aid digestion. When the dessert dishes are cleared, espresso is offered—served with sugar but without milk. And if you smoke—as so many Italians still do—it's time for a cigarette.

UMBRIA'S MICROCUISINES

Over the last dozen years of eating my way around Italy—from the Alto Adige at the Austrian border to Tuscany and Umbria in central Italy to

Rome in Lazio—I discovered that the cuisine of each region has a distinct personality.

While living in Umbria, I realized that within the region there are many microcuisines. Around Lake Trasimeno, lake fish replaces meat in traditional ragù. In Cannara, a town famous for onions, cooks use an inordinate amount of the bulb. Around Norcia and Cascia, lentils are adored, and in the hills above Foligno, squab is commonplace. In towns near the region's borders, the cuisine (as well as the language, sense of humor, and demeanor of the people) is influenced by its neighbors. Italian transplants from other regions are also ingredients in the culinary melting pot.

But what is surprising is just how little fellow Umbrians know about the dishes of neighboring villages. For example, *crescionda,* a dessert common in Spoleto, is virtually unheard of in my town of Umbertide, about an hour away. To complicate matters, the names of dishes are often in the dialect of the village, not in standard Italian. So the same dish might go by a different name just a few kilometers away.

It does not appear that recent immigrants, such as those from Eastern Europe and Muslim countries, have influenced the local cuisine. The biggest threat to traditional Umbrian cuisine is the changing lifestyle—long commutes, busy dual-career families, and a new generation that has less time for and interest in cooking.

What Is Umbrian Cuisine?

As you read about Umbria's cuisine in this book, you will notice that the Etruscans are mentioned over and over again. Many of Umbria's culinary traditions can be traced back to those ancient peoples who populated the region some two thousand years ago—roasting meat on a spit, fermenting grapes to make wine, cultivating saffron, eating cheese with honey, pressing olives to make oil, making pecorino cheese from fresh sheep's milk, and eating farro (emmer wheat). Over the course of centuries, ingredients have gained and lost favor. Chickling peas, farro, and saffron, for example, were almost abandoned but are now in vogue.

The wealthy Etruscan table—and later the *tavola Romana*—was abundant and lavish. While the culinary traditions in Umbria are linked to that period of millennia ago, present-day cuisine has its roots in the recent poverty of Umbria's rural sharecroppers. The farmers cooked what they had—lentils, beans, cornmeal, wheat flour, and vegetables from the garden. Meat was scarce, so nothing was wasted. For example, when a pig was slaughtered, the *contadini* (farmers) used every part, from the blood to the ears to the lungs to the intestines. They cured the meat—turning fresh pork into salami, prosciutto, and pancetta. Umbrians adore pork, but they also enjoy hare, rabbit, goose, duck, squab, wild game, chicken, turkey, beef, lamb, and veal.

The landlocked region's diet doesn't include much fish. In the past, when Catholics couldn't eat meat on Fridays, they ate dried salted fish or canned tuna. Around Lake Trasimeno, carp, perch, eel, and snails are traditional. And the Nera River is famous for its trout. Eggs are popular, but they used to be precious and rare, and were often bartered for salt, pepper, and sugar.

The Umbrians are great foragers. During lean times, they gathered chestnuts in the forests to make a thick, hearty soup. Today they still scour forests and fields for chestnuts as well as blackberries, black and white truffles, wild asparagus, edible mushrooms, wild greens, wild fennel, and juniper berries. And many people still keep bees for the honey.

Umbria produces some of Italy's finest extra virgin olive oil. It is used in cooking and is the main fat in baked goods, including desserts. And it is used *crudo* (raw), drizzled over soups, salads, vegetables, meats, pasta, and bruschetta (garlic toast). In the recent past, not every farmstead had olive trees, so pork fat was used instead, and many cooks still use it.

Wine vinegar and wine (usually white) add acidity and brightness to dishes—and help mellow the flavors of strong game. Fresh rosemary, sage, parsley, basil, wild fennel (flowers and fronds), juniper berries, bay leaves, and red pepper flakes are typical seasonings. Black pepper used to be common in farm kitchens but it seems to be losing favor—it isn't good for you, some people say.

Even today in Umbria the best cooks are the grandmothers who take these simple, wholesome ingredients from the earth and turn them into delicious meals.

The Magnificent Landscape

The Umbrian landscape is magical. Its endless undulating green hills and mountains are dotted with monasteries, Gothic and medieval towns, restored and crumbling castles and towers, and ancient farmhouses. Tiny stone chapels—whose congregations have moved to town—are found along the most remote dirt roads. Hillsides are striped with rows of olive trees and grapevines. Tall abandoned buildings, formerly used for drying tobacco, are evidence that this crop was once important. Soaring cypress trees line long driveways, and "lollipop" pine trees stand stark against the brilliant blue sky painted with puffy clouds. Hilly green forests butt up against fields of corn, tobacco, lentils, potatoes, onions, barley, farro, saffron, and garbanzo beans. From season to season, these cultivated crops create an ever-changing patchwork of colors in the landscape.

In towns, glorious cathedrals and churches, filled with Gothic and Renaissance art, are juxtaposed with modern cranes that reach up into the sky—a sign of the constant renovation, retrofitting, and new construction. In residential and commercial neighborhoods, lovingly tended vegetable gardens fill every undeveloped space.

Umbria is landlocked, but it has plenty of water. There are three major rivers—the Tiber, the Topino, and the Nera—plus a network of smaller rivers and several lakes, with Lake Trasimeno being the largest. The region of Toscana borders Umbria on the west. The Marche region and the snow-capped Apennines form the eastern boundary, and Lazio surrounds Umbria in the south.

The Seasons

The four seasons in Umbria are all beautiful. Each season offers something special. But after spending a lifetime in sunny, temperate Northern California, I needed time to adjust to Umbria's cold winter. I arrived in Umbertide at the end of January to stay for the year. Within a few days, white blanketed the ground after a rare snowstorm. When the snow melted, the air stayed frigid throughout the winter, and the sky was often a dull, dreary gray all day. The thick stone walls of my apartment didn't thaw until mid-May.

The cost of fuel is prohibitive in Italy, so people bundle up and live in cold stone houses—my neighbors considered 60 degrees Fahrenheit a warm room temperature! Firewood is affordable, so I delighted in sitting by a cheery fire while I worked on my book. That winter I discovered that it takes at least three days for socks and blue jeans to air-dry.

In mid-March, the first signs of spring appeared—fruit trees flowered and my neighbor's barn cats roamed the property after hiding all winter. But it was still cold and wet. In the Upper Tiber River valley, at almost any time of year, clouds can quickly gather and darken. Then, *kaboom,* there is a flash of lightning bright enough to turn night into day—followed by booming thunder, torrential rain, and fierce winds.

In June, the days were warm—not hot like they would be in late summer.

The nights were cool, and rain was rare. The landscape was at its prettiest. The hills were a patchwork of colors. Bright yellow sunflowers and golden carpets of grain covered the flatlands in an otherwise emerald-green landscape of corn and tobacco. After harvest, round bales of hay lay like enormous beasts in mowed fields. Grapevines were covered with leaves and filled with bunches of tiny green grapes. The *ginestre* (broom) was covered with bright yellow flowers. Red poppies and a rainbow of wild flowers lined the sides of roads. At night in the countryside, the dark sky twinkled with fireflies.

Autumn is beautiful in Umbria, but the days are shorter and the evening air is chilly. With the fall come the grape and olive harvests—and coveted porcini mushrooms and white truffles are in season! Then the holiday season arrives—a bright spot before the long, cold winter.

COOKING NOTES

Before making the recipes in this book, please read this section to learn about the salt used in cooking and to understand how to measure.

ABOUT SALT—IMPORTANT

Lei è una persona sciapa—She isn't very smart.

When a dish seems dull, Umbrian's declare, *è sciapo* (it needs salt). To many Umbrian cooks, salt is the most important seasoning in the kitchen. *Sale grosso* (coarse sea salt) and *sale* (fine sea salt) are used in Umbria. If you are sensitive to salt or on a salt-restricted diet, you might want to reduce the amount of salt in the recipes.

What Salt to Use: The recipes in this book are based on Diamond Crystal Kosher Salt, which has about half the sodium content per teaspoon of other brands of kosher salt and table salt. On occasion, I call for "grey sea salt" (I tested with Sea Star brand). If you use different brands or different types of salt, you should start with half of the specified amount. And if a recipe says to be generous with kosher salt, you'll need to be less so. This is not an endorsement for any brand of salt, just information you'll need to know so your recipes turn out.

Sodium Content of Salt: Below are the sodium levels of several brands of salt (per package label). The differences in sodium content are so dramatic that if you substitute one type or brand for another without making adjustments, the dish might be ruined. That's because other salts, such as Morton's table salt, can have more than twice the amount of sodium per quarter teaspoon compared to Diamond Crystal.

Diamond Crystal Kosher Salt: ¼ teaspoon (0.7 gm) equals 280 mg sodium.

Sea Star Sea Salt, Natural Light Grey Crystals: ¼ teaspoon (1.5 gm) equals 320 mg sodium.

Morton Coarse Kosher Salt: ¼ teaspoon (1.2 gm) equals 480 mg sodium.

Morton Iodized [table] Salt: ¼ teaspoon (1.5 gm) equals 590 mg sodium.

Why Kosher Salt? Kosher salt has a more pleasant flavor than table salt, and it is more reasonably priced than sea salt. The fluffy structure of Diamond Crystal Kosher Salt provides better coverage than table salt. For example, when seasoning a steak, you will use twice the amount of kosher salt (compared with table salt), so more of the surface is salted—without an increase in sodium.

How to Measure, When to Chop

Italians do not use measuring cups and spoons—they cook by eye, aroma, feel, and taste. For precise baking, they weigh the ingredients. Unless your Italian *nonna* (grandmother) is nearby, you'll probably need to measure.

When to Measure, When to Chop: If the ingredient list says "½ cup chopped parsley," chop and then measure. If the recipe says "½ cup packed parsley, chopped," pack the parsley leaves or sprigs into a half-cup dry measuring cup; chop after measuring.

How to Measure Liquids: Use a clear liquid measuring cup with a pour spout and extra space above the measuring line to accurately measure liquids. Read the cup at eye level to the measuring mark.

How to Measure Dry Ingredients: To measure dry ingredients, such as flour and sugar, lightly spoon the ingredient into the appropriate dry measuring cup—do not tap. A full measure comes to the top of the cup; run a straight-edge spatula across the cup to level it off. If you have a kitchen scale, weigh rather than measure when weights are given in the recipe. Flour is one ingredient that should be weighed whenever possible.

The Dog Who Ate the Truffle

1 🌿 Two Sisters—*Le due sorelle*

Si stava meglio quando si stava peggio

(You were better off when you were worse off)

THE TWO RAMACCIONI SISTERS, PAOLA AND SILVIA, BECAME MY CLOSEST friends during my year and a half in Umbertide. I rented my country apartment from Silvia, and Paola's son Mario, my Italian tutor, lived next door.

Paola, the quintessential Italian mother, carries the family's recipe book in her head. And when she isn't in the kitchen preparing one of her mother's recipes or concocting a new dish, she is taking care of her family. Her three-year-old granddaughter, Giulia, is her apprentice. Covered in flour, Giulia delights in playing with and eating bits of dough stolen from *nonna*'s cutting board. Near the end of my yearlong stay with the Ramaccionis, Paola's second grandchild, Bruno, was delivered.

Silvia, a middle-aged tomboy, avoids the kitchen. Over time, I discovered that although she professes to know nothing about cooking, she knows all about good food and traditional dishes—where to buy the freshest ricotta, how to make fresh pasta. But she prefers to play outdoors with her grandson Simone or work on her country property. On our almost daily hike or bike ride in and around Umbertide, Silvia liked to tell me about the people and the history of the area.

I left my own family at home, but I found a new one in Umbertide. Silvia and Paola welcomed me into their lives and treated me like a sister.

THE WORKHORSE

Silvia is an attractive woman with thick salt-and-pepper hair, muscular arms, and shapely legs that show when she wears short skirts. She has large hands, man's hands, that she uses to haul and stack firewood, prune the vineyards, bundle kindling, and fill potholes with gravel. While I lived at Silvia's country house, I watched her working on the property under the summer's sun and in winter's icy wind—and often with an aching back.

"She's a workhorse," Paola said. "She's always worked like a man."

The other side of Silvia is the doting *nonna* to Simone, a three-year-old. *Maialino, tesoro* (little piggy, treasure), she squeals when she sees him. She covers him with kisses and pinches his chubby cheeks until, giggling uncontrollably, he begs her to stop.

Silvia seems to remember every event dating back to the Etruscans, and she has read most of literature's great books. Her English, spoken with a charming British accent, is as good as mine. (But don't expect her to speak English to you. After teaching English for more than twenty years, she considers it work.) On our frequent Sunday outings to restaurants, museums, and festivals, she has her wallet out and pays the entire bill before anyone else has a chance. When we offer to reciprocate, she says she will stay home if we do.

She refuses to eat off paper plates or to use paper napkins. Lizards and snakes petrify her, but she doesn't flinch when she crushes a scorpion or centipede (which terrify me). She has a twinkle in her dark eyes and an upturned mouth that always seems to be laughing at a private joke. Her usually friendly face flashes in anger whenever anyone with a camera tries to get near.

Silvia, a widow, inhabits the second floor of the ancient three-story house she was born in. The town now surrounds the grand old house, which used to be in the country. Her sister, Paola, lives with her oldest son on the top floor, and a cousin owns the ground floor. Silvia's son, his wife, and Simone live in the house next door, in what used to be the family's *cantina* (winery). The several abandoned houses on the property are owned by cousins who live elsewhere. A tall stone building, once used to dry tobacco, is utilized for storage.

Silvia humbly denies it, but several townspeople have confirmed it—the Ramaccionis are descendants of an old aristocratic Umbrian family. At one time, they owned most of the land in and around Umbertide—block after block in the city and vast expanses of forest and fields outside town. As people died or someone needed money or when things got too complicated with too many owners, the family sold off bits and pieces of land.

Many afternoons, Silvia and I explored the maze of *strade bianche* (dirt roads) that crisscross the hills surrounding Umbertide. She can find the road to any tower, castle, or monastery hiding in the forests and hilltops. On our hikes, she rattled off the architectural styles of nearby castles and the year they were built. Each country house has a name and a history, all of which she remembers. She recalls the last family to move out, leaving a castle to crumble. One day, Silvia told me about the poor farm family who had lived in a house above me. "Poor?" I asked, looking at the large, beautifully restored stone house with magnificent views.

"The house was like a barn for animals, not what you see today," she said. "It probably had a kitchen and one big room for sleeping, and I am sure it was immaculate—farmhouses always were. The farm women worked like beasts. They got up around four on summer mornings and worked hard all day. They were poor but happy. We say, *Si stava meglio quando si stava peggio* [You were better off when you were worse off]. They were happier in their poverty than they are today with their money." Silvia always wanted to talk history, but I kept bringing up recipes.

"I never cook," Silvia told me when I asked her for recipes.

"What do you eat?" I asked.

"Bread, cheese, fruit, a little prosciutto."

"But I've heard you tell Paola how to make several recipes," I persisted.

One night I invited Silvia to dinner. "Why didn't you tell me you were making lasagne?" she asked when I pulled the hot dish out of the oven.

"What difference would it have made?" I asked.

"I would have made the pasta for you."

Another night, when I was cooking the gnocchi for dinner, I heard Silvia say to Mario, "You roll the potato dough into snakes and cut them into short pieces." Next she told him how to push a finger into each *gnocco* to make an indentation. "To hold the sauce," she explained.

One day, after eating *polenta con sugo* at her house, I realized that she didn't just have an opinion about cooking—she really could cook. Here is her excellent recipe for Polenta with Ragù—plus a few more of her favorite recipes.

Polenta with Ragù

Polenta con sugo

ॐ

My friend Sabrina, who spent a lot of time at her grandparents' farm, talks about eating soft polenta from a communal board in the center of her nonna's dining table—everyone dug in with their own silverware. She swears that polenta doesn't taste the same on ceramic dishes, so today she serves it on individual wooden plates.

In Umbria, sugo di salsiccia (sausage ragù) and sugo di carne mista (mixed meat ragù) are two traditional sauces for polenta. For this recipe, a thick polenta is cooled until it can be cut and layered in a casserole with sauce and cheese—diced mozzarella can be added between the layers for a heartier dish. To make a vegetarian polenta, substitute Classic Tomato Sauce (see recipe, page 26) for the meat sauce. To serve soft polenta, rather than baking it, add extra water, milk, cream, or broth near the end of cooking to make it creamy— but not so much that the polenta loses its flavor. Spoon the polenta into individual bowls and top it with sugo and grated cheese. For a more flavorful polenta, substitute whole milk or cream for part of the water or use broth instead of water (but add the salt to taste at the end).

Yield: 4 servings

5 cups cold water

1 tablespoon kosher salt (*important:* see "About Salt," page xxv)

1½ cups uncooked coarse, fine, or instant polenta

1 ounce plus 3 ounces grated Parmigiano-Reggiano cheese (see "Grated Cheese," page 6)

2 tablespoons butter plus more for pans

3 cups Umbrian Ragù (see recipe, page 7)

GETTING STARTED: Preheat the oven to 350°F. Butter a large jelly roll or sheet pan and a 7 × 11 × 2-inch baking dish. Fill a large glass with cold water to dip a wooden spoon in.

1. In a large, heavy pot, bring the 5 cups of water to a boil; add the kosher salt. Be ready with a wire whisk—let the polenta slowly "fall like rain" (that's how the Italians describe it) into the boiling water while beating with the whisk (be sure to whisk as soon as the polenta hits the water and continue until all of the polenta has been added). Return to a boil over high heat while whisking, but stand back—polenta spits and can burn. Reduce the heat to low; cook 25 minutes (if using instant polenta, cook 10 minutes), stirring frequently with a wooden spoon. Add the 1 ounce of cheese and 2 tablespoons butter; stir until the butter melts.

2. Immediately pour the polenta into the buttered jelly roll pan. Dip a clean wooden spoon into the glass of cold water; use the back of the wet spoon to spread the polenta into an 11 × 14-inch rectangle (double the size of the baking dish). When the polenta is cool enough to touch, use wet hands to smooth and shape the rectangle. Let the polenta cool until it is firm, about half an hour; cut the polenta in half crosswise to get two 7 × 11-inch pieces. Cut each half into four pieces.

3. Use four of the polenta pieces to cover the bottom of the buttered 7 × 11-inch baking dish (overlap the polenta as needed to fit it into the dish). Cover with half of the sauce and half of the remaining 3 ounces of cheese. Make a second layer, using the rest of the polenta, sauce, and cheese. Bake uncovered until the polenta is hot and the top is well browned, 45 to 60 minutes. Let stand 10 minutes before serving.

NOTE: To reheat leftovers, preheat the oven to 400°F. Put the polenta on a buttered baking pan; bake until hot and bubbly. Or reheat in a microwave oven. Plain or baked polenta with sauce freezes well. To freeze, cut the polenta into individual portions and space them half an inch apart on a baking sheet lined with parchment paper; freeze until firm. Transfer to freezer bags and seal tightly; store in the freezer up to three months. Reheat frozen polenta in the microwave or a 350°F oven, covering with foil as needed to prevent overbrowning. Thawed plain polenta can be grilled or sautéed—it's delicious as a side with stew or topped with ragù and cheese. ❧

GRATED CHEESE

The recipes in this book give weight rather than a cup measure for grated aged cheese because by-the-cup volume changes dramatically depending on the grater, and whether the cheese was grated by hand or machine. But generally one ounce of store-bought finely grated (not shredded) Parmigiano-Reggiano pretty consistently measures about ⅓ cup. At home, one ounce of Parmigiano cubes yields about ¼ cup when processed until very fine in a food processor. But an ounce of cheese grated by hand might measure significantly more. To use hand-grated cheese, the most accurate method is to weigh the cheese, but measuring cubes of cheese with a ruler works too. For example, a 1½×1-inch piece of Parmigiano-Reggiano weighs about one ounce.

HOW TO MAKE *POMODORI PASSATI*

Pomodori passati (tomatoes put through a food mill), either store-bought or home-canned, are a main ingredient in many Umbrian dishes. To get an equivalent product in the United States, use an immersion blender to mince canned whole tomatoes with their juice. (Alternatively, pulse in a food processor.) For convenience, make big batches; store in the freezer up to three months in small, tightly sealed freezer containers (canning jars are ideal).

Umbrian Ragù

Sugo di carne mista
❧

This is the quintessential Umbrian meat sauce for pasta, gnocchi, polenta, lasagne, and cannelloni. In the past, when families were large and lived on farms, prosperous cooks made the sauce with goose and served it with homemade tagliatelle. Poorer families made a soupy tomato sauce with less meat or used rigaglie (chicken giblets) instead of meat. To make the sauce more complex, most cooks use a combination of meats—thus the name carne mista (mixed meat). Duck, rabbit, goose, lamb, veal, chicken, pork, beef, sausage, marrow bones, and chicken giblets are all popular. Although every family has its own recipe, the "chopped seasonings" almost always include un battuto of celery, onion, and carrot. During cooking, the battuto is often mashed into bits so it practically disappears.

Although this is basically Silvia's recipe, it is embellished slightly—I had too many recipes for sugo to settle on just one. I have added milk and butter as optional ingredients—Silvia's mother always stirred them in near the end. Several cooks I know add chicken and pancetta—they are both flavorful and traditional. This is a fluid recipe with lots of room for variation. For example, you can replace the white wine with red, or add one or more of the following: chopped garlic, a sprig of rosemary, 1/2 teaspoon freshly ground nutmeg, or a handful of dried porcini mushrooms (rinse the mushrooms to remove any dust, soak them in hot water until soft, chop them, and sauté with the battuto).

Yield: 7 to 8 cups

1/3 cup extra virgin olive oil

2 medium celery stalks, very finely chopped

1 medium onion, very finely chopped

1 medium carrot, very finely chopped

1/2 cup water

1 pound ground beef

1/2 pound Umbrian Bulk Sausage (see recipe, page 202) or ground pork

1 bone-in chicken thigh or 6 ounces chicken necks and/or wings

3 ounces sliced pancetta, diced (see "Pancetta versus Bacon," page 9)

2½ teaspoons kosher salt (*important:* see "About Salt," page xxv)

¼ teaspoon freshly ground black pepper

¼ teaspoon red pepper flakes

1½ cups dry white wine, such as pinot grigio or sauvignon blanc

2 cans (28 ounces each) whole tomatoes with juice

¼ cup whole milk (optional)

2 tablespoons butter (optional)

1. Heat the oil in a large pot over medium heat. Add the celery, onion, carrot, and ½ cup water. Simmer/sauté, stirring occasionally, until the water evaporates and the onion is tender, about 10 minutes. Add the beef, sausage, chicken, and pancetta. Sprinkle with the kosher salt, black pepper, and red pepper. Sauté over medium heat (stirring and chopping with a wooden spoon to break the ground meat into tiny pieces) until no longer pink but not browned, about 10 minutes.

2. Stir in the wine; simmer over medium-low heat about 1 hour, stirring occasionally. During this time, smash the ground meat and vegetables with a wooden spoon—there should be no chunks of meat or vegetables in the sauce (except the chicken, which will be finely chopped later).

3. Mince/pulse the tomatoes with juice using an immersion blender or food processor; pour into the pot. Cover and bring to a boil; reduce the heat to low and position the lid so that it is open about half an inch. Simmer, stirring occasionally, over low heat until the sauce has thickened and become flavorful, 2 to 2½ hours. Remove the chicken. If there is meat on the bones, discard the skin and bones; chop the chicken meat and return it to the pot. Adjust the salt to taste. (If using milk and butter, stir them in now.)

NOTE: The best styles of pasta for this sauce are fresh tagliatelle or pappardelle or dry spaghetti, penne, and rigatoni. Allow ½ to ¾ cup of sauce (or more to taste) per serving. See "Eight Steps to Perfect Pasta" (page 28). ❧

Pancetta versus Bacon

Bacon can be substituted for pancetta, but the two cook and taste different. Pancetta is not smoked (except *pancetta affumicata*), but it is seasoned with spices. American bacon is smoked, but it is usually not seasoned with spices. And although pancetta might seem as fatty as bacon, it doesn't release enormous amounts of liquid fat like bacon does while cooking. When substituting bacon for pancetta, test several brands to find the one with the least amount of smoke.

Cooking Tips: Pancetta and bacon are easier to dice when the slices are partially frozen. A ⅛-inch thick slice of pancetta weighs about one ounce. When cooking with bacon, start off with a little less salt and drain off some of the excess fat—if there is too much.

Fava Bean and Chard Soup
Baggiana
༒

In Umbrian dialect, baggiano is the name used for a foolish, simple person. "He is a real baggiano!" This minestra (soup) is just as simple, thus the name baggiana. In various towns in Umbria, baggiana is also known as scafata. Some cooks add carrots, celery, and tomatoes, or they omit the broth and serve it as a side dish.

Silvia grew up with a vegetable garden filled with fava beans, so baggiana, a classic Umbrian dish, became one of her favorites. Silvia tells me I always undercook the chard and favas—generally, Italians cook their vegetables a little longer than I do. Cook them to suit your taste.

Yield: 6 to 8 servings

4 ounces sliced pancetta, diced (see "Pancetta versus Bacon," above)

1 medium onion, diced

2 tablespoons extra virgin olive oil plus more for garnish

8 cups coarsely chopped, packed chard (1 bunch, about 1½ pounds)

2 cups shelled fava beans (4 to 5 pounds fresh pods) (see "How to Prepare Fava Beans," page 11)

2½ to 3 cups hot homemade Meat Broth (see recipe, page 118) or canned chicken broth

Kosher salt (*important*: see "About Salt," page xxv)

6 thin slices Italian or French bread (not sourdough), toasted

1 whole garlic clove, peeled

Freshly ground pepper

1. Sauté the pancetta and onion in a large pot in the oil over medium heat, stirring frequently, until the onion is soft, about 8 minutes. After thoroughly washing the chard, leave a little water clinging to its leaves; add the chard to the pot. Cook, stirring frequently, until the chard is tender, 10 to 15 minutes. Stir in the fava beans and 2½ cups of the hot broth; simmer for 5 to 10 minutes. Add the remaining ½ cup broth, if needed. Adjust the salt to taste.

2. Meanwhile, rub one side of each slice of toast lightly with the garlic. To serve, put a piece of toast in the bottom of six bowls. Drizzle the toast with olive oil. Ladle the soup over the toast. Garnish each serving with pepper and a little olive oil.

VARIATION: For a side dish, omit the toast and add just a little of the broth, if needed, to moisten the vegetables. Drizzle each serving with extra virgin olive oil. ❧

FAVA BEANS—*LE FAVE*

Some cooks compare fava beans to lima beans, suggesting limas make an acceptable substitute. They don't. I rarely eat (dry, mealy) lima beans, but cannot stop eating *le fave*. Starting in mid-April, I eagerly await the arrival of my beloved bean. They have a silky texture and an incomparable flavor, reminiscent of fresh peas, but more complex and intriguing.

In the Mediterranean, people have eaten fava beans for millennia. Until the mid-1900s, *contadini* in Umbria ate raw favas with fresh or aged pecorino cheese for their mid-morning meal. Fava beans are not as common on American tables, but they are well worth searching for. Look for them at farmers' or gourmet markets or grow your own— they are easy to cultivate.

Fava beans grow nestled in bulky, velvety pods, so it takes a lot of beans—and a bit of time—to get enough for a dish. Five pounds of pods, for example, yield two to three cups of shelled beans, about enough for one recipe.

Fava beans are best when young—plump and tender with soft, green pods. Older pods tend to be faded, spotted, and rigid, but they are still edible.

How to Prepare Fava Beans

Early in the season, when fava beans are tender, you can remove the beans from their pods and cook them without shelling them. But I prefer to shell them even when young because they are more delicate, not at all bitter, and have a nice bright green color.

To shell fava beans, invite a couple of friends over, open a bottle of wine, sit on the porch with a couple of big bowls, and get to work. Tear the pods open and scoop out the beans. Discard the pods. Drop the beans into boiling water and reduce the heat. Simmer until tender, 3 to 6 minutes. Drain the beans and plunge them into ice water; drain again. To remove the light green shell, hold a bean between a thumb and finger. Squeeze it to force out the inner bean. Discard the shells. The beans are now ready to use in any recipe. They can be held in the refrigerator a day or two, but are best used immediately.

Fava Bean Purée

In Umbria, dry fava beans are used to make a puréed soup or a spread for crostini. During their fleeting season—late April through June—I use fresh beans instead. To make an exquisite spread, shell the beans and mash them with an immersion blender or food processor until they are creamy, but still lumpy (add a few drops of water, if needed).

Season to taste with extra virgin olive oil, kosher salt, and freshly ground pepper. Serve on toasted crostini (rubbed lightly with raw garlic; see "To Toast Crostini," page 67) with a glass of chilled grechetto or pinot grigio. *Cin cin!*

Roast Chicken with Potatoes
Pollo arrosto con le patate
∞

Roasting is one of the most popular methods of cooking poultry in Umbria. Although this recipe is very simple, it is often served as a second course on special occasions. When Silvia bakes the chicken in her wood-burning oven, it is especially wonderful. Silvia doesn't butterfly the bird, but I prefer to because it browns better. She also roasts duck, guinea fowl, and goose in the same manner.

Some cooks rub seasoned strutto *(lard) over the chicken rather than using olive oil, but the lard must be homemade. And many Umbrian cooks bake the giblets with the chicken. I sometimes vary the recipe by squeezing a lemon over the chicken before seasoning it. In Umbria, cooked chicken is often cut into small pieces before serving. For example, the breast is cut into four pieces (rather than two), and the thighs might be cut into halves.*

If you prefer to bake the chicken without potatoes, see the recipe for Roast Chicken or Smoky Grill-Roasted Chicken on pages 14.

Yield: 4 to 6 servings

1 whole chicken (about 3¾ to 4½ pounds with giblets)

Coarse grey sea salt (*important:* see "About Salt," page xxv)

Freshly ground pepper

6 (3-inch) sprigs rosemary

1 sprig sage

2 large garlic cloves, peeled

4 medium yellow potatoes (about 1¼ pounds)

¼ cup extra virgin olive oil

¼ cup dry white wine, such as pinot grigio or sauvignon blanc

YOU'LL ALSO NEED: Heavy-duty kitchen shears.

1. Preheat the oven to 450°F. Butterfly the chicken (see "How to Butterfly a Chicken," page 15). Put the chicken with the interior cavity facing up in a large baking pan (9×13×2 inches is ideal); pat the chicken dry with paper towels. Rub ½ teaspoon of the sea salt over the inside cavity of the chicken; sprinkle with freshly ground pepper as desired. Flip the chicken over. Tuck one of the sprigs of rosemary and the sage under the chicken.

2. Remove the needles from one of the sprigs of rosemary. Cut each garlic clove into four slices lengthwise. Use a sharp paring knife to cut deep slits in the thickest parts of the chicken—four in the breasts, one in each leg, one in each thigh. Push 1 slice of garlic into each of the slits. Push a pinch of the sea salt and three rosemary needles into each slit.

3. Rub 1 teaspoon of the sea salt over the outside of the chicken; sprinkle with pepper, as desired. Lift the wing tips up and back, tucking them in to secure them; push a rosemary sprig between the wing bones. Tuck a rosemary spring between each leg and breast. Set aside (refrigerate if not baking within a half hour).

4. Peel the potatoes and cut each potato into 8 lengthwise wedges. (To prepare up to 2 hours ahead, submerge the potatoes in a pot of cold water; just before baking, drain the potatoes well.) Arrange the potatoes around the chicken; sprinkle the potatoes with ¼ teaspoon of the sea salt. Drizzle the oil over the chicken and potatoes. Pour the wine into the pan (not over the chicken).

5. Bake uncovered, spooning pan drippings over the chicken and potatoes every 15 minutes, until the chicken is well browned and the potatoes are tender, 1¼ to 1½ hours. The internal temperature, measured in the thickest part of the thigh and breast, will probably exceed the 165°F required

for food safety. Test the potatoes for doneness by piercing with a sharp knife.

6. If the potatoes are not tender or are not well browned when the chicken is done, transfer the chicken to a cutting board; tent with foil. Return the potatoes to the oven; bake until tender inside and well browned outside. After the chicken has rested 10 minutes, use clean kitchen shears to cut the chicken into pieces. Arrange the potatoes and chicken on a platter; drizzle with pan drippings, if desired.

Roast Chicken—*Pollo arrosto* (without potatoes)

Prep: To bake chicken without potatoes, prepare the chicken following steps 1 through 3 on page 13 with the changes that follow. Drizzle the interior of the chicken with 2 teaspoons white wine before seasoning with salt and pepper; drizzle with 1 tablespoon oil. Drizzle 2 tablespoons white wine over the outside before seasoning; drizzle with 3 tablespoons oil (thereby reducing the oil by a tablespoon). Do not add any more wine.

Roast: Roast uncovered in a preheated 450°F oven for 30 minutes. Spoon pan drippings over the chicken and rotate the pan.

Finish: Continue baking, spooning pan drippings over the chicken every 15 minutes, until the chicken is well browned and no longer pink at the bone, 30 to 40 more minutes (total 60 to 70 minutes).

Smoky Grill-Roasted Chicken

Follow the variation for Roast Chicken *without potatoes* per the Prep (above), but without the sprigs of herbs (at this point, use rosemary only in the slits). Preheat the oven to 450°F. Grill the chicken over a moderate charcoal or gas fire for 15 minutes, turning frequently to prevent burning. Transfer the chicken (skin side up) to the baking pan used for Prep; put the sprigs of herbs in place per original recipe directions (step 3, page 13), and drizzle the chicken with 2 additional tablespoons of oil. Pour ¼ cup dry white wine into the pan. Cook the chicken in the preheated oven per the Finish (above), 45 to 55 minutes (total 60 to 70 minutes, including grill time). ❧

How to Butterfly a Chicken

Put the chicken on a cutting board with its back facing up. Use kitchen shears to cut parallel and as close as possible to one side of the backbone from the tail to the head opening. Repeat on the other side, cutting to remove the backbone. Turn the chicken over and press firmly on the breastbone with both hands to slightly flatten the chicken.

Slow-Roasted Tomatoes with Bread Crumbs
Pomodori al forno

Quanti buoni *(how delicious)*, said each and every guest at dinner the night Silvia and I made pomodori al forno. Even Paola had to admit that her sister Silvia makes the best roasted tomatoes. What makes Silvia's tomatoes exceptional is baking them until they are semidry. During the slow roasting, they develop a rich tomato flavor. The drier, the better, advises Silvia.

The tomatoes make an ideal side dish with grilled or roasted meats, fish, or poultry. They can also be served on an antipasto platter, alongside olives, caprese, marinated artichokes, roasted peppers and onions, grilled zucchini, prosciutto and melon, or cold cuts such as salami and mortadella.

Yield: 6 to 8 servings

Olive oil for the pan

3 pounds small Roma tomatoes (16 to 25 of equal size)

Kosher salt *(important:* see "About Salt," page xxv)

1½ cups homemade dry bread crumbs (page 16)

½ cup packed Italian parsley, chopped

3 medium garlic cloves, pushed through a garlic press

¼ teaspoon freshly ground pepper

1 tablespoon plus 3 tablespoons extra virgin olive oil

GETTING STARTED: Arrange a shelf in the center of the oven. Brush a large baking pan with oil (an 11×16-inch jelly roll pan is perfect). Line a large tray or baking pan with paper towels.

1. Put a sieve over a 2-cup liquid measuring cup. Cut the tomatoes in half lengthwise. Use a melon baller to scoop the tomato seeds into the sieve; set aside. Put the tomatoes side by side on the paper-towel-lined tray with their cut side facing up. Sprinkle the tomatoes lightly with kosher salt; set aside for half an hour. Turn the tomatoes over to drain on the paper towels; let stand 5 minutes.

2. Mash the tomato seeds/pulp with a fork, pushing the juice into the measuring cup below; discard the seeds/pulp. You will need ¾ cup tomato juice— add water if necessary to get ¾ cup. Put the bread crumbs into a medium bowl; stir in the tomato juice, parsley, garlic, pepper, and 1 tablespoon of the oil; season to taste with kosher salt.

3. Arrange the tomatoes side by side in the oiled baking pan with the hollow side facing up (put smallest tomatoes in the center of the pan to help prevent burning). Lightly season the tomatoes with kosher salt. Use a teaspoon to fill the tomatoes with bread crumbs—using all of the crumbs; lightly press the crumbs into the tomatoes with your fingers. Sprinkle the tomatoes lightly with kosher salt; drizzle evenly with the remaining 3 tablespoons oil.

4. Put the pan of tomatoes on the center shelf in a cold oven; set the temperature to 350°F. Bake for 1½ hours. The tomatoes will be slightly leathery and semidry when done—if they are not, reduce the temperature to 325°F. Continue baking; check for doneness at least every 10 minutes until done (depending on personal taste, tomato size, moisture, and sugar content, it might take an additional 15 to 30 minutes). Serve warm or at room temperature. ❧

HOW TO MAKE BREAD CRUMBS

The Umbrians, who rarely waste anything, use stale bread in a variety of dishes. It is a main ingredient in *panzanella*, *pancotto*, and *passatelli* (bread salad, bread soup, and bread crumb pasta). *Pangrattati* (bread crumbs) are used in meatballs, in stuffing, and on baked toma-toes. They are used to coat fish for the grill or for pan-fried breaded cutlets or chops. They are sprinkled on casseroles and on grilled zuc-chini and eggplant. They are tossed with a variety of pasta dishes and are sautéed with cabbage.

Homemade bread crumbs, with their coarse, irregular texture, are much better than store-bought crumbs. A coarse-textured Italian-style bread, such as Pugliese or ciabatta, or French bread (not sourdough) work best. Starting with fresh bread is the simplest way to make bread crumbs because the bread is easy to handle. But making crumbs from stale bread is doable, and it is a good way to use up dry bread. You can store bread crumbs in a tightly sealed container in the freezer for a month or two.

Using Fresh Bread: Cut the bread into 2-inch cubes. Put a hand-ful of cubes into a food processor; process in batches until almost fine (this may take several minutes). Use the crumbs "as is" for recipes calling for fresh crumbs. For dry crumbs, spread the crumbs into a thin layer in a large baking pan. Cover the crumbs with a clean dish-towel and let them dry overnight (or until dry), or put the pan into a preheated 325°F oven until the crumbs are crisp, stirring once or twice (avoid browning), 8 to 10 minutes. Cool.

Using Stale Bread: While the bread is still easy to slice, cut it into 2-inch cubes. When the bread is dry (but not too hard), drop a hand-ful of the cubes at a time into a food processor; process until almost fine (it may take several minutes). Or put dry bread cubes into a clean, sturdy plastic bag. Put the bag on a cutting board and pound the bread into crumbs using a flat-bottom meat pounder.

Focaccia with Onions and Rosemary
Schiacciata con cipolla

Schiacciata (pressed or smashed) is the name used in many parts of Umbria for what is called focaccia in other parts of Italy. It is also called ciaccia in some places in Umbria; Città di Castello is one such town.

This flat bread, topped with salty onions, is found in bakeries around Umbria. A bakery in downtown Umbertide near the hospital made one of the best—but it sells out early. Schiacciata makes a nice snack or nibble with wine before dinner.

Paola and Silvia always bake schiacciata *in their wood-burning oven—that is the traditional method and also the most delicious. From a baker I learned the secret of salting the onions before baking. A flavorful, fruity olive oil and good salt are important to this recipe. I recommend kosher salt, but sea salt is also ideal—they both have a nice flavor. A handful or so of fresh sage leaves can be substituted for the rosemary.*

From Paola, the cook at Caffè Accademia in Città di Castello, I learned to make ciaccia d'olio*—a simple focaccia with lots of olive oil and salt. To make it, leave out the onions and drizzle the dough generously with extra virgin olive oil and sprinkle it with kosher salt just before baking.*

Yield: 2 pans (11×17 inches each)

5 cups (25 ounces) unbleached bread flour plus more for kneading

1 package (2¼ teaspoons) instant yeast (see "About Yeast," page 20)

¾ teaspoon sugar

Kosher salt (*important:* see "About Salt," page xxv)

2¼ cups very hot water (120 to 130°F)

Extra virgin olive oil

2 large red onions, cut into halves and thinly sliced

2 (10-inch) sprigs rosemary, needles removed from stems

You'll also need: An instant-read thermometer and parchment paper.

Getting started: Line two 12×17-inch baking pans with parchment paper; spread oil over the parchment paper.

1. Lightly flour a large board. Fit an electric mixer with a paddle attachment (alternatively mix by hand). Put 3 cups (15 ounces) of the flour into a large mixing bowl; sprinkle with the yeast, sugar, and 1¾ teaspoons of the kosher

salt. Mix on low speed until well combined, about 30 seconds (or mix with a fork).

2. Slowly add the 2¼ cups of hot water (120 to 130°F) and 2 tablespoons of the oil; immediately mix on low speed (or stir with a fork), stopping to scrape the sides of the bowl as needed. Add the remaining 2 cups of flour in two batches; mix until the dough forms a ball, about 1 minute. Let stand 5 minutes. Replace the paddle with the dough hook. Knead on low speed until the dough is smooth, about 7 minutes (if mixing by hand, transfer the dough to the floured board and knead by hand until smooth, about 8 minutes).

3. Rub oil generously over the inside of two large, clean bowls. Use a wet knife to cut the dough in half. With wet hands (to prevent the dough from sticking to them), form two balls of dough. Put a ball of dough into each bowl; turn the dough over in the bowl to coat it with oil. Cover the bowls with plastic wrap and set aside to rise in a warm, draft-free place until doubled, 45 minutes to 1 hour.

4. Using wet hands, transfer the dough to the prepared baking pans. Working with one pan at a time, drizzle 1 tablespoon of the oil over the dough. Starting in the center, gently press fingertips into the dough to dimple it— at the same time gently press the dough toward the edges of the pan (the dough will not fill the pan yet). Let the dough rest 20 minutes. Preheat the oven to 475°F.

5. Meanwhile, put the onions into a large bowl. Sprinkle with 2 teaspoons of the kosher salt; toss to coat. Let stand 10 minutes. Drain the liquid given off by the onions; pat the onions dry with paper towels. Toss the onions in 2 teaspoons of the oil.

6. After the dough has rested, drizzle 1 tablespoon of the oil over each pan. Again gently press fingertips into the dough, making dimples and gently pushing the dough to the edges, filling the pan. Let rest 10 minutes.

7. Spread the onions over the dough, dividing them between the two pans. Sprinkle with the rosemary needles and generously season with the kosher salt; lightly press into the dough. Drizzle each pan with about 1 tablespoon

of the oil. Put the pans in the oven; immediately reduce the temperature to 450°F.

8. Bake until well browned, about 20 minutes, rotating the pan after 10 minutes. Cool on a wire rack for 10 minutes before cutting into squares (clean kitchen shears are ideal). *Schiacciata* should be pleasantly salty—if needed, sprinkle with more kosher salt. Refrigerate or freeze leftover bread (will keep in the freezer about one month). To reheat, spritz lightly with water; heat in a preheated 350°F oven until hot.

ABOUT YEAST: RapidRise is a trademarked name for instant yeast. If you use a different kind of yeast (i.e., dry active yeast), follow the label instructions for method and water temperature. ❧

WHEN IN UMBRIA

On a cold, rainy afternoon when Silvia and I were eating pizza, she suddenly pointed behind me, leaned into the table toward me, and whispered in disbelief, "Do you see what they're drinking?"

In Umbria, where *caffè corretto* (coffee with liquor) is a common morning drink, it was hard to imagine what to expect. I turned and saw two elderly women, each with a frothy drink in front of them. I could hear them chatting in English—British English.

"Cappuccino?" I asked.

"Yes, it's strange to drink milk after lunch," she said.

I knew the Italian "rules" for drinking milk with coffee, but I never understood them. "But Italians eat gelato after lunch," I pointed out.

"You're right," she conceded, "but we usually don't drink cappuccino after ten in the morning and certainly not right after lunch!"

"If you ask me, coffee gelato is like cappuccino—coffee, milk, sugar."

Silvia nodded but didn't say anything.

The waiter arrived with dessert menus filled with pictures of gelato sundaes and specialty desserts.

"*Dolce, caffè?*" he asked, clearing our plates.

"Nothing for me, thanks," I said.

He turned to Silvia.

"Due cappuccini," she said, looking directly at him.

The waiter didn't flinch, but I knew he was as surprised as I was. Tourists were one thing, but an Italian! He left and I turned to Silvia.

"Cappuccino after lunch, Silvia?"

"Yes," she said, "it's too cold for gelato."

THE ULTIMATE MOM—*L'ottima mamma*

Paola is the quintessential Italian mother, but away from home she is a professional woman. She used to teach Italian conversation classes to foreign students at the Università per Stranieri (University for Foreigners), a beautiful school in an old palazzo perched on a hill in Perugia. Now she gives language-competency exams to students in Italy and around Europe.

On the days when Paola doesn't work, she plays the adoring *mamma* to her three grown sons, Amilcar, Luciano, and Mario. She often heads to Mario's at seven in the morning to help her granddaughter, Giulia, get ready for nursery school. To get Giulia to eat breakfast, Paola draws pictures of Pippi Longstocking and sings Pippi's songs. After Michela, Giulia's mom, and Mario leave for work, Paola feeds Mario's eight cats and puts a large pot of water with beef bones on the stove. She softens hunks of stale bread in the broth. When it's ready, she feeds it to Mario's two dogs, Paco and Peri.

Like most moms, Paola freely dispenses advice to her kids, asked for or not. "Mario, it's too cold to go for a bike ride with Giulia." "Amilcar, it's too late to go out." "Luciano, don't have another beer." Often they listen, but when they don't, it's not because they resent her well-intended mothering. Before Michela moved in with Mario, I often saw Paola's and Michela's cars parked in front of Mario's house on Sunday mornings. Paola ironed Mario's clothes, played with the dogs, or tidied while Mario and Michela slept in upstairs. My grown son would have had a fit, but Mario didn't mind.

When Michela leaves laundry in the washer, Paola hangs it to dry on the clothesline outside. She waters the potted plants and cleans up the ones the dogs have knocked over. After the plumber finishes unblocking Mario's sink or toilet, she pays him (with her own money) when he leaves. She washes last night's dirty dishes. When neighbors or friends drop by, she makes them coffee. At noon, if she has time, she watches her favorite cooking show while making a delicious lunch—*spaghetti alla carbonara, l'arista con pancetta e funghi*, potatoes, and mixed salad, for example—for her sons. I am often invited to join them.

Paola divorced when her boys were young, and now she is occasionally mother to eleven-year-old Max, her ex-husband's son by a second marriage. When Max visits, he stays with her and she cooks all of his favorite dishes. To the genuine Italian *mamma*, food is love, and it is true for Paola.

"Have some more, Suzanne," she insists whenever my plate is empty. When I turn down seconds, she says, "At least have a little cheese," and drops a huge wedge on my plate.

She prefers the life of the *casalinga* (homemaker) to that of the professional, so she is planning an early retirement. In fact, she is excited about devoting all her time to the duties of *la mamma*.

A few recipes from Paola follow. She's such a good cook that I could have filled a book with all the fabulous dishes I ate at her house. ❧

Spaghetti Carbonara
Spaghetti alla carbonara
☙❧

Many Italian cookbooks have a recipe for spaghetti alla carbonara, *but a lot of the recipes are either not authentic or not very good. This is an easy dish to make, but the method, timing, and ingredients need to be right—then it's an extraordinary dish. The trick to a creamy sauce is adding the egg mixture to the just-drained pot of spaghetti—off the stove—so the heat from the pasta cooks the eggs without scrambling them.*

Every cook has his or her own version—but it's always practically a pantry dish. Paola's recipe calls for aged pecorino cheese, but others use Parmigiano-Reggiano. Onions are common in Umbrian recipes, but not necessarily elsewhere. Some cooks defend guanciale, *a pancetta-like meat made from pork jowls, as authentic; other says pancetta is. Garlic is rare. Black pepper, rather than red pepper flakes, which are popular in Umbria, is the pepper of choice. Some beat a tablespoon or so of chopped Italian parsley in with the eggs. No one adds cream—it is a definite no-no.*

Alla carbonara means in the style of the charcoal makers, but there are many stories about the recipe's origin. Some say it hails from Rome, but many attribute it to the charcoal makers, who had few ingredients available while working in the forest. Supposedly black pepper represents the charcoal dust that inevitably fell into the dish.

Paola makes spaghetti alla carbonara often, but almost without exception she makes it when her middle son, Luciano, comes to visit—it is his favorite pasta.

Yield: 4 main-dish servings (or 6 first-course servings)

½ cup water

1 medium onion, finely chopped

6 ounces sliced pancetta or *guanciale,* diced (see "Pancetta versus Bacon," page 9)

3 tablespoons extra virgin olive oil

¾ teaspoon kosher salt plus more to cook the pasta (*important:* see "About Salt," page xxv)

1 pound dry spaghetti

3 large eggs

2 ounces grated aged Umbrian or Tuscan pecorino cheese plus extra to pass (see "Grated Cheese," page 6)

Freshly ground pepper

1. Put the ½ cup water into a medium saucepan with the onion, pancetta, oil, and kosher salt. Simmer over medium heat, stirring frequently, until the onion is tender and the pancetta is slightly crisp, 15 to 20 minutes. Remove from the heat; cover to keep warm.

2. Meanwhile, bring about 3 quarts cold water to a boil in a large pot to cook the pasta (page 28); add about 1½ tablespoons kosher salt to the boiling water. Add the spaghetti; cook, stirring occasionally, until *al dente*—taste for doneness a couple of minutes before the time recommended on the package. Shortly before draining the pasta, reserve about 1 cup of the cooking liquid; set aside.

3. Just before draining the spaghetti, crack the eggs into a medium bowl; beat in the cheese. Slowly beat in about ⅓ cup of the reserved cooking liquid.

Drain the spaghetti, but save the remaining ⅔ cup cooking liquid. Immediately return the spaghetti to the pot so it stays hot, but keep the pot off the stove. Immediately and quickly pour the egg mixture into the spaghetti while stirring the pasta. Stir in the hot onion mixture, adding the reserved cooking liquid by the tablespoon as needed to make the dish saucy. Adjust the salt and season with pepper to taste. If the dish seems bland, it needs more salt. Serve immediately—pass extra cheese at the table.

NOTE: *Spaghetti alla carbonara* is best eaten immediately—it doesn't reheat well. ❧

Eggplant Parmesan
Melanzane alla Parmigiana
∞

Although you will find melanzane alla Parmigiana *throughout Italy, it is also a classic dish in Umbria. A variation of this recipe—*gobbi alla Parmigiana*—is a traditional Umbrian Christmas dish. Gobbi is dialect for the popular Italian vegetable* cardi *(cardoons). This long thistlelike vegetable, which resembles the stalk of an artichoke plant, replaces the eggplant. Some cooks drizzle nutmeg-scented* besciamela *(béchamel) over each layer of cardoon or eggplant.*

Paola's recipe is one of the Ramaccioni family's favorite dishes—and mine, too. Her rendition is surprisingly light and fluffy. She serves melanzane alla Parmigiana *as a first course, but it can be a hearty entree, served with green salad and bread.*

Yield: 8 main-course servings (or 12 first-course servings)

3 medium eggplants (about 1 pound each)

Kosher salt (*important:* see "About Salt," page xxv)

¾ cup flour plus more as needed

5 large eggs

Vegetable oil for frying

Classic Tomato Sauce (see recipe, page 26)

12 ounces fresh mozzarella cheese, sliced

3 ounces grated Parmigiano-Reggiano cheese (see "Grated Cheese,"
   page 6)

USEFUL EQUIPMENT: A deep-fry thermometer.

1. Trim off the eggplant stems; slice the eggplants lengthwise into ⅜-inch-thick slices. Arrange the slices in a single layer in a large baking pan (9 or 10×13×2 inches is ideal). Sprinkle both sides with the kosher salt; continue to layer and salt until all the slices are salted. Let stand 1 hour.

2. Preheat the oven to 375°F. Spread the flour over a large plate. Beat the eggs in a shallow dish (a pie pan is perfect). Heat the oil (2 inches deep) in a large wok or skillet over medium-high heat until it reaches 375°F; adjust the heat as needed throughout frying to maintain this temperature (briefly remove the wok from the heat if the oil becomes too hot or begins to smoke). Dry the eggplant slices with paper towels, pressing them to remove excess water. Dredge one eggplant slice at a time in the flour to lightly coat both sides; shake to remove excess. Dip slices one at a time into the eggs, turning until well coated; shake to remove excess. Carefully lower one slice at a time into the hot oil, frying 3 or 4 slices at a time (too many will cool the oil). Fry until golden brown on both sides, 1½ to 2 minutes per side. Drain on a wire rack or paper towels.

3. Spread about 1 cup of the sauce over the bottom of the baking pan (used earlier to hold the salted eggplant); arrange a layer of eggplant slices over the sauce. Generously spoon sauce over the eggplant. Top with half of the mozzarella; sprinkle with about one third of the Parmigiano. Repeat the layering (you will probably have enough to make two more layers; the third layer will not have mozzarella). At this point, the dish can be covered and held in the refrigerator for several hours (see Note, below). Bake uncovered until well browned, hot, and bubbly, 45 to 60 minutes. Remove from the oven; let stand about 15 minutes before serving.

NOTE: If the dish was assembled ahead and refrigerated, it may take longer to bake; if the top starts to get too brown, cover the pan with foil. There will be leftover sauce; refrigerate or freeze it.

To Freeze Eggplant Parmesan: When cool enough to cut, slice into individual portions. Arrange the pieces 1 inch apart on a baking sheet lined with parchment paper. Cover and freeze until firm. Transfer to freezer bags; seal tightly. Store in the freezer for up to 3 months. One or more portions can be defrosted in the microwave and reheated in a conventional, microwave, or toaster oven until hot. ❧

Classic Tomato Sauce
Sugo di pomodori
❦

Tomato sauce, like this one, is used in many traditional recipes, including ravioloni, Eggplant Parmesan, and sugo di piselli (pea sauce). It is also delicious on pizza or polenta, or tossed with penne, or used for a variation of saltimbocca. Small amounts can be added to soup, beans, green beans, or zucchini dishes. For variety, stir in a dozen or so torn fresh basil leaves or a handful of chopped parsley, after the sauce is puréed. Simmer 5 minutes.

Typically, the sauce is passed through a food mill, but an immersion blender or food processor work well. For more ideas, see "Five Tomato Sauces" (page 27).

Yield: about 4½ cups

½ cup extra virgin olive oil plus more for finishing

4 garlic cloves, lightly crushed with a knife blade, and peeled

2 cans (28 ounces each) whole tomatoes with juice

1¾ teaspoons kosher salt (*important:* see "About Salt," page xxv)

¼ teaspoon red pepper flakes

¼ teaspoon freshly ground pepper (optional)

1. In a large saucepan, heat the oil over medium-low heat; sauté the garlic (without browning it), stirring frequently, 4 minutes. Carefully pour the tomatoes with juice into the saucepan. Add the kosher salt and red pepper

(if using pepper, add it now). Cover and bring to a boil over high heat. Reduce the heat to medium low; simmer uncovered, stirring occasionally, until slightly thickened and flavorful, 45 to 60 minutes.

2. Use an immersion blender or a food processor to coarsely purée the tomatoes (neither smooth nor chunky—do not overprocess or the sauce will emulsify). If the sauce is too thick, thin it with a little water. Adjust the salt to taste. If desired, finish the sauce with a drizzle of the oil—*crudo* (raw, without cooking it). ❧

FIVE TOMATO SAUCES

Here are some simple ways to expand your tomato sauce recipe file. All of these versions are delicious with spaghetti, penne, or penne rigate. Start with the Classic Tomato Sauce (page 26) and make one of the following changes:

1. *Sugo di magro:* Sauté (whole or finely diced): 1 medium stalk celery, ½ medium carrot, and ¼ small onion with the garlic for several minutes. If the vegetables are whole, discard them before puréeing the sauce.

2. *Sugo di piselli:* Follow variation 1 with the following changes: Sauté 2 ounces diced pancetta with the diced celery, carrot, and onion until tender. Mince/pulse the tomatoes with juice using an immersion blender or food processor before adding them to the sauce. Five minutes before the sauce is ready, add a cup or so of frozen peas; simmer until hot and tender. Serve with lots of grated aged pecorino or Parmigiano-Reggiano cheese.

3. *Sugo di verdure:* Coarsely chop ¾ pound mushrooms. Sauté the mushrooms with the garlic until the liquid evaporates and the mushrooms are lightly browned. Add 1 stalk (diced) celery and 1 medium (diced) carrot; sauté until tender. Pulse/chop the tomatoes with juice in a food processor before adding to the sauce. While the sauce simmers, cut two or three kinds of vegetables—cauliflower, zucchini, asparagus,

peas, green beans—into small pieces (³⁄₈-inch cubes etc.). You will need 4 to 5 cups of mixed diced vegetables. Boil each vegetable separately in salted water until tender; add to the sauce and simmer 5 to 10 minutes. Serve with lots of grated aged pecorino or Parmigiano-Reggiano cheese.

4. *Sugo all'Amatriciana:* Mince/pulse the tomatoes with juice using an immersion blender or food processor before adding to the sauce. Sauté 6 ounces diced pancetta and ¹⁄₂ small (diced) onion in the oil. (Omit the garlic, if desired). Toss the pasta with the sauce and grated aged pecorino cheese.

5. *Sugo di pomodori e panna:* Add about ¹⁄₃ cup of the Classic Tomato Sauce and a little extra red pepper flakes per cup of heavy cream; simmer a few minutes until saucy. Stir in several handfuls of torn basil leaves. ❧

EIGHT STEPS TO PERFECT PASTA

Lei è una buona pasta—She has a good mind!

In Umbria, sauce is never poured on top of pasta. Instead pasta is tossed with just enough sauce to lightly coat and flavor each strand. Cooks try to prepare just the amount of pasta to be eaten at that meal. (Leftovers usually go to the dogs—or cats!) To determine how much pasta to cook, my friend Paola fills an individual pasta bowl three quarters full with dry pasta, such as penne, adding one bowlful for each serving to the boiling water. It is a clever method, but you may want to weigh the pasta, allowing 3 to 4 ounces per main-dish serving. To warm the serving dish, ladle some of the cooking liquid into the dish just before draining the pasta—toss it out as soon as the dish is warm.

The Umbrians like their pasta *al dente*, slightly firm but not hard in the center. They say if the pasta has *l'anima* (the soul), a white center or a dotted white line around tubular pasta when it's cut into, it is not done.

Here is the method for cooking pasta as the Umbrians do it.

1. Have the cheese grated and the sauce heated.

2. Per pound of pasta, bring about 3 quarts of cold water to a boil in a large pot (don't fill it more than three quarters full or it might boil over).

3. When the water boils, add about 2 tablespoons of kosher salt (*important:* see "About Salt," page xxv) per 3 quarts of water. Do not add oil—you want the sauce to cling to the pasta, not slide off it.

4. Call everyone to the table and drop the pasta by the handful into the rapidly boiling water. Stir it immediately, and then stir it several times during cooking. Push long pasta such as spaghetti into the boiling water, bending it and submerging it as it softens—don't break it.

5. Start the timer as soon as all the pasta is in the water. Use the package instructions as a guide for cooking time, but taste for doneness a couple of minutes early. When time is almost up, scoop out and reserve about 1 cup of the cooking liquid (per pound of dry pasta) to use later. Usually the pasta is drained when it is a little undercooked because it finishes cooking in the sauce—so it is often ready a couple minutes before the package recommends. The pasta is ready to serve when it is *al dente*—when it gives some resistance when bitten into. It should not be soft.

6. Drain the pasta (you should have already reserved 1 cup of the cooking liquid) and return the pasta to the pot. Immediately stir in just enough sauce to lightly coat the pasta, adding a little reserved cooking liquid to make it saucier. (Some cooks say this starchy water helps the sauce cling to the pasta.) For more flavor, cook the pasta in the sauce for a few minutes until the pasta is *al dente,* adding cooking liquid as needed to keep it saucy.

7. Stir in cheese to taste. Grated hard cheese, usually Parmigiano-Reggiano or aged pecorino, is the secret ingredient in pastas with meat sauce. Cheese is not typically served with seafood, and it is usually used sparingly with tomato- or vegetable-based sauces.

8. Serve the pasta at the table directly from the pot or serving dish rather than plating it in the kitchen, so that it stays hot longer. Pass around a bowl of grated cheese.

In Umbria, they say the last person to be served pasta is the luckiest because the sauce and bits of vegetables, pancetta, and meat fall to the bottom of the pot (but to be polite, they always serve the most important guest first).

Paola's Adventures with Paco and Peri

No one loves Mario's dogs, Paco and Peri, as much as Paola does. Paola was there when Mario rescued Peri, a starving, abandoned dog covered with ticks and sores. She was there when Peri gave birth to Paco. When Peri escaped, broke her leg, and needed months of physical therapy, Paola kept her checkbook handy.

Paola, whose doctor says she must exercise and lose weight, refuses to take walks—unless it is for the dogs' benefit. So several times a week, she heads outside to fetch the two dogs. Without fail, they jump up and lick her face, leaving muddy footprints on her clean clothes.

"You bad dogs," she always scolds.

Then she laughs and gives them kisses as the three of them stand nose to nose. When the dogs make one of their frequent escapes, she drops everything to find them. From Mario's house, she scans the hills for a glimpse of them.

One day, I found Paola standing motionless in the driveway. "I'm looking for Peri," she explained. "Her white coat is easy to spot."

When she saw Peri in the hills above, we sped up the hill in her car. It was hopeless—the dogs ran farther away when they heard us calling. When Amilcar joined us a few minutes later, his commanding voice brought them racing obediently to his car. Peri collapsed at Amilcar's feet—she looked near death.

"She's ashamed," explained Paola when she saw my alarm. "She knows Amilcar is mad. She always does this."

Paola and Amilcar lifted Peri, limp and lifeless as a rag doll, into the car. At home, Paola made arrangements to pay for the dogs' adventures. Two hundred euros to the truffle hunter to pay for the chickens they had killed. A hundred euros for the visit to the veterinarian and ten more for the antibiotics he prescribed.

A few weeks later, driving home from town, I saw several fire trucks and police cars parked at the riverbank near the house. I didn't think too much about it until I got home and went straight to Mario's, where I'd been invited to dinner.

Paola was talking on the phone. "Yes, we own two big dogs," she said into the receiver. "Right, a white female and a reddish-brown-and-white male. *Per carità* [good heavens]—I'll be right there!"

"The dogs?" I asked.

"The police just pulled Peri out of the river—she was drowning!"

Paola dashed out in a panic to pick up the rescued dogs. Peri looked terrible, but she and Paco were okay—this time.

(After I returned home to California, both Peri and Paco were poisoned. Peri, like a cat with nine lives, survived. Paco wasn't so lucky.)

Pork Chops with Rosemary and Sage

Braciole con rosmarino e salvia

Pork has a natural affinity for rosemary and sage—two herbs grown in every Umbrian garden. In the region, cooks also season pork with bay leaves and ginepro (juniper berries), gathered in the countryside. But juniper berries are also sold in the spice aisle. If you'd like, sauté one bay leaf and six juniper berries with the garlic, rosemary, and sage.

This is one of my favorite pork recipes—it's very simple and incredibly flavorful. Today's pork is very lean, so even when the chops are cooked until just done, they tend to be a little dry. But that is exactly how the Umbrians like their meat—on the dry side. The pork needs to be cooked slowly and long enough to pick up the flavor of the rosemary, sage, and garlic.

Yield: 4 servings

4 (¾-inch thick) bone-in pork chops (about 2 pounds)

½ teaspoon kosher salt (*important:* see "About Salt," page xxv)

¼ teaspoon red pepper flakes

Dash freshly ground pepper

3 tablespoons extra virgin olive oil

10 large fresh sage leaves

2 (5-inch) sprigs rosemary

2 large garlic cloves, lightly crushed with a knife blade, and peeled

1¼ cups dry white wine, such as pinot grigio or sauvignon blanc

1. Pat the chops dry with paper towels; sprinkle both sides with the salt, red pepper flakes, and pepper. Heat a large skillet (roomy enough to accommodate all of the chops in a single layer) over medium-low heat, about 3 minutes; swirl the oil around the skillet. When the oil is hot, add the sage, rosemary, and garlic. Sauté 30 seconds (do not brown).

2. Arrange the chops in a single layer in the skillet; sauté until well browned on both sides, about 8 minutes per side. Add the wine; simmer uncovered over medium heat until the wine turns syrupy and saucy and the pork is no longer pink at the bone, 8 to 10 minutes. Remove from the heat. Turn the chops over; cover and let stand 5 minutes to absorb the flavors. To serve, drizzle the sauce over the chops.

Hunter's Chicken—Pollo alla cacciatora

Follow the recipe for Pork Chops with Rosemary and Sage (page 31), but substitute a whole, cut-up chicken for the pork chops. When the chicken is well browned, add about 1½ cups of white wine; cover and simmer until the chicken is tender and no longer pink at the bone. The sauce should be thick and syrupy—if needed, remove the chicken from the skillet when it is done and reduce the sauce until it is thickened. Boneless, skinless chicken can also be used—remove the chicken as soon as it is done; reduce the liquid, if needed. ❧

Chicken with Red Peppers
Pollo con peperoni

In the summer, when red and yellow bell peppers are abundant and less expensive, this recipe from Paola is one of my favorites. Paola often serves it with rice. Before steaming the rice, she sautés it in extra virgin olive oil with a little garlic

and a dash of salt. I also like to eat it with bread so I can scoop up every drop of sauce on the plate (without having to lick it off).

Although you can use any mix of chicken pieces, thighs are ideal because they don't become dry during the long simmering required to make the peppers melt in your mouth.

Yield: 4 main-dish servings (or 8 second-course servings)

8 chicken thighs (or 3 pounds chicken pieces)

2 tablespoons extra virgin olive oil

2 garlic cloves, lightly crushed with a knife blade, and peeled

1 (6-inch) sprig rosemary

1½ teaspoons kosher salt (*important:* see "About Salt," page xxv)

¼ teaspoon freshly ground pepper

½ cup plus ⅓ cup water

1 medium onion, thinly sliced

¾ cup dry white wine, such as pinot grigio or sauvignon blanc

1½ pounds red bell peppers, cut into ½-inch wide strips

1 large Roma tomato, grated (see "How to Grate Tomatoes," page 34)

1. Remove and discard the chicken skin. Heat a large skillet over medium heat (roomy enough to fit all chicken pieces in a single layer). Swirl the oil around the bottom of the skillet. When the oil is hot, add the garlic and rosemary; cook 30 seconds. Arrange the chicken pieces in the skillet; sprinkle with the kosher salt and pepper. Sauté the chicken until golden brown, about 10 minutes per side. Pour the ½ cup water into the skillet to help loosen the chicken.

2. Use a slotted spoon to transfer the chicken to a bowl. Add the onion to the water in the skillet; simmer, stirring frequently, until the onion is tender and the liquid has almost evaporated, about 8 minutes. Return the chicken and accumulated juices to the skillet; add the wine. Simmer over medium-high heat, stirring occasionally, until the wine evaporates, about 8 minutes.

3. Add the peppers, tomato, and remaining ⅓ cup water; toss to distribute the ingredients. Cover and bring to a boil; reduce the heat to medium low. Simmer, stirring and turning the chicken occasionally, until the chicken is very tender and the peppers almost "melt" into a sauce, about 50 minutes. Discard the rosemary stem. Adjust the salt and pepper to taste. To serve, spoon the sauce and peppers over the chicken. ❧

HOW TO GRATE TOMATOES

Grating is a quick, easy way to purée fresh tomatoes. Cut a tomato in half crosswise; use a small spoon or narrow spoon handle to scoop out the seeds. If the tomato is firm, use a knife to make a ¼-inch-deep X in the cut face of each tomato half. Hold a tomato half with the cut face against a coarse box grater—grate the tomato down to the skin. Discard the skin.

PICKING PEACHES AT PIA'S

Silvia and I parked in a peach orchard near a restored stone farmhouse at the foot of Monte Corona near Umbertide. We got out of the car, and Silvia shouted, *"Permesso, permesso?"* (People often ask permission before entering a store or house, even when they have already been invited to come in.) A few minutes later a robust woman, well past middle age, appeared. We asked if she sold peaches.

"*Sì, sì,* I sell peaches," she said. "But I will have to pick them." We followed her between rows of peach trees while she selected the ripest fruit, filling a big bucket. When the bucket was full, Silvia reached for it.

"*Signora,* let me carry it," said Silvia.

"*Scherza* [are you joking], *signora?*" she replied. She acted insulted.

"*Signora,* can you tell me how to make peach jam?" I asked.

She gave me her recipe and told me to ripen the peaches first or the *marmellata* would be *cattiva* (bad). While she weighed the peaches on a large antique scale inside the barn, she told us a story.

"I was making jam when a woman came for peaches. I told her, 'I am in a hurry. I'm cooking jam.' The woman exclaimed, 'You must be *pazza* [crazy] leaving jam on the stove!'"

Silvia nodded as though she understood.

"I told her I knew what I was doing," the *signora* continued. "She asked my secret for leaving jam unattended, so I invited her into the kitchen. When she saw my wood stove with a big pot of jam on top of a stack of six flat stones, the lady laughed. She'd been making jam for years and never thought of doing that."

When I paid, I asked for her name. The *signora* looked apprehensive. She shook her head and didn't say anything. Silvia explained that I was writing a cookbook and would like to use her name with the recipe. She remained silent.

"Just your first name, not your last name," I said.

She looked toward Silvia and back at me, and finally said, "Pia. Just Pia."

By the time I got home, I decided to make Paola's Peach-Fig Jam (below). Together the two fruits make a more interesting jam than either does when used alone. ❧

Peach-Fig Jam
Marmellata di pesche e fichi
∞

My first September in Umbertide, I encountered Paola almost daily in front of the five grand fig trees that lined my patio.

"I'm making jam again," she said when she saw me. After a week or so of these daily encounters, she said, "I am so embarrassed about coming again." By the end of the month my cupboard was full of Paola's peach-fig jam.

On my next trip, I eagerly awaited fig season. In spring, I watched as thousands of tiny green pea-sized figs popped out on the trees' branches. In midsummer, Paola and I talked about how much jam we would make together with the big crop of figs. But when August arrived, the trees were not just heavy with figs—they had become infested with wasps. Thousands and thousands of them swarmed the trees and terrorized me when I sat on my terrace. Near September, when the fruit was almost ripe, the situation was insopportabile (intolerable). Silvia called an exterminator who sprayed the trees with gallons of pesticides; we lost the enormous crop.

Only delicious, ripe fruit makes good jam, so do a taste test first to see if it is worth the trouble. After all, making jam is a labor of love. But I enjoy carrying on the tradition—spending a day the way my grandmother and great-grandmother spent summer days when their orchards were ripe with figs, peaches, and plums.

For an easy but elegant dessert, put a wedge of Roquefort cheese on a serving plate; drizzle the cheese with honey. Spoon a large dollop of jam next to the cheese. Scatter roasted almonds or hazelnuts around the plate; serve with sliced bread. This jam also makes an excellent filling for crostata (page 53) or fagottini (page 216). The jam is ready to use when it has cooled, without canning it first.

Yield: *About* 7 *or* 8 *(half-pint) jars*

2 pounds firm but ripe peaches (4 to 5 large)

2 pounds fresh figs, stems trimmed, diced

4 cups sugar

Finely shredded zest of 1 lemon (see "About Zest," page 37)

⅓ cup fresh lemon juice (about 1 large, juicy lemon)

GETTING STARTED: Read "Jam to Jars" (page 37).

1. Fill a medium saucepan half full of water; bring to a boil. Use a slotted spoon to lower the peaches into the boiling water; leave about 30 seconds. Transfer the peaches to a board. When cool enough to handle, pat dry with paper towels and use a paring knife to lift off the skin. Pit and dice the peaches. In a large, tall, heavy nonreactive pot, toss together the peaches, figs, sugar, lemon zest, and juice; let stand 30 minutes.

2. Meanwhile, follow the directions in "Jam to Jars" to sterilize the jars (or use the jar manufacturer's instructions).

3. Bring the fruit to a boil over high heat, stirring frequently. Reduce the heat to medium high; cook and stir 15 minutes. Remove from the heat; use an immersion blender or potato masher to break the fruit into small chunks, but do not purée.

4. Return the pot to the stove; cook at a rapid boil—but be careful, as sugary mixtures become extremely hot and can cause severe burns. Stir constantly,

reducing the heat as needed to prevent splattering, until the jam is very thick, 15 to 20 minutes. Now the hot jam is ready to use or can. See "Jam to Jars" and "Storing Jam" (below and page 38).

NOTE: Jam must be cooked in small batches to retain its fruity flavor and to thicken properly. If you want to make a larger amount, cook each batch separately—one recipe per pot. Do not vary the ingredients—a large quantity of sugar is necessary to get a thick consistency. ❧

ABOUT ZEST

Several recipes in this book call for lemon or orange zest. The zest is the colored outer peel of the fruit—avoid the white pith, which lies under the zest. When "finely shredded" zest is needed, use a rasp-style grater. Microplane is one brand that makes this type—it is available at most kitchen shops.

JAM TO JARS: SIX EASY STEPS TO SAFE CANNING

Our grandmothers' method of sealing jam jars with wax is no longer considered safe, so I provide you with detailed but simple instructions for canning jam.

YOU WILL NEED:

- Glass jars (expressly for canning) with new lids
- Large pot with a rack and lid (see Note, page 39)
- Medium pot, for sterilizing the lids
- Jar tongs
- Jam funnel
- Teakettle filled with boiling water, to add water to pots as needed

Setting Up: Arrange a clean dishtowel on a large tray. Set the jam funnel inside a bowl (to hold when not being used). Dampen several clean paper towels for wiping off filled jars. Have a few clean dishtowels handy.

Sterilizing Jars: Before sterilizing the jars and lids, wash them in hot, soapy water. Use the jar manufacturer's instructions or the method that follows to prepare the jars. Fill the large pot (fitted with the rack) about three quarters full of water; bring to a boil. Use tongs to slowly fill and submerge one jar at a time in the boiling water; boil 10 minutes. Fill the medium pot about three quarters full of water; heat to just below the boiling point. Heat the lids in the water for 10 minutes (do not boil the lids). Keep lids and jars hot throughout the canning process. You will use the large pot filled with boiling water later to process the jars.

Filling Jars: Use tongs to lift one jar at a time from the boiling water, tilting to empty the water into the pot. Stand the jar on the dishtowel-lined tray. Put the funnel in the jar; fill with hot jam, leaving ½ inch headspace. Set the funnel aside. Clean the jar's rim and threaded sides with a damp paper towel. Remove a lid from the hot water. Hold the jar with a dry dishcloth and seal the jar but do not overtighten the lid. Keep the jar level from now on. Finish filling and sealing only the number of jars that fit into the large pot at one time (with jars spaced ½ inch apart). Fill, seal, and process in batches, as needed, depending on the size of the pot.

Processing Jars: Use tongs to carefully put the filled jars into the pot of boiling water (the same pot used for sterilizing jars), adding as many jars as possible, leaving ½ inch between jars. Add boiling water, if needed, to cover the jars with at least 2 inches of water. Cover the pot and bring to a boil. When the water boils, set the timer and boil for 10 minutes (add boiling water if needed to keep it 2 inches above the jars). Keeping the jars level, transfer them from the water bath to the dishtowel-lined tray, leaving 1 inch between jars. Pat lids dry with a clean towel. Cool the jars for 24 hours without disturbing.

Storing Jam: Check the seals, following the jar manufacturer's instructions. Here is one method for two-piece lids—remove the ring from the jar and gently try to pry off the lid with a finger. If the lid holds firm, replace the ring—the jar is properly sealed. One-piece lids usually sink in the center when sealed. Immediately refrigerate or freeze any jars with faulty seals. Store properly sealed, unopened jars in a cool, dark place for up to one year. Once opened, jam usually keeps in the refrigerator for several weeks. If jam is moldy, discard the entire contents of the jar.

NOTE: The large pot needs to be tall enough to hold 2 inches of water above the jars, plus have enough space to prevent overflowing when boiling. A silicone hot pad can replace the rack (jars can also be put directly in the pot, but there is risk of breakage).

2 🌿 My Professor and the Two Cousins—
Il mio professore e le due cugine

Gallina vecchia fa buon brodo

(An old hen makes good broth)

SOON AFTER MY ARRIVAL IN UMBERTIDE, I MET MY NEIGHBOR MARIO, who became my Italian tutor. With Mario's patience and determination, after almost five months of daily lessons, I began to understand and speak Italian. Mario, a *buona forchetta* (literally "a good fork," a hearty eater), was just developing an interest in cooking. He and his partner, Michela, taught me to make simple, everyday dishes that Umbria's busy dual-career families have time to make.

Not long after I met Mario, I was introduced to his cousin Gabriella. She is famous within the family for the traditional Umbrian desserts that she bakes using her grandmother's recipes. We made her *nonna's torcolo* (nut cake) and *crostata* (jam tart) in her historic house with frescoed walls. On a hike, I bumped into another cousin, Tomaso. He isn't a cook, but he is married to Anna, one of the best cooks in the family. I finally got a cooking lesson from Anna, so you'll meet her, too.

MARIO—*IL MIO PROFESSORE*

A day or two after arriving for the first time in Umbertide, I sat on the bench outside the apartment I had just moved into. I watched as an old red Volkswagen Golf bobbled up the long, steep gravel driveway to my house, dipping and turning in the deep ruts like a boat in a choppy sea. As soon as the car neared the house, my neighbor's dogs began barking wildly and jumping on the fence that surrounded their kennel. A half dozen or so barn cats and their kittens fled for cover. Mario got out of the car and introduced himself.

"I am your next-door neighbor," he said in good English.

I told him in broken Italian who I was and that I had already met his mother, Paola.

"So you speak Italian?" he said.

"*Magari* [I wish]! I am here to study Italian and to write a cookbook."

Mario's aunt Silvia told me that as a child, Mario was everybody's favorite. He was a bit of a devil, too, she added. As a young adult, he is lively, and at times unconventional, but he is not the rebel he had been. Mario is *in gamba* (literally "in leg"), which means he is bright and on the ball. He was the first among his siblings to earn a university degree and to get a job, although he is the youngest of Paola's three kids.

He is a handsome young man with prominent black eyebrows, dark chocolate eyes, smooth olive skin, and closely cropped salt-and-pepper hair (he started to go gray in his twenties). A small tattoo adorns one arm, and when we met (he was twenty-three) one ear was studded with a tiny silver earring—it disappeared a few years later. When he talks about himself, he says he is more European than Italian. He spent his high school years in Brussels with his Portuguese father, leaving his mother, two brothers, and friends at home.

When I first met Mario, he was a student in Perugia at the Università per Stranieri. I had plans to attend the university's three-month Italian immersion program. When I found out he was home, writing his thesis on international marketing, I asked him to tutor me until classes started.

"Sure, I have time," he replied. "And my mom can help. She used to teach Italian conversation at the university."

We agreed on a fee and began lessons the next day. Mario had never taught but he knew the agony and ecstasy of learning a language. He speaks Spanish, English, French, and Portuguese. Paola orchestrated my lessons, coaching Mario on how to teach and what homework to assign. Mario's family and friends provided me real-life practice. From then on, everyone spoke to me only in Italian.

The student-tutor relationship is very intense. We spent two or three hours a day talking about everything. Politics, religion, crime, soccer, relationships, love, work, culture, film, education, wine, and food. Through Mario, I became part of the family. One day, several of us went to his cousin's for a swim. Mario rang the buzzer. When his cousin's voice boomed over the intercom, Mario wasn't paying attention, so I piped in, "It's us, the Ramaccionis." Everyone heard me. Michela laughed and said, "Well, I guess you are one of us."

Mario loves the old country house that he and I shared. In his spare time, he helps Silvia haul and stack firewood. He prunes, gardens, and picks grapes. Mario's apartment is the place to hang out. During my first tenure in Umbertide, his many friends would arrive from two in the afternoon (just up out of bed) until midnight. Who knows when they left? Now that Mario is a father, and he has a job with a long commute, his friends usually stay away on weeknights.

Mario was a very good teacher. He was fun, patient, and supportive. "*Prova, prova* [try, try]," he always said. For the first time, I didn't care about sounding stupid when I spoke a foreign language. Going to the university had lost its appeal. I knew Italian teachers' reputation for being less than forgiving when students make mistakes. Mario agreed to continue our lessons, but after three months he came to me with a proposal.

"There is a level-one test at the university in a month," he said. "My mom thinks you should take it."

"Mario, what if I don't pass?"

"My mother thinks you will."

I understood Mario, but outsiders, with accents slightly different from his, were hard for me to comprehend. I had a limited vocabulary, and I would be competing with the young students who had finished the university's three-month all-day immersion program. With hesitation, I finally agreed.

So the lessons that had been leisurely were accelerated. We spent the next month reviewing, and for homework, I did practice exams.

The day of the exam arrived and everyone in the family was excited, except me. I had found the practice exams difficult, and I still made many mistakes when I spoke. And answering questions after listening to tapes would be a big challenge without any visual cues.

At the exam, I was asked to write about a picture of a robbery. My vocabulary didn't include the words I needed, but I muddled through. Then I listened to the tapes several times before darkening a circle with my best guess. Before my oral exam, I started to relax—I was almost done. For the orals, I was directed to a room to meet my examiner. There sat Paola, Mario's mother! Seeing her unnerved me. I didn't want to make a fool of myself in front of her! I spoke worse than I usually did.

That night, I warned Mario that I was pretty sure I had failed. Although Mario tried to be positive, I knew he would take my failure personally. I felt terrible. His mother gave us no clues one way or another. We just had to wait.

One afternoon Mario called with the results of the exam.

"My mother says you passed!" he said.

"I did? Are you sure?"

I never got written confirmation from the university, although Silvia had promised to pay to get my grade (there was a fee). Sometimes I think that Paola told Mario I had passed to make us both happy, but that in reality I hadn't really passed. Maybe someday I'll ask.

Spaghetti with Tuna and Tomatoes

Spaghetti con tonno

∞

In the past, when Catholics were not allowed to eat meat on Fridays, this dish was even more common in Umbria than it is today. Sugo di tonno is one of Michela's favorite sauces, so she and Mario make it often.

The beauty of this dish is its simplicity and short ingredient list. I call for spaghetti, but several other styles of pasta work well, including fusilli and spaghettini. My favorite pasta for this sauce is sedanini or mezze penne—tiny, ribbed penne.

Sometimes Mario sautés a few teaspoons of capers and a couple of mashed anchovy fillets with the celery and garlic, but he says it is more Umbrian with-out them. Parsley and garlic are essential to the dish—cheese is forbidden. The celery should be chopped very fine so that it almost disappears.

Yield: 4 main-dish servings (or 6 to 8 first-course servings)

1 can (14 ounces) whole tomatoes with juice

¼ cup extra virgin olive oil

1 medium celery stalk, finely chopped

3 large garlic cloves, peeled

1½ teaspoons kosher salt plus more to cook the pasta (*important:* see "About Salt," page xxv)

⅛ to ¼ teaspoon red pepper flakes

1 pound dry spaghetti, *sedanini,* spaghettini, penne, or fusilli

1 can (6 ounces) water-packed tuna, drained

⅓ cup packed Italian parsley, finely chopped

Freshly ground black pepper

1. Mince/pulse the tomatoes with juice using an immersion blender or food processor; set aside. Bring about 3 quarts of cold water to a boil in a large pot to cook the pasta (see page 28).

2. Heat the oil in a large saucepan. Sauté the celery and garlic over medium-low heat, stirring frequently, until soft, about 6 minutes (do not let the garlic brown). Stir in the puréed tomatoes, 1½ teaspoons of the kosher salt, and red pepper; cover and simmer over low heat for 15 to 20 minutes, stirring frequently.

3. Meanwhile, add 2 tablespoons kosher salt to the pot of boiling water. Add the pasta; cook, stirring occasionally, until *al dente*—taste for doneness a couple of minutes before the time recommended on the package. Shortly before draining the pasta, reserve about ½ cup of the cooking liquid; set aside.

4. About 5 minutes before the pasta is ready, add the tuna and parsley to the sauce. Use a fork to break the tuna into shreds; cover and simmer 5 minutes, stirring frequently. Remove and discard the garlic. Drain the pasta and return it to the empty pot.

5. Add the sauce to the pasta; toss to evenly coat. As needed, add the reserved cooking liquid by the tablespoon to moisten the pasta. Adjust the salt and season with black pepper to taste. Remove from the heat; let the pasta stand 2 minutes to absorb the flavors of the sauce. Serve immediately. ❧

LUNCH *DA ME*—AT MY PLACE

On my first visit to Umbertide, Mario taught me to send text messages from my cell phone. My phone was intuitive—when I started to type an Italian word, the *telefonino* tried to guess what word I was entering. I loved watching how the words changed as I keyed in more letters.

It was near noon, and I had just sent Mario a text. "Coming for lunch?" it read.

"Yes, at one," he texted back.

Several times a week I made lunch for Mario. At that time, he worked for a local producer of cured meats—prosciutto, salami, mortadella—just a few minutes from home. Mario's brother Amilcar often joined us—and when he did, we always had wine with lunch. At 12:30, I turned on the stove under the pasta water. I was eager to hear Mario's and Amilcar's critiques of my meat sauce. Mario gets exuberant about dishes he likes, but Amilcar is like many Italian men who take it upon themselves to point out what isn't perfect, ignoring what is.

Just before 1:00, Amilcar sat down at my table, and I poured each of us a glass of red wine. It was Friday—Mario would probably have *un goccio* (a drop), too. When Mario arrived, I served the spaghetti with meat sauce.

"*Ho una fame del lupo* [I am as hungry as a wolf]!" Mario said. "Who made the sauce?"

"I did."

"It's perfect," he said. "Some people use too much cheese."

"Hmm," Amilcar mumbled. "Well, it is really good."

One day, three-year-old Giulia stayed home from school with a fever, so she came to lunch. While we were finishing our espressos, Mario kissed Giulia goodbye and told her he had to leave.

"*Non andare a lavoro* [Don't go to work]!" she sobbed.

"I have to go back to work. My boss is expecting me." He picked her up and kissed her, wiping the tears off her cheeks.

"I'll come too," whimpered Giulia.

"What will you do at work?"

"*Mangio prosciutto* [I'll eat prosciutto]."

Of course, Mario drove those few miles back to work without Giulia, who had settled down to take a nap. Amilcar cleared the wineglasses and plates off the table, while I put the leftover meat sauce away.

Scaloppine with Prosciutto and Provolone
Saltimbocca

Saltimbocca is so delicious it "jumps in the mouth" (the literal meaning of the Italian name). Mario's specialty is making quick, tasty dishes—this is one of my favorites. He uses veal, but I use thinly sliced top round (beef), sometimes called scaloppine. But pork cutlets and turkey or chicken breasts—all thinly sliced—are good choices. If the meat is thicker than ⅛ inch, you will need to pound it—the bonus is that pounding makes the meat more tender. To pound, put one slice of meat at a time inside a heavy plastic bag; pound the bag with a meat pounder until the meat is about ⅛ inch thick. Take care not to pound too much or the meat will tear.

You might need a few more slices of cheese and prosciutto, depending on their thickness and the surface area of the sliced beef. To be safe, buy extra slices of each. If you'd like, substitute mozzarella, preferably fresh, for the provolone cheese, but cut the mozzarella into ⅜-inch cubes and sprinkle them over the meat. The cheese will spread as it melts.

Yield: 4 main-dish servings (or 8 second-course servings)

1 pound sliced (⅛ to ¼ inch thick) beef, such as round steak (about 8 large slices)

6 to 8 ounces thinly sliced provolone cheese

8 to 10 thin slices prosciutto

4 to 6 tablespoons extra virgin olive oil

10 to 15 large sage leaves

2 or 3 (6-inch) sprigs rosemary

2 or 3 garlic cloves, lightly crushed with a knife blade, and peeled

Kosher salt

Freshly ground pepper

2 or 3 tablespoons dry white wine, such as pinot grigio or sauvignon blanc

You'll also need: A flat-bottom meat pounder or a heavy glass (to pound the meat).

Getting started: Since the thin beef cooks very quickly, you will need to have all of the ingredients ready to go before you start to cook—and you will need to work fast once cooking begins.

1. Pound the meat, if needed, to about ⅛ thick. Have enough cheese and prosciutto prepared to cover each slice of beef (but avoid contact with the raw meat); set aside. Heat a large skillet over medium-high heat. (You'll sauté the beef in two or three batches, depending on the size of the skillet.) Per batch, swirl 2 tablespoons of the oil around the bottom of the skillet; add 5 sage leaves, 1 rosemary sprig, and 1 garlic clove. Sauté until the garlic begins to sizzle, but do not brown it.

2. Arrange the sliced beef side by side in the skillet; season one side lightly with kosher salt and pepper. As soon as the beef is lightly browned, 1 to 2 minutes, turn it over and add 1 tablespoon of the wine. Immediately top each beef slice with a slice of prosciutto and cheese (the beef should be almost covered).

3. Cover and cook until the beef is done and the cheese melts, about 1 minute. Transfer the beef to a large, warm platter. Spoon the pan drippings and sage over the beef; discard the garlic and rosemary. Cover tightly with foil and hold in a warm oven (150 to 200°F).

4. To cook subsequent batches, wipe the skillet clean, if needed. Repeat steps 1, 2, and 3, using the same amounts of oil, sage, rosemary, and garlic for each batch, until all of the beef is prepared.

VARIATION: After topping the meat with prosciutto (see step 2), spread several tablespoons of Classic Tomato Sauce (see recipe, page 26) or store-bought marinara sauce over the meat. Cover with provolone and sprinkle with grated Parmigiano-Reggiano, to taste. Finish cooking per recipe instructions. ❧

HAMBURGERS DA MARIO

Mario knocked at my door one hot June evening. "Come for dinner," he said. "We're having hamburgers—I bought them at the grocery store." I envisioned frozen, perfectly formed thin beef patties of questionable quality. Instead I ate one of the best burgers I've ever eaten—plump, juicy, and well seasoned. The burgers at the market are not the factory-made variety; local butchers prepare them daily. The secret ingredients: ground veal, Parmigiano-Reggiano cheese, bread crumbs, lemon zest, milk, nutmeg, and salt.

"You cook them like a steak or a chop," Mario advised. "Brown them in extra virgin olive oil and then add a splash of white wine."

While Mario cooked the burgers, Michela prepared the condiments. She picked the lettuce—a delicate curly red leaf—and plump, red tomatoes fresh from the garden. She sliced the tomatoes and seasoned them with salt and pepper and a generous drizzle of fruity olive oil. She melted slices of *caciotta* cheese on the inside top of each dense, white bun. At the table, mayonnaise and mustard were absent, but not missed. Ketchup was passed, but not needed. Now I go *volentieri* (willingly) for hamburgers *da* Mario.

GALLINA VECCHIA FA BUON BRODO

"The game is more important than I am," sighed Michela. She was mad that Mario was going to a soccer game in Rome with friends.

"He adores you," I said. "Be patient." Off Mario went. Michela was cross, but she quickly got over it. She always did.

Mario liked to tease Michela about being the older woman; he was a few years younger. "*Gallina vecchia fa buon brodo* [an old hen makes good broth]," he would tell her. Mario says the proverb applies to women—an older, more experienced woman is better.

Michela makes a *bella figura* (a good impression), which is important to Italians. She is tall and slender with long, dark hair and dark eyes. She is always stylish. Even to walk the dogs, she dressed fashionably—a short skirt, zany tights, a lime-green sweater, and matching knee-high boots. I relied on her opinion when we shopped for bargains at the market.

During one of my stays in Umbertide, Michela's life turned upside down when her father fell off a ladder. "Between work and taking my mother to the hospital every day," she said, "I didn't have time to eat." Having at least one good, solid meal is really important to Italians, so she was worried her health was at risk. Michela still sees her parents almost daily, and calls her mother a couple of times a day.

When I called Mario and Michela from home one day, Mario sounded near tears. "I am very excited," he said. "Michela is pregnant."

"Is everyone else happy?" I asked.

Everyone was. Michela would soon move to Mario's, he said.

"Will you get married?" I asked.

"No," he said. Mario had always been against marriage. Michela was neutral.

"Michela's parents are traditional," he added. "They would like us to marry."

Mario and Michela led a busy life, and it was about to get more hectic. Michela worked full-time as a pharmacist at a *farmacia* in town. Mario was a university student. Mario took his relationship with Michela and his impending fatherhood seriously. After graduation, he accepted the first job offer (one that he would leave within a year after not being paid any wages for months).

Later, when I lived next door to Mario and Michela for a year, Giulia was two, going on three. Whenever Giulia saw me on my terrace, she ran for the stairs. We screamed at her—the concrete steps were dangerous. Giulia was a very lively and stubborn child—she never listened. When she reached the terrace, triumphant, she would politely ask me for chamomile tea.

During that year, Michela and I saw each other almost daily. I'd drop by to see if she needed anything in town or to ask if Giulia felt better. When I had stomach troubles, I consulted her. I valued her knowledge, but most of the family had the usual Italian distrust of medicine—they frequently ignored her advice.

Shortly after I arrived in Umbertide, Michela announced that she was *incinta* (pregnant) with baby number two. Soon her belly swelled, and everyone talked to Giulia about the new baby. One day, when I visited Michela, Giulia came charging at me, screaming and throwing punches.

"Susanna, *sei brutta* [you're ugly]! Go home!"

Soon when anyone spoke to Michela, Giulia threw a tantrum. Just when Michela needed peace, she got none. She was working on an advanced degree and now worked six days a week at a pharmacy forty-five minutes from home. The pharmacy had computer troubles, so it hadn't issued paychecks in months. I asked her why she went to work when she wasn't being paid.

"Nobody is getting paid," she said. "Not the doctors or nurses. That's just how it is."

When I cooked with Michela's mother, she told me more about her daughter. "Michela was always at the top of her class," her mother said. "She's ambitious and very competitive." To make her point, she led me to shelves in the family room where more than thirty of Michela's track trophies were on display.

Unlike Michela's mother, who is an exceptional cook, Michela doesn't like to cook. Her mother often sends dinner home with Michela. Or Mario cooks. Michela is the food critic—she can tell you how to make her mother's recipes or tell you how a dish should taste. She was one of my valued taste testers.

During the summer, I often found Michela wearing a bikini, lying in the sun on a chaise in the garden. "I would rather be at the beach, but Mario is working today." Michela wanted to spend every summer weekend at the beach.

As Michela's pregnancy progressed, family and friends got so "ugly" that Giulia wouldn't let any of them near her mother.

"Maybe it's the terrible twos?" I offered.

"I think it's Bruno," said Michela. Bruno was the name they had given to the soon-to-be-born baby boy.

Bruno arrived a week before Christmas. The day after he was born, Silvia, Paola, and I went to visit Michela. She had delivered at an old hospital in the heart of Perugia, perched on the top of a hill. From the large window in her room, there were stunning views of the city's old churches, ancient houses, and red tile rooftops.

When Michela returned home, I went to see the baby. I braced myself for Giulia's assault. She came running up to me, but this time she smiled and reached for my hand.

"Susanna, you must come see my brother Bruno!"

Peace returned to the house—punctuated only by Bruno complaining of hunger or a wet diaper.

Since I have been back home, I hear that Giulia is a little mother to Bruno. And Mario recently accepted a more lucrative job—he is much happier. Michela completed one advanced degree and is working toward a second one. Mario still watches soccer with his friends, but now Michela invites their wives and kids to join them. She orders pizza and everyone watches the game together on the television in Mario and Michela's living room.

WATCH YOUR LANGUAGE!

I was living my dream, living in Umbria and speaking Italian. But I found memorizing thousands of new words—and their genders—difficult. (At my age, the brain was full.) Throw in the formal and informal "you," the irregular verbs, and the *passato remoto* verb tense, which English doesn't have, and you can see that Italian is a complicated language. But I had one advantage that I didn't have as a teen studying Spanish—I was not afraid of sounding dumb. So I spoke without hesitation.

One afternoon some Italian friends and I were listening to an American tell a story about her visit to the Great Wall of China. I was translating. "There were many women sweeping the steps," she said.

When I translated the sentence from English into Italian, my friends Paola and Silvia both looked horrified.

"That's enough, Suzanne," said Silvia. "You'd better stop."

"Why?" I asked.

"Never mind," said Paola. "Let's talk about something else."

I knew I had used some word or phrase incorrectly. So the next day I told Mario what I had said.

He laughed loudly. He said, "You said the women were f—king."

"No, I said 'sweeping'—s-c-o-p-a-r-e, 'to sweep,' right?" I asked.

"Yes and no. Today it means 'f—k.' Use *spazzare* for sweeping."

I had sounded more vulgar than dumb, but I didn't lose my courage to speak. In the future, I avoided new words until I was certain I knew them well—and I never spoke of sweeping again!

THE ELECTION

Most of the Italians I know aren't what I would call patriotic. For cultural and historical reasons, loyalty to the family is number one. Identity with their village or town is next. And most people have a strong attachment to their region.

Mario's cousin Gabriella is different. Although she is devoted to her family and local community, she is also very patriotic. "She has a patriotic fervor," said Silvia. "It's reminiscent of the Fascists of the 1930s." She is dedicated to her political party and what it stands for. Also, Gabriella is unlike most middle-aged Italian women I know, because she has never married or had children.

"She was very beautiful as a young woman." Silvia said. "But I think her father scared off any would-be suitors."

"How?" I asked.

"I remember him screaming at any beau who showed up."

Her father, who was very attached to her, is now dead. Gabriella's life is full. With a law degree, she found a good job with the municipality of Perugia. During off-work hours, she shares a beautiful apartment with a plump Siamese cat, whom she adores. She is very close to her large extended family and is one of the regulars at Casa Caldese on Sundays, when friends and family often come calling and stay to play cards.

During card games, I had noticed she sometimes talked politics, but no one listened. What did arouse curiosity was the dessert that Gabriella had brought. She has an old collection of family recipes of Umbria's traditional desserts—*torcolo, tozzetti, crostata*—and everyone loves them. One Sunday, shortly before a local election, Gabriella arrived carrying a freshly baked *crostata* (jam tart) and a stack of political flyers.

"Grow Umbertide with Gabriella Ramaccioni," the flyer said in big, bold print. "One Interest—Umbertide." Gabriella was running for office! This time during the card game, everyone listened to Gabriella talk and to the promises she was making as a candidate. Gabriella sounded self-assured and intelligent.

Billboards in downtown Umbertide were plastered with political posters. I walked by without paying attention, but the red posters with the distinctive hammer and sickle—the Italian Communist Party's symbol—made me nervous. When I was growing up in the United States during the 1950s and '60s, any association with communism was dangerous. And here were posters with pictures of real Communists—their headquarters was in the main piazza.

"This town is run by Communists," said Mario. "If you're not a Communist, it's nearly impossible to get elected—or hired. Gabriella doesn't stand a chance of winning."

The morning of the election, Silvia and Paola headed to town to cast their votes for Gabriella. If I could have voted, I, too, would have written in Gabriella's name as her flyer instructed. Instead, I would have to hope the *cittadini* (citizens) of Umbertide would vote for her.

The next day, Mario arrived with the election news. "The Communists won—just about everything." Gabriella had lost. The town was still red— along with most of the rest of Umbria.

Jam Tart

Crostata di marmellata

∞

This tart is very popular in Umbria. Its cookie-crust dough is called pasta frolla, *which means tender or short. Some cooks make the tart with a thick crust and lots of jam, but I prefer a thin crust and a thin layer of jam. Gabriella's grandmother's original recipe called for lard, but Gabriella adds butter. Gabriella sometimes fills the tart with pastry cream instead of jam.*

The crostata *is baked until quite brown and dry, which is typical of Umbrian desserts. My neighbor Michela came for coffee when I was baking the tart. Every time I brought it out of the oven, thinking it was done, she told me to put it back. When it looked overbaked to me, she said it was perfect.*

Yield: 8 to 12 servings

2¾ cups (12½ ounces) all-purpose flour plus more for rolling

Finely shredded zest of 1 lemon (see "About Zest," page 37)

½ teaspoon double-acting baking powder

½ teaspoon kosher salt (*important:* see "About Salt," page xxv)

⅔ cup (3½ ounces) granulated sugar

½ cup soft butter plus more for the pan

¼ cup lard, softened

2 large eggs

1 to 1½ cups Peach-Fig Jam (see recipe, page 35) or any thick jam

2 to 3 tablespoons unsifted powdered sugar

GETTING STARTED: Butter the bottom and sides of an 11-inch tart pan (preferred) or a large pie pan. Lightly flour a large wooden board.

1. In a medium bowl, toss together the flour, zest, baking powder, and kosher salt; set aside. Put the granulated sugar, butter, and lard into a large mixing bowl; mix well. Add the eggs; mix well. Add the dry ingredients in two batches, mixing well after each addition. Use hands to form a ball. Transfer the dough to the lightly floured board; knead about 30 seconds.

2. Form one third of the dough (about 8 ounces) into an 8-inch-long cylinder; shape the remaining dough into a 7-inch flat disk. Individually wrap the disk and cylinder in plastic. Chill dough until firm but not hard, about 1 hour.

3. Preheat the oven to 350°F. Roll the flat disk of dough into a circle slightly less than ¼-inch thick (it should be large enough to fit into the pan and come ½ inch up the sides). Carefully fold the dough in half; transfer it to the buttered pan. Gently press the dough into the bottom of the pan and about ½ inch up the sides (repair tears by pressing dough together with fingers). Spread the jam over the dough (the amount of jam needed will depend on the size of the pan and personal preference—I like a thin layer). If needed, trim the dough so it is no more than ¼ inch above the level of the jam; roll dough scraps into a ball.

4. You'll use the scraps and the cylinder of dough to make a decorative top. Slice off a small piece of dough at a time; use hands to roll pieces of dough into ⅜-inch diameter snakes. Set aside the number of snakes needed to go around the perimeter of the pan.

5. Arrange half of the remaining snakes in parallel lines about 1 inch apart across the top of the tart, adjusting the length of the snakes as needed; arrange the other half at right angles to create a crisscross pattern on top of the tart. Gently press snake ends into the dough around the edges of the

pan. Arrange the reserved snakes around the perimeter of the pan to cover crisscross ends; press to seal.

6. Bake in the center of the oven until the crust turns a rich golden brown, 50 to 60 minutes. While the tart is still warm, sift the powdered sugar over the tart.

NOTE: Instead of rolling snakes by hand, you can roll the cylinder of dough (shape it into a disk first) into a circle the diameter of the pan. Use a zigzag pastry wheel to cut the dough into 1/2-inch-wide strips. Arrange in a criss-cross pattern on top of the tart (see step 5). ?❧

Almond-Orange Biscotti

Tozzetti

Tozzetti *are known as biscotti (twice baked) in other parts of Italy. It's my guess that Umbrians love dry baked goods such as* tozzetti *because it gives them an excuse to serve* vinsanto, *a favorite dessert wine that they dunk cookies and cake into.*

Making this cookie dough goes quickly using a heavy electric mixer, but it is also easy to mix by hand.

Yield: About 5½ dozen cookies

4½ cups (20 ounces) all-purpose flour plus more for kneading

2 teaspoons double-acting baking powder

Finely shredded zest of 1 orange (see "About Zest," page 37)

1 tablespoon anise seeds (optional)

1¾ cups (13 ounces) sugar

½ cup (4 ounces/1 cube) soft butter

5 large eggs

8 ounces (1½ cups) whole almonds

You'll also need: Parchment paper

Getting started: Preheat the oven to 350°F. Line a large baking pan (an 11 × 16-inch jelly roll pan is perfect) with parchment paper. Put a damp towel under a lightly floured wooden board.

1. In a medium bowl, combine the flour, baking powder, and orange zest (if using anise seeds, add them now); set aside. In a large mixing bowl, beat together the sugar and butter. (If using an electric mixer, always use low speed and stop occasionally to scrape the sides of the bowl with a spatula.) Beat in the eggs, one at a time. Add the reserved dry ingredients in 3 batches; mix well after each addition. Stir in the almonds; mix well. Shape the dough into a ball.

2. Turn the dough out onto the floured board. Dust your hands with flour; knead the dough about 1 minute, dusting with flour, if needed. The dough should be soft and slightly sticky. Divide the dough into 4 equal pieces; roll each piece into a log about 1 inch in diameter by 15 inches long. Arrange the logs about 2 inches apart in the parchment-lined pan.

3. Bake at 350°F until lightly browned and firm but still cake-light when gently pressed, 20 to 25 minutes. Cool in the pan until firm enough to move without breaking, about 10 minutes. Carefully transfer the logs to a cutting board (you'll need the pan again); cut the logs at a 45-degree angle into ½-inch-thick slices (a serrated knife works well).

4. Arrange the cookie slices on the same parchment-lined baking pan with cut edges facing up. Reduce the oven temperature to 300°F; bake until dry, about 20 minutes. For really dry cookies, turn off the oven and let the cookies stand in the oven an additional 15 to 30 minutes. When completely cool, store in an airtight container. The cookies freeze well for a month or two. ❧

The Long-Awaited Dinner

I knew Tomaso, Silvia and Paola's cousin, long before I met his wife, Anna. Silvia and I encountered Tomaso frequently near his country house on Monte Acuto. Silvia consulted with him when we wanted to make *vinsanto*.

And at his recommendation, she replaced her ancient white-wine barrel with a new tank.

I'd heard stories of Anna's exquisite cooking for years. "She's the best cook in the family," Silvia told me. In December, when my year in Umbria was almost up, I was worried we wouldn't meet, but shortly before Christmas, Silvia, Paola, their cousin Gabriella, and I received an invitation to dinner.

Walking into Anna's living room that night in Città di Castello made me think of stepping into an Edith Wharton novel, the scene a nineteenth-century dinner party with New York's elite. A fire flickered in the beautiful old marble fireplace. Elegant centuries-old furniture gleamed with polish. Fresh flowers filled crystal vases. Artwork adorned the room: Anna's paintings of her beloved dogs; intricately carved gilded frames with family portraits from the 1800s; two huge ceramic vases, each with a portrait of one of the two sisters who had owned the family's pharmacy long ago. Beyond the vases, the dining table was set with crisp white linens, sterling silverware, long-stemmed crystal, and tall candlesticks.

On the bookshelf near the fireplace was a collection of antique ceramic jars from the pharmacy that had been in Anna's family since the mid 1800s. The name of the drug it had held was hand-painted on each jar—codeine, cannabis, morphine. Family photos in sterling silver frames were scattered on tables around the room. A delicate oval portrait on the wall caught my eye.

"Who is that?" I asked.

"That's Marianna," Anna said. "When I was growing up, my father frequently told us the story of Marianna, our relative the marchesa—a noblewoman." Pulling a book from a table, Anna opened it to a portrait of Marianna. "'The marchesa was considered one of the most beautiful and cultured women of the [nineteenth] century,'" read Anna. "She was the king of Bavaria's lover—Ludovico the First. He gave this painting to Marianna. The king's copy is in a museum." Ludovico (Ludwig/Louis I), who ruled from 1825 to 1848, was famous for his escapades with women.

Anna put the book away and she, Paola, and I headed to the kitchen to cook. Silvia, Gabriella, and Tomaso remained on the sofa in front of the fire—Tomaso with his fluffy white dog on his lap.

"You might know someone who used to be a regular at my table," Anna said while tying her apron around her waist. "He was always happy to accept my lunch invitations. He loved my cooking."

He was the man I had envied because he rented one of Anna's houses every summer—an idyllic farmhouse nestled in the woods on Monte Acuto. I did "know" him: Ralph Fiennes. I loved him in *The English Patient.* I had seen (or rather shamelessly stared at) him at a bar downtown.

Anna turned her attention to a sheet of paper. Reading out loud, she said, "The ingredients for *piccione in salmì.* Three *piccione* [squab], one and a half cups of *olio di oliva,* 133 grams of chicken livers, two cups red wine, half a cup of red wine vinegar . . ."

Never before had someone given me precise measures for a savory dish—most Italians cook by *occhio* (eye). But of course, she is a pharmacist and a former science teacher.

"Here in Città di Castello—only sixteen kilometers from the Tuscan border—our food has had a mix of influences," Anna explained. "From the Marche, Toscana, and Emilia-Romagna. Because there are so many hills and forests near Castello, we eat more game than people in southern Umbria. *Salmì* is for game—hare, squab, guinea hen, pheasant, wild boar—because its sauce is very assertive."

"All that vinegar and wine make anything tasty," I said.

Soon the kitchen was fragrant with the smell of rosemary, garlic, sage, and meats simmering. With all the conversation in the kitchen, it seemed like dinner was ready quickly, but a few hours had passed when we finally sat down to eat. When Tomaso lifted a forkful of *penne con sugo,* Anna turned to watch him. "He's my food critic," she said. Tomaso pronounced the pasta *perfetta.* Later he sampled the squab. "*Squisito* [exquisite]," he said. We all nodded in agreement.

"I learned to cook Umbrian dishes from his mother—an excellent cook." Anna said. "I didn't know much about cooking when we married, but for his sake, I learned."

With dinner, we drank Tomaso's wine. It was *vino novello*—the new wine from October's harvest. It was light and sweet—one of the best homemade wines I had tasted. I was glad he was advising Silvia.

After dinner, we followed Anna to a room off the entry. "This is my room," she said. "I come here when Tomaso watches soccer and I don't want to." It breathed good taste and old elegance. A fire in the marble fireplace made the room warm and inviting on that cold winter night. An antique wooden cabinet with glass doors revealed a collection of books and an extraordinary sculpture of a young girl. An off-white glaze showed the delicate features of her face, a dainty nose, a thick head of shoulder-length hair.

"My first attempt at sculpture," said Anna. "I was twelve."

"If you had told me it was by a famous Italian sculptor, I would have believed you!" I said, and I meant it.

A few minutes later, we said our good nights. Leaving Edith Wharton's world, we stepped outside, back into the twenty-first century in what is now a middle-class neighborhood.

Squab in Red Wine and Vinegar
Piccione in salmì
∞

Don't be intimidated by the long ingredient list—this is one of those Umbrian recipes that require very little preparation. Everything goes into the pot together and at the end the vegetables and giblets are puréed to make a delicious sauce for the squab and a pâté for crostini.

Since squab is expensive and difficult to find in the States, you might want to try duck or chicken thighs or legs (to replace the missing squab giblets, increase the chicken gizzards and livers by about one ounce each). Don't be tempted to leave out the giblets—they add an intriguing complexity to the dish and provide the backbone for the pâté.

Salmì is a very typical dish in Città di Castello, a small town near the Tuscan border (referred to as Castello by locals). But salmì is also popular in many places in Tuscany and Umbria, including my town of Umbertide.

Yield: 4 servings (including about 1½ cups pâté)

2 tablespoons drained and rinsed capers

2 tablespoons plus ⅓ cup red wine vinegar

½ cup extra virgin olive oil

2 squab (about 1 pound each) with giblets

4 ounces chicken gizzards

2 ounces chicken livers

1 large red onion, quartered

1 large celery stalk, quartered

1 medium carrot, peeled and cut in half

10 large fresh sage leaves

1 (5-inch) sprig rosemary

1 large garlic clove, peeled

8 juniper berries (see Note, page 61)

1 teaspoon kosher salt (*important:* see "About Salt," page xxv)

1/4 teaspoon freshly ground pepper

2 cups cold water

1 1/2 cups dry red wine, such as sangiovese, merlot, or cabernet sauvignon

1 thin slice prosciutto

1 tablespoon fresh lemon juice

Sweet baguette or Italian bread, such as ciabatta or Pugliese, sliced
    1/4-inch thick

1. Marinate the capers in the 2 tablespoons vinegar; set aside. Heat the oil in a large pot over medium heat. Add the squab and giblets, chicken gizzards and liver, onion, celery, carrot, sage, rosemary, garlic, juniper berries, kosher salt, and pepper. Pour the 2 cups water, wine, and remaining 1/3 cup vinegar into the pot. Cover and bring to a boil over high heat, stirring occasionally. Reduce the heat to medium; simmer, covered, 1 1/2 hours, turning the squab occasionally.

2. Remove the squab from the pot. Add the prosciutto and reserved capers in vinegar to the pot; simmer uncovered over high heat, stirring frequently, until the sauce is thick and the liquid is almost gone, 15 to 20 minutes. To make the pâté, use a slotted spoon to transfer the prosciutto, vegetables, and giblets left in the pot to a meat grinder fitted with a coarse blade or a food processor (leave the oil in the bottom of the pot); carefully check for and discard bones and rosemary stem. Grind or pulse until almost puréed but still slightly chunky; set aside.

3. When the squab is cool enough to handle, cut it into pieces (discard the back and tip of wings). Return the squab to the oil in the pot; sauté on

medium-high heat until the squab is lightly browned. Transfer the squab to a platter, but leave the drippings in the pot. Lightly season the squab with salt; set aside.

4. Stir the lemon juice into the pâté; mix in several tablespoons of reserved pan drippings. Adjust the salt and pepper to taste. Generously spread some of the pâté over the pieces of squab. Serve the remaining pâté with the bread (the pâté can be spread onto the sliced bread up to a half hour ahead or it can be served in a bowl alongside the bread at the table). If desired, drizzle a bit of the pan drippings over the squab and crostini (bread spread with pâté). Serve the *salmì* warm or at room temperature.

NOTE: Juniper berries can be found in the spice section of supermarkets. ❧

3 ❧ The Grandmothers—*Le nonne*

Quando c'è troppo carne al fuoco qualcosa si bruccia

(When there is too much meat on the fire, something will burn)

WHEN I ASKED PEOPLE TO INTRODUCE ME TO UMBRIA'S BEST COOKS, without fail, I was told to find *le nonne* (the grandmothers). Not one person referred me to a restaurant chef. This chapter is filled with tales and traditional recipes from the grandmothers I met in various towns in Umbria—Umbertide, Perugia, Magione, and Monte Acuto. My friend Michela's mother is one of the *nonne*. Her mother gets up early every Sunday to prepare a traditional *pranzo* (lunch) for her grown family. She refuses offers of help and she doesn't sit down until everyone has gone home. All the grandmothers have interesting stories and delicious recipes to share.

TUTTI A TAVOLA!

Monday was my favorite day for lunch with Mario. I would always ask Mario, "*Cosa hai mangiato ieri da Bruna* [what did you eat yesterday at Bruna's] at the family lunch?" We would talk about what Bruna Pauselli, Michela's mother, had cooked—rabbit in wine, polenta with mushroom sauce, lasagne with meat sauce. Sunday lunch is a tradition that goes way back in Umbria, and to Bruna it is an important institution. She expects everyone—her grown daughter and son, spouses, and grandchildren—to come to Sunday lunch.

For Bruna, Sundays start out like any other day. She gets up early and begins the day by cleaning the bathroom and tidying. But on Sundays, after doing her daily chores, she cooks a multicourse lunch for the family.

When I asked Michela about a cooking lesson with her mother, she sounded positive. Several weeks passed before Michela gave me the answer—no. "I tried several times," she said. "My mother is too shy." But Michela and her mother were often together, so I became acquainted with Bruna. Still, months went by with no mention of a lesson. About two weeks before leaving Umbria, Michela asked if I could come for dinner at her parents' on Sunday.

On Saturday Michela called to cancel. I suspected that her mother had cold feet, but then Michela said her father was in a serious condition after falling off a ladder. Her father, Silvio, remained in the hospital for the next five months. Bruna spent every day with him. Fortunately, the news of Michela's pregnancy a few months later gave Silvio a reason to live. When I returned to Umbria, Michela and Mario's baby, Giulia, was six months old. Silvio was better, but he had a long recovery ahead. I knew there would be no meal at Bruna's—all I could do was hope that on my next visit I would get the long-awaited lesson.

A year and a half later, I returned to stay for one year. About four months passed before Bruna mentioned a dinner. The invitation was vague, so I hoped it would materialize. Another month went by without setting a date. Bruna was busy taking care of her husband and granddaughters Giulia and Jessica. She had a house and large vegetable garden to tend. And besides hosting Sunday lunches, she also managed to make enough cappelletti for her granddaughters to eat regularly.

At last, Bruna set a date. When Michela and I arrived, Silvio was watching TV and trimming lettuce. "A bit of rest and entertainment," he said, motioning us to sit. Bruna asked, "*Signora*, what can I get you? *Caffè?* Orange soda or juice? Maybe white wine? Biscotti?"

I said *niente, grazie* after each offering and we headed to the kitchen. "Michela, please offer the *signora* chocolates!" said Bruna. She turned to me and said, "*Senza complimenti* [without compliments]. Please have something."

When I saw her disappointment, I asked for an espresso. She poured the dark, frothy coffee into a tiny cup, put a slice of homemade jam tart on a plate, and handed them to me. "*Senza complimenti,*" she said again.

Michela left and Bruna began. "Put the meat and wine in a pot."

"*Vino bianco* [white wine]," added Silvio.

"That's right," she said. Silvio continued to interrupt to provide important details. Finally, Bruna laughed and said, "He is telling you how to cook!"

"If you like to eat, then knowing about cooking is important," he said.

"He doesn't cook," said Bruna. "I cook by eye and Silvio tastes for me."

Later, Silvio critiqued the filling—it needed salt and nutmeg, he said. Bruna made the adjustments, and told me what time to come back the next day.

I returned at 2:30 on Wednesday. First, we would make cappelletti and then gnocchi with duck sauce. The day would culminate with a dinner for nine—Bruna's family and me. Bruna dropped ten eggs into the center of the flour on a wooden board. She mixed the flour and eggs using her hands, and then secured the pasta machine to the table. "I don't like the *macchinetta*," she said, "but with the grandkids and a bad back, I cannot roll pasta by hand." Bruna recently stopped making tagliatelle for Sunday lunch. "The machine ruins tagliatelle," she said.

"The texture is wrong," said Silvio.

"But the machine is okay for cappelletti and lasagne," she said.

Bruna rolled the dough and cut it into small circles. Silvio pinched off bits of filling with his huge fingers, putting a pea-sized dab on each circle. When he finished, he left the room. "Come back," Bruna called after him. "You do the filling. When I do it, it isn't good." Bruna's daughter-in-law and I shaped the pasta into "little hats." It took four adults three and a half hours to fill and shape the cappelletti. Bruna put the cappelletti in the freezer and we took a short break.

Bruna and Silvio live upstairs in a two-story flat in Umbertide. Her son, his wife, and their daughter, Jessica, live on the ground floor. Bruna's terrace is filled with potted plants, and all were in bloom. Every plant was flawless—no fading blossoms, no yellow leaves, no bugs. Bruna had transformed the entire side yard into a vegetable garden. That June day it was filled with perfect rows of tomatoes, lettuce, peas, and squash.

Back in the tiny kitchen, Bruna cooked the potatoes. I ran water to wash dishes, but she stopped me. She said, "I have my system." Her method involves hand washing and drying everything by herself. She has refused Michela's offer to put in a dishwasher. It is hard to believe that such elaborate meals come out of such a small space. On one wall there is a small work table next to the refrigerator. On the opposite wall there is a sink. Two stoves—

one gas and one wood-burning—take up the rest of the kitchen. Bruna uses the dining room fireplace to grill meat and cook griddle bread.

By the time we finished cooking, I was exhausted, but I offered to set the table. Bruna didn't argue; maybe she was tired, too, but she didn't show it. The table is disproportionately large for the room—it comfortably seats fourteen. Bruna planned dinner for 8:00, but at 8:15 Michela called. "We're shopping. We'll be there soon." At 8:30, she phoned to say they would arrive shortly.

Bruna hung up and said, "*Tutti a tavola* [everyone to the table]!" She added water to the pot for the third time to replace the water that had boiled away. When Mario and Michela arrived, we were all seated and Bruna was serving. She returned to the kitchen, even though we begged her to stay.

"*Complimenti* [compliments], Bruna," I said, facing the kitchen. "The gnocchi are so light and fluffy and the sauce is *squisito* [exquisite]!"

Bruna sat to eat a few bites of gnocchi. Then she checked the meat on the grill—fresh pancetta, pork ribs, and sausage. Earlier that day she had seasoned the meat with white wine vinegar, thinly sliced garlic, rosemary, and salt. Bruna picked up her barely touched plate, so I got up to help. "Signora, no, no," she said. "Please sit." But while she plated the meat, I managed to clear the plates. After Bruna passed the meat, she said *buon appetito,* and dashed to the kitchen.

"Please eat with us," I said.

"I will, *signora,* after I make the salad." At the table, she passed a salad of garden lettuce and sweet onion, seasoned with lots of olive oil, a whiff of vinegar, and salt. When she carried dishes to the sink, I followed, but she shooed me out.

Bruna nibbled on a rib and Michela served the gelato. We ate dessert, while Bruna washed fruit for the last course. She offered coffee, but we all declined. It was 10:30, and I was *stanca morta* (dead tired)—but I wanted to help. Bruna again told me about her system, so I gathered my things to go. Bruna transferred the cappelletti to a bag and plunked it on the scale. "We made two and a quarter *chilogrammi* [five pounds]," she said. If everyone in the family ate moderately, our two-day project would supply enough cappelletti for two Sunday lunches. But after you taste the cappelletti, you'll see that it was time well spent!

Crostini with Liver Pâté
Crostini con fegatini
∞

These are the crostini of Umbria—when people talk about crostini, they are often referring to crostini con fegato (liver; fegatini means "little liver"). This is the crostini served on special occasions such as Christmas. Bruna's recipe is really flavorful—and not too strong, if you are new to liver.

At my local grocery store, chicken hearts and gizzards are sold in a mixed package—the ratio of each isn't important. Chicken livers are sold separately. Juniper berries are found in the spice section of supermarkets. The pâté freezes well—defrost it and bring it to room temperature in the microwave before serving.

Yield: About 3½ cups

2 medium celery stalks, cut into halves

1 large onion, quartered

1 medium carrot, cut in half

9 large fresh sage leaves

9 juniper berries

2 (6-inch) sprigs rosemary

⅓ cup plus 2 tablespoons extra virgin olive oil

12 ounces chicken livers

12 ounces chicken hearts and gizzards

1 tablespoon kosher salt (*important:* see "About Salt," page xxv)

2 cups dry white wine, such as pinot grigio or sauvignon blanc

3 tablespoons white wine vinegar

3 anchovy fillets

1½ tablespoons drained capers

2 to 3 tablespoons fresh lemon juice

Freshly ground pepper

Sliced baguette (not sourdough)—toasting is optional

1. Put the celery, onion, carrot, sage, juniper berries, and rosemary in a large saucepan; drizzle with the ⅓ cup oil. Sauté over medium heat, stirring occasionally, until tender, 8 to 10 minutes. Rinse the livers, hearts, and gizzards under cold water; add them to the saucepan. Sprinkle with the kosher salt.

2. Cover; cook over medium-high heat, stirring frequently, until no longer pink, 10 to 15 minutes. Add the wine and vinegar; partially cover and simmer over medium-low heat, stirring frequently, until the gizzards are tender and most of the liquid has evaporated, 45 to 60 minutes. (The object is to cook the gizzards until tender and at the same time cook away the wine— remove the lid if needed to evaporate the liquid or add water if the wine evaporates too quickly.)

3. Discard the rosemary sprigs. Transfer the entire contents of the saucepan to a food processor; add the anchovies and capers. Pulse until almost smooth. (Alternatively, coarsely grind using a meat grinder.) Stir in 2 tablespoons of the lemon juice and the remaining 2 tablespoons of oil. Adjust the salt and lemon juice and season with pepper to taste. Spread a thin layer of pâté over the slices of bread or toast (the pâté can be chilled or at room temperature). Serve open-faced. ❧

To Toast Crostini

Preheat the oven to 350°F; arrange the sliced bread side by side on a large baking sheet. Bake until lightly toasted, 10 to 12 minutes (if the bread isn't quite crisp, let it cool in the pan to finish toasting). The bread can also be brushed with olive oil before toasting, but watch it carefully—it toasts more quickly.

CROSTINI—ANYTHING GOES!

In Umbria, most traditional meals start with crostini. Like French canapés, crostini are sliced bread topped with something, usually savory—pâté, cheese, mushrooms, anchovies. Crostini are served open-faced. The word *crostini* probably has its roots in the Italian word for crust (*crosta*). *Crostini* does not mean "toasted bread," as some Americans believe—in Umbria, it is usually not toasted. Bruschetta, on the other hand, is always grilled or toasted.

To make crostini, cut a baguette (not sourdough) into ¼-inch-thick slices. (Alternatively, slice Italian bread such as Pugliese or ciabatta ¼- to ¾-inch thick.) Cover each slice with one of the toppings that follow—plan on two or more toppings per platter for festive occasions.

There are several crostini recipes in this book. The classic Liver Pâté (page 66); Mushroom-Truffle Pâté (page 318); Fava Bean Purée (page 11); Lentils with Garlic (page 258); and Bruschetta/Crostini with Tomatoes (pages 200 and 318). Some other suggestions follow—toast the bread, if you want (see "To Toast Crostini," page 67).

• **Tuna:** Put 6 ounces of well-drained, water-packed tuna, ½ cup soft butter, 1 tablespoon extra virgin olive oil, 4 anchovy fillets, 2 tablespoons capers, and a dash of freshly ground pepper in a food processor; process until light and fluffy.

• **Taleggio Truffle:** Toast bread topped with Taleggio cheese until the cheese melts. Finely grate black truffles over the cheese; return to the oven to warm the truffles. Or spread soft butter over crostini; top with shaved white truffles.

• **Anchovy:** Butter crostini (toast before buttering, if desired) and top each slice with an anchovy fillet and a couple of capers (optional). Or instead of butter, spread mascarpone cheese over the bread and top with chopped anchovies.

• **Cauliflower:** Drizzle cauliflower florets lightly with extra virgin olive oil and sprinkle with kosher salt in a large baking pan; toss to coat. Spread the florets evenly over the pan (without crowding). Roast in a preheated 450°F oven until very tender and partially browned, about 20 minutes. Pulse/process in a food processor with enough olive oil to make smooth. Season with freshly ground pepper; adjust the salt to taste. Spread over crostini.

• **Smoked Salmon:** Cut a quarter of a small red onion into 6 pieces. Put the onion into a food processor; pulse until finely chopped. Add 8 ounces sliced smoked salmon, 3 sprigs Italian parsley, 1 tablespoon capers, and the juice of ½ small lemon; pulse until finely chopped. Add 2 tablespoons olive oil; pulse several times. Season with freshly ground pepper. Spread over toasted, buttered (and cooled) crostini.

• **Mortadella:** Process several slices of mortadella and/or prosciutto with ¼ cup softened butter and a dash of freshly ground pepper in a food processor until almost smooth. Add ¼ of an anchovy fillet (mashed), if desired. (Alternatively, use mascarpone cheese instead of butter.)

• **Black Olive:** Finely chop pitted black ripe or kalamata olives in a food processor with a small garlic clove, an anchovy fillet, and a few sprigs of Italian parsley. Add just enough mayonnaise to moisten; pulse a few times. Season with black pepper.

• **Sausage:** Spread a layer of fresh Italian sausage (casing removed) over thick slices of crostini; bake until the sausage is cooked and the bread is toasted. Top with thin slices of smoked cheese; bake until the cheese melts.

• **Egg:** Called *crostini alla mimosa*. Spread a little mayonnaise over slices of crostini. Top each *crostino* with a slice of hard-cooked egg. Garnish with a dollop of mayonnaise and season with salt and pepper.

Tiny Potato Dumplings
Gnocchi di patate

The original gnocchi were probably made from water and flour, but today the most traditional dumplings are made with potatoes and flour. In Umbria, grocery stores sell bags of potatoes labeled "for gnocchi." The potatoes are similar in texture

and color to our yellow potatoes, such as Yukon Gold. Pietralunga, near Umbertide where I lived, and Colfiorito, above Foligno, are famous for red potatoes, so local cooks use those to make gnocchi. Dumplings are also made with semolina, polenta, spinach, cheese, bread crumbs, or winter squash instead of potatoes.

My favorite sauces for potato gnocchi are sugo d'anatra *(duck ragù) and* sugo di carne mista *(mixed-meat sauce), see recipes, pages 72 and 7. For other serving suggestions, see "Ways to Serve Gnocchi" (page 74).*

The recipe instructions are long, but the gnocchi are not hard to make. After the potatoes are cooked and riced, it takes a little more than one hour to make the dough and roll and cut the gnocchi.

Yield: About 6 servings (about 3¼ pounds; allow 7 ounces per serving, less for a first course)

2½ pounds yellow potatoes, such as Yukon Gold

4 teaspoons kosher salt (*important:* see "About Salt," page xxv) plus more to cook the gnocchi

4 cups cake flour or unbleached all-purpose flour (17½ ounces)

1 large egg

You'll also need: A ricer (preferred) or a potato masher. Parchment paper.

Getting started: Read "Tips for Gnocchi" (page 72). Line 2 large trays with parchment paper and lightly sprinkle with flour (recommended). (Alternatively, generously sprinkle trays with flour.) Put a damp towel under a lightly floured wooden board.

1. If the potatoes are chilled, bring them to room temperature. Fit a large pot with a steamer rack; add water up to the rack. Put the potatoes on the rack. (Alternatively, without a rack, cover potatoes with water.) Bring to a boil. Reduce the heat to medium; cook the potatoes until tender when pierced with a knife, 35 to 50 minutes—test individual potatoes for doneness (remove as soon as tender). (If boiling potatoes covered in water, do not overcook or potatoes will absorb water.)

2. When the potatoes are cool enough to handle, use a paring knife to peel them. Push the potatoes, half a potato at a time, through the ricer into the

pot. (Alternatively, mash the potatoes with a potato masher.) Sprinkle the 4 teaspoons kosher salt over the potatoes; mix lightly with a fork. Make a well in the center of the warm potatoes. Add half of the flour and the egg; mix with a fork—throughout the entire process, mix and handle the dough as little as possible. When the flour is almost combined, add and mix in the remaining flour. Work the dough by hand for 30 seconds.

3. Transfer the dough—it will be crumbly—to the floured board. Knead the dough just enough to fully incorporate the flour and form a firm dough, about 2 minutes. Do not overwork or the dough will become sticky and unusable. (As the dough cools it feels wet—do not add flour.) Shape the dough into a loaf; cover with a bowl (keep covered during gnocchi making).

4. Wipe the flour off the half of the board closest to you; dust the top half with flour. Slice off a handful of dough; knead it once or twice. Working on the unfloured portion of the board, roll the piece of dough into a long ½-inch-diameter snake. Arrange the snake horizontally near the top of the board. (At this point, cut a few gnocchi to do a test; see "How to Test," page 72.)

5. When you have four long snakes, arrange them all horizontally in parallel rows about ¼ inch apart. Use a long, sharp knife to cut across all of the snakes to form ½- to ¾-inch logs. Sprinkle with flour; with flat fingers and the palm of your hand, gently roll gnocchi to slightly round the edges and lightly coat with flour. (Alternatively, see "How to Shape" on page 72.)

6. Transfer the gnocchi to the floured trays (do not stack or pack tightly); as more gnocchi are added, shake the trays to separate and coat gnocchi with flour. Let the gnocchi dry at room temperature 30 minutes (but not longer—they are perishable). Cover and freeze or refrigerate (see "How to Store," page 72).

7. To cook gnocchi, bring about 3 quarts of water to a boil in a large pot; add 2 tablespoons kosher salt to the boiling water. Drop several handfuls of fresh or frozen gnocchi into the rapidly boiling water (cook large amounts in batches), stirring occasionally. Once the gnocchi rise to the surface, cook fresh gnocchi about 1 more minute, about 4 minutes total (cook frozen gnocchi

about 2 more minutes, about 5 minutes total). For serving suggestions, see "Ways to Serve Gnocchi" (page 74). ᐩ

TIPS FOR GNOCCHI

How to Test: Boil a few gnocchi about 4 minutes—they are ready 1 minute after they rise to the surface. Cool slightly and taste; if they fall apart, work another 1/2 cup of flour into the dough, handling the dough as little as possible. Test again.

How to Shape: The Tiny Potato Dumplings recipe (step 5) explains the simplest method for shaping gnocchi. Three other methods follow: first, cut the snakes into 3/4-inch logs. Choose one of the following (1) roll each *gnocco* diagonally across the back of a fine cheese grater, or (2) roll over the back of a fork, or (3) push a finger into each *gnocco* to make a small indentation.

How to Store: Refrigerate covered trays up to 4 hours. Or freeze covered trays until firm; transfer to freezer bags. Seal tightly and freeze up to 3 months. Cook from the frozen state.

Duck Ragù with Braised Meat

Sugo d'anatra e carne in umido

This meat-scented—but meatless—sauce is the classic Umbrian sugo to serve with potato gnocchi (see recipe, page 69). The ragù is also delicious with pasta, polenta, or cheese ravioli. The meat that simmers in tomatoes to make the gnocchi sauce is served as the second course, carne in umido *(braised meat).*

Although when Bruna and I made this sugo, we used veal and duck, she sometimes substitutes rabbit or chicken thighs for the veal—she likes the fat that they add. (I have substituted beef for the veal.) Another friend uses sausage links, pork ribs, and cubes of pork shoulder, beef chuck, or veal—add whatever meat you'd like to serve for a second course. Unlike pasta, which is served with a thin coating of sauce, the gnocchi should swim in this soupy sugo. The sauce is also delicious with penne or homemade tagliatelle.

Yield: 4 to 6 servings of meat and 7 cups of sauce
(allow about ½ cup sauce per serving of gnocchi or pasta)

2 whole duck legs (about 1 pound)

1½ pounds beef chuck, cut into 1½-inch cubes

2 medium celery stalks, quartered

1 medium carrot, quartered

1 medium onion, cut into 6 wedges

½ cup extra virgin olive oil

3 tablespoons butter

1 ounce sliced pancetta or *lardo,* minced (see "Pork Fat," page 205)

4 teaspoons kosher salt (*important:* see "About Salt," page xxv)

¼ teaspoon freshly ground pepper

¾ cup dry white wine, such as pinot grigio or sauvignon blanc

2 cans (28 ounces each) whole tomatoes with juice

1 cup water

1. Pat the duck dry with paper towels; refrigerate uncovered ½ hour to dry it out. Put the duck, beef, celery, carrot, onion, oil, butter, and pancetta into a large pot; sprinkle with the salt and pepper. Sauté over medium heat, stirring occasionally, until the meat is no longer pink, about 10 minutes.

2. Add the wine; simmer over medium-low heat, stirring occasionally, until the sauce thickens, about 40 minutes. Purée the tomatoes with juice using an immersion blender or food processor. Add the tomatoes and the cup of water to the meat; cover and bring to a boil. Simmer over low heat, stirring occasionally, until the beef is tender, 1½ to 2 hours. Adjust the salt to taste (it needs a lot of salt because gnocchi are bland).

3. Turn off the heat; let stand ½ hour. Discard the vegetables. Remove the duck skin; cut the duck legs in two, separating the drumstick from the thigh. Transfer the beef and duck to a platter; sprinkle lightly with salt and pepper.

Ladle some of the sauce over the meat; cover tightly with foil and hold in a warm oven (150 to 200°F).

4. Refer to "Ways to Serve Gnocchi" (below) to use with gnocchi. Serve the meat as a second course.

NOTE: The meat and sauce can be frozen (separately) up to 4 months. ❧

WAYS TO SERVE GNOCCHI

Gnocchi are popular all over Italy, but their size, shape, ingredients, and name often change from region to region. In Umbria, besides meaning dumpling, *gnocco* also means "idiot" (*gnocco* is the singular of *gnocchi*). In the neighboring region of Tuscany, gnocchi are affectionately called *topini* (little mice). Below you'll find some of the memorable gnocchi sauces from Umbria's kitchens. Unless otherwise specified, use Umbrian or Tuscan pecorino or Parmigiano-Reggiano whenever grated cheese is called for.

Duck or Umbrian Ragù: These two are my favorite sauces for gnocchi (see recipes, pages 72 and 7). Layer hot, cooked gnocchi with sauce and grated cheese in a warm serving bowl, repeating the layers until all the gnocchi are used.

Gorgonzola Cheese: Heat half-and-half (or half milk and half cream) until warm but not hot; remove from the heat. Whisk in bits of Gorgonzola *dolce* cheese and a little grated Parmigiano-Reggiano cheese until the cheese melts (it should be flavorful and saucy, not thick). Add hot, cooked gnocchi; let stand a minute. Sprinkle with additional grated cheese and finely chopped walnuts (optional).

Buttery Tomato: Simmer cooked gnocchi in Classic Tomato Sauce (see recipe, page 26) for one minute. Add several tablespoons of butter; stir until melted. Serve with grated cheese. Or instead of butter, use lots of cream and just enough tomato sauce to make it pink and flavorful. Add red pepper flakes to taste.

Sausage-Porcini Cream: Rinse off a small amount of dried porcini mushrooms; soak in boiling water until soft. Drain and mince.

Sauté the porcini in a little olive oil with bits of Umbrian Bulk Sausage (see recipe, page 202). Add cream; simmer a few minutes. Stir in cooked gnocchi; simmer one minute. Serve with grated cheese. Diced ham or bacon can be substituted for the sausage.

White Truffles: Toss cooked gnocchi in melted butter; top with freshly shaved white truffles and grated cheese.

Porcini Cream: Sauté a whole garlic clove in butter and extra virgin olive oil until lightly browned. Discard the garlic. Add chopped fresh porcini (or dried, rehydrated porcini or any combination of fresh mushrooms); sauté until lightly browned. Stir in a little cream; simmer a few minutes. Add cooked gnocchi; simmer one minute. Stir in grated cheese.

Sage Butter: See recipe on page 272.

Lasagne with Ragù

Lasagne con sugo
〇〇

Lasagne *is plural for* lasagna, *which is the name of the pasta—and the casserole is made up of many sheets of lasagna, thus lasagne. Umbrian lasagne is much lighter than the cheese-laden American versions. The pasta is thinner and there is less cheese, but the dish has more layers and uses two sauces instead of one—meat sauce and béchamel.*

Bruna always makes her own pasta—her only concession to an ailing back is rolling with a machine rather than by hand. If you prefer to use store-bought lasagne, fresh is best. If fresh pasta isn't available, De Cecco's dry lasagna larga doppia riccia *(wide with rippled edges) is a good substitute—and the thin noodles cook quickly. De Cecco's lasagne are thinner than American brands, so if you use a different brand, all five layers might not fit in the pan. If the dried noodles have rippled edges, after boiling them use kitchen scissors to cut them off. Use the "ripples" in soup or toss them with sauce.*

It is hard to know exactly how much pasta you will need, because it depends on the thickness of the pasta and the exact size of your pan. To be safe, I recommend having extra pasta (fresh or dry) on hand. So that making lasagne doesn't feel burdensome, make it over the course of two or three days. Make the pasta one day, and cook the ragù and béchamel the next day. Assemble and bake the lasagne on the third day.

Bruna frequently serves this lasagne as a primo piatto *(first course) for Sunday lunch, but it is hearty enough for a main course—serve it with a green salad.*

Yield: 6 to 8 main-course servings (or 12 first-course servings)

1 pound, 10 ounces Fresh Lasagne (see Fresh Egg Pasta, pages 84 to 90) or two 1-pound packages dry lasagne

8 ounces Parmigiano-Reggiano cheese, cut into ½-inch cubes

2½ cups Béchamel (see recipe, page 94)

Extra virgin olive oil

6 to 7 cups Umbrian Ragù (see recipe, page 7)

2 tablespoons kosher salt (*important:* see "About Salt," page xxv)

12 ounces mozzarella cheese (preferably fresh), cut into ⅜-inch cubes

GETTING STARTED: To prepare for assembly, have a large bowl of ice water handy to cool the pasta. Cover a large cutting board with a wet (wrung-out) nonterry dishtowel.

1. Preheat the oven to 350°F. Bring 3 or 4 quarts of cold water to a boil in a large pot to cook the pasta. Trim the fresh pasta sheets to fit into a large baking pan (around 9×13×2 inches is ideal). You'll need five layers of pasta. (If using dry pasta, trim after boiling it.)

2. Put the cubes of Parmigiano into a food processor; process until very fine. Stir ½ cup of the grated cheese into the béchamel. Rub a little oil over the sides and bottom of the baking pan; spread about 1 cup of the ragù evenly over the bottom of the pan. Just before cooking the pasta, add the kosher salt and 3 tablespoons of the oil to the boiling water.

3. (You will cook only enough pasta at a time to make one layer; when that layer is sauced and so on, cook enough for another batch.) Cook 2 fresh

pasta sheets at a time in the boiling water; cook 30 to 60 seconds (if using dry lasagne, cook 4 to 6 pieces at a time—cook 1 minute less than the package recommends). Use a skimmer or slotted spoon to transfer one sheet of pasta at a time to the bowl of ice water.

4. Let the pasta cool briefly in the water. Transfer the pasta to the board lined with the wet dishtowel, arranging lasagne side by side so they don't stick together. (If the noodles stick together at any point, dip them briefly in hot, then cold water.) Immediately arrange a layer of pasta in the pan to cover the bottom.

5. Spread about 1 cup of ragù evenly over the lasagne. Pour (or drop by the spoonful) about ½ cup of the béchamel over the ragù (do not spread the béchamel). Sprinkle about ¼ cup of the Parmigiano evenly over the pan. Dot with one quarter of the mozzarella.

6. Continue layering in the same manner until four layers are done (finish the mozzarella on the fourth layer). Make the fifth and final layer of pasta using enough of the ragù to cover the top. Use the remaining béchamel and Parmigiano.

7. Bake uncovered until the entire top is bubbling and well browned, about 1 hour (if the sauces or casserole were chilled, additional time will be needed—when properly reheated, the internal temperature should reach 160°F). If needed, cover the lasagne with aluminum foil near the end of cooking to prevent burning. Let stand 10 minutes before cutting. ❧

As Fast as a Racehorse

About halfway up Monte Acuto, on the way to Bruna Cecchetti's, there is a small valley. It is there that I feel like I've stepped into the pages of one of my favorite books, *The Betrothed* (*I promessi sposi*) by Alessandro Manzoni. Most of the farmhouses and castles that dot the sparsely inhabited hillsides were constructed before the novel's maiden, Lucia, was pursued by the wealthy Don Rodrigo in the mid-1600s. Could any of the landowners in this idyllic place have been as cruel and brutal as Rodrigo? (You'll have to read the book to decide.)

Bruna lives farther up the mountain, where the road narrows, the curves sharpen, and the number of houses diminishes. There are no street signs or house numbers in the country. Houses are identified by name, and the locals know the name of each house. Finally, I came to an entry that I thought was Bruna's. When I drove up the steep, muddy driveway, and saw Bruna's old racehorse, I knew I was right. I drove up to the house and parked in front. Bruna came out escorted by her little black barking dog. I got out of my car and said to Bruna, "What views! They take my breath away."

Bruna turned her head toward the panorama beyond her house and said, "Hmm, I never notice." Silvia says that old-time farmers see only the work and hard labor that need to be done when they look over the landscape.

From where I parked, I could see the magnificent Castello Polgeto—an enormous castle owned by an American couple—and two other towers from twelfth-century castles, and way off in the distance I could see the town of Umbertide.

Bruna kissed me on both cheeks and motioned to me to go inside. By the time I had taken off my scarf and heavy jacket, Bruna had emptied my grocery bag, putting the carrots, celery, meat, and cans of tomatoes on the granite dining table. I had just managed to jot her name and the date in my notebook, when she put the meat and vegetables I had just delivered to cook on the wood-burning stove. That done, she began cracking eggs over a mound of flour on a wooden board. Minutes later, while she kneaded the dough, she asked what I wanted for lunch. "You don't need to feed me," I said, "but if you insist, then let's eat the cannelloni."

"No, no," she said, shaking her head. "What do you want? I have tagliatelle and *sugo di piselli* [pea sauce]. Gnocchi? Or *cappelletti* [tiny filled pasta]? I have everything—all homemade. What shall we have?"

"Pasta with pea sauce, please." I had never eaten the traditional sauce. Bruna put the dough to rest, and she left the room. She returned with a jar of home-canned tomatoes and a fatty sliver of prosciutto.

"Your store-bought tomatoes might be better than mine," she apologized, "but we use these because we have tomatoes in the garden." She insisted I take my tomatoes home. Within minutes, she had a saucepan with tomatoes, prosciutto, carrots, onion, and celery simmering on the stove.

In the tiny kitchen, a windowless alcove off the dining room, she filled a pot with water to cook the cannelloni. Before the water came to a boil, she had rolled out the pasta. While she cooked I took photographs of her in action.

"I look terrible in photographs," she laughed. Bruna is shorter than my five feet. She has short salt-and-pepper hair—thick and gorgeous—that makes her look younger than her years. Bruna put the rolling pin down to show me a photo album. She laughed heartily at the pictures, bending over, slapping her legs. In one photo her eyes were closed. In another, her mouth was open.

"It's not you," I said. "The camera caught you in a bad moment."

"No. Look, I am *proprio schifa* [really disgusting]!" She suddenly looked stricken. "Where are my manners? You must have something. Bruschetta with *olio*?" She held up a green bottle. "*Nuovo* [new]. Just pressed in our *frantoio*."

"I cannot resist bruschetta with new oil!"

Bruna poured the rich green oil over toasted bread, and filled a short glass with a pale yellow liquid. "Without wine, bruschetta is nothing," she explained, handing me the glass and the plate of bruschetta. Half past nine in the morning is earlier than I usually drink wine, but I graciously toasted Bruna, and we ate together.

Well before noon, Bruna had cooked and ground the meat for the cannelloni filling and together we had stuffed the cannelloni. By the time we sat down for lunch, she had made the tomato and *besciamela* sauces for the cannelloni and two casseroles of cannelloni. Before one o'clock, we were sitting at the table with her husband, drinking homemade wine and eating antipasto—crostini topped with a slice of hard-cooked egg and a generous dollop of mayonnaise, another kind buttered and topped with a fillet of anchovy, and a third spread with liver pâté.

Her husband is a quiet man with a slow walk and a tentative, careful manner. Bruna is just the opposite. She laughed gaily and told story after story while we cooked and ate. When Bruna got up to serve the pasta, she pushed the remaining two crostini onto my plate.

"You live next door to Michela and Mario, don't you?" Bruna's husband asked.

"Yes, I do."

"I have known the family since Mario's mother was a little girl," said Bruna. "I babysat his mother and aunt when they were little. Watching the girls at the beach was better than working in the tobacco fields!"

"Mario's dogs came up here and killed several of my chickens," her husband said.

"They sure get around," I said

Bruna wanted me to try her *gnocchi con funghi porcini* (with porcini mushrooms), so she served that dish, too. Earlier in the kitchen, I was relieved that she had used frozen mushrooms for the sauce. I am leery of eating mushrooms gathered in the forest.

At the table, when Bruna handed a plate of gnocchi with mushrooms to her husband, he shook his head and refused the plate. "I got sick from mushrooms once," he explained to me, "so I stopped eating them."

"It's true," Bruna said. "Mushrooms can make you sick."

I became distracted by visions of the poster I had seen at the Umbertide hospital emergency room with photos of each poisonous mushroom found in Umbria.

"Where did you get the mushrooms?" I asked. I hoped they were frozen, certified wild mushrooms from the store.

"My daughter found them in the forest."

"Oh, I thought they were frozen."

"*I* froze them."

I politely finished the mushrooms. Supposedly nothing poisonous resembles the porcini. I hoped that was true.

For our third course, Bruna served thin slices of steak that she grilled outside near the kitchen. "From our own cow," Bruna said. "Until my husband was badly injured when he fell off a ladder, we had about ninety cows." Bruna had picked in her fields the sautéed wild greens that accompanied the meat.

"Did you eat like this when you were growing up?" I asked.

"No, no. Although we were luckier than many," Bruna said. "We ate what we had, what we raised and grew. Fruit from our trees. And these same wild greens that we found in the fields, usually with *brustengo*." All over Umbria, people made a simple bread like *brustengo*. "You make a thin batter with flour and water and cook it in a skillet with oil.

"When the landowners took all the grain and left us only with cornmeal, we made *torta al granoturco* [a rustic flat cornbread made on the griddle]. It was better than no bread. We ate boiled chestnuts that we gathered in the forests for dinner. We drank coffee without milk, or if we were lucky, used goat milk. We made pasta without eggs and seasoned it with pork fat. But when we slaughtered a pig, we ate fresh pancetta. We toasted garbanzo beans over the fire."

Since her in-laws died, her sister-in-law moved away, and her two daughters and their families moved to Umbertide, Bruna and her husband live alone on their country property in the main two-story farmhouse. One of the daughters and her family left behind the beautiful second house on the estate, preferring to live in town. "I don't think they'll ever come back," said her husband. "They like town, but they come every Sunday for lunch." So the partially restored beautiful old stone farmhouse across from the *frantoio* sits empty.

As late as the 1950s, the property didn't have electricity or water in the house. "Winter was really hard on us women," she said. "Back then we got a lot of snow on the mountain—and the women had to go out to the well and carry back water to do everything. It was a nightmare raising the children without water in the house—fetching water to wash diapers by hand. In the winter, the diapers never quite dried so my daughter always had a rash. We couldn't afford to buy medicine for the rash, so we made our own salve."

Bruna brought a bowl of fruit and a plate of sliced cake to the table. "Please," she begged, "you ate nothing. At least have an orange." Before I could answer, she said, "Well, then have some *spumante* [sparkling wine] and a little cake."

I took a slice of chocolate cake and held out my glass for wine. A few minutes later, Bruna brought out a bottle of homemade *limoncello* (lemon liqueur). I had some of that, too.

After lunch Bruna put the two casseroles of cannelloni near my bag, insisting that I take them both. She and her little black dog walked me to my car. I took one last glance at Bruna's bucolic landscape, waved goodbye, and drove down the mountain to my apartment.

Pasta and Beans
Pasta e fagioli
ᖇᖇᖇ

If you haven't eaten pasta e fagioli, *you might think the combination of pasta and beans seems odd. But I love the way the beans turn into a creamy, delicious sauce that coats the silky homemade* maltagliati *pasta. This recipe, a cross between a soup and a pasta dish, is one of my favorites. Maltagliati pasta, which means badly cut, is cut into a variety of shapes, from trapezoids to parallelograms to rhombuses or squares. Tagliatelle, cut into 3-inch lengths, are another classic pasta for this dish. Some cooks serve grated cheese with* pasta e fagioli— *Bruna does not (and I prefer it without). The perfect garnish is a generous drizzle of extra virgin olive oil and freshly ground pepper.*

This recipe makes a big batch, but both the sauce and raw pasta freeze well (separately). If you need fewer servings, cook the amount of pasta to be eaten at the meal (allow 2 to 3 ounces of fresh pasta per serving) and add sauce to the pasta as needed. Leftovers can be reheated, but the dish is best when eaten immediately.

Yield: 8 main-dish servings or 12 first-course servings
(makes about 10 cups of bean sauce)

1 pound dry *borlotti* (cranberry) or pinto beans

1/2 cup extra virgin olive oil plus more for garnish

1 medium carrot, finely chopped

1 medium stalk celery, finely chopped

1/2 medium onion, finely chopped

2 ounces sliced pancetta, finely chopped (see "Pancetta versus Bacon," page 9)

1 can (14 ounces) whole or diced tomatoes with juice

3½ teaspoons kosher salt (*important:* see "About Salt," page xxv) plus more for cooking pasta

1½ pounds fresh *maltagliati* pasta (Fresh Egg Pasta, pages 84 to 90)

Freshly ground pepper

1. Sort and rinse the beans; put them into a large pot. Add water until it reaches several inches above the surface of the beans. Cover and bring to a boil over high heat; simmer 4 minutes. Turn off heat; let stand about 1 hour. (Alternatively, soak beans in cold water, refrigerated, for 8 hours.) Drain and rinse the beans well under cold water. Return the beans to the pot; add 8 cups cold water (do not add salt). Bring to a boil; cover and simmer gently until tender (mash easily with a fork—check several beans) but skins are still intact, 40 to 45 minutes (pinto beans or old beans may take longer). Drain the beans; set aside.

2. Meanwhile, in another large pot, heat the oil over medium heat; add the carrot, celery, onion, pancetta, and 1/2 cup water. Cook, stirring frequently,

until the onions are soft, about 12 minutes. Purée the tomatoes with juice using an immersion blender or food processor. Add the tomatoes and kosher salt; partially cover and simmer over low heat, stirring occasionally, ½ hour. Stir in the beans and 4 cups cold water; cover partially. Bring to a boil; reduce the heat to medium low and gently simmer, stirring occasionally, until flavorful and slightly thickened, 30 to 45 minutes.

3. Meanwhile, bring about 3 quarts of cold water to a boil in a large pot to cook the pasta; add 2 tablespoons kosher salt to the boiling water. Cook the fresh pasta until *al dente,* 30 to 60 seconds (do a taste test). Drain the pasta and add it to the pot with the beans. Let stand 1 minute, stirring twice. Adjust the salt to taste (beans need a lot of salt, so don't be shy). Add water to thin the bean sauce, if needed to make it soupy. Drizzle each serving with some of the oil and season with pepper.

Substitutions: Instead of homemade pasta, make *maltagliati* from store-bought fresh lasagne. Dry lasagna works too—break it into 1-inch pieces. Dry orecchiette is also good. (To determine the quantity, put pieces of dry pasta into a pasta bowl—the bowl should be about one quarter full, per serving. Follow package cooking instructions.) To substitute canned beans for dried, use three 15-ounce cans *borlotti* or pinto beans (drained). (Note: canned beans are high in sodium.) Skip ahead to step 2—but do not add the measured amount of salt. Instead, salt to taste at the end of step 2. (See "About Salt," page xxv.)

VARIATION: In step 2, reduce the kosher salt to 1 teaspoon. Replace 2 of the 4 cups of water with 2 cups of homemade broth (canned chicken broth is okay but high in sodium); add the broth with the tomatoes. Just before serving, adjust the salt to taste (depending on the broth, the dish may need a lot more salt). ❧

PASTA FROM UMBRIA'S KITCHENS

Stringozzi, **umbricelli,** *strangozzi,* and *strengozzi* are Umbria's oldest, most traditional styles of pasta, all made from flour and water. Although the name of the pasta varies from village to village, the eggless pasta is basically the same—rustic, thick, and spaghetti-like. Today dry versions are sold commercially (mostly to tourists).

In the past, when eggs were on hand (Mother Nature controlled availability), wealthy families used eggs rather than water to make fresh pasta. And goose eggs were favored over chicken eggs. With increased prosperity and commercial egg production, *pasta all'uovo* is more common than its eggless cousin.

The names of pasta change from region to region—and so do preferences. In most of Umbria, tagliatelle—called fettuccine elsewhere—is the favorite cut, except in a few places such as Montefalco, where five-eighths-inch wide pappardelle is preferred. Dry pasta, which was once a luxury, is rapidly replacing handmade pasta because it is so convenient—and finally affordable.

Fresh Egg Pasta

Pasta all'uovo

This is the traditional recipe for egg pasta. I use it for most kinds of pasta—tagliatelle, cannelloni, lasagne, pappardelle, cappelletti—but I prefer to use the Filled Pasta Dough recipe on page 86 for ravioli and ravioloni.

To me, making homemade pasta is therapeutic. I love the way the crumbly mixture of eggs and flour miraculously turns into soft, pliable dough under my hands. In Umbria making pasta, from mixing to rolling, is done on a wooden board called la spianatoia. When making pasta was a daily activity, kitchen tables—the workstation in the Umbrian kitchen—had storage under the table-top for the board and long rolling pin called il matterello. Many kitchens still have this kind of table.

Italian eggs have bright, deep orange yolks, so Italian pasta has a rich yellow color that we cannot get—unless we increase the ratio of yolks. American un-bleached all-purpose flour is a good substitute for the Italian "0" flour that is used to make pasta. If you have a scale, for speed and accuracy, weigh the flour.

Since the two ingredients—eggs and flour—used in making pasta vary con-siderably, your dough might be dry one time and sticky the next. One reason is that protein in flour varies by type and by brand—this affects how the dough handles. How the flour is stored is another factor. In a sealed canister, flour absorbs less humidity than it does in a paper bag. Large eggs can differ, too. All sizes of eggs are classified by a minimum weight, rather than by an exact weight. Read on—there are simple solutions.

The number of servings depends on end use. For example, the recipe makes about five main-dish servings or eight to ten first-course servings of tagliatelle.

Yield:1 pound, 10 ounces fresh pasta

4 cups (17½ ounces) unbleached all-purpose flour

6 large eggs (or 5 large eggs plus 3 large yolks)

Flour for kneading and rolling

DIRECTIONS FOR MAKING PASTA DOUGH

1. Put the flour into a large bowl. (If making Filled Pasta Dough, page 86, mix in the semolina now.) Make a well in the center; drop the eggs— yolks and whites—into the well. (If making Sun-Dried Tomato Pasta, page 86, add the tomatoes now.) Use a fork to mix—the mixture will be crumbly.

2. To prevent slipping, put a damp towel under a large wooden board. Turn the bowl of dough out onto the board—set aside the bowl to use later. Set the timer for 15 minutes and begin kneading the dough to mix in all of the crumbs. When the crumbs are incorporated, knead by pushing and rolling the dough into a cylinder and folding it into a ball.

3. If the dough is too dry after six minutes of kneading, dampen hands and continue kneading. If the dough sticks to the board, dust it with flour as often as needed. Continue kneading until the crumbly mess turns into a soft, smooth dough—if not ready when the timer rings, knead 5 minutes more.

4. Shape the dough into a ball. It might be a little sticky, but it should not stick to the board. (At this point, the dough can be tightly wrapped in plastic and refrigerated up to 24 hours.)

5. Use the set-aside bowl to cover the dough on the board. Let the dough rest about 10 minutes (if rolling by hand, rest ½ hour). The dough is now ready to roll. See "How to Roll and Cut Fresh Pasta," page 87.

NOTE: I mix by hand because in my mixer the bowl constantly pops out of its stand. If you want to try, use a heavy-duty mixer with a paddle attachment to mix the dough on slow speed for 2 to 3 minutes. Replace the paddle with the dough hook; knead until smooth and elastic, about 10 minutes. Knead by hand for 2 minutes. ❧

FILLED PASTA DOUGH

In the old days, cooks didn't have semolina (coarse Durham wheat flour), so they made egg pasta—flat and filled—with all-purpose flour (Italian "0"). But for ravioli, ravioloni, and most filled pasta—except for cappelletti—I like the addition of semolina. It adds strength to the dough.

Yield: 1 pound, 10 ounces fresh pasta

3½ cups (15½ ounces) unbleached all-purpose flour

½ cup (3 ounces) semolina flour

6 large eggs

Flour for kneading and rolling

Follow the "Directions for Making Pasta Dough" on page 85. ❧

SUN-DRIED TOMATO PASTA

Flavored pastas are not that common in Umbria. Ira (see Chapter 5) gave me this recipe—she serves the pasta with lentils and truffles (page 165).

Yield: 1 pound, 10 ounces fresh pasta

2 tablespoons boiling water

¼ cup sun-dried tomatoes (semisoft, not oil-packed)

4 cups (17 ½ ounces) unbleached all-purpose flour

5 large eggs

Flour for kneading and rolling

Pour the 2 tablespoons boiling water over the dried tomatoes in a small bowl; let stand ½ hour. Drain the tomatoes, reserving the liquid. Use a mortar and pestle to purée the tomatoes; stir in the reserved liquid. (Alternatively, chop the tomatoes for several minutes with a knife until almost puréed; combine the tomatoes with the reserved liquid.) Finish the pasta following the "Directions for Making Pasta Dough" on page 85. ❧

How to Roll and Cut Fresh Pasta

Grandmothers in Umbria, who have been hand-rolling pasta for decades, can quickly roll out a sheet of pasta the size of a kitchen table—it is marvelous to see. But hand-rolling requires skill and lots of energy, so I recommend using a hand-cranked pasta machine. The *macchinetta* is reasonably priced, durable, and easy to use. It's an investment that will save you hours in the kitchen—and reward you with delicious pasta. If you follow these simple but detailed instructions, you'll be rolling pasta as quick as the *nonne*. Although I like the rustic appearance of hand-cut pasta, cutting by machine is much quicker—the quarter-inch-wide cutters make perfect tagliatelle.

1. **Setting Up:** Line several trays with parchment paper and sprinkle lightly with flour (preferred) or sprinkle trays generously with flour. Have a cup of flour handy. Cover a large work area with a clean tablecloth or dishtowels. Clamp the pasta machine near the right end of the work area. Put a large wooden board to the left of the machine.

2. Prep for Machine: Cut the dough into 8 equal pieces; dust each lightly with flour. Put one piece of dough on the board and cover the rest with a bowl or plastic wrap. **For all styles of pasta (except *ravioloni*):** Shape the piece of dough into a ⅜-inch-thick rectangle so that when it is positioned horizontally on the machine it is about 2 inches narrower than the width of the rollers. **For *ravioloni*:** Shape the piece of dough into a ⅜-inch-thick rectangle (about 2½×5 inches); feed it through the machine vertically. The end goal is to end up with a long strip of pasta that is about 3½ inches wide.

3. Roll by Machine: (If the dough is too soft, the pasta sheets will end up too thin—and when they come out of the machine the ends of the dough will curl and stick together. If you cannot roll the pasta to the second- or third-thinnest setting without it tearing, you will probably have to knead in more flour.) If making flat pasta, lightly dust the piece with flour (do not flour filled pasta unless it is really sticky). Set the dial on the machine to the widest setting (usually 1). Position the dough horizontally on the rollers (for *ravioloni*, position it vertically) and feed it once through the machine. Turn the dial to the next setting. Feed the pasta one time through each successively thinner setting (usually a higher number), gently pulling the dough through the rollers, until the dough is thin. (Pulling gently is important. Without pulling, the pasta is too thick; pulling too hard makes the dough too thin.) Flat pasta is usually rolled one stop thicker than filled pasta. For example, on my Marcato Ampia 150, I roll tagliatelle, pappardelle, *and* cannelloni to 7 (9 is the thinnest), and cappelletti, *ravioloni,* ravioli, *and* lasagne to 8 (for cannelloni with a light filling, such as the *ravioloni* filling, I roll the cannelloni thinner, to 8). Your pasta machine may be different. For future reference, keep notes on what numbers work best with your machine. To make filled pasta, see the recipe's directions.

4. Using Scraps: Keep scraps covered until needed. Knead large quantities of scraps as long as necessary to make the dough smooth again; roll again and cut as desired. Cut small scraps of rolled pasta into ¼- to ½-inch squares—dry and freeze. Add to your favorite soup.

5. Prep Flat Pasta: As the long sheets of flat pasta come out of the machine, arrange them side by side (but not touching) on the tablecloth. If the dough is sticky, dust it lightly with flour. Flip the pasta sheets over after 10 to 15 minutes to dry the other side. When slightly leathery, the edges just beginning to dry, the pasta is ready to cut. On humid or cold days, position a fan to blow lightly over the drying pasta.

6. Cut by Machine: Drag a sheet of the leathery pasta across a lightly floured board. Trim about ¼ inch off one end of the pasta—the straight edge is easier to feed through the cutters. Feed the cut end through the cutters and catch the pasta ribbons as they come out underneath. The ¼-inch-wide cutters make tagliatelle; the ⅛-inch cutters make *tagliolini,* also called *tagliarini.*

7. Cut Flat Pasta by Hand: Many styles of pasta have to be cut by hand. First, drag a sheet of pasta across a lightly floured board. Cut across both ends of the pasta to form a long rectangle.

• *Cannelloni:* Put a clean 4-inch-square paper template on top of a sheet of pasta (or cut a size that works best with your baking pan). Use a pastry wheel to cut the pasta sheets into neat 4-inch squares—or guesstimate, without a template.

• *Lasagne:* Cut pasta sheets to fit into the baking pan.

• *Maltagliati:* Use a pastry wheel to cut the pasta into 1- to 1¼-inch-wide ribbons and then cut them crosswise at a slight diagonal to create "badly cut" squares, rhombuses, parallelograms, or trapezoids.

• *Quadrucci:* Use a pastry wheel to cut the pasta into ⅜- to ¾-inch squares. (Alternatively, to save time, feed short sheets of pasta through the ¼-inch cutters on the pasta machine; hand cut the ribbons crosswise into squares.)

• *Tagliolini, tagliatelle, pappardelle:* To make ribbon-style pasta, cut long sheets of dough in half. Start at a narrow end of the rectangle and roll into a tight cylinder, leaving a 1-inch tail. Cut through the cylinder every ³⁄₁₆ inch for *tagliolini;* ⅜ inch for tagliatelle; or ⅝ inch for pappardelle. Grab several rolls by their tails and shake them to unfurl the ribbons of pasta.

8. Drying Pasta: Dust the cut pasta with a little flour. Let dry on the tablecloth or in trays. Toss ribbon pasta occasionally, and turn over sheets of pasta (i.e., lasagne) after 15 minutes. Continue drying until no longer sticky, about 30 minutes (but not more than 60 minutes—and less time in hot weather because pasta and filling are perishable).

9. Freezing Pasta: For ribbon or filled pasta, freeze on parchment-paper-lined or floured trays until firm (space filled pasta ¼ inch apart); transfer to freezer bags. To freeze sheets of lasagne and cannelloni, when semidry and leathery arrange them in a stack, separating each piece with a sheet of parchment or waxed paper. Store in freezer bags up to 2 months.

10. Cooking Fresh Pasta: Fresh or frozen (not thawed) flat pasta cooks in 30 seconds to about 2 minutes, so check for doneness often. Filled fresh or frozen (not thawed) pasta can take up to 5 minutes, but it is usually ready 1 to 2 minutes after it rises to the surface—*quando vengono a galla.*

Cannelloni
∞

Cannelloni are pasta squares stuffed with vegetable or meat filling and rolled into "cigars." In Umbria, meat filling—pork, beef, chicken—seasoned with Parmigiano cheese, lemon zest, and nutmeg is traditional. The meat-loving Umbrians usually smother cannelloni with meat sauce, but Bruna's family says ragù is too heavy. So instead Bruna uses tomato sauce, flavoring it with carrot, onion, and celery. Mozzarella is optional, but Bruna and I like it better with the extra cheese. For a lighter filling, substitute the ravioloni *filling (page 268) for this one.*

The beauty of this recipe is that all the components—the pasta, filling, and sauces—can be made ahead and refrigerated or frozen. I usually make the pasta and sauces one day and assemble the cannelloni the next. To simplify the recipe, you can buy fresh lasagne or sheets of pasta instead of making your own. Cut the sheets into a size that fit neatly into your baking pan (somewhere between 3½- and 5-inch squares).

As with all filled pasta recipes, it is impossible to ensure you'll have just the right amount of filling for the amount of pasta. When making cannelloni, it helps if you roll and cut the pasta into squares as you go, rather than letting the sheets dry before cutting. With this system, you will have lots of fresh scraps to reroll and make into squares. Of course, the number of cannelloni you end up with will also be determined by the thickness of the dough.

Yield: 7 or 8 main-dish servings (or 12 first-course servings); makes three 7 × 11-inch (or two 9 × 13-inch) baking dishes, about 36 cannelloni

7 ounces Parmigiano-Reggiano cheese, cut into ¾-inch cubes

6 ounces boneless beef, such as round or sirloin

8 ounces boneless pork loin chops

6 ounces boneless, skinless chicken breasts

1 medium carrot, cut into 1-inch rounds

1 medium celery stalk, cut into 1-inch pieces

½ medium onion, cut into 3 wedges

1½ teaspoons kosher salt (*important:* see "About Salt," page xxv) plus more for cooking pasta

¾ cup dry white wine, such as pinot grigio or sauvignon blanc

⅓ cup extra virgin olive oil

¼ cup water

2 tablespoons soft butter

1 teaspoon freshly ground nutmeg

Finely shredded zest of ½ small lemon (see "About Zest," page 37)

1 to 3 tablespoons milk

Oil, for pans and cooking pasta

36 to 40 (4-inch) fresh cannelloni squares (see Fresh Egg Pasta, pages 84 to 90)

5½ cups Classic Tomato Sauce (see recipe, page 26)

1½ cups Béchamel (see recipe, page 94)

8 ounces fresh mozzarella cheese, cut into ⅜-inch cubes (optional)

YOU WILL ALSO NEED: Parchment or waxed paper. A meat grinder, if you have one (it makes a slightly lighter filling than a food processor does).

1. Process the Parmigiano cubes in a food processor until fine. Put ⅔ cup of the cheese into a medium bowl; set aside. Put the rest of the cheese into a small bowl; refrigerate. Cut the beef into 1-inch squares (leave the pork and chicken as is).

2. Put the beef, pork, chicken, carrot, celery, and onion into a medium saucepan. Sprinkle with the salt; add the wine, oil, and ¼ cup water. Cover and bring to a boil; simmer over medium-low heat, stirring occasionally, until the pork and chicken are no longer pink when cut into, about 15 minutes. Transfer the pork and chicken to a cutting board; let cool.

3. Continue cooking the beef and vegetables, uncovered, over medium-high heat, stirring frequently, until the liquid is almost gone and mostly oil is left, 15 to 20 minutes. When the pork and chicken are cool enough to handle, cut them into 1-inch cubes. Transfer the pork, chicken, beef, vegetables, and any oil/sauce in the saucepan to a meat grinder fitted with a medium-grind template; grind once. (Alternatively, pulse in a food processor until minced—do not purée.)

4. Transfer the filling to the medium bowl with the ⅔ cup cheese. Stir in the butter, nutmeg, and lemon zest; stir until the butter disappears. Mix in 1 to 3 tablespoons of the milk to moisten—do not make it soggy. Adjust the salt to taste. Cover and refrigerate up to 24 hours.

5. Setup for assembly: Line two large trays with parchment paper. Put a clean, wet (wrung out) nonterry dishtowel over a large board. Have a large of bowl of ice water handy. Bring 3 quarts of water to a boil in a large pot; add 3 table-spoons oil and 2 tablespoon kosher salt. Drop 4 sheets of pasta at a time into the water; cook 30 to 60 seconds (if using store-bought pasta, cook until barely al dente). Use a skimmer or slotted spoon to transfer the pasta to the ice water and then lay the pasta sheets side by side on the wet dishtowel.

6. Put about a third of the filling into a small bowl; refrigerate the rest of the filling (refill the bowl as needed—this keeps it fresh). Work in an assembly line, with 4 sheets of pasta on the board—drop about 1½ tablespoons of

filling onto each square of pasta. Per square, starting about ½ inch from the edge nearest you, shape the filling horizontally into a "cigar" (without packing it)—end the filling about ¼ inch from the outer edges. Starting at the edge of pasta nearest you, roll the pasta tightly to enclose the filling and form a slender "cigar." If the filling oozes out, push it in. With the seam down, gently press across the length of the cannelloni to help secure it; let stand on the wet cloth about 10 seconds.

7. Arrange the cannelloni (seam down) ¼ inch apart on the prepared trays. As soon as each tray is filled, cover it and refrigerate it up to 24 hours. (Alternatively, put the covered tray in the freezer until the cannelloni are almost frozen. Transfer the cannelloni to freezer bags. Store in the freezer up to 3 months.) To serve, see "How to Prepare Cannelloni" (below). ❧

HOW TO PREPARE CANNELLONI

You can cook a single serving of fresh or frozen cannelloni or serve all two or three casseroles at one meal. To assemble the casseroles ahead, chill the cooked pasta and sauces first. When baked properly, cannelloni are tender and delicate, unlike lasagne, which is better when the top is browned and crispy.

To Cook Fresh Cannelloni: Preheat the oven to 375°F. Oil one to three (7×11×1¾-inch) baking dishes (or one or two 9×13×2-inch)— make as many pans as you need and individually freeze the rest of the cannelloni (see step 7, above). Cover the bottom of the dishes with a thin layer of tomato sauce. Arrange a layer of cannelloni in each pan. Dividing the sauces and cheeses evenly among the pans, completely cover the pasta with the tomato sauce; drizzle with the béchamel and sprinkle with the reserved Parmigiano. If using, dot the tops with the mozzarella. Bake uncovered until the cheese melts and the interior temperature reaches 165°F, about 20 minutes. If needed, cover with foil and bake until hot, about 5 minutes. Do not brown.

To Cook Frozen Cannelloni: Preheat the oven to 375°F. Assemble the casserole following the directions for cooking fresh cannelloni, substituting frozen (not thawed) cannelloni. When the dish is assembled, cover it with foil; bake until the interior temperature reaches 165°F, 30 to 40 minutes. Do not brown.

To Cook an Individual Serving: Put one portion (3 to 5 cannelloni) on a microwaveable plate (if frozen, defrost first in the microwave). Cover with the tomato sauce and drizzle with the *besciamela*; sprinkle with the cheese(s). Cover and microwave until the interior temperature reaches 165°F—do not overheat or the pasta will be tough.

Béchamel
Besciamela

Besciamela is an essential ingredient in many traditional dishes, from lasagne to cannelloni to eggplant Parmesan. It is usually the base of the sformato— *a vegetable dish baked in a casserole or mold, sometimes with a timbale-like texture.*

Yield: About 2½ cups

3 cups whole or 2% milk plus more as needed

3 tablespoons butter

3 tablespoons all-purpose flour

1 teaspoon kosher salt (*important:* see "About Salt," page xxv)

¼ teaspoon freshly grated nutmeg

1. Heat the milk in a small saucepan until warm but not hot; cover and set aside. Melt the butter in a nonreactive (i.e., stainless steel) medium saucepan over medium-low heat. Use a wooden spoon to stir in the flour, salt, and nutmeg. Cook, stirring constantly, until smooth, bubbly, and golden yellow, 1 to 2 minutes. Remove from the heat; let cool 5 minutes.

2. Whisk the warm milk into the flour mixture. Simmer over low heat, stirring frequently with a wooden spoon, until the flavor is developed and the

sauce has thickened, about 20 minutes. Adjust the salt and nutmeg to taste. If the sauce is too thick, thin it with a little milk. If it is lumpy, strain it.

3. Use immediately or keep warm over a water bath up to 1 hour, stirring occasionally to prevent a skin from forming. The sauce can be made ahead, but it should be cooled quickly over a bowl of ice water, whisking it often. Refrigerate up to two days or freeze up to one month. ❧

JUST THE THREE OF US

Monia invited me to dine at Il Cantico, her country inn. When I arrived that summer evening, Monia was busy with chores, so I joined her eighty-three-year-old grandmother, Rita, and Monia's three-year-old daughter, Aurora, on the front porch. Rita was peeling pears from a big wooden crate and Aurora was playing with the family's new puppy. Rita had already prepared a crate of figs to make jam, which was boiling away on the stove inside the house. I sat down with Rita, and Monia went back to her chores.

"Figs and sugar," Rita said. "Pears and sugar. My jam recipes are nothing fancy."

Rita had said the same thing about her recipes a few years earlier when I had been a guest at her home on the outskirts of Perugia, but everything was delicious. She prepared several traditional dishes—*fagioli con le cotiche* (beans with pork rind), *barbabietola* (yellow beets with lemon juice and olive oil), *cavolo e pane mollicche* (cabbage sautéed in oil with garlic and bread crumbs), *polpette* (meatballs seasoned with grated pecorino cheese, fresh bread crumbs, pine nuts, and raisins simmered in puréed tomatoes and broth), and a flavorful but soupy pasta sauce, *sugo di pollo e anatra* (duck and chicken ragù). And she taught me how to make fresh pasta, roll it by hand, and cut it into tagliatelle.

She began making pasta for the family when she was seven years old—she had a short-legged table especially for that purpose. From then on for many, many years to come, Rita made pasta every day. While in her mid-seventies, she made a batch of pasta using 120 eggs (and rolled the dough out by hand)! The tagliatelle was for Monia's wedding dinner.

There was no such extravagant dinner at Rita's wedding in 1941. The custom at the time required that the bride bring a wedding gift to the groom's family. "I walked to church with my gift of two live chickens," Rita said. "And I carried a basket with all my belongings—a few towels and a couple items of clothing." After being wedded, she and her new husband walked from the church to his house.

"How very happy we were," Rita said. "It was a different happiness. Today's young people are not as contented as we were."

In the kitchen of her new abode, a huge pot for cooking pasta hung above the fire at the hearth. That was the only pot they owned. "I used empty five-kilogram tomato cans to cook in," she said.

At the age of seventeen, Rita was pregnant. Due to a terrible storm—and the lack of a car or a phone—the doctor arrived three days after Rita had gone into labor. Enduring what seemed like endless pain, the doctor finally delivered (without painkillers) an eleven-pound baby. Unfortunately, it was too late for her firstborn. Her three subsequent pregnancies each produced a healthy newborn.

Rita's mother gave birth to thirteen babies, but only eight survived childhood. Rita was the eleventh-born. To support the large family, Rita and her siblings helped their father gather wood in the forest, which he made into charcoal. Besides charcoal, her family sold much of what they produced. The wealthy drizzled the family's rich green olive oil over salad; Rita's mother used melted lard instead.

"When there was nothing to eat at home," Rita said, "on the way to school I would steal an onion for breakfast."

Rita was allowed to go to school only on those days when she didn't have to feed the farm animals. It was a three-hour walk each way—and she did it without shoes.

"At the stream near school, I washed my bare feet and put on my shoes." At nine years of age, Rita was confirmed in the Catholic Church. "That day I had the privilege of riding to church on a donkey," she said. But there was no joy. "I was scared the whole way. I had heard the priest was pounding nails into the foreheads of children."

In January, her family used to slaughter a pig and hang it above a pan to collect the blood. They mixed the blood with wine, fat, raisins, pine nuts, and bread crumbs to make a sausage called *sanquinaccio*. From the pork, they made cured meats—prosciutto, *coppa*, and salami. Rita's father kept these delicacies locked up so the kids wouldn't eat them. He brought them out for special occasions and holidays. The pig's intestines were cleaned and dried near the fire. At mealtime, they would cut off and cook a piece of the pig intestines. They filled their stomachs with fava beans and *cicerchie* (chickling peas) and lots of bread. In the fall, they dried grapes to eat during the winter.

At harvest people in the village came together to help their neighbors. The day started with a simple meal of *borlotti* and garbanzo beans. After harvest, they celebrated with a feast, which by tradition usually included *pasta e fagioli* (pasta and beans). During the olive harvest, they ate a lot of tiny fried fish and salt cod.

"The fisherman came from Lake Trasimeno and traded fish for olive oil," explained Rita. "We also ate chestnuts and drank *vino nuovo*. Or we roasted tiny potatoes under ash and ate *torcolo* [a simple cake] that we dunked in wine. And we sang and danced to the accordion."

As the sun set on that warm summer evening at Monia's, Rita and I ended our conversation and headed indoors. We were to dine at Monia's rather than going to the inn's restaurant. Monia played waitress, running up and down the stairs to the restaurant to deliver each new dish and return the plates from the last course. It was a quiet dinner—Aurora and her baby brother were already in bed and Monia's husband was still at work. Rita's loud sighs punctuated the lulls in conversation.

"Look where we have arrived!" she finally burst out. "Just the three of us for dinner. How much fun we used to have. There were always fifteen to twenty people at dinner."

"*Nonna,* you've told Suzanne so many sad stories, please say something positive," begged Monia.

"Well, my life has been difficult. I was widowed at forty-eight and I didn't have much fun," Rita began.

Monia gave her grandmother a look.

"But my life is good now. I am independent and healthy. And I still don't wear glasses."

Beets with Lemon

Barbabietola con limone

I was very surprised when Rita served beets—I had never seen fresh beets at the store or at the weekly market. She told me that beets were usually fed to the pigs. When there wasn't much else to eat, I suspect that is when the family ate beets.

Rita boiled yellow beets and tossed them with lemon juice, oil, salt, and a little pepper. Although the boiled beets were delicious, roasting intensifies the flavor. The beet greens are edible too—cook them like chard (see "Chard," page 162).

Yield: 4 servings

2 bunches small beets, preferably yellow (about 10)

1 tablespoon plus 1 tablespoon extra virgin olive oil

½ teaspoon kosher salt (*important:* see "About Salt," page xxv)

2 teaspoons fresh lemon juice or more to taste

Dash of freshly ground pepper

GETTING STARTED: Preheat the oven to 450°F.

1. Cut off the tops of the beets to completely remove the stem from the root. Peel the beets and cut them into quarters (or halves, if they are very small). Put the beets into a large baking pan. Drizzle with 1 tablespoon of the oil and sprinkle with the kosher salt; toss to coat evenly. Turn the beets so that a flat edge is against the bottom of the pan; spread them out so they are not crowded.

2. Bake until lightly browned and just tender when pierced with a knife, 30 to 35 minutes. Put the beets into a bowl. Drizzle the lemon juice and remaining tablespoon of oil over the beets; toss to coat. Season with the pepper and adjust the salt and lemon juice to taste; toss again. Serve warm, chilled, or at room temperature. ❧

Chickling Pea Soup

Zuppa di cécere
ᑕᕮᏮ

Cicerchie (Italian) or cécere (Umbrian dialect) are a legume in the pea family that has been cultivated for thousands of years. In many countries around the world, they are the food that has staved off starvation because they grow well under extreme conditions—droughts and floods. These irregularly shaped peas that grow wild among cultivated crops are once again in vogue in Umbria, along with other poverty-born dishes from the region's rural past. When Rita was young (and her family was poor), she ate this dish for breakfast. The zuppa di cécere recipe is hers.

The scientific name for these tan pebblelike peas is Lathyrus sativus, *but in the United States they are commonly called chickling peas, fava chickpeas, grass peas, or vetch.* Cicerchie *make a nutritious, yummy soup, but with a caveat—when they are a mainstay of the diet, they cause a serious nervous system disease called lathyrism. Eaten infrequently in small amounts, they are considered healthful and safe.*

I love the small Umbrian cicerchie *that are about three eighths of an inch across, sold at my market under the Bartolini label. In my tests, the cooking times varied dramatically, but several times I simmered them three hours (after soaking) and then cooked them another hour with the tomato sauce.*

Yield: 6 servings

1 pound dry chickling peas (*cicerchie*), sorted and rinsed

⅓ cup extra virgin olive oil plus more for garnish

½ large onion, finely chopped

¾ cup canned whole tomatoes, with juice, puréed

2 teaspoons kosher salt (*important*, see "About Salt," page xxv)

1. Put the peas into a large pot. If the peas need soaking (consult the package label), add water until it reaches several inches above the surface of the peas. Cover and bring to a boil over high heat; simmer 4 minutes. Turn off heat; let stand about 1 hour. (Alternatively, soak peas in cold water, refrigerated, for 8 hours.) Drain and rinse the peas well under cold water.

2. Return the peas to the pot; add 6 cups cold water (do not add salt). (Add water if needed during cooking to keep them covered.) Bring to a boil; cover and cook gently, adjusting the heat as needed to keep them at a gentle simmer. Cook until just tender (they cook unevenly, so test several)—it could take 3 or more hours to get to this point (and it could take less); drain the peas. Return them to the pot; set aside.

3. Meanwhile, when the peas are almost tender, heat the oil in a small saucepan. Sauté the onion in the oil over medium-low heat until soft, about 8 minutes. Add the tomatoes and kosher salt; cover and simmer for about ½ hour, stirring frequently. Do not let it burn.

4. Stir the tomato sauce into the pot of beans; add 6 cups of water. Cover and bring to a boil; simmer 1 hour, adding water as needed to keep it soupy. Adjust the salt to taste. Drizzle a little of the oil over each serving.

VARIATION: Lightly rub one side of six thin slices of toasted Italian bread, such as Pugliese or ciabatta, with raw, peeled garlic. Before serving the soup, put a slice into the bottom of each bowl; ladle soup over the toast. Drizzle with olive oil. ❧

THE SETUP

Lake Trasimeno has a few dishes that aren't found outside the lake region: *tegamaccio*—fish stew with eel and perch; *sugo di pesce*—pasta sauce made of lake fish; *regina in porchetta*—carp with fennel and rosemary (see Fish with Fennel, page 222). So I wanted to find a cook to teach me a few of these specialties. One day, I had lunch at a traditional restaurant near the lake. Before leaving, I asked the owner if I could return to cook with the chef. So, as agreed, a few weeks later I went for the lesson. The owner welcomed me, but escorted me to the dining room, where he opened an old cookbook.

"Many of our restaurant recipes are in this book," he said. Then he explained his plans to host culinary vacations at the restaurant, but he needed the recipes translated into English. "I propose," he said, "that you write my book and drop yours."

"Your plans are intriguing," I said, "but I need to finish my book."

He closed the old book and said, "Well, I am sorry you drove all this way today. It's a bad day for us to have you. The health inspector is coming, and you cannot be in the kitchen." No invitation for a subsequent visit was offered.

Out of guilt (I think), he introduced me to Anna—a grandmother and good cook who lives a few minutes away. I visited Anna that day and took detailed notes on a few recipes, with the hope of returning to cook with her. I never got the chance, so I tested her recipes and served them to my Umbrian neighbors. The recipes met with their approval—in fact, they loved them. I've included two of her recipes, but neither of them are specialties of Lake Trasimeno.

Fresh Tomato Sauce

Battuto e pomodoro
ᐠᔓ

Battuto con tagliatelle is a very old recipe from Umbria's countryside. Anna makes the battuto *(chopped seasonings) in the traditional style. "I use fresh pork fat, which is how the recipe was originally made," said Anna. Using olive oil in place of pork fat is a newer style of cooking. "You put the pork fat and all of the* odori—*garlic, onion, basil—together on a board and chop. In the old days, we even chopped the tomatoes, skin and all, because we didn't have a* passatutto *[food mill]." A food mill removes the skin and seeds while it purées the tomatoes. A food processor is quicker; however, I prefer the texture of the sauce when the tomatoes have been peeled and seeded first—extra but simple steps. For the best texture the "pulse" feature on the processor works better than the "on" switch.*

Fresh pork fat is hard to come by in the States, so I recommend salt pork or pancetta. For a vegetarian version, use ⅓ cup extra virgin olive oil instead of the pork. In Umbria many soups and sauces start with a pork-fat battuto. *The sauce is traditionally served with homemade tagliatelle, but dry fettuccine or penne pasta are also good choices (use one pound dry pasta). Or use the sauce with polenta, cannelloni, ravioli, or scaloppine (spread the sauce on the cooked meat, and top with cheese). Or stir some into risotto at the end of cooking.*

This particular battuto *with tomatoes and basil makes a delicious soup base for Tuscany's pappa al pomodoro (tomato-bread soup). To make the soup, add some sauce (to taste) to simmering chicken broth. Then add torn bite-size pieces of stale Italian bread to the pot—the soup should be thick with bread. Simmer a few minutes until the bread is tender. Drizzle extra virgin olive oil over each serving (or pass oil at the table). Serve with grated Parmigiano-Reggiano cheese.*

Yield: *About 3⅓ cups (enough for 4 or 5 servings of pasta)*

4 ounces salt pork or sliced pancetta (see "Pancetta versus Bacon," page 9)

2¾ pounds fresh Roma tomatoes (about 13 medium)

2 large garlic cloves, peeled and cut into halves

¼ teaspoon freshly ground pepper

½ medium onion, coarsely chopped

½ cup packed fresh basil leaves (about ½ of a small bunch)

2 tablespoons extra virgin olive oil plus more for garnish

Kosher salt (*important:* see "About Salt," page xxv)

1 pound, 10 ounces Fresh Tagliatelle (see Fresh Egg Pasta, pages 84 to
   90)

1. Cut the salt pork into three pieces (if using pancetta, coarsely chop it and set it aside until step 3, and skip ahead to step 2). Put the salt pork into a large saucepan; cover with water and bring to a boil. Reduce the heat and simmer for 15 minutes. Discard the water; repeat with fresh water. Drain; let cool. Cut into ½-inch cubes. Rinse out the saucepan to use later.

2. Meanwhile, peel and seed the tomatoes (see "How to Peel and Seed Tomatoes," page 103). Cut the tomatoes into quarters. Pulse the tomatoes in a food processor until very finely chopped (but not puréed). Transfer tomatoes to a bowl; set aside.

3. To make the *battuto,* pulse the salt pork (if using pancetta, add it now), garlic, and pepper in a food processor until finely chopped. Add the onion and basil; pulse until finely chopped, scraping the sides with a spatula as needed. Transfer the *battuto* to a large saucepan (the pan used for the salt pork); add the olive oil. Sauté the *battuto* over low heat, stirring frequently, for 15 minutes.

4. Add the tomatoes to the *battuto;* cover and simmer over low heat for about ½ hour, stirring frequently. Adjust the salt to taste.

5. Meanwhile, bring about 3 quarts of cold water to a boil in a large pot to cook the pasta (see pages 28 to 29); add 2 tablespoons kosher salt. When the sauce is almost ready, cook the pasta in the boiling water, stirring occasionally, until it is *al dente*—gives some resistance when bitten into. Tagliatelle takes between 30 seconds and 2 minutes (if using dry pasta, follow package directions), but taste for doneness early. Before draining the pasta, reserve about 1 cup of the cooking liquid; drain the pasta and return it to the pot.

6. Stir the sauce into the drained pasta; if needed, add cooking liquid (a few tablespoons at a time) to moisten the pasta. If desired, drizzle a couple tablespoons of extra virgin olive oil over the pasta; toss. Adjust the salt to taste; let the pasta stand 2 minutes to absorb the flavor of the sauce. Serve immediately. ❧

HOW TO PEEL AND SEED TOMATOES

Have ready a large bowl three-quarters full with ice and cold water. Carefully drop the fresh tomatoes into a pot of boiling water; simmer about 1 minute. With a slotted spoon, transfer the tomatoes to the ice water. When cool, peel the tomatoes with a paring knife—the skin almost slips off. Cut the tomatoes crosswise into halves; scoop out and discard the seeds—a small espresso spoon or a narrow spoon handle makes a good scoop.

Grilled Marinated Lamb Chops
Agnello a scottadito

In Umbria, every cook has his or her own version of scottadito—*all delicious— but Anna's recipe is unusual. In addition to the classic seasonings—rosemary and garlic—she uses wild fennel in her* battuto, *which I love.*

*In Umbria (and in the Napa Valley, where I live), wild fennel—*finocchio selvatico—*grows everywhere. If it doesn't grow near you, substitute commercially grown fresh fennel stalks and foliage—and use the bulb to make* insalata di finocchio *(see page 295). Gourmet and farmers' markets often have fresh fennel available.*

In Italian, scottadito *literally means "burn finger." If you grab a* scottadito *off the hot grill, you will burn your finger! And* scottodito, *when made with tiny rib lamb chops, is finger food. Lamb steaks can be substituted for chops.*

Yield: 4 servings

1 thin (10-inch) stalk wild fennel with foliage (optional)

1 (8-inch) sprig fresh rosemary, stem discarded

2 medium garlic cloves, peeled

1 bay leaf

2½ pounds rib or loin lamb chops (½- to 1-inch thick)

1 large, juicy lemon, cut in half

¼ cup white wine vinegar

2 teaspoons kosher salt (*important:* see "About Salt," page xxv)

½ teaspoon freshly ground pepper

¼ cup extra virgin olive oil

1. To make the *battuto* (seasoning), finely mince together the fennel, rosemary, garlic, and bay leaf; set aside. Arrange the lamb chops side by side in a shallow nonreactive dish, such as stainless steel or glass (use two dishes if necessary). Squeeze one of the lemon halves over the chops; drizzle with half of the vinegar. Sprinkle with half of the salt, pepper, and reserved *battuto*. Drizzle with half of the oil; rub the seasonings in with the back of a spoon. Turn the chops over and season the other side in the same manner. Cover; marinate in the refrigerator at least 2 hours, but preferably at least 12 hours (up to 24 hours is okay—the longer the lamb marinates, the saltier it will get).

2. Grill the chops over a medium-hot fire, turning as needed, until well browned and a bit crispy on the outside (thin chops require a hotter fire to brown the outside by the time they are done). To test for doneness, make a small cut at the bone. In Umbria, lamb is eaten well done (internal temperature 165°F), but I prefer it pink in the middle (internal temperature 150 to 160°F). The chops take from 8 to 20 minutes total cooking time, depending on the fire, the cut and thickness of the lamb, and personal taste. ❧

IL BATTUTO—THE FLAVORS OF UMBRIA

Il battuto (chopped seasonings) is the flavor base of Umbria's dishes. The ingredients vary but often include garlic, onion, carrot, celery, salt, pepper, pork fat or *lardo,* and often fresh herbs such as wild fennel, rosemary, sage, or basil. The name comes from the Italian verb *battere,* to beat. In the past, the *battuto* ingredients were chopped together on a cutting board with a large cleaver, both called *la battilarda.* Sometimes the wooden board was built into a small portable cabinet, much like a nightstand; it had a hinged lid that covered it when not in use. Years of chopping carved inches-deep gouges into the thick board.

My friend Silvia remembers hearing the sound of *la battilarda* beating on the board in the first half of the twentieth century, when mothers and grandmothers cooked large meals for their families of twenty to thirty people. The noise filled the house and filtered into the yard.

Anna gave me this recipe for *battuto.* Very finely chop the following: 2 ounces sliced *lardo* (it looks like bacon, but it is all fat) or pork fat, needles from a 6-inch sprig of rosemary, a 6-inch sprig of fresh fennel foliage (preferably wild), and 1 medium garlic clove. Put the chopped ingredients into a bowl; season with 1 tablespoon extra virgin olive oil, 2 teaspoons white wine vinegar, 1 teaspoon lemon juice, and a little salt and pepper. Rub the mixture over the inside and outside of guinea hen, pork roast, rabbit, chicken, goose, duck, or lamb. You can also make small slits in the flesh and push some of the *battuto* into them. Grill, roast, or rotisserie.

4 ❧ My Acquaintances—I *miei conoscenti*

Quell che 'nn amazza, angrassa

(What doesn't kill you will make you fat)

THE STORIES AND RECIPES IN THIS CHAPTER ARE FROM PEOPLE I MET while living in Umbertide. On a walk in the hills above town, I bumped into the famous truffle hunter Il Simba, who took me with him in search of the famous white truffle. A friend's father, Luigi, showed me how to hunt for wild asparagus in a forest filled with dangerous vipers. And Adriano and Silvana Bottaccioli taught me to cook some of Umbertide's oldest, most traditional dishes. The culinary teacher Melchiorre took me to buy a rabbit for dinner from his friend Cesarina. Through Melchiorre I met Stefano, who loves to cook. Andrea, the zany baker I met at a bread class in Perugia, showed me how to make the best pizza I've ever eaten. And the Umbrian cookbook author Rita Boini made some special dishes for me from her hometown of Torgiano.

MEET MELCHIORRE

Remember Game Boy's Mario—the little energetic man with dark bushy eyebrows and a thick black mustache? My friend Melchiorre could have been the inspiration for that character. I met him through my American friend Elizabeth at the Sagra del Pesce in Calzolaro, a village northwest of Umbertide. I sat across from Melchiorre under the humid dining canopy, sipping homemade *vino* and eating a mediocre dinner of overcooked *risotto di mare* and fried fish. As night fell and a cool breeze wafted through the dining tent, everyone moved outside to the blacktop dance floor.

"Would you like to dance?" Melchiorre said as he took my hand.

"Let's wait," I replied, nodding to the empty floor.

He pulled me onto the floor despite my refusal. He sang *rah tah tah, dum dee dum* in a loud voice as we danced—everyone stared. The song changed and Melchiorre left me for Elizabeth. The music slowed and several more couples joined them on the dance floor. The other couples looked like graduates of the same dance school. Each pair danced with perfect precision. They stared straight ahead with blank faces except for Elizabeth and Melchiorre, who smiled and laughed.

When the band began a tune everyone recognized, hundreds of dancers swarmed to the floor. Then, like marionettes guided by a puppeteer, they moved in unison. One, two, three. Four steps forward. Turn right. Four steps back. Turn again. I couldn't catch on to the steps they knew so well, so I moved to the sidelines to escape their spiked heels and hard-soled shoes. It looked like fun, but the dancers still wore serious faces—except for Melchiorre, who smiled broadly and stamped his feet. He laughed out loud in between boisterous *rah tah tahs*. What a glorious time we had.

By the end of the evening, Melchiorre, a cooking teacher by profession, had agreed to share some of his recipes at my house. The next day I invited Paola, Silvia, and the rest of my adopted family to join us. I felt a little anxious about the dinner. Melchiorre is so lively and my friends are reserved—I suspected it would be an interesting evening.

HOW TO MAKE BREADED MEAT

Carne panata

At a dinner at Melchiorre's, he served *scottadito a panata*—tiny bread-coated rib lamb chops—as an appetizer. The secret to great *carne panata* is homemade bread crumbs with an uneven texture that most store-bought crumbs don't have. And the bonus is you can get by with less meat because the crispy bread crumb topping adds bulk.

The small lamb rib chops were delicious, but bone-in rib veal chops are classic. In Umbria, boneless pork cutlets are just as popular. Thin slices of boneless beef, duck, chicken, or turkey are also good choices. Allow 6 to 8 ounces of bone-in meat per serving or 4 to 6 ounces for boneless.

1. Pound the meat to a thickness of about ¼ inch using a flat-bottom meat pounder. (If the slices are tender and already ¼-inch-thick, skip the pounding.) Season the meat with salt and pepper.

2. Lightly dredge each slice of meat in flour (shake off the excess), then dip each slice in beaten eggs (allow about one egg per two servings), and finally dredge the meat in dried bread crumbs (seasoned with a little grated Parmigiano-Reggiano or fresh, minced parsley, sage, or rosemary, if desired).

3. Heat about ¼ inch of olive oil (or half oil and half butter) in a large skillet over medium heat. Sauté the meat in batches (without crowding) until golden brown on both sides and no longer pink in the middle. (Alternatively, deep-fry the tiny chops in vegetable oil, as Melchiorre does.)

4. Squeeze a lemon over the meat (if you want) and serve with lemon wedges. (For variety, when the meat is done, spoon Classic Tomato Sauce over each slice of meat and cover with mozzarella cheese. Cover the pan; let stand a few minutes to melt the cheese.)

NEVER BUY A HEADLESS RABBIT

The day of our dinner party Melchiorre and I gulped down espresso, as the Italians do, standing at the bar next to La Coop, a large chain grocery store. We met to talk about the menu for *la cena* (dinner). Prosciutto with melon, wild asparagus with eggs, gnocchi with duck sauce, and rabbit on the rotisserie. We headed to La Coop to shop, but Melchiorre insisted we buy the rabbit from Cesarina, who raises them. "It's better to know what we're getting," he confided. "Here in Umbria we say, 'Never buy a rabbit without its head—it might be a cat.'" I wasn't excited about purchasing a rabbit with its head intact, but I couldn't bear the possibility of buying a cat.

After putting away the groceries we'd bought at La Coop—cherry toma-toes, asparagus, duck, potatoes, flour, and eggs—and eating a grilled pro-sciutto and pecorino panino, Melchiorre and I drove to Cesarina's farm.

On the drive, I found out that Melchiorre had grown up and lived as a shepherd on the island of Sardinia. But for many years now, he has lived in downtown Umbertide in a large, modern apartment building. He lives alone, not with his mother, as many unmarried Italian men of any age often do. His mother, sisters, and brother live nearby. As the oldest of eight children, he worked at a young age to put his siblings through school. One sister is a doctor, another is an engineer, and one brother is a surveyor. For several years, Melchiorre and his friend Elizabeth, an American expatriate, have taught Italian cooking to American tourists in various vacation houses around Umbria. (A good career choice for a gregarious man.)

We approached Cesarina's via a long, curved driveway. The house sits on a knoll surrounded by fields of grain and forested hills. We parked next to a cluster of ancient stone sheds—a small lean-to housed several pigs, and a shed had two calves inside. We left the animal sheds and walked toward the house.

Cesarina looked like one of the typical Italian grandmothers I often saw riding a bike in town or working in the garden. She looked robust, but not plump, in her floral apron. As Cesarina led us from the yard to the open kitchen door, a large black-and-white rooster and several brown chickens crossed our path. A huge gray goose met us near the house, stretched out his neck, hissing, and chased us inside as Cesarina invited us in. She turned to scold the goose and quickly closed the door behind her.

Cesarina's kitchen had a long wooden table that doubled as a prep area, and a few cabinets and cupboards along the wall. The small built-in refrig-erator had a wooden panel that matched the cupboards. But what caught my attention was the bucolic scene framed by the kitchen window. The view looked like a painting by Pietro Vannucci, the fifteenth-century Umbrian painter known as Perugino. Every window boasted such a view.

"*Prego*," said Cesarina, motioning us to sit down at the table. "*Caffè?*"

"*No, no grazie*," I said. Melchiorre told her we had just had coffee.

Disappointed, she passed a bowl of chocolates. We each took a couple of pieces. In Umbria, the more you eat, the happier you make the hostess.

"A glass of *vinsanto*?" she offered next.

"*Sì, un goccio*." I said. A "drop" of wine was plenty on a hot afternoon.

"You know how to cook rabbit?" Cesarina asked Melchiorre, but she didn't let him answer. "Make slits in the meat and fill them with *rosmarino, lardo tritato,* and *sale.*" Of course, he already knew the recipe; she had taught it to him during the time when he ate both lunch and dinner at her house. If he stayed home, she would phone to ask, "*Stai bene* [are you okay]?"

When it was time to go, Cesarina left to get the rabbit. I hoped it would be cleaned and skinned. Buying meat directly from a farmer isn't for anyone with a weak stomach. I once bought a chicken at a farm in Tuscany. The *contadina* broke its neck, drained the blood, dipped the chicken into boiling water, and plucked its feathers while we watched and waited. The disemboweling was left to us to do at home. I wasn't looking forward to gutting a rabbit.

Cesarina returned to the kitchen with the rabbit—skinned and cleaned, frozen stiff, and sealed in a plastic bag. She handed the rabbit to Melchiorre.

"*Senza testa* [without a head]?" Melchiorre said, looking at the rabbit.

The color rushed to Cesarina's already ruddy cheeks.

"Without a head, it could be a cat," joked Melchiorre.

"I'll get you another one," she said, reaching for the rabbit.

"*No, no, signora.*" Melchiorre tightened his grip on the rabbit.

"*Sì, sì, sì. Insisto!*"

"*No, no, no. Stavo scherzando* [I was joking]."

With each round of *no, no, no* and *sì, sì, sì,* Cesarina's face turned redder.

"*Basta* [enough]," announced Melchiorre, finally. Cesarina seemed amenable, so I pressed money into her hand to pay for the headless rabbit and kissed her on both cheeks as we said our goodbyes.

With a ready-to-cook rabbit in the backseat, I would be able to enjoy the drive home through Pietro Vannucci's magnificent landscape.

THE CHARACTER

The night of our dinner, Melchiorre roared up my steep, potholed driveway on his vintage 1960s Vespa. He wore a helmet, baggy black-and-white-checkered pants, and a chef's jacket. I ran down the stairs to help him carry up his boxes filled with wild asparagus, a blowtorch, and a portable rotisserie. We immediately started to cook. I sliced the melon and wrapped a slice of prosciutto around each wedge. Melchiorre seasoned the rabbit with rosemary and lard. He blasted the hair off the duck with his blowtorch and put the potatoes, covered in water, on top of the stove. Paola arrived in time to peel the potatoes for gnocchi.

When Melchiorre went outside to get something, Paola grabbed my arm and tried to stifle a laugh. "He's like a character in a *fumetto* [comic strip]," she snickered. After that, every time she caught my eye, she chuckled.

Silvia came to set the table. "How many of us are there?" she asked.

"Twelve," I said. "I'll help you with the plates."

When we got to the patio, Silvia said, "He is like someone in a *cartone animato* [cartoon]!" Silvia and Paola giggled whenever they saw me, or each other.

Elizabeth came at eight o'clock, just as Melchiorre and I were wrapping the asparagus and eggs in Sardinian bread—an exquisite dish from Melchiorre's home island. When the rest of the Ramaccionis arrived, Mario took the melon with prosciutto to the table. And Michela passed around the platter of gnocchi with fresh tomato duck sauce, and finally, the perfectly roasted *coniglio* (rabbit).

To my relief, Silvia and Paola had regained their composure by dinnertime. The subject of Melchiorre went on for days after the dinner—what he'd said, what he'd done, how he'd spoken, and how much they had liked him.

"He has the kind of personality you see on television," said Mario.

"On a comedy show," added Silvia.

"Is he really that unusual?" I asked.

"You meet people like him in Umbertide," said Paola, "but not often."

"Paola," contradicted Silvia, "I have never met anyone like him in Umbria!"

I could see how the typically reserved Umbrians might view Melchiorre as a character, but I bet he'd go unnoticed in his hometown on the multicultural island of Sardinia. I was glad that Silvia and Paola hadn't seen Melchiorre at the Sagra del Pesce, dancing with glee. They never would have made it through dinner with straight faces.

Fried Zucchini Blossoms

Fiori di zucca fritti

❦

I went to a fabulous dinner party at Melchiorre's—that's when I learned his recipe for fiori di zucca fritti. The fried blossoms have a light, crispy exterior contrasted with a soft, cheesy filling; they are delicious and simple to make. Melchiorre stood at the stove frying them, and he passed them out as soon as they were done. Instead of an appetizer, they can also be served as a side dish with grilled meat.

During the summer, farmers' markets are a good place to buy zucchini blossoms—if you don't grow your own. In the garden, be sure to pick male blossoms, those with a thin stem. Leave the thick-stemmed female flowers; they produce the squash. The blossoms are best the day they are picked, but can be held in an open plastic bag in the refrigerator for a day.

Yield: 6 to 8 servings

20 to 24 zucchini blossoms

8 ounces low-moisture mozzarella (not fresh), scamorza, or Swiss cheese

1 cup all-purpose flour

1 teaspoon kosher salt plus more for seasoning (*important*: see "About Salt," page xxv)

1 cup ice-cold sparkling water

Vegetable oil for frying

USEFUL EQUIPMENT: A deep-fry thermometer.

GETTING STARTED: Line a platter or tray with several layers of paper towels.

1. During preparation, handle the blossoms carefully. Break off the stem at the end of each blossom and carefully reach inside to pinch off the long yellow stamen. On the outside base of each blossom trim off the little triangular greens. Gently rinse the blossoms inside and out under cold water; drain on paper towels. Pat them dry with paper towels.

2. Cut the cheese into ⅜-inch-thick slices; cut each slice lengthwise into ⅜-inch-thick "fingers," about ½ inch shorter than the inside of the blossoms (you'll need a piece for each blossom). Carefully put a piece of cheese inside each blossom, gently twisting the tip of the flower to enclose the cheese (be gentle but don't worry if the flower tears).

3. Just before frying, combine the flour and kosher salt in a large bowl; use a wire whisk to beat in the chilled water. The batter should be lumpy; set aside. Heat about 2 inches of the oil in a large wok or skillet over medium-

high heat until the oil is moderately hot (about 365°F); adjust the heat as needed throughout frying to maintain the temperature. Briefly remove the wok from the heat if the oil becomes too hot or begins to smoke.

4. Dip one stuffed blossom at a time in the batter to lightly coat the entire blossom; shake to remove excess batter. Carefully lower a blossom into the hot oil, frying up to four at a time (too many will cool the oil). Fry, turning once, until light golden on both sides, about 1 to 1½ minutes total.

5. Use a skimmer or slotted spoon to remove and hold the blossoms briefly over the wok to drain the excess oil; finish draining on the platter lined with towels. While hot, sprinkle lightly with the kosher salt. For best results, serve immediately. (Alternatively, hold the fried blossoms on a baking sheet in a 300°F oven for up to 10 minutes.)

VARIATION: To make *fritto misto* (fried mix), in step 3 beat an egg yolk in with the chilled water. Suggestions for the mix: large Bergamont sage leaves (homegrown or from a farmers' market); shelled prawns and/or bite-size pieces of calamari; and/or wedges or slices of vegetables—artichoke hearts, red bell pepper, fennel, cauliflower, onions. ❧

SUMMER'S PERENNIALS

During the summer, when tomatoes are abundant and luscious, one of the simplest (and best) antipasto dishes shows up on Umbria's tables—*insalata caprese* (tomatoes with mozzarella). And when temperatures soar, *insalata di riso* (rice salad) is a favorite, served as an antipasto, first course, or side dish.

Insalata caprese: Slice equal amounts of ripe, flavorful tomatoes (preferably heirloom) and the best fresh mozzarella cheese you can find. Arrange the tomatoes, slightly overlapping, on a plate. Tuck a slice of cheese between each slice of tomato, letting the cheese peek out from under the tomatoes. (Alternatively, scatter halved cherry tomatoes such as Sweet 100s and *bocconcini*—tiny balls of fresh mozzarella—on a plate.) Sprinkle generously with kosher salt and freshly ground pepper; drizzle generously with fruity extra virgin olive oil. Garnish with torn bits of fresh basil leaves.

Insalata di riso: Toss cooked, cooled white rice (medium grain is ideal) with diced pickled vegetables (red peppers, carrots, and cauliflower), chopped marinated artichoke hearts, bite-size marinated mushrooms, diced ham, diced Emmentaler cheese (or fresh pecorino or mozzarella), sliced black and green pimento-stuffed olives, diced fresh tomatoes, diced hard-cooked eggs, canned tuna, extra virgin olive oil, mayonnaise, and a splash of white wine vinegar—salt and pepper, to taste.

HUNTING THE WILD ASPARAGUS

In mid-April wild asparagus fever hits Umbria. Hunting asparagus, I had heard, is an addiction. The promise of finding the next asparagus makes it almost impossible to give up the hunt and go home. So when Silvia's friend Luigi offered to take us hunting, I was eager to go. But when I showed up alone, Luigi's face fell. "Where's Silvia?" he asked.

"She is scared of lizards, snakes, and wild boars," I said. We both laughed.

"You're wearing shoes?" he asked. "Don't you have boots?"

"No, *ma vanno bene* [but these are okay]," I replied, pointing to my sturdy walking shoes. I figured the mud wouldn't be bad—it hadn't rained for a couple of days.

We drove into the hills above Magione and parked in the woods. It was a clear day, so we could see across Lake Trasimeno to the opposite shore. Outside the car, Luigi tapped the toe of a boot with a stick. "Metal-toed boots are good for the forest. Usually the vipers hide in the brush and attack below the knee."

"You wear boots because there are vipers?" I asked, surprised.

"*Certo* [of course]," he said. "Did you bring a walking stick?"

I hadn't, so he handed me one, and we left the dirt road to enter *il bosco*.

"You know, it's safer to look for asparagus in the morning—you're less likely to see vipers." I didn't ask why we were there in the middle of the day.

"Vipers freeze when they hear you and attack when you reach into the grass." He taught me to beat the grass with a stick and watch for movement.

"How poisonous are vipers?" I asked, feeling anxious.

"The ones that are *marroni, marroni* [really brown] are the most poisonous," he said. "The man I saw bitten by one was dead within thirty minutes, but you don't always die." Suddenly every stick or twig looked like a viper to me.

To my untrained eye, the lanky asparagus—some over four feet tall—blended into the forest's underbrush and were hard to see. The thin green branches and thick blades of grass that were everywhere looked like asparagus.

"Do you ever get lost?" I asked. I had no idea where we were.

"No, but people do get lost."

Luigi had already found plenty of asparagus by the time I picked my first stalk. It was about three feet tall and more slender than a plastic drinking straw. I looked for a cluster of asparagus, but instead found it scattered over the forest floor among the weeds.

Hiking up and down the hills, trudging through scrubby brush, and fighting off low tree branches was hard work. Small lime-green lizards scurried everywhere, moving the brush and startling me. Wild rose bushes with their thorny, gangly branches grabbed at my sweater and pierced my pants, stinging my legs. A couple of times, I stepped into a grass-covered hole and fell backward, landing in the domain of the snake with the triangular head and deadly fang.

"Look!" called Luigi from below. To my horror, he reached his hand into some moving weeds. "Did you see it?"

"*O Dio!* The viper?" I asked, but then I saw a foot-long bright green lizard scamper away.

"When you see that lizard—*il ramarro*—you usually see vipers," he warned.

"Does your wife ever come with you?"

"No, but sometimes my son comes."

"Why doesn't your wife come?" I wanted to know.

He didn't reply because some droppings had caught his eye. "*Cinghiale* [wild boar]," he said. "They're dangerous, but they only come out at night." Then he said, "Both my wife and daughters are too afraid to come."

"How often do you see vipers?" I asked.

"I've probably killed at least five over the years, but you always have to be wary."

Two hours passed without seeing a viper (*per fortuna*). By then we had collected at least two pounds of *asparagi selvatici* so we decided to head back. I was eager to get home and make asparagus lasagne.

That evening, following Michela's mother's advice, I simmered crumbled sausage in white wine; sautéed asparagus rounds in olive oil; stirred the sausage and asparagus into a thin béchamel with grated Emmentaler and Parmigiano cheese; and topped each layer of lasagne with the rich sauce and fresh mozzarella cheese.

The asparagus stalks were tougher than their cultivated cousins and took longer to cook than expected. Their flavor was strong and distinctive. I loved them—I was hooked. I made plans to hunt for wild asparagus the following weekend. Before going, I found a walking stick and bought rubber boots and leather gloves. I wasn't going to let the vipers win.

LIVER AND SUCH

When I lived in Umbria, I told everyone I met I was writing a cookbook and looking for cooks. Someone gave me Rita Boini's name and number, but her name was not new to me. I already had a copy of her cookbook *La Cucina Umbra*—and I had devoured the tidbits of culinary history that accompanied her traditional recipes. I regularly read her weekly food and culture articles in the *Corriere dell'Umbria*, Umbria's most important daily newspaper. So I was eager to meet Rita and talk about our mutual passions—Umbrian food and culture.

Rita and I shared several meals, including an American Thanksgiving and a cooking-lesson dinner, both at my place. We lunched at the truffle festival in Gubbio, and I attended a goose festival where she was one of the speakers. We met for dinner at a culinary competition where she was a judge.

One night, Rita suggested that we dine at La Mulinella, a traditional restaurant outside Todi—Rita's favorite hill town in central Umbria. It was a very dark, cold November night, which made the rustic restaurant seem all the more cozy and inviting. The menu consisted of several dishes I'd read about in Rita's book, and many of them I had not yet tasted—*spezzatino di cervo, piccione alla ghiotta, sugo d'oca con umbricelli*. I asked Rita to choose the dishes for dinner. So she ordered. *Gnocchetti rustici con sugo d'oca* (flour dumplings with goose sauce). *Torta al testo con spinaci e mozzarella* (flat bread filled with spinach and mozzarella). *Filetto* and *piccione alla ghiotta* (steak and roasted squab—each simmered with liver in red wine with vinegar, olives, anchovies, capers, and sage).

We shared tastes of everything. The *gnocchetti* were light and delicious in the goose sauce, and the filled bread was really good, too. But the two dishes with liver sauce—well, I didn't love liver then like I do today. After dinner, I thought a lot about the kind of recipes I'd gathered up to that point. Chicken liver pâté; pork liver wrapped in caul fat; ragù made from chicken innards; squab stuffed with liver; and goose stuffed with pig ears and liver. By the time I finished my research, would I end up writing *Umbria's Fifty Best Liver Dishes*? What publisher would buy that book? What cook would?

Most Umbrians adore liver, but where there is liver there is meat for roasting, grilling, stuffing, and sautéing—pork chops, sausage, chicken, guinea fowl, squab. I needed to find out how cooks prepared the rest of the creature—not just the ears and *interiora*. And I wanted to track down cooks who prepared the other delicious meals I'd eaten—gnocchi with duck sauce, cannelloni, *spaghetti alla carbonara*. The dinner with Rita was a turning point in my research. Instead of requesting the most traditional farmhouse dishes, I began asking for recipes of the family's favorite meals—as well as those recipes with a longer history. And Rita was one of the cooks to teach me several special recipes from her hometown of Torgiano.

My recipe collection expanded along with my palate—I learned to enjoy liver. Now I actually crave liver crostini and dishes such as *piccione alla ghiotta*.

Parmesan Egg-Drop Soup
Stracciatella
∞

In the past, stracciatella *was a rich man's soup. "Eggs were precious in Umbria," said Rita Boini, "so people ate very few. They needed the money eggs would bring to buy salt, sugar, and pepper." At Easter, when eggs were plentiful, wealthy families served this soup. "People also ate* stracciatella *when they were cold or sick and wanted something comforting. And they served it to unexpected guests because it was quick."*

Although stracciatella *is made all over Umbria, this version hails from Torgiano, where cooks add lemon zest. In other towns, cooks add flour or bread crumbs to the egg mixture—I like both, but Rita uses neither. Homemade broth makes this soup extraordinary, but canned broth will do. It is easy to reduce or increase the recipe—for a single serving, use 1½ cups of broth, ½ ounce grated cheese, 1 tablespoon bread crumbs, a dash of lemon zest and nutmeg, and a sprig of parsley.*

Yield: 6 servings (about 10 cups—1¾ cups per serving)

9 cups Meat Broth (see recipe, page 118) or canned chicken broth

3 ounces grated Parmigiano-Reggiano cheese plus more for the table (see "Grated Cheese," page 6)

Finely shredded zest of ½ lemon (see "About Zest," page 37)

¼ teaspoon freshly grated nutmeg or more to taste

⅓ cup homemade dried bread crumbs (page 16) or flour (optional)

6 large eggs

6 sprigs Italian parsley, finely chopped

Kosher salt

1. Bring the broth to a boil in a large covered saucepan (the Meat Broth recipe may yield only 8 cups; if so, add 1 cup of water). Turn off the heat. In a medium bowl, toss together the cheese, lemon zest, and nutmeg (if using, add the bread crumbs or flour now); use a fork to beat in the eggs.

2. Bring the broth to a simmer over medium low. While beating the broth with a fork, gradually drop spoonfuls of the egg mixture into the saucepan, forming tiny wisps of egg. Remove the saucepan from the heat; stir in the parsley. Adjust the salt and nutmeg to taste. Let stand a few minutes. Pass additional cheese at the table. ❧

Meat Broth

Brodo di carne

In Umbria homemade broth is usually made from a mix of meats—veal, chicken, and gallina, an old hen that is too tough to roast. While every supermarket in Umbria sells gallina, most in the States don't—so I use chicken. Although veal is often available here, beef is less expensive, so I use it. If you prefer, you can omit the beef and increase the amount of chicken by one pound. Turkey and pork make good broth, but with a flavor too strong for use in most recipes. For Umbria's delicate recipes—stracciatella, cappelletti, risotto—this mild, all-purpose broth is ideal.

Rita adds tomatoes, like the contadine did, to the simmering broth. "Sometimes they also added whole, peeled potatoes near the end of cooking," she said. "When the potatoes were tender, they chopped them and served them as a side dish—they were delicious. The potatoes absorbed the flavor of the broth, so they didn't need any other condiment." The night Rita and I cooked together, she served carne bolita (boiled meat leftover from making broth) as a second course (see recipe, page 120).

Yield: 8 to 10 cups (depends on evaporation,
additions of water, and duration of cooking)

2½ to 3 pounds chicken with bones, such as thighs, legs, wings, backs, necks

1½ pounds beef with bones (more meat than bones)

3 medium celery stalks, quartered

2 large carrots, peeled and quartered

1 medium onion, quartered

1 tablespoons kosher salt (*important:* see "About Salt," page xxv)

¼ teaspoon freshly ground pepper

2 Roma tomatoes, quartered (optional)

5 sprigs Italian parsley (optional)

4 quarts cold water

1. Put the chicken, beef, celery, carrots, onion, kosher salt, and pepper into a large pot (if using, add tomatoes and parsley now); add the 4 quarts water. Cover and bring to a boil over high heat. Immediately reduce the heat to low; simmer, partially covered, 2 to 3 hours, stirring occasionally (add water, if needed to keep ingredients covered).

2. To strain the broth, put a sieve or colander over a large bowl; ladle the broth into the sieve. Discard the solids (and reserve the meat for another use, if desired). If using the broth right away, skim off and discard the fat floating on the top (if making the broth ahead, skim it later). Adjust the salt to taste (it may need a lot more). The broth is now recipe-ready.

To Store Broth: Cool the broth quickly—select a bowl or pot that is large enough to rest the bowl of broth inside. Fill the empty bowl halfway with ice; add a couple cups of cold water. Put the bowl of broth in the ice bath; stir the broth frequently to help cool it. When cool, spoon off and discard the fat. Cover and refrigerate it immediately—broth is very perishable. Use within 2 days or freeze up to 3 months.

VARIATION: Umbria's *brodo* is light in color and delicate but flavorful. For a richer flavor and darker color (and a different use), sauté the chicken and beef in oil in the pot until well browned; add the rest of the broth ingredients and simmer per recipe directions. ❧

BOILED MEAT— *CARNE BOLITA*

When cooks in Umbria make broth, they often serve the *carne bolita* that flavored the broth for a second course. One Umbrian friend makes chicken salad instead, serving it as a second course—cut the chicken into bite-size pieces and dress it with mayonnaise seasoned with diced celery and red onion, minced garlic, chopped parsley or basil, fresh lemon juice, salt, and pepper. Of course, the meat can be saved for a variety of uses, from cannelloni filling to hearty soups to tacos.

To make *carne bolita,* prepare Meat Broth (see recipe, page 118) with the following changes. (1) For the meat, use 6 large bone-in chicken thighs and 1½ pounds boneless beef chuck cut into six pieces. (2) Simmer the beef with the rest of the ingredients—except the chicken—for 1 hour. (3) Add the chicken; simmer until the beef is tender and the chicken is done, about 1 hour. Transfer the meat to a platter. To finish making the broth, follow the recipe directions, starting with step 2. Serve the meat or cool it about 45 minutes. Refrigerate (cover when cool) up to 2 days or freeze up to 3 months.

PATATE IN SALMÌ

In Torgiano, *carne bolita* is often served with *patate in salmì* (potatoes simmered in wine and vinegar). The tangy potatoes complement the bland boiled meat, but they are also a good accompaniment to sautéed, roasted, or grilled meats, fish, and poultry. To make Rita's *patate in salmì,* sauté 8 large sage leaves in ½ cup olive oil in a large pot until almost crisp. Add 2 pounds yellow potatoes (peeled and cut into ¾-inch cubes), 1 sliced medium onion, ½ cup dry white wine, 3 tablespoons white wine vinegar, and 1 lemon wedge. Add water to just cover the potatoes. Bring to a boil; reduce the heat and simmer until the potatoes are tender and the cooking liquid is thick and saucy.

IN THE DARK

Just minutes outside most Umbrian towns, gravel roads branch off the main thoroughfares and street signs vanish. So landmarks—an old tree, a pink house, a yield sign—offer the only navigational aids. To get to Stefano's, he told me to look for the 5.5 kilometer sign, blinking arrows indicating a curve in the road, and the names of two houses—Casa Bianca and Casa dei Fiori.

"Make a sharp right there," said Stefano, "and head up the hill. It will seem like forever. Go right at the first fork."

"Is there a sign at the fork?" I asked.

"No, no. Pass Casa dei Fiori and turn right at the sign for Casa Bianca. At the fork in the road veer left. Drive between two pillars. My house is just ahead on the left."

When I left the paved street, the streetlights disappeared. Under the blackness that blanketed the mountain, I had the sensation I might drive off a cliff. It seemed like many miles passed before I left the main gravel road and entered the dirt drive to Stefano's. Just after I turned and drove a short way down a narrow road, I was walled in—I knew I had made a wrong turn. The road, barely wide enough for my tiny Lancia, hugged a vertical overgrown forest wall on one side and a tall fence on the other. I was in complete darkness.

I stopped to call Stefano and was told I should have turned left when I went right. I got out and tiptoed around the car—scared I might attract one of Umbria's ferocious wild boars. The only way out was to back up, but after driving several yards in reverse the narrow road became too steep to manage well. So inch by inch, putting on the hand brake, releasing the clutch, turning the steering wheel, and doing it all over again, I managed to turn the car around in a space where the road had widened by a couple of feet. Once I was driving forward again, I arrived at Stefano's in minutes, but with my heart racing and my arms exhausted.

Stefano's house was surprisingly warm (most houses are cold in the winter). And the aromas from the kitchen were wonderful. By the time I had taken off my winter coat and gloves, I was already laughing at one of Stefano's stories. Not only is he funny and witty—and a bit of a flirt—at sixty-something, he is handsome. He is slim with thick dark hair and a dark mustache. While Stefano stirred a saucepan of sausages simmering in tomato sauce and sautéed pork ribs in a skillet with garlic, rosemary, and bay leaves in olive oil, he told me about his new love, a woman from Belarus.

"I'm lucky to find someone," he said. "At my age, a man wants a woman."

"I know what you mean," I said. "I would like to find someone, too."

"You? Well, that will be very difficult," he said, shaking his head.

"Difficult? Why?" I asked, surprised.

Before answering, Stefano poured a splash of white wine over the ribs and said, looking me in the eye, "Italian men want someone to take care of them and keep house."

"I didn't say Italian. Besides, I don't want to be someone's mother."

"You're right. Many Italian men are looking for a *mamma*."

"What about [our mutual friend] Melchiorre's new American love?" I asked. "Have you met her?"

Stefano opened his eyes wide as though I had shocked him, and he shook his head. "Yes, yes, I met her. It will never work! Never! He is fifty-five years old. He wants a housewife, but he needs a mother."

"Melchiorre has taken care of himself for years," I objected.

"She will never do. American woman don't even iron, for heaven's sake."

"That's not true. We iron. Well, never kitchen or bath towels or sheets. Never underwear and rarely blue jeans or T-shirts. My grandmother did but we don't."

"That's what I mean. American women don't iron. Ironing is an art. Women here to go to the 'University of Ironing' to learn to do it right."

"Well, I might not iron much, but I am a good cook."

"Well, at least that," he said. "A good cook is important to a man."

Dinner was ready, so I carried the plates to the table while Stefano opened the wine. The glass of sagrantino and the delicious meal assuaged my hurt feelings. I loved the tender braised sausages. The sauce was so lovely that I mopped up every last bit with a thick slice of rustic bread. And then I joined Stefano in picking up a pork rib to nibble on the bone.

At the end of dinner, Stefano selected two antique dessert wineglasses from a china cabinet shelf dedicated to his glass collection. He filled each glass with sweet Sicilian muscat. When our glasses were empty, he filled two thimble-size glasses with grappa. I refused his subsequent attempts to refill any of my three glasses with something *alcolico*. I wanted to be sober when I hit the dark maze of dirt roads that would take me home.

Fish Soup
Zuppa di pesce
∞

The origins of this dish are in poverty. Fisherman used whatever was in their nets to make a flavorful broth—often the fish that was too bony to eat. But with today's seafood prices, zuppa di pesce *can be a very expensive dish. With that in mind, you may want to base your selection of seafood on price. For example, buy the least-expensive firm white fish at the market or drop the prawns in favor of using more of the less-pricey mussels or squid. If money isn't a concern, choose your favorite seafood—crab, scallops, prawns.*

For the white fish, I have specified Alaskan rock cod or Pacific halibut, but mahimahi from the United States and Pacific cod or Alaskan red snapper are also good choices. These fish are abundant and on the environmentally friendly list (see Resources, page 351). If you choose not to use prawns, you can skip the step of making broth by adding water when broth is called for.

In Umbria, supermarkets sell frozen packages of zuppa di pesce *that include the raw ingredients for making a couple of servings of soup—diced tomatoes, parsley, clams, mussels, calamari, prawns, and bits of fish.*

Yield: 6 servings

18 large prawns in shells (about ¾ pound) (see "Tips for Seafood," page 125)

3 cups water

3 plus 3 large garlic cloves, peeled

1 pound small squid (see "Tips for Seafood," page 125)

1½ pounds firm white fish fillets, such as Alaskan rock cod or Pacific halibut

1 can (14 ounces) diced tomatoes with juice

1/2 cup extra virgin olive oil

1 large celery stalk, finely diced

1 medium carrot, finely diced

1/2 medium onion, finely chopped

1/2 cup packed Italian parsley, finely chopped

1 anchovy fillet, minced

1 bay leaf

1/8 to 1/4 teaspoon red pepper flakes (use 1/4 teaspoon for more spice)

1/2 cup dry white wine, such as pinot grigio or sauvignon blanc

1 teaspoon kosher salt (*important:* see "About Salt," page xxv)

1/8 teaspoon freshly ground pepper

1 tablespoon all-purpose flour

1/2 pound tightly closed live mussels (see "Tips for Seafood," page 125)

1/2 pound tightly closed live clams (see "Tips for Seafood," page 125)

12 slices (3/4-inch thick) Italian or French bread, toasted

GETTING STARTED: Prepare the prawns, squid, mussels, and clams according to the directions in "Tips for Seafood" (page 125).

1. Shell and devein the prawns—set aside the shells. Refrigerate the prawns. Put the shells into a small saucepan with the 3 cups water and 3 of the garlic cloves. Bring to a boil; cover and simmer over low heat for 10 minutes. Strain; discard the solids. Return the broth to the saucepan. Cover; keep warm. Clean and cut the squid into bite-size pieces; refrigerate.

2. Cut the fish into 1-inch cubes; cover and refrigerate. Finely chop/pulse the tomatoes with juice using an immersion blender or food processor; set aside. Mince the remaining 3 garlic cloves. Heat the oil with the garlic in a large pot over medium heat. Add the squid, celery, carrot, onion, parsley, anchovy, bay leaf, and red pepper; sauté, stirring frequently, 2 minutes.

3. Add 1 cup of the prawn-shell broth; cover and simmer over low heat, stirring occasionally, until the squid is tender, about 15 minutes. Add the tomatoes, wine, kosher salt, and pepper. Simmer over medium heat, stirring occasionally, 5 minutes. Sprinkle with the flour; cook and stir over medium-low heat 2 minutes.

4. Add the mussels and clams; cover and simmer over medium heat for 2 minutes. Add the fish and prawns. Simmer until the mussels and clams open (discard any that don't), the fish is tender when pierced with a knife, and the prawns turn opaque, about 3 minutes. Add prawn-shell broth if needed to make it saucy. Adjust the salt and pepper to taste. Serve with the bread. ❧

TIPS FOR SEAFOOD

Clams and Mussels: Buy closed mussels and clams with intact shells (not broken or chipped). At home, completely open the bag so they can breathe (they are alive). Store them in the coolest part of the refrigerator. About 20 minutes before cooking, soak in cold water to remove any sand. Remove the hairy "beard" from the mussels by yanking the threads toward the pointed end of the shell. Scrub the shells with a stiff brush. Rinse well.

Prawns: Look for prawns from the United States for the best quality—these are usually sold at the fish counter. (Bags of frozen prawns from foreign countries often have an off flavor and a mushy texture.) Store prawns in the coldest part of the refrigerator under ice. To prepare for cooking, peel off the shells and run a sharp paring knife about ⅛ inch deep down the center of the curved back, from top to tail. Rinse under cold water, pulling out the black vein.

Squid: Store squid covered in ice in the coldest section of the refrigerator. Squeeze near the eye to pop out the small round beak hidden inside the tentacles; discard the beak. Pinch the head off just below the eye—discard the eye but save the tentacles. Lay the body on a cutting board. Starting at the pointed end, push and scrape across the body with a paring knife to remove the colored outer skin, fins, and guts. Use a finger to reach inside the body to remove the long, paper-thin, transparent quill and any remaining guts. Rinse out the body.

TIED WITH RIBBONS

My next-door neighbor Mario introduced me to his colleague Adriano, an artist and graphic designer. I invited Adriano and his wife, Silvana, to lunch—rather, a cooking lesson (for me) followed by lunch. Silvana planned to teach me to make *pancotto,* a very old peasant soup made from stale bread, water, and olive oil. Adriano wanted to show me his recipe for trout with rosemary and potatoes. To complete the meal, I planned a salad. But then someone decided that we should invite Mario and Adriano's boss, Signor Renzini.

When Mario's mother, Paola, heard what I was going to serve, she was mortified. "We cannot serve him *pancotto!* Not a country dish. Not the first time he dines with our family!" she said.

So Paola and I embellished the menu. Before Silvana and Adriano arrived, I made braised fennel baked in béchamel and two large potato pancakes. Paola made a turkey breast and a veal roast, both stuffed with prosciutto; risotto with mushrooms and asparagus; a salad; and two apple strudels.

When Silvana and Adriano arrived and heard about the revised menu, Adriano said, "We're having *un pranzo coi fiocchi* [special lunch, tied with ribbons]." It seemed insane for the three of us to cook the trout and soup, but I had the ingredients, so we did. It was a grand feast.

Several months later, Silvana and Adriano invited me to experience a very traditional farm dinner at their home. Since Silvana had grown up on a farm near Umbertide, and Adriano's hobby is food history, I knew the conversation would be interesting and the meal authentic. When I arrived at their modern single-story apartment not far from historic downtown Umbertide, the kitchen door was closed.

"The *budelli* stink," explained Silvana. It was true, they did! To prepare the smelly intestines, they were thoroughly cleaned and seasoned with garlic, wild fennel (sprigs and flowers), salt, and pepper. Then they were left in a cool place for a week to absorb the flavors and then hung above the fireplace for several days. Typically, the dried *budelli* are grilled over the fire, cut into pieces, and served really hot. We nibbled on the *budelli secchi di maiale* (dried pork intestines) before dinner. And, yes, they were surprisingly tasty. Silvana also served small, round red peppers stuffed with tuna, anchovies, and capers and a large platter with five kinds of crostini. I made one of them—topped with braised *roveja,* a tiny dried pea that grows wild in the fields near Cascia in southwestern Umbria. There were two kinds of liver toppings, one mushroom and one with hard-cooked eggs called *crostini mimosa.*

While we ate, Silvana and Adriano talked about growing up in Umbria. Before World War II, most people lived in the country—and many lived far out of town in the hills on very remote, isolated farms. "My family was really lucky living in the country," said Silvana. "It was a hard life—everyone had to work, even the children. But we lived better on the farms because we had food."

It was her father's job to work in the fields and care for the large animals, the sheep and oxen. But her mother's life was even busier—she had nine children to care for, plus the house to keep. She tended the chickens, pigs, geese, guinea fowl, rabbits, and pigeons and worked in the fields. She returned home a little before lunch to cook for the family and workers, fifteen to twenty in all.

"Every day my mother made fresh pasta—like we're eating today," said Silvana, passing around plates filled with tagliatelle with meat sauce. "But everything we ate was more delicious than it is today because the food was so high in quality. The chicken roamed free and the pork was more flavorful because the pigs were so well cared for."

Adriano served the rest of the meal while Silvana and I cleared the table. "*L'anatra in porchetta*—a traditional duck recipe," he announced, "with roasted potatoes and eggplant Parmesan." Adriano had cooked pig ears and pig feet for several hours and then chopped them and seasoned them with garlic and wild fennel before stuffing the mixture inside the duck. Using a hot oven (425°F) and rubbing the skin with wild fennel flowers, salt, pepper, and seasoned *lardo tritato* (ground pork fat) were his secrets to making the incredibly flavorful duck with crisp skin.

For dessert, Silvana served *celiata,* a traditional fried cookie made during Carnival. She also prepared *mijaccio,* a very old farmhouse treat made from the blood of a just-slaughtered pig, broth, almonds, flour, milk, nutmeg, cinnamon, sugar, pine nuts, bread crumbs, and lemon zest. It looked like a rich chocolate tart (today chocolate is sometimes added), but it tasted like blood pudding. Although Adriano grew up with his three siblings and parents in Umbertide, his passion for food and history has made him adore dishes such as *mijaccio* that some of my city-dwelling friends turn up their noses at.

After Silvana had finished explaining how the desserts were made, she said, "You can see that on the farm we didn't waste anything, not the pig's blood, ears, or feet. We didn't have much but we were better off than the city folk because the only things we had to buy were salt, sugar, and pepper."

"But the townspeople had to buy almost everything," added Adriano. "If they didn't raise chickens or rabbits, they had it really bad." Adriano's family could afford to buy what they needed—his father worked for the railroad, so they had a regular income.

"And you city folks had to pay with money," Silvana said. "We paid with eggs or pigeons."

At the end of dinner, I heartily thanked Adriano and Silvana. "What fascinating stories and what a lovely dinner!" I said on the way to the door. "The evening has been every bit as special as the lunch we shared with Signor Renzini. Two wonderful meals, both *coi fiocchi*."

UMBRIA'S SALT-FREE BREAD

Adriano has a book of laws from Umbertide published in 1521 that includes rules about food. "Food was so precious that there was a great respect for it," said Adriano. "That is probably why they were so exacting in their regulations." For example, the book states that bread must not be held on a table but in clean linen—the table might be dirty.

A dozen or more years after the book was written, Pope Paul III levied a tax on salt that lead to a rebellion in Umbria—*la guerra del sale* (the salt wars). In protest, Umbrians baked bread, the mainstay of their diet, without salt—the traditional bread is still made without it.

"My mother made bread once a week," said Silvana. "I came from a large family—plus we fed our workers. So we went through a lot of bread."

A major feature in the *contadini* kitchen of yesteryear was the *mattra*, a large waist-high cabinet that held a wooden board for kneading dough and space for storing the flour and loaves of bread underneath it. At about 8:30 in the evening, her mother would add flour and water to the piece of dough left from the week before.

"She would form the dough into a huge ball and make a cross on the top. Then she would cross herself, like Catholics do when they enter a church. She did this to bless the bread and to give thanks to God for the food."

Bread was a very important part of the diet—it filled up hungry families when there wasn't much else to eat.

"My mother would close the hinged lid of the *mattra* with the dough inside and let it rise overnight. Then, at five thirty in the morning, she would knead some flour into the dough and shape it into sixteen loaves of bread."

Her mother put the bread in the wood oven, and she sealed the oven's iron door with mud (it helped to hold in the heat). Again Silvana's mother made the sign of the cross, but this time, in the mud.

People tell me that the smell of bread in the *contadini* kitchen was very strong—you could even smell it outside the kitchen. It was an intense, but pleasant, delicious smell.

CAH-RUNCH!

I signed up for a two-day professional pizza-, focaccia-, and bread-making course at the Università dei Sapori (of Flavors) in Perugia with Andrea Pioppi. It was late June and we were having a heat wave in Umbria—it was over 100°F. The class was held in a small room without air-conditioning. A huge pizza oven dominated the space, and by noon it felt like the classroom itself was a *forno*. Being a professional baker by trade, Andrea seemed unfazed by the heat—but the rest of us newbies were dripping wet and lifeless.

Andrea's family has a large, well-respected bakery in the small town of Mantignana, not far from Perugia. He, his wife, and their kids live upstairs in a modern apartment with hip decor. But he left the family business to work as a consultant to other bakeries, and to teach. He is a young, sturdy-looking man. His chef's jacket, trimmed in yellow piping one day and in red the next, was crisply ironed and pristine. A kerchief that matched the trim on his jacket covered his shaved head. While he spoke, he paced and used his hands to punctuate each sentence. His voice was loud and forceful one minute, quiet the next—but he always spoke in rapid-fire Italian. He spent at least the first hour talking passionately about flour, using very technical yet poetic phrases. "Every sack of flour is different because flour is a complex ingredient." "Gluten [the protein in flour] is like the frame of the house." "The amount of enzymes is important—it can be like preparing dinner for three and three hundred show up."

Later the topics Andrea covered included salt, yeast, and water (how mineral content affects outcome). He taught us about thermometers and pH meters—and how to use them. And he told us to weigh everything, from the flour to the water. The discussions were interesting, but I admit we all perked up when Andrea put the mixer on the table and invited us to help make dough. Over the course of two days, we learned to make crackers, bread sticks, dinner rolls, braided bread, a couple of kinds of focaccia, and two kinds of pizza—individual pizza and pizza baked in sheet pans (*pizza al piatto* and *pizza al taglio*).

When he took the *pizza al taglio* out of the pan to dry, the smell of baked crust and whiffs of hot olive oil, cheese, and tomato filled the stifling room.

The wait we had to endure for him to cut it was unbearable. He had put off sampling until the end of the day—and earlier in the day we had watched him donate half of the baked goods to the school's lunch. Then he made a show of slicing the pizza. "Listen," he said as he started to cut into it. A loud "cah-RUNCH" escaped the pizza as the blade made its way through the crust. *"Perfetta!"* he said, making a snapping sound with his fingers. "See, the crust is light, well-browned, and crisp. Not soggy. Just as it should be."

The pizzas he made were some of the best I have ever eaten—so I pass along Andrea's recipe for *pizza al piatto* and give you some advice for baking great pizza at home. And my first tip—avoid making pizza on the hottest day of the year!

Pizza "On the Plate"
Pizza al piatto
ᏅᎬᏅ

Andrea's pizza class was eye-opening. In university culinary classes, I had been taught that yeast required warm to hot water to activate it. In class, Andrea used chilled water because the flour was room temperature (hot). His original recipe used fresh cake yeast, but I have adapted it for dry active yeast, which is more common and less perishable. Do not substitute instant yeast such as RapidRise. The secrets to Andrea's chewy yet crisp pizza al piatto *are using a small amount of yeast, allowing resting periods during mixing, and letting the dough rise slowly.*

The recipe looks long but it is easy—and it works on the "dough" cycle in a bread machine! Just bring the ingredients to the right temperature and toss everything into the machine. Then follow the instructions for rising the dough and baking the pizza. A heavy-duty mixer makes it easy, too, but you can mix by hand.

This is very traditional pizza made with a thin crust and minimal cheese and sauce, but boy, is it delicious. If you want to add other toppings, be frugal—the thin crust was developed for a lightly topped pizza. If you want to put more toppings on the pizza, make the Quick Dough (see recipe, page 281) with bread flour instead of using this recipe.

To find your favorite cheese, the first time you make the recipe use a different mozzarella on each of the four pizzas. In Italy, where mozzarella di bufala *(buffalo-milk cheese) is really fresh and affordable, that's my favorite cheese. But in the*

United States, I usually buy locally made fresh mozzarella or our standard low-moisture mozzarella—both are good. I prefer the softer texture of the fresh cheese.

At least once a year, my family—my son, my brothers, their wives and kids—gets together to make pizza. Everyone rolls and tops his or her own pizza. It is great fun.

Yield: 4 individual pizze (1¾ pounds dough)

- 4 cups unbleached all-purpose flour (17½ ounces) plus more for kneading/rolling

- 4 teaspoons kosher salt (*important*: see "About Salt," page xxv)

- 1¼ teaspoons sugar

- ½ teaspoon active dry yeast (*do not use instant yeast such as RapidRise*)

- 1⅓ cups water at room temperature (75 to 80°F)

- 1 tablespoon extra virgin olive oil plus more for pans

You'll also need: Parchment paper. An instant-read thermometer, pastry blade, pizza stone, and pizza peel (paddle) are recommended.

Getting started: Bring the flour to 75 to 80°F. For example, put the measured flour into a warm oven (on the lowest setting) or into the refrigerator (tightly wrapped) for a few minutes—toss the flour and check the temperature. Put a damp towel under a large, lightly floured wooden board to prevent slipping.

1. Fit an electric mixer with a dough hook attachment (alternatively, mix by hand). Put the flour, salt, sugar, and yeast into a large mixing bowl; mix to combine. Pour the 1⅓ cups (75 to 80°F) water and the oil over the dry ingredients. Immediately mix on low speed until the mixture forms a ball, about 9 minutes—scrape the sides and bottom of the bowl as needed. (Alternatively, beat with a wooden spoon.) Let the dough rest in the bowl for 10 minutes.

2. Knead on low speed until the dough is smooth, about 10 minutes. (Alternatively, turn the dough out onto the floured board and knead by hand.) At

this point, do a windowpane test: cut off a small piece of dough. Use both hands to gently stretch it in all directions—the center should become thin and almost transparent without tearing. If it tears, knead a few minutes more.

3. Use slightly wet hands to scoop the dough out onto the floured board (set aside the bowl to use later); shape the dough into a ball (the dough will be sticky). Lightly dust the board again with flour; put the dough on the board and cover it with the bowl. Let the dough rest for 5 to 10 minutes.

4. If the dough is stuck to the board, use a wet pastry blade or large knife blade to scrape it off (set aside the bowl to use later). Rub a little flour over the board. Knead the dough by hand for 5 minutes; shape it into a ball. Dust the board with flour again. Cover the dough with the bowl; let stand 30 minutes.

5. Rub oil over a large baking sheet. Use a wet knife or pastry blade to cut the dough into four equal pieces. With wet hands, shape each piece of dough into a ball. Put the balls about 3 inches apart on the oiled baking sheet. Roll the balls in the pan a few times to coat with oil.

6. Cover the pan of dough loosely with plastic wrap; set aside to rise in a warm draft-free place until doubled, about 4 hours. For a slower rising period (and chewier crust), put the dough in the refrigerator for several ½-hour periods. (Alternatively, cover the pan tightly with plastic wrap and let the dough rise 24 to 48 hours in the refrigerator.)

7. When the dough has doubled, it is ready to bake; or refrigerate for up to 2 days; or freeze for up to 2 months. See "Making Pizza" (below) for directions on preparing and baking the pizza. To top the pizza, see the Pizza Marinara recipe (page 133) and "Pizza Toppings" box (page 135). ❧

MAKING PIZZA

Preparing the Dough: Before rolling dough that has been chilled, let it stand at room temperature 1½ to 2 hours (frozen dough requires about 3 hours, or less in a warming or proofing oven set on low).

Preheating the Oven: If using a pizza stone, put the stone on the middle shelf in the oven. Allow about 1½ hours to preheat the oven and stone. If baking in a pan, arrange an oven shelf in the highest position (or the hottest place in your oven) and preheat the oven for about ½ hour. For either method, preheat the oven to 550°F or the oven's highest setting.

Shaping the Pizza: In Italy, the *pizzaiolo* (pizza maker) uses the palm of his hand to start to shape the pizza, and then pushes it out with his hands. He tosses the dough across one bare forearm and then over the other, back and forth. Every so often, he twirls the dough in the air—I don't recommend that to a beginner. Do what works for you—use a rolling pin and/or hands and arms (scrubbed, please!)—to roll and stretch the dough. If you use a rolling pin, you'll need to flour the dough and board frequently to prevent the soft dough from sticking.

Directions for Baking on a Stone: Shape the dough into a 10- to 12-inch circle (between ⅛ and ¼ inch thick). Put a 12-inch square sheet of parchment paper on the pizza peel; arrange the crust on the paper. With scissors, cut the paper close to the pizza to remove the excess paper.

Directions for Baking in a Pan: Per pizza, oil a baking sheet or pizza pan. Shape a piece of dough into a 12-inch circle or 10×13-inch rectangle, whichever fits into the pan. Arrange each pizza in an oiled pan.

Pizza Marinara
🕉

Homemade pizza baked directly on a preheated pizza stone comes close to pizza baked in a pizza oven. The thin pizza bakes quickly, and the crust gets crisp and well browned. If you make pizza often, the stone and peel (paddle) are a good investment. If you use a pizza stone, unless you have more than one, you will bake one pizza at a time. This pizza is also good baked in a pan.

Although this is my favorite pizza, there are many other delicious variations— see "Pizza Toppings" (page 135). The classic Pizza Marinara typically has garlic—this one does not. To make pizza margherita, season it with fresh basil instead of oregano.

Yield: 4 individual pizze

4 ready-to-top Pizza "On the Plate" crusts (see recipe, page 130)

12 ounces mozzarella cheese (fresh or low moisture), sliced ⅜-inch thick

1 cup (canned) crushed or ground tomatoes (see Note, below)

1 teaspoon dried oregano or 16 fresh basil leaves, torn

Kosher salt

8 teaspoons extra virgin olive oil

GETTING STARTED: Prepare the oven (see "Making Pizza/Preheating the Oven," page 133).

1. Prepare and shape the pizza crusts per directions in "Making Pizza" on pages 132 to 133. Cut mozzarella slices into ⅜-inch wide "fingers."

2. Per pizza: spread ¼ cup of the crushed tomatoes over each pizza, leaving about ½ inch free around the edges; sprinkle with ¼ teaspoon of the oregano (if using basil, add it later) and season lightly with kosher salt; dot with about ¼ of the mozzarella; drizzle with 2 teaspoons of the oil.

3. To bake on a stone, do this step as quickly as possible—open the oven and shake the peel to slide the pizza with the parchment onto the stone. Immediately close the oven. (If baking in a pan, put it in the hottest part of the oven.)

4. Bake until the crust is browned on the bottom and around the edges (6 to 8 minutes on a stone; 7 to 8 minutes in a pan). Thin crust bakes quickly, so watch the pizza closely, but avoid opening the oven unnecessarily (thicker crusts and heavier toppings take longer to bake).

5. Remove the pizza from the stone with the peel (aided by a metal spatula). If using basil, toss it over the pizza when it comes out of the oven. Use kitchen shears (like Andrea does) or a pizza wheel to cut the pizza into wedges. Serve immediately.

NOTE: The tomatoes should be closer to a purée than to diced tomatoes. "All Purpose Ground Tomatoes" made by the 6 in 1 brand are ideal. ❧

Pizza Toppings

The classic *pizza margherita*, topped with tomato sauce, mozzarella, olive oil, salt, and fresh basil, is on every pizzeria menu. Below you will find some of Umbria's other popular pizzas and some new inventions. Go lightly on the toppings for an authentic pizza—and finish the pizza by drizzling with extra virgin olive oil and seasoning with kosher salt.

White Pizza (*BIANCA*)

Spinaci: Bits of sautéed spinach with tidbits of cooked sausage or diced pancetta or bacon. Good with sautéed onions and tomato sauce, too.

Pomodorini: Mozzarella and halved cherry tomatoes—top the pizza with a handful of baby arugula as soon as it comes out of the oven.

Patate: Cooked bits of yellow potato with mozzarella, Parmigiano-Reggiano, and oregano (optional).

Pizza with Red Sauce (*ROSSA*)

Spread ¼ cup (canned) ground or crushed tomatoes over the pizza dough; season with salt. Top with any of the following.

Caprese: Sprinkle a little oregano over the tomatoes; bake. As soon as it is out of the oven, top the crust with slices of fresh mozzarella; put a ripe tomato slice on each piece of cheese. Top with arugula or fresh basil. Drizzle with extra virgin olive oil; sprinkle with kosher salt and pepper.

Con accuighe: Add several anchovy fillets to Pizza Marinara. Can also add capers and small black olives (with the pit).

Quattro formaggi: Pick four of your favorite cheeses—Emmentaler, pecorino, fontina, Gorgonzola *dolce*, *scamorza* (a firm, smoked cheese similar to our mozzarella), Parmigiano-Reggiano, fresh mozzarella.

Quattro stagioni: The toppings on the "four seasons" are divided into four sections, one for each season. First top the pizza with sauce and mozzarella cheese, then cover one quarter with thin slices of prosciutto; dot another quarter with small black olives (often with the pit); sprinkle the third quarter with sautéed sliced mushrooms; and add cooked, quartered artichoke hearts to the last portion. After baking, plunk half of a hard-cooked egg in the center.

Peperoni: This pizza has surprised many an American: *peperoni* pizza is topped with sautéed sweet bell peppers, usually red or yellow.

THE DOG WHO ATE THE TRUFFLE

I read about Vincenzo—also known as Il Simba—in the newspaper after he won a prize for finding the most *tartufi* (truffles) in a contest. With his dog Ravan, he found five truffles in the record time of fifty-two seconds! He is one of four thousand licensed truffle hunters in Umbria's Upper Tiber River valley—and he is reputed to be one of the best. I guess you'd expect him to be exceptional after more than fifty years of experience hunting truffles.

My friend Silvia knew Il Simba, so I begged her to arrange a hunt with him. Truffle hunters are very secretive, she told me. She doubted he would take me along. One day on a hike, we bumped into the *tartufaio* (truffle hunter). I gave Silvia the eye, but she ignored me, so I asked him myself. Sure, I'll take you, he said. Come see me in November. When I asked for his phone number, he declined to give it, saying that Silvia knew where to find him. I thought he was putting me off, but I wasn't about to give up. In November, I pestered Silvia almost daily to take me to Vincenzo's. Early in the month, she was too busy, and as the month drew to a close, she was too sick to leave the house. I pleaded with my neighbor's brother Amilcar to take me, and he finally got directions from Silvia. So one afternoon, we drove off to find Il Simba. When Amilcar pulled up in front of the house we thought was his, a woman opened the front door.

I called out the car window, "We're looking for Vincenzo the truffle hunter."

"You're in the right place," she said, "but you just missed him. I am his wife. Please come in."

Amilcar parked and we followed *la signora* into the kitchen. She excused herself to call her husband. When she returned she said, "He'll be here in a minute. Please sit down." She was pouring espresso into three tiny cups when Vincenzo came in. He is a big, tall man with a face tan from spending his days outside. He had on the Aussie-style cowboy hat that he was known for. The hat, his stature, and his confident demeanor give him a commanding presence. His wife poured him an espresso, and she asked if we wanted *caffè corretto.* The three of us held out our cups, and she poured a generous splash of anise liqueur into each espresso.

When we finished our drinks, Vincenzo took us outside to the kennels to see his fifteen dogs. That morning one of the bitches had given birth to eight puppies. Vincenzo picked up a puppy—the furry creature fit perfectly in the palm of his big hand.

When Vincenzo and his wife retired, he converted the pigsty into dog kennels. "For fifteen years, we raised pigs for our butcher shop in town," he said. "It was such a sacrifice, spending all day inside." He and his wife made everything themselves—prosciutto, pancetta, sausage, *zampone* (boneless leg filled with sausage), *porchetta* (slow-roasted pig). When the large grocery stores opened in town, they closed their shop.

Vincenzo put the puppy back, and we left the kennels and headed back to the car. Vincenzo said he would pick me up at seven the next morning.

When Vincenzo arrived with two of his dogs, the sky was dark gray. The temperature outside was close to freezing, and a dense, drippy fog made the morning dreary. I was bundled up in warm winter clothes, and I had on fur-lined gloves and knee-high snow boots. "You look like you're dressed for the North Pole," he said when I got into the car. Vincenzo wore knee-high rubber boots, water-repellant chaps, camouflage pants, and a mud-colored jacket. On his head, he wore his big hat.

Fifteen minutes later, Vincenzo parked on a grassy knoll and opened the back to let the dogs out. In the forest, the dogs wove around the oaks, spindly poplars, and deciduous trees that had recently shed their leaves—and we followed. The fallen leaves and muddy ground were a dangerous, slippery combination. In some areas, the underbrush was dense with climbing ivy and thorny wild roses that caught on my wool scarf with a fierce tenacity.

"Why did you choose these two dogs?" I asked.

"They are good at finding white truffles, others are better at black."

Sara, a small black-and-white dog with a light brown nose and short curly fur, was the novice at just fourteen months. The robust black-and-white male named Ravan was three years old. The two dogs raced about in circles, a bit crazed, sniffing with their noses about a foot off the ground. Vincenzo made a clucking sound—a noise between the cluck of a chicken and the squeal of a pig. It made the dogs more frantic. Within minutes, just ahead of us on the trail, Sara began to dig rapidly.

"Watch her," Vincenzo said. "*Cosa c'è, c'è qualcosa* [what's up, is there something]?" he said to the dog. Sara pushed her nose into the ground and snorted like a pig. She dug frantically with her front paws, tossing clods of wet, claylike earth up behind her. Vincenzo ran after her, clucking and saying, "*Brava, brava* [well done]!" "Look," I shouted. "The dog ate the truffle!"

"She is a *vagabonda*!" he said. "She is young, she doesn't know what she is doing." He shook his head and withheld the treat that Sara was begging for. He wasn't mad, and he didn't scold her.

"She's an expensive dog," I said.

Vincenzo shook his head. "When she learns not to eat truffles, she will be a champion hunter."

"How do you train them?"

"I begin by putting a piece of cheese into a hole in the ground, but leave it uncovered. I give them a treat when they find it." He always keeps his right pocket filled with treats, and he stores truffles in his left pocket. After the cheese lesson, he taught the dogs to find sausage, and finally *tartufi*. Dogs love to eat truffles, so even when they are trained, he rewards them after they relinquish the tuber.

After the dogs found a handful of black truffles, we drove to another forest to look for "precious white" truffles. We parked and walked into the forest for a few minutes. The dogs walked slowly. They seemed bored.

"There are no truffles here," Vincenzo said. "Look, there have been at least ten people here already."

"How do you know?"

"We're like Indians—I look at the ground. See the different boot prints, the different dog prints?"

We returned to the car and drove to a hillier location. We left the car and followed the dogs down a muddy bank. There was a creek at the bottom of the steep slope. Branches grew up on the sides of the path. I grabbed them often to steady myself when I started to slip. One time I had a firm grip on a branch, but I continued sliding down toward the ice-cold stream below. I could feel the branch in my hand, but when I looked down I realized it had come uprooted. I grabbed another and it came loose, too. Vincenzo looked up in time to extend his walking stick to me. With his strong, steady hand, he was able to stop me. At the bottom, when I reached the creek, Vincenzo picked me up and tossed me over his shoulder like a sack of potatoes—not bad for a sixty-five-year-old man!

"Vincenzo, I'll break your back."

"Don't you worry," he said. On the other side of the stream, he put me down. I tiptoed along the edge of the creek on a very narrow leaf-covered path.

He waded in the water next to me—it was less slippery than the trail, he explained. The dogs ran in and out of the water. Vincenzo left the path, bending down where one of the dogs had started to dig. He used his truffle shovel to start digging, but then he used his bare hands to dig up a chunk of wet clay. "If there is a truffle in here, I will smell it." He sniffed deeply. "*Niente* [nothing]." He tossed the clay aside and rinsed his hands in the icy stream.

It had recently rained, which was a good thing, Vincenzo said. The rain clears away the odors in the forest—people, dogs, and wild animals all leave behind scents that confuse and distract truffle dogs. But the rain had turned the paths into a muddy mess. The dogs were wet and filthy. I looked like I had been rolling in the mud myself. Every now and then, the dogs jumped up on my blue jeans to say hello or to ask for a treat. Vincenzo, in his camouflage clothes, looked as spotless as he had when he picked me up that morning.

The dogs wore bells on their collars, so whenever they ran we could hear their constant jingling.

"Do the dogs wear a bell so you know where they are?" I asked.

"No, for the vipers. When the snakes hear the bells, they hide. Years ago, my old dog Tiba was bitten by a viper—and hit by a car."

She survived both, but Vincenzo has lost seven dogs in the few last years to what he calls the "truffle hunter dog wars." Unscrupulous hunters leave meatballs laced with poison in hunting areas so other hunters' dogs eat them and die. Fewer trained dogs means less competition for truffles.

We had been following Sara when Vincenzo realized that Ravan was missing. We heard a jingle above us—he was across a ravine, high up on the side of a steep hill. He was digging furiously. "Wait, wait. *C'è, c'è?*" Vincenzo ran up the hill, coaxing the dog to wait. Finally he bellowed, "Ravan, come!" The dog dashed down the slope to meet Vincenzo. Together they climbed the hill, and Ravan resumed digging. Several minutes later Vincenzo held up a good-size white truffle in his muddy hand. "Notice he waited for me?" he said. "Ravan is an expert." He tucked the truffle into his left pocket and pulled a doggie treat from the other pocket. Ravan swallowed it without chewing.

Ravan ran ahead again, sniffing intently, but Sara meandered along. Suddenly she started to dig and snort. Vincenzo reached her immediately, and made it in time to pull a large white truffle out of her mouth. "This pays for the day's outing," he said. "I bet it weighs a hundred grams [about 3½ ounces]." A few minutes later, Sara started pawing the ground again.

"She's making a nest," I said.

"*C'è, c'è,* Sara?" Vincenzo started clucking to encourage her hunting.

Sara turned around twice over the hole she had dug and then curled up on the ground to take a nap.

"She's a baby," he said. "And as always, a *vagabonda.*"

At that point, I was as tired as the dog. We'd been hiking up and down slippery hills for close to five hours. Fortunately, it was lunchtime, so we headed home. At my apartment, Vincenzo brought the truffles out of his pocket. He sniffed the two big white truffles, and then handed them to me to smell. Truffles have an utterly indescribable fragrance—earthy, intense, pleasant, delicious. Vincenzo set aside a dozen or so truffles for me—mostly black, but a couple of white ones.

"If Sara hadn't eaten a half dozen or so, you'd be a wealthy man," I said.

"She'll learn," he said. "Now, I'll head home. My good wife will make me tagliatelle and serve me a *buon vino*—the sweet life. I'll come back at one thirty."

I brought a pot of water to a boil to cook tagliatelle, and I sautéed a grated black truffle in olive oil with garlic. Vincenzo arrived for the afternoon hunt as I put the last bite of *tagliatelle con tartufi* in my mouth. The sun was out and the air was finally warm. It would be a much more pleasant afternoon.

That evening, I wrapped three hundred grams (10½ ounces) of truffles individually in paper towels and sealed them in coffee tins. I put one tin in the freezer and the other in the refrigerator. For days, my apartment smelled like truffles—the aroma that escaped when I opened the refrigerator was exhilarating.

The white truffle Sara found that morning weighed seventy grams (2½ ounces). At wholesale prices for white truffles of 1,500 to 2,000 euros a kilogram ($870 to $1,162 per pound), even Vincenzo had to agree that the *vagabonda* had earned her keep.

Umbria's Black and White Gold—Truffles

The ancient Romans adored *tartufi* (truffles)—and Italians today do, too. Truffles are edible members of the Fungi kingdom, *Tuber* genus. They have a symbiotic relationship with the trees they live under—oak, poplar, beech, and hazelnut, to name a few. In Umbria, serious truffle hunters scour hilly forests nine to ten months out of the year with their trained dogs to find truffles buried beneath the forest floor. Black truffles, the more common of the tubers, live close to the surface. When freshly dug up, they resemble a clod of dirt or a lumpy potato. Black truffles have a bumpy, rough exterior and a brown or black marbled interior. In Umbria, six varieties of black truffles are prized for their aroma and flavor.

Umbria is one of the few regions in Italy where the precious white (*bianco pregiato*) truffle grows—Piedmont, Tuscany, and Marche are the others. White truffles—rarer than black varieties—live deeper in the ground. Their exterior color ranges from white to pale tan to yellowish to almost orange. Inside they have marbled white veins. Their surface is smooth and their aroma and flavor are intense and intriguing.

Here's a story that illustrates the powerful aroma of white truffles. A friend was cleaning a large purchase of white truffles in a hotel room when he heard a knock at his door. A voice through the door explained that the guest in the next room, a foreigner, had called the front desk to report a strange odor, maybe gas. My friend opened his door, and the clerk started to laugh—he immediately recognized the smell of truffles.

Truffle Season: The precious white truffle (*Tuber magnatum pico*)—the most important and delicious variety—is available only from the first of October through December. The precious white is found mostly in the Upper Tiber River valley and central Umbria. The other white truffle found in Umbria, called the *bianchetto,* is collected from mid January through April. The precious black truffle (*Tuber melanosporum Vittadini*), mature from mid-November to mid-March, is diffuse in Umbria, but the most famous come from Norcia and Spoleto. Although each black variety has its own season, at least one is available during most months of the year.

Where to Buy Truffles: In Umbria, truffle vendors sell at truffle festivals during the fall—in Montone, Gubbio, Città di Castello, and other towns. Specialty stores sell fresh truffles in season in various places around Umbria—Gubbio and Norcia are among them. Year-round, grocery stores carry jars of whole truffles and truffle sauce. In the States, gourmet shops sometimes sell fresh truffles as well as jars of whole truffles and truffle sauce. Truffle oils are often artificially flavored, so read the label—or do a taste test when possible. (See Resources, page 351, for where to buy truffles.)

How to Buy Truffles: Examine the truffle to make sure it doesn't have clumps of dirt or pebbles stuck to it (you don't want to pay for them). Gently squeeze it—it should feel firm and feel heavy (truffles are about 70 percent water). And most important—smell it. All of Umbria's truffles are fragrant, but white truffles should be intensely so. If the price seems cheap, it is probably a bland truffle from China—not worth the money. Fresh truffles are sold by weight—smaller truffles sometimes command a lower price. The rare *bianco pregiato* is the most expensive.

How to Wash and Store Truffles: Soak truffles in tepid water for a couple of minutes, and then gently use a soft brush to remove the dirt. Rinse and pat dry with paper towels. Wrap each individual truffle in parchment paper or a paper towel and store them in a tightly sealed jar or tin. Truffles are best used immediately, but white truffles will keep about five days in the refrigerator and black about a week (change the paper daily). Or freeze in the sealed containers a month or two.

How to Prepare Truffles: Wait to prepare the truffles until just before using them. Both types of white truffle are used raw—and complement butter better than olive oil. Use a truffle shaver or a vegetable peeler to shave the white truffle at the table over risotto, buttered pasta, buttered Italian toast, fluffy omelets. If the black truffles have a hard exterior, peel off whatever is hard (not too much). Then grate with a cheese grater or shave with a vegetable peeler. Briefly heat black truffles to bring out the flavor—sauté shaved or grated black truffles in extra virgin olive oil with garlic over low heat for a couple of minutes. Add garlicky truffles to mashed potatoes, sautéed mushrooms, sautéed white fish, or scaloppine. Use store-bought truffle sauce (usually a mix of mushrooms and black truffles), layered with béchamel and cheese, to make vegetarian lasagne. Or serve the sauce over grilled polenta. Or mix some with ricotta and Parmigiano-Reggiano cheese to fill ravioli.

5 ❧ The Young Cooks—*Gli giovani cuochi*

L'abito non fa il monaco

(Clothes don't make the monk)

THROUGH MY TUTOR MARIO, I MET SEVERAL OF HIS TWENTY-SOMETHING friends—Ira, Baldo, Claudia—all passionate about good food and cooking. I bought the tiny Lancia car that I adored from Claudia. When she heard I was looking for good cooks, she introduced me to her friend Sabrina, a young mother of two. Sabrina longs to spend her days in the kitchen and garden, like her grandmother did, but she has to work outside the home. And finally, I met my youngest cook, eleven-year-old Alberto, at a harvest party where I overheard him explaining to a friend how to make ravioli. All of these young people learned to cook from their mothers and grandmothers. Baldo, who says he was born to cook, comes from a family of cooks. Both he and Ira, who have worked in restaurants, like to experiment using familiar ingredients in new ways.

LET'S MAKE LATE-NIGHT SPAGHETTI—
FACCIAMO LA SPAGHETTATA

"Late at night—as late as midnight—my friends and I would make *la spaghettata*," said Mario. "We could always improvise something with spaghetti—every Italian pantry has spaghetti. The simplest *spaghettata* is made with *aglio, olio, peperoncino, e prezzemolo*—all ingredients we usually have in the house."

Spaghetti with garlic, oil, red pepper, and parsley is one of Italy's most delicious dishes—so simple it's served without grated cheese. To make the dish, sauté 4 garlic cloves (minced or whole, peeled) in ⅓ cup extra virgin olive oil with ¼ to ½ teaspoon red pepper flakes over low heat for 2 to 3 minutes (do not brown the garlic). Remove from the heat, and stir in several tablespoons of minced Italian parsley. Meanwhile, cook a pound of spaghetti until *al dente*; drain. Pour the garlic mixture over the pasta; toss to coat the spaghetti. Let stand a minute. Season to taste with salt. (If you used whole garlic cloves, discard them.) Makes enough for four hungry *ragazzi* (young men). *Buon appetito!*

(ITALIAN) TIME TO EAT

It wasn't often that I met someone in Umbria who had been to the United States—or even had the desire to visit, although I had met a few young people who wanted to see New York or Los Angeles (they thought LA was groovy). So when I met Baldo through Luciano (my neighbor's brother), I enjoyed hearing about his five-week trip around the States. He and a friend had picked up a rental car on the East Coast and headed west to their final destination, the Grand Canyon. They couldn't get a room at the Grand Canyon so they drove on to Las Vegas.

"We were so exhausted," said Baldo. "We'd already spent three hours on horseback and hours in the car. So we splurged on a huge room with a giant bathtub. We loved Vegas, but I wouldn't want to stay too long."

The next topic of discussion was food, of course. I had heard Luciano and his girlfriend, Ira, talking about Baldo. He worked in a restaurant near their apartment in historic downtown Perugia. The day Baldo came to teach me a few recipes, it was his last day of vacation before he resumed classes at the culinary school he attended.

"I come from a family of cooks," Baldo said. His mother has been working as a restaurant chef for the last fifteen years—and after culinary school, Baldo hoped to find a job as a chef, maybe in Switzerland. "My grandmother got up at six in the morning and cooked all day. She lived to cook, but I was born to cook."

So after that passionate interview, Baldo and I decided on a menu and he agreed to come to my house on Sunday afternoon around three. That way we can cook *con calma* (calmly), he said. It was an ambitious meal—stuffed leg of lamb, guinea-fowl terrine, roasted potatoes, and salad—so starting early was a good idea. Three o'clock came and went, and Baldo had not shown up. Shortly after three thirty, my neighbors dropped by to say they had seen Baldo. He had told them that he would arrive around four thirty that afternoon. They had all been together at a birthday party the night before. The party ended around four in the morning—when I saw my neighbors they were just getting out of bed. At five in the evening, Baldo dropped by to say he would be over in a few minutes, after visiting with Mario next door. He returned at five thirty.

Baldo began the lesson with the tedious process of removing the white membrane covering the leg of lamb. While he did that, he asked me to make the pork-sausage filling for the lamb. Baldo stuffed the lamb, rolled it, and tied it with string.

"The lamb needs to sit at least two hours before baking," he said, "so the lamb absorbs the flavors."

It was already seven o'clock—and the twelve dinner guests were arriving at eight. He saw me consulting the clock and said, "Maybe a half hour will do."

"Now, we can make the *terrina di faraona* [guinea-fowl terrine]," he said. "We have plenty of time." He pulled the skin off the fowl and cut the meat off the bones. He chopped the meat in the food processor with the seasonings— parsley, salt, pepper, and cream. While he worked, I tidied. "Don't take the bones," he said. "They're for the sauce. I'll make that now—it needs to simmer at least an hour."

I helped layer the ground fowl with chicken tenders on top of the layer of spinach that would enclose the terrine, as Baldo had instructed me to do. As soon as I put the terrine in the oven, Baldo said, "Now it's time to make the bread."

"Bread?" I asked. "What bread?"

"The bread that covers the lamb—*in crosta* [en croûte]. That's what the fava beans are for."

The beans were simmering, but they were far from done. The time was eight thirty. I finally accepted that dinner was a long way off, so I took the cauliflower crostini—which I had made between assignments from Baldo—downstairs to the dining room, where all the guests were waiting. Everyone was hungry, but since they were all family—and they knew Baldo—they just shrugged when I explained the delay. I ran back upstairs to my apartment. In my kitchen, I checked on the roasting potatoes—they were as hard as rocks. The sauce was still simmering, and Baldo said it needed at least another half hour. At nine thirty, he took the lamb out of the oven.

"It's done but it needs to rest at least a half hour," Baldo said, "before I can wrap it in the bread dough."

"I'll give you ten minutes," I said.

Ten minutes later, he wrapped the roast in dough, and I sighed with relief.

"Now, we let the bread rise a half hour," he said.

"Baldo, you'd better give it just ten minutes," I said. "How long does it take to bake the roast now?"

"Twenty-five minutes."

While the *agnello in crosta* baked, I sliced the *terrine di faraona,* plated the potatoes, and tossed the salad. I carried everything downstairs to the dining room below.

"If I take the lamb downstairs when it comes out of the oven," Baldo said, "I can slice it—just like a turkey—at the table. And that will give it the rest it needs before slicing."

So that's what we decided to do. At ten o'clock, Baldo stood at the head of the table, slicing the lamb. I plated it and drizzled the sauce over the meat. We passed the rest of the dishes around the table, family-style. At that point, everyone was so hungry that they emptied the platters in minutes. I was as exhausted as Baldo must have been in Las Vegas after his horseback ride and long trip in the car. I wished that I had a huge bathtub to soak in like he'd had in Vegas—but alas, I only had a shower.

Roasted Potatoes

Patate arrosto

Baldo's mother taught him to make this version of roasted potatoes. Every Umbrian cook has a favorite recipe for patate arrosto, *and most recipes call for*

the classic seasonings—extra virgin olive oil, salt, sage and/or rosemary, and garlic. Some cooks toss in chopped wild fennel, several juniper berries, a few tablespoons of dried bread crumbs, or several strips of lemon zest. The nonne tend to make the most decadent—and delicious—potatoes. They season the potatoes with lard, goose fat, or seasoned ground fresh pork fat, instead of—or in addition to—olive oil. But Baldo douses the potatoes with dry white wine, which adds flavor and makes the potatoes more tender inside. When the wine evaporates, the olive oil left in the pan gives them a crispy exterior. Another fabulous method for making roasted potatoes is to toss peeled potato wedges in the pan when roasting meat or poultry—the potatoes baste in the drippings. Buonissime! See the recipe for Roast Chicken with Potatoes (page 12).

If the potatoes have been refrigerated, it is best to bring them to room temperature several hours ahead.

Yield: 6 servings

2¾ to 3 pounds yellow potatoes, such as Yukon gold (8 or 9 medium)

15 large fresh sage leaves, torn into bits

2 (6-inch) sprigs fresh rosemary, stems discarded

3 large garlic cloves, peeled and sliced

1¾ teaspoons kosher salt (*important:* see "About Salt," page xxv)

⅓ cup extra virgin olive oil

½ cup dry white wine, such as pinto grigio or sauvignon blanc

Freshly ground pepper

GETTING STARTED: Arrange a shelf in the middle of the oven; preheat the oven to 425°F.

1. Peel the potatoes; cut them into 6 wedges each (if extra large, cut them in half crosswise and cut each half into quarters). At this point, the potatoes can be submerged in cold water and held at room temperature for about 2 hours.

2. (If the potatoes were held in water, drain them well.) Spread the potatoes out in a large jelly roll or shallow baking pan without crowding them. Sprinkle

the sage, rosemary, garlic, and kosher salt over the potatoes. Drizzle the oil over the potatoes; toss to coat. Pour the wine into the side of the pan.

3. Bake the potatoes: turn, scraping with a metal spatula after 15 and 30 minutes. Continue baking until well browned outside and tender when pierced with a knife, 55 to 65 minutes. Let stand in the pan 5 minutes; scrape with a metal spatula to remove. Adjust the salt to taste and season with pepper; toss well. ❧

Mixed Salad—*L'insalata mista*

This simple salad is served in homes and restaurants everywhere in Umbria (ask for it if it isn't on the menu). The most basic—and common—*insalata mista* is made with lettuce, shredded carrots, and tomatoes. Embellishments often include sliced onion, sliced fennel, torn radicchio, and arugula. In restaurants, the waiter brings (cheap) extra virgin olive oil, wine vinegar, and salt to the table so you can dress the salad yourself. Most home cooks season the salad in the kitchen—but not with a prepared dressing. They spoon lots of fruity extra virgin olive oil over the salad. Some cooks add a splash of wine vinegar or fresh lemon juice, while others don't. Pepper is optional, but the salad is always seasoned generously with salt. *Basta* (that's it). You'll never need to buy bottled dressing again.

Clothes Don't Make the Monk

While Franca (see Chapter 10) was preparing the meal for Chiorri winery's harvest *festa* (party), I was watching and taking notes. The old kitchen in the farmhouse was packed—many of the guests had already arrived and migrated to the kitchen. Several university students were among them. They had been hired to pick grapes and were there to celebrate the end of harvest. A group of younger kids was hanging around, too. There were a dozen conversations going on around the room, but I was intrigued by the discussion between two boys. The younger of the two was telling the other one how to make ravioli.

"You chop the spinach really fine," he said. "Then you mix it with the cheese. Of course, you add nutmeg and salt. Plenty of salt—I don't like things that are *sciapo*."

He went on to explain how to shape and cook the dumplings in minute detail. "They float to the top when they are done," he explained. I was dumb-founded.

I knew if I interrupted they would realize I had been eavesdropping, but I cut in anyway. (I am shameless in the pursuit of a good recipe and an interesting story.) "*Mi scusa,* but where did you learn how to make the ravioli?"

"My *nonna,*" he said. "I stayed at her house for several days and she taught me."

At that moment, Franca asked us all to leave. She wanted to do the last-minute cooking alone, but I couldn't let the kid go without talking to him. So I said, "Could you teach me how to make ravioli?"

"*Certo* [sure]," he began. "You cook spinach . . ."

"No, no, I want to watch you cook at your house—do you think it would be okay with your mother?"

"I think so," he said. He turned around. His mother was behind us, putting a jacket on her smallest child. I introduced myself and explained that I was writing a cookbook. Her name was Marta, and her eleven-year-old son whom I had been speaking to was named Alberto. We set a date to cook.

Alberto lives with his parents, his six-year-old brother, Carlo, and three-year-old sister, Margherita, in the town of Mantignana. They live in a modern two-story flat. His father's parents live downstairs. The day I arrived, Alberto's father was out of town on business and the grandparents weren't speaking to Marta—still upset over a dinner at their house she had missed.

When I arrived, the first thing Marta did was apologize for the state of the house. "You know I work every day at the winery. I don't have time to clean." I assured her the house looked fine, and it did. It looked like every other Umbrian house did during the cold months—there were racks of clothes, towels, and sheets drying everywhere. "We have a lot of laundry," she said, "and it never dries outside this time of year—too much rain and fog." Although everyone I knew had an automatic washer, I had never met anyone in Umbria who had a clothes dryer.

While Marta hung up my coat, she whispered, "Alberto is nervous about cooking for you. It's the first time he will make the ravioli by himself."

"But he'll do fine," I said.

"Well, he is excited—he invited his best friend to come over."

Marta had also asked one of her good friends to come, a newcomer from Holland (I think), the mother of five young kids—two girls, nine and ten years old, and three boys, a six-year-old and four-year-old twins.

"So for lunch there will be three adults and nine children," she said. *"Una festa!"*

In the kitchen, Alberto was chopping the spinach in a food processor, and he had already lined up the rest of the ingredients on the table—ricotta, Parmigiano-Reggiano, eggs, flour, nutmeg. He dumped the ingredients into a large bowl, announcing the exact amount of each item he added. He mixed it well and covered the bowl with plastic wrap.

"We cannot roll the ravioli until just before we cook them," said Alberto. The doorbell rang, so he went to the door. He returned with his best friend, and they excused themselves to go play.

I told Marta that I had eaten ravioli before, but I had never heard of this pastaless version called simply "ravioli." "In Toscana, where my mother and I are from, that's what they're called. The ravioli in pasta are called *tortelli.*"

While I watched, Marta prepared the rest of the lunch dishes—we would eat the ravioli as a first course. For the antipasto, she made liver crostini with a twist—she stirred in a little mustard and mayonnaise at the end.

"These *alici* are for the second course," she said. She held up a platter filled with very large anchovies. "They're canned. You buy them at the deli. In the winter, when we are all very busy, we eat this dish often because I can make it ahead—it's even better the next day."

Marta cut a large onion into thin slices and spread the rings over the fish. She sprinkled the plate with chopped parsley and seasoned the fish with red pepper flakes, salt, and black pepper. Then she doused it with red wine vinegar and lots of extra virgin olive oil. "It's best to make it ahead, to marinate the fish and give the onions time to mellow."

Alberto came back to roll the ravioli. As soon as he had several ready, he dropped them into a pot of boiling water. When they rose to the surface, he scooped them up and put them into a bowl. He looked at the ravioli and made a worried face. He said, *"L'abito non fa il monaco."*

"The clothes don't make the monk?" I repeated.

"You might think the ravioli look awful, well, something can be ugly but it is really beautiful and good."

"We say, 'Don't judge a book by its cover,'" I said. The ravioli looked wonderful to me.

By the time Alberto had finished rolling and cooking the ravioli, Marta was taking the skewers of pork liver wrapped in caul fat out of the oven. She covered the pork with foil and put a bowl of meatballs in the microwave oven to heat. All the guests had arrived, so she called everyone to the table. The formerly tranquil kitchen became loud and boisterous. With so few adults, lunch felt very much like a child's birthday party. After we finished the crostini, Alberto brought the ravioli to the table. They were light and delicious.

"*Complimenti* [my complements], Alberto," I said. "*Sono buonissimi* [they are really good]." Six out of the nine kids loved the ravioli, too. They wolfed them down and asked for seconds. The other three refused to try the green dumplings.

We adults sat mixed in among the kids, so conversation was impossible. Consequently, we ate quietly, sipping wine (it was a party, after all), listening to the kids talk and giggle. When Marta passed the bottle of wine around, Alberto's friend said, "Sometimes I drink red wine with dinner." He was telling the truth—he was ten.

"I like beer better," said Alberto.

The kids left the table as soon as they finished eating—some headed outside and some stayed inside to play computer games. While the kids played, the three of us adults sat at the table, eating Marta's homemade biscotti, which were firm but slightly spongy—but best of all, instead of plain nuts, she had used chocolate-covered nuts. Marta poured thimblefuls of her homemade *nocino*.

"At the end of June, I began soaking green walnuts with their shells in pure alcohol. Then I added sugar, cinnamon, and nutmeg."

In October, when the liqueur was a deep, dark brown color, she strained and bottled it. It is one of the Italian *digestivi* (liqueurs called digestives) that is bitter and medicinal tasting. But by the thimbleful, it wasn't bad.

Alberto is the youngest cook in the book, but he knows how to cook and throw a party as well as any of the others! What a memorable day.

Spinach-Ricotta Dumplings with Classic Tomato Sauce

Ravioli con sugo di pomodoro
ↂ

These light, fluffy "naked" ravioli—without a pasta wrapping—are Alberto's favorite first-course dish. Similar dumplings are made all over Italy—they go by a variety of names. Alberto's nonna, who comes from Tuscany, calls them ravioli, but they are also called ravioli nudi and gnocchi. In Umbria, they are often called bigoli, which is confusing because one of Umbria's eggless pastas also goes by that name. Alberto's mother, Marta, said the sauce should be delicate, so she recommends tomato sauce or sage and butter (see page 272). Although Alberto said he likes the ravioli with meat sauce, we ate them with his mother's tomato sauce.

Starting with frozen spinach makes these ravioli quick, but most grocers sell bags of fresh spinach leaves that are tastier and almost as fast to prepare. Of course, bunches of spinach are fine, too—and often less expensive—but a lot more work. Using a food processor to chop the spinach speeds up preparation, but Alberto told me his nonna, who taught him to make the ravioli, insists on hand chopping it.

These dumplings are typically served as a first course instead of pasta, but they also make a great vegetarian entree. They are an ideal dish to serve to company or to take to a potluck—the ravioli can be boiled ahead and reheated in the sauce (see "To Make Ahead," page 154).

Yield: 4 to 6 main-dish servings (or 10 first-course servings), about 32 ravioli

2 (9 ounce) packages fresh spinach leaves, 3 large bunches, or a 16-ounce package frozen spinach (about 18 cups packed fresh leaves)

4 ounces Parmigiano-Reggiano cheese, cut into ½-inch cubes

15 ounces ricotta cheese

2½ teaspoons kosher salt (*important*: see "About Salt," page xxv) plus more for boiling water

¾ teaspoon freshly grated nutmeg

¼ teaspoon freshly ground pepper

2 large eggs

1 large egg yolk

¾ cup plus ¾ cup all-purpose flour

4½ cups Classic Tomato Sauce (see Note, page 154)

1. (If using frozen spinach, defrost the spinach and skip ahead to step 2.) If using fresh prewashed leaves, rinse the spinach in cold water. (If using bunches of spinach, pick off the leaves; discard the stems. Wash the spinach

in a bowl until no sand remains in the bottom—it usually requires three washings.) Put the spinach with water still clinging to the leaves in a large pot; cover and cook over medium-low heat, stirring frequently, until completely wilted, about 10 minutes.

2. Dump the spinach into a large sieve. (Set aside the pot to use again later.) Use a wooden spoon to force out the excess water. If the spinach is hot, let it cool.

3. Meanwhile, put the Parmigiano cubes into a food processor. Process until very fine. Transfer half of the Parmigiano to a small bowl; cover and refrigerate. Put the remaining Parmigiano into a large bowl. Spoon the ricotta cheese into the food processor; pulse quickly 25 times to make the cheese fluffy and less grainy but not completely smooth. Transfer to the large bowl of Parmigiano. (Set aside the food processor to use again later.) Sprinkle the mixture with the 2½ teaspoons kosher salt, the nutmeg, and pepper; mix well.

4. When cool enough to handle, take one handful of spinach at a time and squeeze out the excess water. Repeat as many times as needed until the spinach is quite dry. Pulse the spinach in the food processor until finely chopped; transfer to the ricotta mixture. Use the side of a wooden spoon to cut in the spinach; mix well. Adjust the salt to taste.

5. Stir in the eggs and additional yolk; mix well. Add ¾ cup of the flour; mix well. Cover and chill ½ hour (at this point, the mixture can be held up to 24 hours, refrigerated).

6. Heat the sauce; cover and keep warm. Bring 3 quarts of cold water to a boil in the empty pot; add 2 tablespoons kosher salt to the boiling water. Spread the remaining ¾ cup flour over a large plate.

7. Using wet hands, take about 1½ tablespoons of the ricotta mixture and roll it into a slender football (about 2 inches long × ¾-inch diameter). Quickly roll the football in flour to lightly coat it. (If the mixture seems very soft, drop a ravioli into the boiling water; simmer about 5 minutes. If it falls apart—it will slough off a little spinach—mix in another tablespoon or 2 of flour.) Continue shaping ravioli, holding them on the plate of flour, until you have 8 ravioli ready.

8. Drop one *raviolo* at a time into the boiling water, cooking about 8 at a time. Boil gently, stirring occasionally, until they rise to the top (about 3 minutes), and continue simmering 2 more minutes after rising. When the ravioli are almost ready, cover the bottom of a large serving bowl with a layer of sauce.

9. Use a skimmer or slotted spoon to scoop the ravioli out of the pot, 2 at a time, shaking gently over the pot to drain well. Drop the ravioli into the serving bowl; sprinkle with some of the reserved Parmigiano cheese. Cover tightly and hold in a warm oven (150 to 200°F). As the ravioli are cooked and drained, continue layering with sauce and cheese in the bowl until they are all cooked. Serve immediately.

To Make Ahead

Boil the ravioli up to 48 hours ahead; cool in two large buttered baking pans (9×13×2-inch pans are ideal). Cover and refrigerate. About 1 hour before serving, preheat the oven to 375°F. Spoon sauce over the ravioli in each pan; sprinkle with the remaining cheese. Drizzle with a little melted butter (optional). Bake until very hot, 30 to 45 minutes.

NOTE: For this dish, use the Classic Tomato Sauce recipe on page 26, but add ¼ large onion, ½ large carrot, and 1 stalk celery (cut in two); sauté with the garlic. Discard the aromatics before puréeing the sauce. ❧

KEEPING SECRETS

On a very dark, cold December night, I approached Gubbio in my tiny old Lancia. It was almost as cold as the day I purchased the car in Gubbio from Mario's friend Claudia almost a year earlier. But driving into town this time, I was awestruck. The entire mountainside that made up the glorious medieval hill town was twinkling with lights. Bright green lights formed the outline of a mountain-size Christmas tree. Red, yellow, and blue lights decorated the tree. It was a well-choreographed effort among neighbors, from the bottom of the town to the highest peak. I parked the car near the hospital, within view of the marvelous tree of lights, waiting for Claudia to pick me up. When she arrived, we drove together in her Smart Car to Marco and Sabrina's house.

At the front door, Claudia introduced me to her friend Sabrina, who led us to her downstairs entertaining kitchen, which opened onto the garden. The family kitchen was upstairs in the main house. Her two young sons,

Andrea and Giaccomo, were doing homework at the table. Sabrina rattled off a list of dishes she had eaten growing up in Gubbio: *coratella di agnello* (braised lamb organs); *tagliatelle con sugo di lepre* (homemade pasta with wild hare sauce); *cappelletti in brodo* (tiny filled pasta in broth); *polenta con sugo* (polenta with meat sauce); *cicerchie* (chickling peas).

"But I decided to teach you a dish unique to Gubbio—*friccò*," said Sabrina. "We'll make it with both lamb and chicken—and we'll eat it with *crescia,* roasted potatoes, and spinach and chicory."

"I'll show you how to make *crescia* [flat bread] and the greens," said Claudia.

Within minutes, Sabrina had the chicken and lamb browning in olive oil with garlic and rosemary—it smelled heavenly. Her husband, Marco, entered the kitchen. He and Sabrina made a handsome young couple. She had smooth skin, short dark hair, and sparkling dark eyes. Marco had thick, prematurely silver hair. His playful side showed up immediately.

"The secret is to cook the meat slowly," Sabrina said, turning the lamb and chicken in the skillet.

"Don't give away all your secrets," Marco said, rolling his eyes.

It would take about twenty minutes for the meat to brown, so Claudia called me over to the *mattra,* an old farmhouse cabinet devoted exclusively to bread and bread making.

"You probably call the bread *torta al testo,*" said Claudia, "but in Gubbio, we call it *crescia.* We call the griddle it's cooked on the *panàro,* rather than *testo.*"

While Claudia rolled out the dough, Sabrina and Marco stoked the fire and heated the heavy griddle. Sabrina sprinkled the *panàro* with flour.

"See, the griddle is hot now," Sabrina said. "The flour has turned golden."

Claudia put the thin round dough on the *panàro* and pricked it with a fork. Marco pushed embers under the stand that held the griddle. When the bottom of the *crescia* was brown, Claudia turned it over and covered it loosely with foil.

"Using foil is my modern secret," said Sabrina.

"Don't tell her everything," said Marco, rolling his eyes again.

Sabrina ignored him. She spread embers and ash from the fireplace over the foil to help it bake evenly. Marco came and went, telling stories, laughing, checking on the bread, or tasting the *friccò* that was now simmering in tomatoes. He would remind Sabrina not to give me all her secrets.

By the time dinner was ready, I had written down as many secrets as Sabrina was able to divulge. Marco poured Uncle Giudo's homemade red wine. It was spritzy—still fermenting from the fall harvest a couple of months earlier. It was an excellent homemade wine.

"Have you ever seen a pig being slaughtered?" Sabrina asked just as I swallowed my first sip of bloodred wine. The vision that question brought to mind wasn't pretty. I think I even grimaced—undetected, I hoped.

"Well," she continued, "I remember it vividly from my childhood on my grandparents' farm."

Her grandmother would get up early the day of the *macello*. For breakfast, she would grill pork ribs and put them on top of slices of bread. The bread would soak up the fat and smoky flavor from the ribs.

"When I got up out of bed in the morning," Sabrina said, "I could smell the ribs grilling. Nonna would put one big plate of ribs on the table—we all ate off the same plate. We'd eat a bite of meat and then a bite of bread."

Sabrina sighed at the end of the story. My stomach calmed down—I was warming up to the idea of being around for the *macello*—a much nicer-sounding word than our English word *slaughter*.

"I always loved being in the kitchen," Sabrina said, "watching my mother and grandmother cook. I really should be a *contadina* [farm woman]."

She and Marco were both accountants—about as far away from the life of *contadini* as you could get.

"At least we have our olive trees," sighed Sabrina. She pointed to two bonsai trees in the garden just outside the kitchen window. "I get enough olives every year to make a batch of dried olives that I season with orange and fennel seeds."

The meal was delicious, down to the last drop of sauce on the plate! The rich, tomatoey *fricciò* sauce played off the slightly bitter note in the chicory. And the bland bread cleansed the palate and the plate.

"The *crescia* is the *scarpetta* [little shoe] to mop up the sauce," said Sabrina.

"Yet another secret revealed," said Marco.

"In the summer and fall," Sabrina said, "I am like an ant getting ready for winter. I make jam, can tomatoes, and collect chestnuts. Marco, the chestnuts!"

Marco went to the fireplace to rescue the chestnuts he had buried in the embers during dinner. In minutes, we were nibbling on warm, slightly smoky chestnuts. Sabrina passed around the red wine.

"My father says that chestnuts need wine."

After the rich, comforting meal and a little too much wine, we were ready to brave the cold. We said our goodbyes, and Claudia and I drove to see the street that by day was a living nativity. At nearly midnight, the famous scene had turned into an icy wind tunnel, so we headed home with *mani gelate* (frozen hands) and chilled bodies.

Spring Garlic Frittata
Frittata con l'aglio
ॐ

This dish is one that everyone in Sabrina's family adores, including her two young kids. Once she used thirty eggs for seven people—there were no left-overs. In California spring garlic (also called green garlic) is planted and harvested in the spring, while ordinary head garlic is planted in the fall. Spring garlic resembles green onions. The head and cloves of the garlic are just starting to develop so the flavor is milder than head garlic. Like the green onion it resembles, both the white and green portions of spring garlic are eaten.

From April to early June, some grocers and farmers' markets sell spring garlic. The garlic tends to be pricey, so you might want to plant your own—it is an easy crop to grow. Green onions plus a garlic clove make an acceptable substitute for spring garlic.

The frittata is Italy's omelet, except the vegetables, meat, cheese, and other embellishments are mixed together with the beaten eggs rather than stuffed inside. Frittate are often served as an appetizer or first course at lunch or dinner, but the eggs can also be a main dish. My favorite way to serve frittata is to put a wedge of it on a slice of toasted Italian bread and eat it like an open-faced sandwich. In Umbria, eggs are not a breakfast dish.

The frittata should be tender, with just the slightest browning. Single-serving frittatas do well on top of the stove, but large frittatas like this one are more moist and delicate when baked. As long as you follow these instructions carefully, using a heavy skillet and heating the skillet before adding the eggs, the frittata should come out of the pan perfectly.

Yield: 4 main-dish servings (or 12 appetizer wedges)

10 medium-large spring garlic (see Note, page 159)

1 tablespoon extra virgin olive oil

4 ounces sliced pancetta, finely diced (see "Pancetta versus Bacon,"
  page 9)

1 teaspoon kosher salt (*important:* see "About Salt," page xxv)

10 large eggs, lightly beaten

GETTING STARTED: Preheat the oven to 350°F and arrange a shelf in the middle
of the oven. Select a large, heavy skillet with an ovenproof handle (a slant-sided
skillet is best)—make sure the skillet fits in the oven with the door closed.

1. Rinse the garlic well under running water, opening up the green portion
to remove dirt. Cut the garlic lengthwise into quarters; thinly slice crosswise,
both the white and green portions. Bring ½ inch of water to a boil in the
skillet (with the ovenproof handle). Simmer the garlic in the boiling water
for 3 minutes. Drain; set aside.

2. Rinse out and dry the skillet. Heat the skillet over medium-low heat. Swirl
the oil around the skillet. Sauté the pancetta in the oil, stirring occasionally,
until it just starts to brown (but do not let it get crisp), 6 to 8 minutes. Scoop out
about 1½ tablespoons of the fat in the skillet; reserve 1 tablespoon of the fat.

3. Add the reserved garlic and kosher salt to the skillet with the pancetta.
Use a spatula to loosen any browned bits in the skillet. Sauté the garlic, stirring frequently, for 4 minutes; remove the skillet from the heat.

4. Lightly beat the eggs in a large bowl. Temper the eggs by adding about a
quarter of the garlic mixture to the eggs at a time, mixing well after each
addition, until all of the garlic has been added. Swirl the tablespoon of reserved fat around the sides and bottom of the empty skillet. Heat the skillet
over medium-low heat until hot; pour the egg mixture into the skillet.

5. Bake on the middle shelf until the surface is no longer wet and the frittata
is firm (but springy) to the touch, 14 to 15 minutes (the size and shape of the
skillet will determine cooking time—the larger the skillet, the shorter the
cooking time). Remove from the oven; let stand for 5 minutes.

6. If necessary, run a knife around the edge of the skillet to loosen the frittata. Put a large plate (slightly larger than the diameter of the top rim of the

skillet) over the skillet; wrap a large thick towel around the plate and skillet. Holding the bottom of both the plate and skillet, flip the skillet upside down to transfer the frittata to the plate. Cut the frittata into wedges. Serve hot or at room temperature (refrigerate leftovers).

NOTE: Typically, the stalk of the garlic is about ½ to ¾ inch in diameter. But the stalk might be as slender as ¼ inch, in which case, double the amount of garlic.

SUBSTITUTION: Use 12 medium green onions and 1 large garlic clove in place of the spring garlic. ❧

FRITTATA IDEAS

There are many vegetables that make delicious *frittate*. In Spoleto, the *frittata di Pasqua* (Easter) is made with diced pancetta, Gruyère, Parmigiano-Reggiano, and a mix of finely diced, cooked vegetables— artichokes, zucchini, eggplant, carrots, potatoes, or whatever is on hand. But *frittate* in Umbria tend to be made with a single vegetable such as wild asparagus, wild greens, spinach, onions, or zucchini. Sautéed, diced pancetta, ham, or onions are also good additions to *frittate*. Mushroom-Truffle Pâté (see recipe, page 318) is wonderful in a frittata. Rather than mincing the mushroom mixture, coarsely chop it and stir some into the beaten eggs with grated Parmigiano-Reggiano cheese (a common ingredient in *frittate*). Truffles and eggs are a classic combination in Umbria.

THE DRIP—*IL PILLOTTO*

I heard about the cooking technique called *il pillotto* from cooks in Umbertide and Gubbio. The method involves using skewers of melting fresh pork fat or baconlike *lardo* to baste meat roasting in the fireplace.

"We lined a piece of butcher paper with strips of *lardo*," explained

Sabrina. "Then we rolled the paper into a cone. We would hold the cone with tongs over the fire—as the paper burned, the fat slowly melted and dripped over the meat grilling below. It was beautiful to see. When the drops of fat hit the coals, the fire burst into bright blue flames."

To try this on the barbecue, thread fatty bacon onto a long metal skewer, intertwining it with sprigs of rosemary and sage, if you wish. Then, grasping the handle of the skewer with a potholder, carefully heat the bacon over the hot coals until it starts to melt. Then move the skewer, positioning it so the fat drips onto the meat cooking on the spit or grill. Meat cooked this way is *meravigliosa* (marvelous)!

In dialect *il pillotto* means "the drip." When a man was a real bore, people called him *un pillotto.*

Chicken and Lamb with Tomatoes and Garlic

Friccò
∽∾

I have never seen friccò, *a dish that comes from the town of Gubbio, elsewhere, but* friccò *is similar to* arrabbiata—*meat braised in tomatoes and wine— which is found all over Umbria.*

Sabrina, who lives in Gubbio, makes friccò *with a mix of meats. "It is more flavorful with two kinds of meat," she said. "You can also make it with rabbit and lamb or just lamb." When Sabrina makes the dish with just lamb, she makes it* bianco—*without tomatoes. The sauce is mopped up with Umbria's traditional flat bread, called* crescia *in Gubbio, but more commonly known as* torta al testo *in most of Umbria. Sautéed chard and roasted potatoes (pages 162 and 146) are also good accompaniments.*

Yield: 4 main-dish servings (or 8 second-course servings)

4 plus 2 large garlic cloves, peeled

1 cup dry white wine, such as pinot grigio or sauvignon blanc

1 (8-inch) sprig rosemary, needles removed from stem

1 teaspoon kosher salt (*important:* see "About Salt," page xxv)

2 (1¼-inch-thick) bone-in lamb steaks (about 1½ pounds)

3 tablespoons extra virgin olive oil

2 pounds bone-in chicken thighs, skinned

Freshly ground pepper

1 can (28 ounces) tomatoes with juice, puréed

Torta al testo (page 296), cut in wedges, or sliced Italian bread

1. Thinly slice 4 of the garlic cloves; put them in a small bowl. Add the wine, rosemary needles, and kosher salt; let stand 10 minutes.

2. Cut the lamb into 1¼-inch cubes leaving the bone in. Heat a large skillet (broad enough to hold the lamb and chicken pieces side by side) over medium heat. Swirl the oil around the skillet. Add the remaining 2 garlic cloves; sauté 30 seconds. Add the lamb; sauté 8 minutes, turning occasionally.

3. Add the chicken, squeezing it in so the lamb and chicken are side by side, not stacked. Sprinkle the chicken and lamb with kosher salt and pepper as desired. Sauté, turning frequently, until lightly browned, about 20 minutes. Add the wine mixture; simmer over medium heat, turning occasionally, until the wine becomes thick and saucy, about 15 minutes.

4. Stir in the tomatoes; bring to a boil over high heat. Reduce the heat to medium-low and simmer until the sauce thickens, about 15 minutes. Cover and reduce the heat to low; simmer until the lamb is tender when pierced with a knife and the chicken is no longer pink at the bone, about 30 minutes. The dish should be saucy—if the sauce is too thick, thin it with a little water. Adjust the salt to taste. Serve with the *torta al testo.* ❧

UMBRIA'S VEGETABLE DISHES

In Umbria, when you step into a grocery store's produce section, you know what season it is. In the winter, you usually won't find zucchini. In the summer, you might not find broccoli. Some out-of-season crops occasionally come in from warmer climates such as Sicily and Africa.

Traditional vegetable dishes feature *verdure* grown in the garden—cabbage, tomatoes, zucchini, eggplant, potatoes, chard, lettuce, fava beans—or wild vegetables gathered in the field or forest, such as asparagus, greens, and mushrooms. The simplest dishes are boiled vegetables—from chard to cauliflower—seasoned with extra virgin olive oil and salt. In the more complicated recipes, vegetables are grilled and dressed or baked in casseroles with tomato sauce or béchamel and cheese. In Umbria, vegetables are cooked until very tender and flavorful, never semiraw like in California. Vegetables are usually served as an appetizer or a side dish, but occasionally they are presented as a first-course dish, such as eggplant Parmesan, or as a second course, such as roasted porcini mushrooms. Although side dishes are served with the second course, they are not plated with it.

Chard (*Bietole*): Slowly simmer the coarsely chopped chard (or a combination of chard, chicory, and/or spinach, adding the spinach last) in about ½ inch of lightly salted water with 2 or 3 crushed and peeled garlic cloves and several tablespoons of olive oil until very tender, about 10 minutes. Drain well. Return the greens to the pot; heat over low heat several minutes to dry the greens out. Drizzle with additional oil, if desired. Adjust the salt to taste. Good with roasted or braised poultry or meat.

Potatoes, Cabbage, and Broccoli (*Patate, cavolo, e broccoli*): Separately, boil an equal amount of potatoes, broccoli, and cabbage until tender; drain. Peel the potatoes; coarsely mash with a fork. Gently squeeze the water out of the cabbage and broccoli; cut into bite-size pieces. Heat ¼ inch of fruity extra virgin olive oil in a large nonstick skillet. Add the potatoes, broccoli, and cabbage; season with salt. Sauté until the vegetables are lightly browned. A very delicious side dish.

Potatoes and Cabbage (*Patate e cavolo*): Follow the recipe for potatoes, cabbage, and broccoli but omit the broccoli.

Cabbage and Bread Crumbs (*Cavolo con pane molliche*): Also called *lo sticcolo*. Boil a quartered cabbage until tender; drain well. Squeeze the water out; chop. Heat ¼ inch of olive oil in a skillet with a garlic clove. Add the cabbage and several handfuls of stale bread crumbs or torn bits of stale bread; season with salt and pepper. Sauté until lightly browned.

Stuffed Zucchini (*Zucchini ripieni*): Mix raw Italian sausage (removed from its casing) with lots of dry bread crumbs and a little parsley. Boil small whole zucchini until tender. Cut in half lengthwise and scoop out the seeds. Brush the zucchini with olive oil and season with salt. Fill the hollow with the sausage mixture. Bake until browned and cooked through. Appetizer, first course, or side dish.

Vegetable Bake (*Sformato di verdure*): To make a vegetable casserole, boil, steam, or braise your favorite vegetable—fennel, cauliflower, radicchio, zucchini, spinach, broccoli—and drain well. Chop the vegetable and combine it with béchamel and grated Parmigiano-Reggiano cheese. (Some cooks add a raw egg.) Bake in a buttered casserole dish until hot, bubbly, and lightly browned. Fennel is my favorite.

Peppers and Tomatoes (*Peperonata*): Also called *la bandiera* (the flag) when made with green bell peppers instead of red peppers. Simmer 1 large, finely chopped onion in ½ cup water and ½ cup olive oil in a large skillet until tender. Meanwhile, slice 1 pound of Roma tomatoes; set aside. Core and slice 4 bell peppers (2 yellow, 2 red) lengthwise into ½-inch strips. When the onion is tender, add the peppers and season with salt. Simmer, stirring occasionally, until wilted. Add the tomatoes; cover and cook, stirring occasionally, until the peppers are very soft, 30 to 45 minutes. Drizzle with olive oil before serving.

Potato Salad (*Insalata di patate*): Boil yellow potatoes until tender; cut them into bite-size pieces. While the potatoes cook, make the dressing. Push a garlic clove through a press. Mix the garlic with fresh lemon juice, salt, and pepper. Add lots of olive oil and some chopped Italian parsley; drizzle over the hot potatoes. A nice side dish with grilled meats.

Peas with Prosciutto (*Piselli con prosciutto*): Also called *piselli di Bettona,* from a town famous for its peas. Sauté some diced onion and a few thin slices (diced) of prosciutto (or pancetta) with a little olive oil and a splash of water until the onion is tender. Add a pound or so of frozen peas and several tablespoons of water. Simmer until done as desired; season to taste with salt and pepper.

MONEY

I remember the first time I heard Paola talking about "Lira," I asked who she was. "You know her," Paola said. "Ira, Luciano's girlfriend." Luciano was my good friend Paola's middle son.

"I thought you just called her *Lira*," I said.

"Yes, la Ira—l'Ira."

"Oh, I forgot about using *la* before a woman's name when you talk about her."

Ira's name with the article in front does sound like *lira,* Italy's former basic unit of money. So when I heard someone talk about l'Ira, I was always thrown off.

Ira was born and raised in the central Umbrian town of Spoleto. At the time I met her, she was a university student living in the historic center of Perugia in a tiny ancient apartment with Luciano and their part–German shepherd mutt named Cooper. Perugia is a lively town with two universities. The historic center, with a thriving nightlife, is always crowded with young people. Luciano and Ira's pad has become a hangout. Friends drop in at all hours and stay to play cards until *le piccole ore* (the wee hours of the morning).

Ira also worked in the oldest herbalist shop in downtown Perugia. She was negotiating with the owners to buy the shop, but the city had stepped in and made a fuss. Something about the closet-size shop—which had been located in the same spot forever—needing to have a bathroom if ownership changed hands. And the city was annoyed that the price was too low!

Ira was the only person I knew from Spoleto, so one day I quizzed her about recipes that were particular to the town.

"Many of the dishes we eat in Spoleto are the same as elsewhere in Umbria," she said. "But there are a few exceptions. *Frittata di Pasqua*—Easter frittata—eggs cooked with pancetta, Parmigiano-Reggiano, Gruyère, and lots of cooked, diced vegetables. And we have *crescionda,* a dessert that is made only in Spoleto."

Ira enjoys cooking, but the passion for food skipped a generation in her family. "My mother has never really cooked much," she said. "My grandmother still cooks a big lunch every day—my mother eats with her." Ira offered to teach me a few dishes, including her grandmother's treasured recipe for *crescionda.* Then she decided on two *nuove* recipes—one based on a dish from a restaurant she had worked in (a job she quit when she didn't get paid).

At my place, we prepared the restaurant's dish for the first course—*maltagliati con lenticchie* (sun-dried tomato pasta with lentils). And we baked salmon fillets layered with thin slices of zucchini, seasoned with lemon juice and sesame seeds, for our second course. And finally, for dessert we made the lovely amaretti-flavored cake called *crescionda.*

Since I returned to the States, "Lira" is finally making money—she graduated from the university and somehow managed to buy the herbalist shop.

Pasta with Lentils and Truffles

Maltagliati con lenticchie e tartufi

෨ඏ

When I discovered the combination of lentils and fresh pasta, I was hooked—
now it is one of my favorite dishes. But Ira's recipe for fresh sun-dried tomato
maltagliati and lentils with truffles is sublime! Other pastas, such as fresh
tagliatelle, dry orecchiette, or dry spaghetti, are also good.

To make Ira's sun-dried maltagliati, follow the instructions on pages 84 to
90. To make the lentils, follow the recipe for Lentils with Garlic (see recipe,
page 258), adding ¼ teaspoon red pepper flakes to the oil with the garlic. Just
before serving, stir in 1 tablespoon of white or black truffle butter (about 12
grams) per serving into the lentils. (Alternatively, heat 6 or more paper-thin
slices of black truffles with the garlic oil for 30 seconds, or shave 6 or more
slices of white truffles over each serving of plated pasta.) Per serving, allow
about ⅔ cup of lentils and 3 ounces of fresh pasta (or 2 ounces of dry pasta)—
and cook only as much pasta as you plan to eat. Cook the pasta separately until
just al dente (fresh pasta cooks in 30 seconds to just under 2 minutes). Save 1
cup of the cooking liquid before draining the pasta. Drain the pasta and return
it to the pot; spoon the lentils over the pasta. Stir to coat the pasta; add reserved
cooking liquid by the tablespoon as needed to moisten the pasta (but don't dilute the flavors by adding too much). Adjust the salt to taste. Let stand 30 seconds before serving. ❧

Amaretti Cake

Crescionda

෨ඏ

This recipe comes from Ira's grandmother who was a teacher. Every year during
carnavale, her students brought sweets from home to share at school. Over the
years, her nonna tasted many versions of crescionda, but this was her favorite
one—so the student gave her the recipe.

"There are many variations of this dessert," said Ira, "but all of them are from
Spoleto. People outside Spoleto haven't heard of this cake."

It is quick and easy to make. Italian amaretti cookies—ground into crumbs—
make up the foundation of the cake. The crisp, light cookies, made with bitter

almond or almond kernel, add an intriguing flavor that complements the cake's thin dark chocolate and cakelike layers. Original versions of this old recipe called for stale bread rather than amaretti cookies and used honey instead of sugar. Ira uses two cups of milk, but I prefer the cake's texture when one cup of cream replaces one of the cups of milk.

If you don't have a scale to weigh the cookies, you can measure the crumbs after processing the cookies in the food processor—you need about 2 cups of cookie crumbs.

Yield: 10 to 12 servings

Soft butter and flour for the pan

7 ounces amaretti or *amorelli* (apricot almond) cookies

6 ounces dark chocolate (71 to 85% cocoa), coarsely chopped

1½ teaspoons double-acting baking powder

¼ teaspoon kosher salt (*important:* see "About Salt," page xxv)

¼ cup granulated sugar

2 tablespoons all-purpose flour

Finely shredded zest of ½ medium lemon (see "About Zest," page 37)

5 large eggs

1 tablespoon extra virgin olive oil

1 cup homogenized heavy cream

1 cup homogenized whole milk

2 tablespoons unsifted powdered sugar

GETTING STARTED: Butter and flour a large heavy skillet with an ovenproof handle (alternatively, use a deep 10-inch glass pie dish or a 9×13×2-inch metal baking pan). Arrange a shelf in the middle of the oven; preheat the oven to 350°F (if using a glass pie dish, reduce the heat to 325°F).

1. Process the amaretti in a food processor until the cookies resemble bread crumbs; transfer to a medium bowl. Process the chocolate in the food pro-

cessor until the texture is slightly coarser than crumbs; transfer to the bowl. Add the baking powder and kosher salt; toss to mix. Set aside.

2. In a large bowl, combine the granulated sugar, flour, and lemon zest; mix with a fork. Add the eggs and oil; beat until smooth with a wire whisk. Whisk in the cream and milk. Add the dry ingredients; beat to mix well.

3. Immediately pour the batter into the prepared skillet. Bake on the middle shelf until the top feels firm but spongy when pressed gently and a toothpick inserted in the center comes out clean (melted chocolate on the toothpick is okay), 40 to 45 minutes (if using a glass pie dish, bake about 50 minutes; if using the 9×13-inch baking pan, bake about 35 to 40 minutes).

4. Cool on a wire rack about 1 hour. Sift the powdered sugar over the cake. Cover lightly with waxed paper; refrigerate until serving time. Cut into wedges (if using a 9×13-inch baking pan, cut into squares or rectangles). ࿏

ABOUT HOMOGENIZED MILK

Most milk is homogenized—the milk and the cream are mixed together, rather than separated, with the cream rising to the top. The Amaretti Cake recipe and Vanilla Cream recipes in this book do not turn out right when made with cream-on-the-top milk—and for the heavy cream, buy it in an ordinary carton, rather than in an old-fashioned glass bottle. The cream label will probably not say "homogenized."

6 ❧ Artisans, Farmers, and Producers of Umbrian Products—Gli artigiani, gli agricoltori e i produttori Umbri

Tanto va la gatta al lardo che ci lascia lo zampino

(The cat that goes to the fat too often leaves a paw print—and gets caught)

FOR THIS CHAPTER, I TRAVERSED THE REGION—FROM THE TOWN OF DERUTA IN central Umbria to the hills of Colfiorito above Foligno to Cascia, a mountain town in the south. I was on the lookout for high-quality small food producers or talented artisans. Along the way, I met Novella, a ceramic artist—and a good cook. I learned to make pecorino cheese from a couple in Campi di Norcia. And some local butchers in Umbertide taught me how to make prosciutto and sausage. I met with other artisans, growers, and producers of lentils and other legumes, saffron, olive oil, porchetta—and discovered their secrets.

LUNCH AT BORGO LA TORRE

I had heard about the famous red potatoes from Colfiorito in the mountains above the town of Foligno. And I often cooked the tiny Colfiorito lentils—they are excellent. So when a friend offered to introduce me to a family who had a *biologico* (organic) farm in the hills, I was eager to go. I spent my second visit to the farm in the kitchen with Rita Fanelli Marini—she owns the business with her husband, Sergio, and their two sons. The sons run their farm, called Torre di Acqua Santo Stefano, and she and Sergio work on the property and take care of the guests at the *agriturismo* (bed and breakfast) Borgo La Torre.

With Rita's explicit directions, I found the property without a problem, even though it is located in the remote hills, and several miles of the trip are on a gravel road. The estate's twelfth-century stone buildings that make up the *agriturismo* are nestled in the hills surrounded by forests. The Marinis restored the buildings, which had been neglected for over thirty years, keeping the integrity and beauty of the palazzo intact. Both Rita and Sergio are artists, and their sense of design is present in every room. The furnishings and floor coverings are exquisite and elegant. The 740-acre property, with an elevation of almost 3,280 feet, is mostly forest and pasture, but 148 acres are cultivated in crops.

The legumes such as garbanzo beans and lentils grown in the area are tiny—but flavorful—because the mountain soils are poor and quick-draining. The red potato, too, owes its lovely flavor and texture to growing in the hills. The family sells what they produce—an ancient variety of garbanzo bean, farro, polenta, lentils, potatoes—in local stores and at Borgo La Torre. All their products are certified organic. In addition to crops, they raise cows.

Rita is an excellent cook. "I learned to cook in the school of life," she said. Her grandmother, mother, and father all had opinions about how to cook various dishes. "One would say, 'Make it like *nonna* did.' Someone else would say, 'In my house, we make it this way.'" Sergio has learned to keep his mouth closed.

"*Mangio solo* [I only eat]," Sergio explained.

On my visit, I watched Rita make several traditional mountain dishes—garbanzo bean and pasta soup, rabbit in porchetta, potato pancakes. Every dish was simple yet exquisite. The *zuppa* (soup) has just a few ingredients—garbanzo beans, garlic, rosemary, extra virgin olive oil, and tomato. Half-inch squares of handmade pasta complete the delicious dish.

By the time Rita's son Andrea arrived, covered in dust from working in the fields, everything was ready—except the rabbit needed to be carved. Rita had waited for Andrea to do it. The rabbit smelled heavenly—the dried wild fennel flowers she'd used for seasoning had an intense, delightful aroma. When Andrea plated the rabbit, Rita called us to the table in the gorgeous dining room, with ancient stone walls and heavy beams in the high ceiling. Rita did everything with elegance. The silverware and white cloth napkins were set on top of a beautiful hand-embroidered eyelet tablecloth. She served chilled white wine with the soup and red wine with the roasted rabbit, potato pancake, and lettuce and basil salad. After lunch, she brought out a *crostata* (jam tart) and *il visner,* Rita's homemade dessert wine.

Rita has a habit of spoiling the guests at Borgo La Torre. When the overnight visitors get up in the morning, she fixes them something to eat—there is no set breakfast hour. And if they ask in the morning, guests may dine with the family at dinnertime. Eating one of Rita's home-cooked meals and sleeping in one of the beautiful rooms is worth the long, twisting drive up to the *agriturismo.*

Garbanzo Bean Soup with Pasta
Zuppa di ceci con quadrucci
◌◦◌

Every Umbrian family has a recipe for ceci con quadrucci. *Some sauté diced carrot, onion, and celery with the garlic. Others enrich it with diced pancetta. And some cooks substitute fresh sage for the rosemary. But Rita's recipe is one of the simplest. "My* zuppa *relies on quality ingredients for flavor," explained Rita. "Good garbanzo beans and fruity olive oil are important. Our* ceci *are tiny [about ¼ inch in diameter], but flavorful, because they grow in poor soil." For the tomatoes, Rita purées and cans tomatoes from the garden.*

Zuppa di ceci is an old recipe from Umbria that is also served with toasted bread instead of pasta. The soup can be made with a handful of dry orecchiette, tagliatelle, or fettuccine per serving (broken into 2-inch lengths), instead of fresh quadrucci. Both the soup and uncooked fresh pasta can be made ahead and frozen, separately. If you want to serve fewer than 6 portions, cook 1 ounce of fresh pasta per person—drain and return it to the pot; add 1⅓ cups soup per serving.

Yield: 6 servings (about 10 cups—about 1²/₃ cups per serving)

1 pound dry garbanzo beans, sorted and rinsed

½ (14-ounce) can whole tomatoes with juice

½ cup extra virgin olive oil plus more for garnish

3 large garlic cloves, peeled

2 (4-inch) sprigs rosemary

2 teaspoons plus 2½ teaspoons kosher salt (*important:* see "About Salt," page xxv) plus more to cook the pasta

Freshly ground pepper

6 ounces fresh *quadrucci* pasta (see Fresh Egg Pasta, pages 84 to 90)

Grated Parmigiano-Reggiano cheese to pass at the table (optional)

1. Put the beans into a large pot. Add water until it reaches several inches above the surface of the beans. Cover and bring to a boil over high heat; simmer 4 minutes. Remove from the heat; let stand about 1 hour. (Alternatively, soak beans in cold water, refrigerated, for 8 hours.)

2. Drain and return the beans to the pot; add 8 cups cold water (do not add salt). Cover and bring to a boil. Simmer gently over low heat until very tender but intact, 2½ to 3 hours (cooking time can vary dramatically; consult the package). Drain the beans; set aside 2½ cups of beans in a bowl. Return the rest of the beans to the pot; set aside.

3. Purée the tomatoes using an immersion blender or food processor. In a medium saucepan, heat the oil, garlic, and rosemary over medium-low heat. When the garlic sizzles, after about 2 minutes, add the tomatoes and the 2 teaspoons kosher salt; season to taste with the pepper. Simmer 5 minutes, stirring occasionally.

4. Add 2 cups cold water and the reserved 2½ cups beans to the saucepan with the tomatoes. Cover and bring to a boil over high heat. Simmer over low heat, stirring occasionally, 30 minutes—add water if needed to keep the beans covered.

5. Meanwhile, add 1 quart of cold water and the remaining 2½ teaspoons kosher salt to the pot with the remaining beans (*not* the beans with tomatoes). Cover and bring to a boil. Gently simmer on low, stirring occasionally, for 30 minutes.

6. Purée the beans (*not* the beans with tomatoes) in the pot using an immersion blender. (Alternatively, use a food processor). Add the tomato mixture to the pot of puréed beans. (Rinse out the saucepan to use later.) Cover and bring to a boil. Simmer over low heat stirring occasionally, about 30 minutes. Discard the rosemary stems.

7. Meanwhile, fill the empty saucepan ¾ full with cold water to cook the pasta. Add 2 teaspoons kosher salt to the boiling water. Cook the pasta until just *al dente,* ½ to 1½ minutes; drain. Stir the pasta into the soup; let stand 1 minute. Add water, if needed, to make it soupy. Adjust the salt to taste. Drizzle each serving with oil, and if using, sprinkle with the cheese. ❧

Rabbit with Fennel

Coniglio in porchetta
∞

In porchetta *means the rabbit is seasoned in the style of* porchetta, *a roast pig seasoned with fennel. Rabbit is popular in Umbria, but especially in the countryside outside Foligno where Rita lives. Fennel makes the rabbit so fragrant and flavorful—and the hot oven and long baking time make it crispy on the outside and tender inside. If you have never eaten rabbit, this is a good recipe to try—it makes the most delicious rabbit I have ever eaten. If you prefer, you can substitute a whole chicken (see Chicken with Fennel, page 174).*

Rita gathers and dries wild fennel for this recipe. Since not everyone has access to finocchio selvatico, *I have substituted store-bought fennel seeds and commercially grown fresh fennel greens. If you have wild fennel growing near you, cut both the flower/seeds and stalks. Dry the weed in a dark, airy place; grind the flower/seeds with a mortar and pestle. Substitute the wild flower/seeds for the store-bought seeds, measure for measure. And use the dry stalks in place of the fresh fennel sprigs. The wild fennel adds a floral, intriguing note.*

*In Umbria, rabbit is also braised—*all'arrabbiata *(with tomatoes), in sugo (*ragù*), and in* salmì *(with vinegar and wine).*

Yield: 4 servings

1 (2²/₃- to 3-pound) rabbit (weight includes giblets but not the head)

2 cups vinegar (inexpensive)

2 quarts cold water

3 teaspoons fennel seeds

¾ teaspoon plus ½ teaspoon kosher salt (*important:* see "About Salt," page xxv)

Freshly ground pepper

2 tablespoons plus ½ cup extra virgin olive oil

2 (3-inch) sprigs fresh fennel greens (optional)

You'll also need: Heavy-duty kitchen shears.

Getting started: Preheat the oven to 450°F.

1. Put the rabbit into a deep, nonreactive pan or bowl (such as glass or stainless steel); pour the vinegar over the rabbit. Add the 2 quarts of water. Cover and refrigerate 1 hour. Drain the rabbit, discarding the vinegar water. Pat the rabbit dry with paper towels.

2. Meanwhile, grind the fennel seeds with a mortar and pestle. Rub ¾ teaspoon of the kosher salt and 2 teaspoons of the ground fennel over the inside cavity of the rabbit and the inside of the legs. Season with pepper to taste. Drizzle the 2 tablespoons oil over the cavity and inside of the legs. (If using the fresh fennel sprigs, tuck them inside the cavity now.)

3. Rub the remaining ½ teaspoon kosher salt and 1 teaspoon ground fennel over the outside of the rabbit; season to taste with pepper. Lay the rabbit on its side; pour the remaining ½ cup oil over the rabbit.

4. Bake uncovered for 30 minutes (total time is about 55 minutes), spooning pan drippings over the rabbit after 15 minutes. Turn the rabbit over and baste again. Continue baking until the rabbit is well browned and crispy on both sides, about 25 minutes more. The internal temperature, measured in the thickest part of the thigh and breast, will probably exceed the 165°F required for food safety.

5. Let the rabbit rest for 10 minutes. Use kitchen shears to cut the rabbit into pieces. To serve, spoon pan drippings over the rabbit.

Chicken with Fennel

Follow the recipe for Rabbit with Fennel (page 172) with these changes. See "How to Butterfly a Chicken" (page 15) to prepare a 3½- to 4-pound chicken (weight includes giblets). Pat the chicken dry with paper towels. Skip recipe step 1. Season the chicken in the same manner as the rabbit, using the same amounts of salt, fennel, and pepper—except reduce the oil to 1 tablespoon inside the cavity and 2 tablespoons on the outside of the chicken. Put the chicken in the baking pan with the skin-side facing up; bake uncovered in a preheated 450°F oven. Spoon pan drippings over the chicken every 15 minutes; rotate the pan after 30 minutes for more even cooking. The chicken is done when well browned and no longer pink at the bone, 60 to 70 minutes total. ❧

Anise Wine Cookies

Roccetti del San Francesco

According to Rita, when Saint Francis was dying, he asked a woman in Assisi to bring him a good dessert. She brought him these cookies. When must (juice from wine grapes) is used instead of wine, the cookies are called mostaccioli. *I recommend zante currants over raisins because the tiny dried currants are easier to handle in this recipe, but raisins are fine.*

I love these fragrant, semidry roccetti—they are perfect for dunking in vinsanto, *Umbria's traditional dessert wine. According to Elisa, the chef at Perbacco in Cannara, these cookies are even more Umbrian than* tozzetti (biscotti).

Yield: About 4 dozen cookies

3 cups (13 ounces) all-purpose flour plus extra for rolling

⅔ cup granulated sugar

2 tablespoons anise seeds

1½ teaspoons double-acting baking powder

¼ teaspoon kosher salt (*important*: see "About Salt," page xxv)

¼ cup zante currants or raisins (optional)

¾ cup dry white wine, such as pinto grigio or sauvignon blanc

½ cup extra virgin olive oil

1 teaspoon vanilla extract

2 tablespoons unsifted powdered sugar

USEFUL EQUIPMENT: A clean plastic ruler.

GETTING STARTED: Preheat the oven to 375°F. Put a damp towel under a lightly floured wooden board to prevent slipping.

1. In a large bowl, toss together the flour, granulated sugar, anise seeds, baking powder, and kosher salt (if using currants or raisins, add them now). Make a well in the flour mixture; pour the wine, oil, and vanilla into the well.

2. Use a fork to slowly mix the liquids and dry ingredients. Turn the dough out onto a lightly floured wooden board (and flour the board as needed); knead about 1 minute. Shape the dough into a ball (the dough will feel slightly oily).

3. Pull off a small piece of dough at a time; roll it into a snake about ⅜ inch in diameter by 5½ inches long. Form the snake into a loop, overlapping the ends and leaving ½ inch tails. Gently press the dough together where the snakes cross to hold the loop together. Arrange the cookies on an ungreased baking sheet, about ½ inch apart.

4. Bake until the cookies are light golden on top and lightly browned on the bottom, 18 to 20 minutes. They should feel firm (but not hard) when pressed gently with a finger. They get crunchier as they cool. While still warm, sift the powdered sugar over the cookies. ❧

THE WONDER OF SAFFRON

I had heard that *zafferano* (saffron) was again being cultivated in southern Umbria around Cascia after being out of favor for several centuries, so I began searching for a grower. One day, I mentioned my interest in saffron to my local butcher. He said I didn't need to leave Umbertide—he jotted down the phone number of Enrico, a grower who was just down the street. When I called, Enrico told me the timing was perfect. It was the third week in August, and the next morning they would be digging up last year's saffron bulbs. He suggested I arrive at nine.

Enrico works for the *comune* (municipality) of Umbertide at a center for the developmentally disabled. The program serves about two dozen *ragazzi* (young men), who come to the center Monday through Friday to do a variety of activities, including growing and selling saffron, vegetables, and flowers.

At nine in the morning, I met briefly with Enrico, who turned me over to Massimo, a young man who was supervising the saffron project that day. When Massimo and I were in the field, he dug up one of the bulbs, brushed the dirt off it, and handed it to me. He asked me to remove the ruffled outer layer of skin.

"Today we're digging up the bulbs," he said. "Then we'll clean them, like you just did. And then we'll put them back in the ground."

"You use the same bulbs year after year?" I asked.

"No, no, the bulbs we planted last year have disintegrated, but each bulb produces one or two *figli* [offspring] by August the following year."

Massimo and two colleagues started digging, using hoes and picks. The operation was too delicate to have the *ragazzi* do it—the sharp implements could easily damage the bulbs. When a bulb appeared, one of the *ragazzi* squatted to finish unearthing it by hand. A few workers started the tedious task of cleaning the bulbs, separating any twins and removing the brown button on the bottom of the bulbs. Two men dug a series of four shallow trenches, three rows for saffron and the fourth for water drainage. Squatting, one of the men arranged the bulbs in single rows in the trenches, spacing them about an inch apart. The work—from digging to cleaning to planting—was tedious, slow, and back-aching.

"In about one month," said Massimo, "there will be green blades coming from each bulb. The bulbs will start to flower in about two months." He handed me a bag of saffron bulbs to plant at home. "Never water them," he instructed. He invited me to come back in October, during harvest.

The *bulbi* that Massimo gave me are officially called *Crocus sativus,* a plant that produces small lavender flowers. Inside each flower are three bright red pistils and stigmata. The spice called saffron comes from the female part of the flower, a thin, inch-long pistil and its pollen receptor, the stigma. Today we think of saffron as a spice, but along with a rich culinary history, saffron has had a multitude of other uses dating back thousands of years. The Etruscans used the red threads to dye clothing, and for centuries artists used it to color paint. Some cultures believed saffron was a powerful medicine and an aphrodisiac. The wealthy added it to bath water, perfume, and cosmetics.

In September, I went to an agricultural fair in Umbertide where I met two growers from Cascia. They were selling lentils, *roveja,* farro, and saffron. In October, when I went to Cascia to meet with Silvana (I had met her husband at the fair), I found out that they are one of the largest producers of saffron in the region of Umbria. And Silvana must be the most passionate of them all—her fervor reminded me of a religious convert. A more accurate description of Silvana's zeal would be to call her a saffron ambassador.

"I like to talk about saffron," she said, "because for years no one in Umbria knew anything about it. Some growers do it only for the money, but we do it for the *meraviglia della storia* [wonder of its history]." Shortly after I arrived, we left her house in the tiny village of Civita di Cascia to go to her seven-hundred-square-meter saffron field. The air was icy cold and the plants were still shaded by the mountain.

"I usually pick around seven in the morning," she said, "but I didn't want you to have to leave at five to get here in time."

"Thanks," I said.

"No problem. The flowers are still closed—that's the important thing."

"Why?"

"The light can alter their aroma."

The crocuses flower for about one month, from mid-October to mid-November. During harvest, Silvana picks seven days a week. Each morning she collects all the blossoms, and by the next morning there are new flowers—they pop up overnight.

Silvana and I crouched down near the ground so she could show me how to pick saffron. Each flower has to be pinched off by hand where it emerges from the dirt, so it was really time-consuming picking the whole field. When we were done, Silvana and I returned to her house to warm up—my hands and ears were really cold. When Silvana opened a kitchen cupboard where she stored dried saffron, the pungent, earthy, indescribable aroma of saffron escaped into the room. A pinch of saffron is fragrant, but the large bowl Silvana brought out was almost overwhelming.

Silvana picked up a just-picked flower, opening its long slender lavender petals to pluck out the three long red stigmata, the saffron threads. She tossed the useless petals into a basket, saying that at least they were pretty.

"Take one saffron thread at a time and pinch off the white end so all that's left is pure saffron," she said. "Next the saffron is dried, weighed, packaged, and labeled."

"No wonder saffron is the world's most expensive spice!" I said.

"But actually in the kitchen saffron ends up being reasonably priced."

"I guess so, when you consider you just need a pinch," I said.

"Just three threads of pure saffron for one serving," said Silvana.

At prices ranging from $9 to $40 per gram (0.035 ounce), the cost per serving can be as low as 10 cents, or as high as $1.25, depending on quality, origin, and the amount used. With the current exchange rate, Silvana's high-end saffron would cost about $900 an ounce! Compare that to the once-exotic clove at $1.50 per ounce.

"From 1300 to sometime in the 1600s, everyone in the area grew saffron," Silvana said. "Back then, *zafferano* was used like money. Three hundred grams could buy a horse. And to enter a convent you had to pay a fee, plus give a certain amount of saffron."

Silvana spread a batch of saffron threads out in a screen-bottomed wooden basket. She put the basket on a stand in the fireplace near the smoldering fire. "This is the traditional method for drying saffron," she said. "The temperature needs to be between thirty-six and forty degrees Centigrade [97 and 104°F]—it takes about six or seven minutes to dry."

Silvana's annual crop yields about a pound of dried threads. It takes about 6,500 flowers to get one ounce of dried saffron threads, so that's another reason high-quality, pure saffron is so expensive.

By late October, I had visited Silvana and returned to pick saffron with Massimo in Umbertide. I had seen such an abundance of flowers—the day I picked with Massimo, we collected 525 flowers in his small plot. Massimo had told me to expect one to six flowers per plant, so I was disappointed in my own yield. I picked my fourth and last flower on November 3. That was barely enough for four servings. Good thing I had bought saffron from both Silvana and Enrico.

Farro Soup with Saffron
Minestra di farro e zafferano
∞

Silvana entered this recipe in a cooking contest at her town's saffron festival— it won first place! Zafferano adds an intriguing earthy note and a lively yellow hue to the soup. This elegant yet rustic soup is quick and easy to make if you have broth—preferably homemade—on hand.

If you won't be serving the entire batch of soup at once, instead of adding the cooked farro to the pot of soup, add some farro to each individual bowl and ladle the soup over it. When allowed to stand for a long time in leftover soup, farro continues absorbing broth and loses its desirable chewy texture. The recipe calls for semi-perlato *(semipearl) farro because that is what is available here. If you find farro labeled "pearl," it might require soaking or a longer cooking time— consult the label for cooking information. If you cannot find farro, pearl barley makes a good substitute.*

Yield: 4 to 6 servings

1/2 teaspoon saffron threads

2 tablespoons hot water

3 medium yellow potatoes (about 12 ounces)

12 ounces Roma tomatoes (about 3 medium-large)

8 ounces uncooked semipearl farro (about 1 1/4 cups)

1 large carrot, finely diced

1 large celery stalk, finely diced

1/2 large onion, finely chopped

3 tablespoons extra virgin olive oil plus more for a garnish

6 cups Meat Broth (see recipe, page 118) or canned chicken broth

Kosher salt (*important:* see "About Salt," page xxv)

Freshly ground pepper

1. Put the saffron threads in a small jar; cover with the 2 tablespoons hot water. Seal and let stand at least ½ hour, but preferably 2 hours. Peel and cut the potatoes into ½-inch cubes. Submerge the potatoes in cold water (they can be held up to 1 hour); drain just before cooking. Seed and grate the tomatoes (see "How to Grate Tomatoes," page 34); set aside.

2. Rinse the farro in cold water; put it into a small saucepan. Add water until it reaches about 2 inches above the level of the farro. Bring to a boil; immediately reduce heat to low. Simmer gently until the farro is *al dente,* 20 to 25 minutes; drain. Rinse in cold water; set aside.

3. In a large pot, sauté the carrot, celery, and onion in the oil over medium heat, stirring frequently, for 8 minutes. Add the drained potatoes; cook and stir 1 minute. Stir in the tomatoes and ½ cup of the broth; cover and simmer over low heat, stirring frequently, until the potatoes are just tender, 6 to 10 minutes.

4. Add the remaining 5½ cups broth to the pot; bring to a boil. Stir in the farro and saffron water with threads; simmer 5 minutes. Season with kosher salt and pepper to taste (if the soup is bland, it needs more salt). Serve immediately. At the table, drizzle a little of the oil over each serving. ❧

THREE MORE FARRO SOUPS

Prepare the recipe for Farro Soup with Saffron, making the following changes:

Farro-Lentil: Omit the saffron, potatoes, and tomatoes. Reduce the uncooked farro to 1 cup. Sauté 3 minced garlic cloves with the carrot, celery, and onion. Add ¾ cup of uncooked, rinsed lentils (preferably tiny green or brown lentils) to the broth in step 4; simmer until *al dente.* Add the cooked farro; simmer 5 minutes.

Farro-Porcini: Omit the saffron. Rehydrate a handful of dried porcini mushrooms; rinse and finely chop. Sauté with the carrot, onion, and celery.

Farro-Chard: Omit the saffron and potatoes. Sauté 1 to 2 ounces of diced pancetta or bacon with the carrot, onion, and celery. In step 4, simmer a bunch of chopped chard in the broth for 15 minutes. Add the cooked farro; simmer 5 minutes.

TEN THINGS YOU SHOULD KNOW ABOUT SAFFRON

Saffron's pungent, earthy aroma and slightly bitter notes complement many foods, but strong, overpowering flavors that mask saffron should be avoided. Foods saffron pairs well with include mild cheese, cream, butter, and eggs; farro, lentils, rice, pasta, and polenta; chicken, lamb, and seafood; tomatoes, potatoes, onions, and garlic; and breads, cakes, and cookies.

1. For good flavor, high-quality saffron threads are a must (see Resources, page 352).

2. Although tiny jars of saffron seem more affordable, one-ounce tins are usually a better deal.

3. Pure saffron threads are bright or deep red from tip to tip.

4. There is no such thing as cheap pure saffron. Ground saffron is often adulterated with turmeric. Although threads can include flavorless flower parts, you're more likely to get good saffron when you buy threads.

5. Although pure saffron threads are always red, they turn hot liquid a rich yellow color. The saffron threads remain red.

6. Use dry hands and utensils when handling saffron.

7. Put the saffron container on waxed paper before opening it; that way flyaway threads are easy to return to the container.

8. For most recipes, leave the threads whole. If threads would detract from a dish, crumble them between your fingers or grind them with a mortar and pestle.

9. To prepare saffron for a recipe, put the threads into a small jar and cover with 2 tablespoons hot water; seal the jar. Steep the "tea" for at least 20 minutes but preferably for 2 hours. Add threads with the liquid as directed in the recipe, but usually at the end of cooking. Avoid using a whisk or the threads will get tangled in it.

10. When saffron is stored in a tightly sealed container in a cool, dark, dry place, it can last for years. Once saffron loses its pungent aroma, it's time to toss it out (or use it to dye fabric or perfume your bathwater).

ROVEJA—A WILD PEA

Farmers and shepherds around Civita di Cascia in southeastern Umbria have eaten *roveja,* a wild pea, for centuries. Today a few farmers cultivate and sell the formerly wild legume. The small, dark brownish-green peas are sold dried for soups and stews. And the dried peas are also ground into meal for polenta, which is served with an assertive sauce of garlic, anchovies, and olive oil. *Pisum arvense* is the pea's scientific name, but it is commonly called *roveglia, rubiglio, corbello,* and *pisello dei campi.* The braised peas make a delicious topping for crostini. To make *crostini di roveja,* sort and rinse the *roveja.* In a pot, cover the *roveja* with several inches of cold water; bring to a boil. Simmer 4 minutes; cover and soak one hour. (Alternatively, soak, refrigerated, overnight in cold water.) Drain the *roveja* and cover with fresh water an inch above the peas; simmer until *al dente,* adding water as needed to keep covered. Season to taste with salt. Lightly rub one side of toasted crostini with raw, peeled garlic. Spoon the *roveja* with a little of the cooking liquid over the toast and drizzle the top generously with extra virgin olive oil.

A DERUTA ARTIST IN THE KITCHEN

On my first trip to Umbria, I bought an expensive hand-painted cup and saucer from Deruta that I treasure. The squat cup with a pixie-ear-shaped handle is an ancient design, so the shopkeeper told me. She had painted the intricate centuries-old *Raffaellesco* design—a pattern specific to Deruta—herself. The dominant feature is a grotesque (a fantasy creature from sixteenth-century art) with a man's face, the forequarters of a hoofed animal, an amphibian-like body, and multicolored wings, painted in blues, yellows, and rust. Flowers, curlicues, and a series of fine lines complete the decoration. In the States, I showed the cup to a friend named Vima. She turned the cup over to discover that her artist friend Novella had painted it. On my next visit to Novella's shop, Deruta Placens, I mentioned Vima's name, and I instantly had a dinner invitation from Novella.

No matter that I have driven on the *superstrada* (highway) past Deruta's frontage road dozens of times before my visit to Novella, I am always in awe of the bigger-than-life ceramic jars and tabletops that beckon shoppers from manufacturers' rooftops. The small town of Deruta, with around eight thousand inhabitants, has hundreds of ceramic studios and shops. In fact, you wonder where residents buy the necessities—its seems as though every business is a ceramic studio. The night of our dinner, I walked past Deruta Placens in the historic upper city, across the piazza, and turned right to go to Novella's daughter's ceramic shop. Annalisa is a skilled painter like her mother—their work is very fine and intricate. I asked her why she had a shop of her own. "It would be too much to work and live together," Annalisa said.

I left Annalisa's to meet Novella so I could follow her home. Novella's house is down in the flatlands, next door to her workshop, where Annalisa's husband glazes and fires the ceramics. Novella used to live in the house with her husband, but he died suddenly while dancing at a festival. No one seems to have gotten over the shock.

When Novella opened the front door, she said, "We're a bit crowded here but it is better living with my daughter, her husband, and two kids than living alone." Annalisa and her husband, Andrea, left their large new house just outside town to move in with Novella when she lost her husband.

After quickly passing through the living room, filled with hand-painted ceramics—a large plate painted by an uncle for a graduation, a half dozen small, delicate plates painted for baptisms, two urns decorated with portraits—Novella took me into her modern kitchen. She tossed off her winter coat and wool scarf and immediately lit a fire—the house was icy cold. Without pausing for a break after working all day, she began assembling the dinner ingredients—sausages, bread, pork, veal, wine, onions, rosemary. The menu included asparagus risotto and *spezzatino* (braised veal and pork).

"I am not a great cook," she said. "I hope everything turns out okay."

"Of course it will," I replied.

Annalisa, who had just arrived, joined in. "My mother gets nervous with company, about how things will turn out," she said. "Don't you, Mamma?"

"Well, I taught myself how to cook," said her mother. "And I didn't learn until I got married. Even then I didn't cook often because my husband was a good cook."

"And there is no reason for me to learn to cook," said Annalisa, "because you're such a good cook."

The night before I came, Novella had stayed up until one in the morning to make *torta al testo* (griddle bread) for the meal we would soon eat. But that is her normal bedtime. Since she is often at her ceramic shop seven days a week, the only time for chores—ironing, tidying, cooking—is after everyone else has gone to bed. "As long as I never stop," she said, "I am not sleepy until then—but if I watch television early in the evening, I am out in seconds."

As we talked, Novella browned chunks of meat with rosemary and onion in a large pot. In a saucepan, asparagus sizzled in a pool of hot olive oil. Whiffs of smoke from the fireplace mingled with the aromatics cooking on the stove—dinner smelled wonderful. Minutes later, Novella spread pork sausage over thick slices of bread and topped it with smoked cheese—she baked it until browned.

When Camilla, Novella's eighteen-month-old granddaughter, came into the kitchen, I turned my camera lens toward her. The bright flash surprised Camilla, so she opened her mouth wide and let out a loud screech that quickly turned into a gurgley giggle. Until dinner, Camilla followed me around, pointing at the camera, squealing. When I pressed the shutter release, she would open her mouth as wide as possible and repeat the screech and chuckle. I never caught her with her mouth closed.

Within two hours of arriving at home, Novella had prepared a four-course meal by herself. *"Brava,"* said Annalisa. "I could never have made this dinner so quickly, and you kept the kitchen in perfect order!"

At the table, Camilla, who ate everything with gusto, kept pace with me—devouring each delicious course. Her four-year-old brother, Giovanni, pushed the meat and sautéed greens around his plate. "He eats nothing," said Novella.

"Mamma," said Annalisa, "he ate the sausage crostini, salami, broth with pasta and cheese. What more do you want him to eat?"

I didn't stay much past dinner because everyone had to work the next day. Annalisa and Novella would paint ancient designs on ceramics with steady hands and wait on customers in their respective shops. Andrea would glaze and fire the painted ceramics, ship a few orders, and pick up the kids after work. And me, I would write up the evening's notes and make Novella's risotto for lunch.

Creamy Risotto

Risotto mantecato

✑

The term mantecato *simply means to stir until creamy—some say it means to stir in butter. Risotto is one of my favorite dishes. I make the creamy rice for a quick one-dish meal on weeknights or as an elegant first course when I entertain. This basic recipe is made with ingredients I always have on hand—rice, broth (homemade frozen or canned), onion, butter, Parmigiano-Reggiano cheese, extra virgin olive oil, and dry white wine. From here, I add whatever suits my mood. Sautéed, grilled, or roasted vegetables—zucchini, mushrooms, tomatoes, cauliflower, asparagus, butternut squash. Pancetta, prawns, garlic, chives, leeks, saffron, fresh herbs, fava beans, mascarpone cheese. Leftover vegetables (see Chard, Peppers and Tomatoes, and Peas with Prosciutto, pages 162 and 163). In Italy, berries or melon similar to cantaloupe sometimes embellish risotto in the summer.*

There are four secrets to making great risotto: (1) use high-quality olive oil and Parmigiano-Reggiano—and don't skip the butter; (2) use mild broth, preferably homemade; (3) cook the rice until just al dente—overcooking ruins it; (4) be sure to season it with enough salt so it doesn't taste bland.

The amount of broth needed varies depending on the rice, the pot and the stove, and personal taste—I like risotto soupy, but you might not. If you run out of broth, add hot water. Since the saltiness of your broth is an unknown, I call for a minimum amount of salt to avoid oversalting.

Yield: 4 main-course servings (or 8 to 10 first-course servings)

6½ cups Meat Broth (see recipe, page 118, and "Substitutions," page 187)

3 tablespoons extra virgin olive oil

½ medium onion, finely chopped

2 cups arborio, *vialone nano,* or *carnaroli* rice (see "Substitutions," page 187)

½ cup dry white wine, such as pinot grigio or sauvignon blanc

1 teaspoon kosher salt (*important:* see "About Salt," page xxv)

2 ounces Parmigiano-Reggiano cheese, grated (see Grated Cheese, page 6)

2 tablespoons butter

⅛ teaspoon freshly ground pepper

1. Heat the broth in a medium saucepan until hot; cover and turn off the stove. As needed, to keep the broth hot, reheat over low heat but do not let the broth boil down. Heat the oil in a large, heavy pot over low heat. Add the onion; sauté, stirring frequently, until the onion is tender, about 5 minutes.

2. Add the rice; cook and stir 3 minutes (do not brown). Stir in the wine; simmer until the wine is almost absorbed, about 2 minutes.

3. Stir in about 2 cups of the hot broth and the salt; set the timer for 15 minutes. Simmer over medium-low heat, stirring every few minutes, until the broth is almost absorbed (do not allow the rice to get dry). Repeat, adding about 1 cup of broth each time it is absorbed, until the rice is *al dente*— taste the rice for doneness at 15 minutes. It is ready when it is slightly chewy, but not chalky.

4. When *al dente,* stir in the cheese, butter, and pepper. Add broth or water, if needed, to make the risotto creamy. (If desired, add enough broth to make the risotto soupy.) Adjust the salt to taste. Cover and let stand 2 minutes. Serve immediately.

SUBSTITUTIONS: Instead of homemade broth, you can substitute 5 cups of water plus 1 can (14 ounces) of regular-strength chicken broth. California medium-grain rice can be used instead of Italian rice.

RISOTTO TIPS

To Get a Head Start, About 1½ Hours Early: After sautéing the rice for 3 minutes in step 2, remove the pot from the heat. About 20 minutes before serving, resume cooking by adding the wine. (Cooked rice is perishable—do not leave it at room temperature over one hour.)

To Get a Head Start, Several Hours Ahead: After the wine has been absorbed (at the end of step 2), spread out the rice in a large baking pan to cool quickly. Refrigerate until about 20 minutes before serving time. Resume cooking at step 3.

What to Do with Leftover Risotto: Make pan-fried risotto cakes to serve as an antipasto or a side dish. To do this, shape the cold risotto into patties about 2½ inches across by ½ inch thick. Dredge the patties in dry bread crumbs; sauté in olive oil in a nonstick skillet over medium heat until browned on both sides and heated through. Serve hot.

RISOTTO WITH ASPARAGUS

Novella's *risotto con asparagi* is unusual because its rich, creamy base is an asparagus purée made from almost two bunches of fresh asparagus. At the height of asparagus season, she freezes fresh asparagus to use over the next several months. She freezes the tips separately from the sliced spears. Novella's original recipe calls for almost a cup of olive oil, but I think it is good with just ⅓ cup.

How to Make Risotto with Asparagus: Follow the recipe for Creamy Risotto (page 185) with the following changes.

Additional Ingredients: 2 pounds untrimmed asparagus; ½ teaspoon saffron threads (optional); ⅛ teaspoon red pepper flakes.

Changes in Ingredients: Increase the olive oil to ⅓ cup; omit the black pepper.

About 20 Minutes to 2 Hours Ahead: If using saffron, put the threads in a small jar; cover with 2 tablespoons hot water. Seal the jar and let steep, preferably 2 hours.

- Cut off the asparagus tips; set aside in a small bowl. Slice the spears into ⅜-inch rounds; set aside in a separate bowl.

- Add the red pepper flakes with the onion in step 1. When the onion is tender at the end of step 1, add the asparagus spears (but not the tips). Cover; simmer 20 minutes, stirring frequently. Use an immersion blender to purée the asparagus in the pot (alternatively, purée in a food processor). At this point, go to step 2 and add the rice to the pot with the asparagus purée. Continue cooking following the recipe's directions—adding the asparagus tips when the wine is absorbed at the end of step 2.

RISOTTO RICE

Most Americans think that arborio rice is the only kind to use for making risotto, but in Italy many cooks prefer *carnaroli, valone nano,* or *ribe*—all medium-grain rice varietals. The Italian rice varieties can absorb a lot of flavorful broth while holding their shape and staying firm, and they release the right amount of starch to help make the risotto creamy. Each type of rice has its own cooking time, from about 15 to 22 minutes. If you cannot find any of these Italian specialty rices, or if you don't want to spend the extra money, you can substitute California medium-grain rice.

Beef and Pork Braised in Tomatoes and Wine

Spezzatino

At the macelleria (butcher shop) in Umbertide, I ordered a kilogram of beef chuck. Next I asked for pork shoulder. "Are you making spezzatino?" the

clerk asked. When I told her I was, she said, "I see you're an Umbrian cook now."

She was right that I had learned the secret to a good Umbrian stew. From Novella, I discovered that the combination of two meats, pork and beef (or veal), makes a more flavorful dish than either meat alone. Sometimes Novella substitutes faraona (guinea fowl) for the pork and beef. Before cooking, she cuts the fowl into small pieces (cutting the breast into quarters, rather than in half, for example) so it is more flavorful.

By the time I made this dish with Novella, I had already learned the other secret to great braised dishes—lots of fat. Novella used almost two cups of olive oil for this dish—I have cut it to a half cup. As always, more oil makes a richer, more luscious dish—use as much as you want.

Novella says that eating torta al testo with spezzatino is an important tradition. As usual, the flat bread is used to mop up sauce on the plate. If you don't want to make bread, serve spezzatino with thick slices of Italian or French bread, mashed or boiled potatoes, or grilled or soft polenta. To add potatoes to spezzatino, cut them into bite-size pieces and boil them until al dente. Add the potatoes to the spezzatino just a few minutes before serving—that way they hold their shape and texture. Braised chard is another good accompaniment to the braised meats.

Yield: 6 to 8 servings

2½ pounds boneless beef chuck

¾ pound boneless pork shoulder

2 medium onions, cut top to bottom into halves

4 large garlic cloves, crushed and peeled

4 (6-inch) sprigs rosemary

½ cup plus 1 cup hot water

½ cup extra virgin olive oil

2 teaspoons kosher salt (important: see "About Salt," xxv)

¼ teaspoon freshly ground pepper

1½ cups dry white wine, such as pinot grigio or sauvignon blanc

1 can (14 ounces) whole tomatoes with juice, puréed

1. Cut the beef and pork into 1×1×2-inch pieces. Finely chop 3 of the onion halves; set aside. Put the remaining half onion into a large, broad pot. Add the beef, pork, 1 of the garlic cloves, 1 of the rosemary sprigs, and the ½ cup hot water.

2. Cover; cook over medium-high heat, stirring frequently, for 10 minutes. Uncover; cook over medium heat, stirring frequently until the liquid evaporates, about 30 minutes. Discard the onion and rosemary.

3. Pour the oil over the meat. Add the reserved chopped onions, the remaining 3 garlic cloves, and the remaining 3 rosemary sprigs. Sprinkle with the kosher salt and pepper. Cover and reduce the heat to low. Sauté 20 minutes, stirring frequently.

4. Add the wine. Simmer uncovered over medium heat, stirring frequently, until the wine evaporates, about 15 minutes. Add the tomatoes and the remaining cup of hot water. Cover and simmer on low heat until the meat is tender and the sauce is thickened (add water during cooking if the sauce gets too thick), 50 to 80 minutes. ❧

Making Cheese in Campi di Norcia

In the Graziosi family, cheese-making traditions have been passed from father to son for five generations, beginning with Giustino's great-grandfather. Now Giustino Graziosi's son is the fifth such apprentice. Today, father, son, and mother, Giuseppina, make cheese at their farm just below Campi di Norcia, where they live. These days Campi is barely a village; it consists of an old church and several dozen houses. But the cheese—and the panoramic views—from the area are spectacular.

"The elevation is 2,625 feet here," Giustino said. "That's important because what the sheep eat in the mountains is different than at lower elevations." A cheese's character depends upon the flavor of the milk—and ultimately on what plants the sheep graze. The flavor of milk, and thus cheese, changes from pasture to pasture and season to season.

Giustino and Giuseppina make *pecorino di Norcia* and sheep's milk ricotta, both *fresca* (fresh) and *salata* (salted/aged). The couple is among the select few who still use natural rennet to curdle the milk—and they make their own rennet. When they butcher a lamb, they use milk found in the stomach to make *latte acido* (acid milk), which contains the enzymes needed for coagulation.

Even without making rennet, dairy life is demanding. The sheep need tending, and cheese making begins at six in the morning. In the winter, they sometimes make cheese twice a day. By July, the milk production starts to dwindle, so they often make cheese every other day. They stop making cheese in mid-July, and start up once more in October when there is milk again.

In mid-July when I visited the cheese makers, it was one of the last days for making cheese until the fall. The Graziosi's 450 sheep had already been transferred to the mountains for the summer.

Giustino and Giuseppina make cheese in an extremely clean bedroom-size space. Stainless-steel tables and vats make the operation seem modern, but the methods they use are antique. Giustino, who is bald with a dark fringe of hair above his ears, looked serious in his lab coat, but it wasn't long before he was laughing and telling jokes. Giuseppina seemed to enjoy his sense of humor, but she focused on talking seriously about cheese. In reality, they are both earnest about cheese-making traditions. They produce cheese in small batches—and the work is all done by hand.

When I arrived that morning, about 180 liters of raw sheep's milk was heating in a pristine stainless-steel vat. It would yield about thirty-five kilograms (seventy-seven pounds) of pecorino cheese. Soon the milk reached 98.6°F, so Giustino added the *caglio* (rennet). "This temperature makes pecorino *fresco* [fresh]," Giustino said. "To make pecorino *staginato* [aged], the milk is heated to forty-two degrees centigrade [107°F]."

While the rennet coagulated the hot milk, the two cheese makers set up sixteen perforated plastic bins on a stainless-steel table. About twenty minutes later, when the cheese curds had formed, Giustino plunged a dowel with long wooden spines into the vat of curds and whey (the liquid left when the milk curdles). He stirred to break the curds into tiny pieces, about the size of coarse cottage cheese. Next he filled the waiting plastic tubs with curds. To speed up the draining process, Giustino pressed the cheese into the bins with his hands, forcing the whey through the holes in the molds. When the cheese was firm enough, he removed one cheese at a time from the mold and tapped it and rolled it around on the table, finally dropping it back into its plastic tub. When he finished the last tub, he waited another half hour before sprinkling *sale grosso* (coarse salt) over the top of the cheese.

Giustino and Giuseppina carted the cheese to the refrigerator. The next day, they would turn the cheese over to salt the other side. They would salt and rotate the cheese daily for two days. After forty-eight hours, the cheese would be removed from the tub and again held in the refrigerator. After four days, the cheese would be moved to a cellar to age for thirty days at 54°F.

With the bins of cheese put away, it was time to make ricotta using the whey leftover from making pecorino. Giustino poured the whey through a strainer that Giuseppina held over the steel vat. "We strain it to catch any pecorino curds," he explained. "Pecorino isn't a good flavor for ricotta."

Next Giustino added some raw sheep's milk to the whey, stirring it constantly, until it reached 176°F. At that point, he stopped stirring, waiting until the temperature reached 203°F—the desired temperature for making *ricotta salata* (fresh ricotta is heated to 185°F). Inside the vat, a mechanical blade stirred the milk. When the curds formed, they poured the steaming-hot ricotta into thick white cotton sacks, tying them closed with cotton twine. They stacked the cotton bags of ricotta on the stainless table, where the cheese would drain for several hours. Later in the afternoon, they would squeeze the sacks to remove the water before putting the cheese in the refrigerator. The next day, the couple would remove the firm cheese from the sacks and salt it. *Ricotta salata* is salted just once, then it is aged for a month or two until it becomes firm and dry.

Spaghetti with Cherry Tomatoes and Ricotta Salata
Spaghetti con pomodorini e ricotta salata
❧

Giuseppina's summer pasta dish comes together in minutes—but it is also good whenever flavorful cherry tomatoes are available. If you have a vegetable garden with tomatoes and herbs, this is practically a pantry dish. If you buy extra cheese, you can freeze it for a couple of months in two-ounce pieces—as long as you wrap and seal it tightly.

Yield: 4 main-dish servings (or 6 first-course servings)

Kosher salt (*important:* see "About Salt," page xxv)

1 pound dry spaghetti

8 large fresh basil leaves or 4 sprigs Italian parsley

16 ounces cherry tomatoes

⅓ cup extra virgin olive oil

2 large garlic cloves, thinly sliced

¼ teaspoon red pepper flakes

2 ounces grated *ricotta salata* cheese plus more for the table

1. Bring about 3 quarts of cold water to a boil in a large pot; add 2 table-spoons kosher salt to the boiling water. Add the spaghetti; cook until *al dente,* checking for doneness at least 1 minute before the package recommends. Shortly before draining the spaghetti, reserve about 1 cup of the cooking liquid; set aside. Drain the pasta and return it to the pot.

2. Meanwhile, stack the basil leaves; thinly slice into a chiffonade (if using parsley, finely chop it); set aside. Cut any small tomatoes into halves and any larger ones into quarters. Heat a large skillet over medium heat; add the oil. Sauté the garlic in the oil, stirring frequently, 30 to 60 seconds (do not brown). Stir in the tomatoes, ¾ teaspoon kosher salt, and red pepper. Cook over medium-high heat, stirring occasionally, until saucy, 3 to 4 minutes. Stir in the basil (if using parsley, add it now).

3. Pour the tomato mixture over the spaghetti; toss to coat. Stir in enough of the reserved pasta cooking liquid to make it saucy (but do not dilute the flavors). Cook and stir over medium heat about 1 minute so the pasta absorbs the flavor of the sauce. Remove from the heat. Add the cheese; toss well. Adjust the salt to taste. Pass additional cheese at the table. ❧

UMBRIA'S CHEESE

At supermarkets in Umbria, many cheeses are simply labeled *cacio,* which is dialect for *formaggio* (cheese). *Cacio* is an ancient food in Umbria. Together with garden vegetables, such as fava beans, *cacio* made a nutritious mid-morning snack for farmers. Although Umbrian cooks regularly use mozzarella, Parmigiano-Reggiano, and a few other kinds of cheese, pecorino and its by-product, ricotta, along with *ca-ciotta*, are Umbria's most important cheeses.

Pecorino: Made exclusively with sheep's milk. Its name comes from *pecora* (sheep). After a one-month aging period, it is sold as pecorino *fresco*. It is similar to Monterey Jack cheese in texture with a more complex, rich yet tangy flavor. Pecorino *staginato* (aged) has a sharper flavor than *fresco* with a firm texture, similar to Parmigiano-Reggiano. Sometimes pecorino is aged in a cave—then it is called *pecorino in fossa* or *in grotta*.

Ricotta: Often made with sheep's milk and whey leftover from making pecorino. Also made with cow's milk. *Fresca* is rich and incredibly creamy—nothing like commercial American ricotta. *Salata* is aged one to six months so it slices or grates.

Caciotta: Made from cow's and sheep's milk. Consumed fresh, after about two weeks of aging. It is semisoft with a sweet, tangy flavor. *Caciotta mista* is made with a mix of milk, from cow to sheep to buffalo to goat. Sometimes *caciotta* is flavored with spices or bits of black truffles.

Scamorza: A firm, salty cheese that is sometimes smoked. It is reminiscent of America's low-moisture mozzarella.

THE OLIVE HARVEST—*LA RACCOLTA*

For people who live to eat, November is probably the best month to visit Umbria. Porcini mushrooms and Umbria's precious white truffles are in season. But equally as enticing is the olive harvest, which usually begins in late October and ends in December. In October I set a date with Jura and Giovana to pick olives at their 148-acre farm above Umbertide in the remote Migianella area. The prior year it had taken forty days to pick the five hundred olive trees. So Jura and Giovana were always glad to have a few extra hands.

The farm's steep hillsides provide the ideal growing conditions for olive trees. Over time, rainwater has carried the nutrient-rich earth down the slopes, leaving behind the rocky, fast-draining soil that olive trees prefer. Some of the trees on the property are more than a thousand years old, but most are between eighty and one hundred. Old trees tend to be pest resistant, and pests are usually not a problem at the farm's elevation of 1,475 feet. With nature's help, Jura and Giovana are able to farm organically.

The morning I arrived at the farm, Vocabolo Ripa, to pick, a thick mist blanketed the rolling hills and the valley below. When the fog cleared, the Apennine Mountains that divide Umbria from Marche were visible. Castello Polgetto, a glorious castle, stood out on a hill to the right, and a medieval tower was visible on another hill.

Giovana met me at the car and took me to find her husband, who was picking olives. Jura climbed down a ladder that rested precariously against a tree. I mentioned that the ladder looked unstable.

"A vertical ladder puts less weight on the tree," he explained. "A ladder can actually break an old delicate tree like this Rosciola."

"Picking olives looks dangerous," I said.

"It is," said Giovana. "That's why I only pick olives that I can reach from the ground."

"Giovana is smart," Jura said. "I fell recently. Fortunately I didn't hit my head too hard, but I still couldn't move for about half an hour. Do you want to pick?"

"*Certo* [sure]," I said.

I helped Jura spread a huge net under a tree and stake the downhill edge up to keep the olives from rolling away. About fifteen minutes later, the net was ready. Jura stood a ten-foot ladder almost vertically against a few thin branches. I carefully climbed up the ladder—it trembled with every step I took.

"Reach up under a branch of olives," Jura said. "And comb your hands through it." I stretched my arm overhead, and even that slight movement caused the ladder to rock. The gray leaves tickled the palm of my hand as I dragged it across a branch. The olives gave little resistance, dropping into my hand and then to the ground. The higher I climbed, the more the ladder swayed. After about five minutes my arm tingled from holding it over my head. When I had picked all the olives within reach, I climbed down to reposition the ladder and continue picking. I moved the ladder about a dozen times.

"*Che fatica* [how exhausting]!" I said, coming down the ladder when we had picked the tree clean. "Climbing up and down."

"Even worse—holding your arms up in the air!" Jura said.

Jura and I shook the net to gather the olives and transfer them to a small plastic bin. An experienced worker can fill about 2½ bins in a day—that's enough olives to make about seven quarts of extra virgin olive oil. After a couple days of picking, Jura had 220 pounds of olives ready for the press.

The next day, I joined Jura and Giovana on the trip to the Marfuga *frantoio* (olive press) in Campello sul Clitunno south of Foligno, about an hour away. We arrived at the appointed time, but the press was running about two hours behind. We browsed around the sales room/store decorated with Persian rugs and overstuffed chairs. Finally, we settled down to drink espresso near the fireplace in the elegant waiting room, where we could watch the goings-on in the press room.

The Marfuga press room is immaculate and ultramodern, but extremely noisy. And the aroma in the room is intense, a mix of fruity, spicy olives and machinery. The traditional presses I had seen were not as efficient or as pristine. At Marfuga a technician watches and controls the entire process from a computer. Another man works the back room, where the stainless-steel tanks of oil are kept, and a third man dumps newly arrived bins of olives into a hopper with a forklift. It's a slick process. Once inside the building, the olives are washed and the stray leaves are removed. A machine crushes the olives and another slowly pushes the dense olive paste to a centrifuge to separate the oil from the water and dry paste. Finally, the extra virgin olive oil flows to a tank, the water goes down the drain, and the paste is taken elsewhere for further processing. About an hour after the olives started their journey at the washer, Jura's containers—about ten quarts—were filled to the top with oil.

"Until about ten years ago," Jura said, "it would have taken all day to press the amount of olives we brought here today."

Jura and Giovana sent me home with a liter of *olio extravergine di oliva nuovo.* It was one of the finest olive oils I have ever tasted. A translucent green color, a tad spicy with a velvety mouthfeel and a lingering taste of fresh, fruity olives. That night, when I drizzled the oil over a plate of bruschetta, I had a new appreciation for *l'olio.* After all, it had taken someone about an hour to pick enough olives to fill the quart bottle with oil.

UMBRIA'S LIQUID GOLD

I laugh when I think of how I used to pour a tablespoon of olive oil into a skillet and feel guilty that I had used so much. In Umbrian kitchens, olive oil is treated more like a nutritious food than a fat. It is used in abundance and with abandon. A cup per eight servings isn't uncommon, for example. But things are changing; young cooks tend to use less oil than their grandmothers do.

Olives are a very old product in the region—the ancient Romans, and the Etruscans before them, cultivated olives. In fact, olive oil production in Umbria is among the oldest in all of Italy.

Olive Oil in the Kitchen: In the Umbrian kitchen, oil almost always means extra virgin olive oil. However, until recently, olive oil was for the rich. In the past, the poor *contadini* (farmers) used pork fat for cooking and baking and to dress salads (melted, of course). Although lard is still popular, today *olio extravergine di oliva* is Umbria's all-purpose fat for sautéing, baking, seasoning, and garnishing, for both savory and sweet dishes. But frying demands *olio per friggere* (frying oil), oil with a higher smoke point. Cooks sometimes call EVOO (extra virgin olive oil) *olio crudo* (uncooked/raw oil) when the oil is used as a garnish, rather than in cooking. Umbrian cooks often recommend *un filo d'olio* (a drizzle of oil) to finish a dish—over risotto, fish, steak, and soup, to name a few. In autumn, when oil is *nuovo* (new), it is the ideal time to feature *l'olio* in simple dishes that highlight it—spaghetti with lots of oil and Parmigiano-Reggiano cheese or bruschetta (rustic garlic bread) smothered in oil.

What Is Extra Virgin Olive Oil? Extra virgin olive oil is the premier category of olive oil, so it tends to be expensive. To be called EVOO, the oil must be extracted by mechanical or physical methods without the use of chemicals. Temperatures during processing must not alter the oil's properties, and the acidity must be under 0.8 percent.

Qualities of Extra Virgin Olive Oil: When just pressed, *olio extravergine di oliva* is a deep green color, and slowly over time it turns golden. EVOO has a velvety, viscous mouthfeel and a pleasant fruity flavor (*fruttata*). Some oils are naturally spicy (*piccante*), pleasantly bitter (*amaro*), and pleasant and balanced (*dolce*). The personality of the oil comes from the character of the olive varietals, the blend of olives, and its place of origin.

How to Store Olive Oil: Olive oil and wine have similar storage needs—light, heat, and air are their enemies. To protect oil, store it in a tightly closed dark bottle or a tin in a dark, cool place (57 to 59°F) such as a cellar. Store only a week's supply of oil in a kitchen cupboard, and keep it away from the stove and oven. Keep the rest in a cool place. Oil decanters need a stopper to seal the pour-spout to prevent oxidation, which destroys flavor. To reuse oil containers, wash them with rock salt and hot water—soap residue may flavor the oil. Olive oil is at its best when it is *nuovo,* right after the *raccolta* (harvest), usually in November or December. When EVOO is stored properly, it will keep for twelve to eighteen months after harvest.

DOP Umbria Olio Extravergine di Oliva: When the European Union created the quality certificate for DOP Umbria Extra Virgin Olive Oil in 1998 (see "The ABCs of the DOP . . . ," below), it gave the designation to the region's entire production area. No other region has an all-encompassing certificate. Of course, only oil produced under DOP guidelines may use the trademark. DOP rules require that the oil be composed of a blend of traditional olive varieties (Moraiolo, Frantoio, Leccino, Dolce Agogia, San Felice). The codes spell out the percentages allowed for each olive. Every olive variety has different characteristics, from assertive to delicate to bitter to sweet to spicy, so oil made from a blend typically produces more balanced flavors than a single varietal does. To qualify for DOP status, a panel of tasters must approve the oil. The maximum acidity for DOP oil is 0.65 percent (versus 0.8 percent for non-DOP extra virgin olive oil). The lower the acidity, the higher the quality.

PINZIMONIO

Pinzimonio (olive oil dip) served with raw vegetables makes a great summertime starter or side dish. Prepare a raw vegetable platter. Wedges of fennel and celery sticks are my favorites, but strips of red pepper, cauliflower florets, and carrot and cucumber sticks are good, too. Pour a couple of tablespoons of fruity extra virgin olive oil into small bowls—preferably one for each person—and mix in a pinch or two of kosher salt and a dash of freshly ground pepper. At the table, diners dip the vegetables into the *pinzimonio*.

THE ABCS OF THE DOP, IGP, AND STG

In Umbria a half dozen or so food and/or agricultural products carry the DOP, IGP, and STG certificates of quality. In order to use these icons on product labels, the producer must follow the stringent rules and guidelines set up by the European Union. The standards have been established to maintain the quality of food products and to give consumers confidence in buying them. There is also a certificate for organically farmed foods—*Prodotto da Agricoltura Biologica*.

Of course, in Umbria many high-quality food products do not bear these trademarks because of limited production. Cannara's onions, Lake Trasimeno's tiny *fagiolina,* Cascia's saffron, and Trevi's "black" celery are just a few examples. Most of the small producers share a culture that honors tradition and quality.

Definitions of the Icons

DOP (*Denominazione di Origine Protetta*): Food or agricultural products must be grown, produced, and processed within specific geographic boundaries, following precise methods of cultivation and/or production. The product's qualities and character must be attributable to place.

IGP (*Indicazione Geografica Protetta*): A food or agricultural product from specific geographic areas. Some part of the production may take place outside of the place of origin.

STG (*Specialità Tradizionale Garantita*): This mark is not connected to geographic origin. These products have strong ties to tradition—in the product and/or in the method of production. Specific quality standards of their country must be followed.

DOP and IGP Products

A list of the current DOP and IGP products from Umbria follows (by now, more products may have been added). STG products are not tied to a geographic area.

DOP: *Olio Extravergine di Oliva Umbria* (extra virgin olive oil from Umbria); *Salamini Italiana alla cacciatora* (small salami in the hunter's style); *Pecorino Toscano.*

IGP: *Vitellone Bianco dell'Appennino Centrale* (white veal from the central Apennine Mountains); *Prosciutto di Norcia; Lenticchia di Castelluccio* (lentils).

You Say *Brews-SHET-tah,* Italians Say *Brews-SKEHT-tah*

I often tagged along with Silvia on outings with her hiking group. We did some fabulous day trips—climbing to the top of Monte Tezio, picking wild asparagus in the forest, hunting for truffles near Montone, hiking to a cliff-hanging ancient monastery. One Sunday in June, after an hour of strenuous hiking on a steep, muddy path up Monte Acuto, we arrived at a group of seventeenth-century farmhouses recently converted into a lovely bed-and-breakfast. From the terrace near the pool, there is a scenic lookout for viewing the Upper Tiber River valley.

A woman was putting salt shakers, plates of peeled garlic, and bottles of oil and water down the center of a long garden table. A man was grilling sliced bread over a wood fire. When the bread was toasted and the edges were lightly charred, the woman brought the bread to the table. We rubbed the toast with garlic, drizzled it with olive oil, and sprinkled the saltless bread with salt. That is how you make authentic bruschetta (grilled garlic bread). Tomatoes and other toppings are add-ons. And for the authentic pronunciation, remember that in Italian "ch" sounds like "k."

To Make Bruschetta: Toast ¾-inch-thick slices of Italian bread— ciabatta, Pugliese, or batard (not sourdough)—side by side on a baking sheet in a preheated 350°F oven until crisp on the outside but soft inside, about 12 minutes (let it cool slightly in the pan). While warm, use a light touch to rub one side of the toast with a peeled, raw garlic clove (the toast acts like sandpaper so it is easy to overdo the garlic). Drizzle lots of fruity extra virgin olive oil over the top, and sprinkle lightly with kosher salt.

To Make Bruschetta with Tomatoes: After rubbing the bruschetta with garlic but before drizzling it with the olive oil, arrange thin tomato slices (preferably heirloom) on top of the toast (trim tomatoes as needed to fit). Sprinkle generously with kosher salt; season with freshly ground pepper. Drizzle liberally with olive oil and garnish with thinly sliced fresh basil. Can be made about a half hour ahead.

2M CENTRO CARNI

2M Centro Carni may be one of Umbertide's largest butcher shops, but it is also one of the most traditional. They do their own butchering, make their own sausage, and cure their own prosciutto. The shop is clean and modern, with a long L-shaped meat counter. Fresh pork commands the most space— thick slices of fresh pancetta (not cured), loin roasts, breaded cutlets, shoulder, chops, liver, sausage. Another section displays house-made cured pork—pancetta, prosciutto, *guanciale, capocollo, lombo* (see page 205). But they also sell veal, beef, lamb, and *ruspante,* a free-range chicken.

Marino and Massimo (2M—two men with names that start with M) own the *macelleria* (butcher shop). Marino's wife, Anna, and Massimo's wife, Gabriella, help customers, but they also roast chickens to order and make other ready-to-go items. Twentysomething Marco, Gabriella and Massimo's son, works alongside his father, Marino, and Stefano, an employee. It feels like one big happy family.

On my first morning at 2M, Massimo showed me the tag on the ear of a half pig he had just dropped onto an immaculate stainless-steel table—it gave the name and address of the farm it came from.

"All of our pigs—and our beef—come from Umbria," he said. "We know the people who raise them and what they feed them. We never buy from people we don't know."

Massimo and Marco worked side by side. They divvied up the work by instinct; they'd done the job hundreds of times before. With a few quick slashes of a sharp knife, they extracted the ribs, then a pork loin, then the ham. They tossed odd bits of meat and fat into a bin and set aside roasts and steaks to cure or sell fresh. Marco reserved the tasty fat from the chops to make *lardo tritato* (freshly ground seasoned fat). Within about half an hour, they'd butchered the entire half pig into perfect cuts of meat. But the work had just begun.

The next day, Stefano would make *porchetta* (boneless roasted pig). In a couple of days, Stefano, Massimo, and Marco would make prosciutto. As needed, they make pancetta, *guanciale, capocollo,* and *lombo.* And Marco planned to show me how to make fresh *salsiccia* (sausage) in just a few minutes.

MAKING FRESH SAUSAGE WITH MARCO

Marco pounded garlic with a little salt on a piece of butcher paper until the garlic was creamy. He knew the sausage recipe by heart. "Two garlic cloves for twenty kilograms of pork," he said. "Twenty-seven grams of salt per kilo of meat and three percent black pepper." He rubbed the garlic over the meat in the bin.

He picked up the bin, and I followed him into a small room. "We use this little grinder," explained Marco, pushing bits of pork and fat through the machine. "The big grinder is faster, but it overworks the meat and heats it up, so the sausage isn't as good." He mixed lots of salt and freshly ground pepper into the coarsely ground pork. "We mix in the seasonings by hand," he said.

"The sausage comes out better than it does if you mix it by machine." Marco pushed and pleated a long *budello* (casing) onto the funnel end of the sausage maker, and fed pork into the machine's chute. As the casing filled and unfurled, Marco massaged the sausage to pack the meat tightly inside the *budello*. He pricked the sausages with pins to release the air bubbles, and he quickly and expertly tied the sausage into three-inch links.

This simple *salsiccia* is the most popular sausage in Umbria, but there are several other traditional sausages. For *salsiccia secca*, the fresh sausage is dried and eaten like salami. The substitution of 4 percent red pepper flakes for the black pepper makes *salsiccia piccante* (spicy sausage). During the fall and winter, different recipes are used to make blood sausage and *zampone* (pig's foot stuffed with sausage).

Umbrian Bulk Sausage
Pasta di salsiccia Umbria
ᐭᐃᐤ

Umbria's fresh pork sausages are like the ubiquitous American hamburger. They're served often and everywhere for a quick dinner or Sunday lunch, at festivals and parties, and in restaurants. People love them. Because they are simple—ground pork, salt, and pepper with a whiff of garlic—they are versatile. In fact, they are the backbone of at least half a dozen traditional Umbrian dishes.

The most popular way to cook sausage in Umbria is over coals in the fireplace—salsiccia alla griglia. They're also delicious simmered with grapes or lentils, eaten between slices of torta al testo *(griddle bread), braised in sauces for pasta and polenta, or roasted with rosemary and potatoes. In Umbria, sausages are cooked until well done and dry inside, with a well-browned, crusty exterior. I prefer them slightly moist inside, but still well done and crispy outside.*

Since making sausage links at home is very time-consuming, this recipe makes bulk sausage for use in the recipes in this book. But patties make a suitable alternative to links. To improve the texture of the patties, sprinkle 2 teaspoons of cornstarch over the pork with the garlic mixture. Never add cornstarch when using the sausage as an ingredient in a recipe—it makes the meat clump together in big chunks.

For the best ground pork, buy a fatty pork shoulder or butt and grind your own. Or for convenience, look for ground pork in the meat department at the supermarket.

Yield: 2 pounds

1 small garlic clove, peeled

2 tablespoons kosher salt (*important:* see "About Salt," page xxv)

2 teaspoons freshly ground pepper

2 pounds ground pork, preferably home ground

YOU'LL ALSO NEED: A mortar and pestle or garlic press.

1. Grind the garlic with the kosher salt and pepper with a mortar and pestle. (Alternatively, push the garlic through a press into a small bowl with the kosher salt and pepper; mix well.) Put the pork into a large bowl. Sprinkle the garlic mixture over the pork. Mix with a fork until the seasoning is evenly dispersed, but do not mix more than necessary (overmixing makes ground meat tough).

2. Cover and refrigerate at least 2 hours to develop flavors (or up to 24 hours). At this point, the sausage is ready to use as an ingredient in recipes calling for bulk sausage.

3. To store the sausage, divide it into ½- to 1-pound portions; flatten each portion into a 1-inch-thick disk. Use or freeze within 24 hours. To freeze, store the sausage in tightly sealed freezer bags (wrap each portion in plastic wrap before storing in freezer bags). Store in the freezer for up to 3 months. ❧

OGGI PORCHETTA

Every Monday, Stefano descends the stairs to make *porchetta* (roast pig) in 2M's cold basement. One Monday, I came to watch. When Massimo and I arrived at the basement, Stefano poured a thick layer of rock salt on a stainless-steel table. "Salt tenderizes the skin," he explained. "It makes it easier to sew the pig closed."

Massimo pulled a huge headless half pig along the track in the ceiling and dropped it onto the table with the skin side against the salt. "Alive, this pig probably weighed about one hundred and thirty five *chilogrammi* [350 pounds]," Massimo said. "The bigger, the more flavorful." Massimo started the laborious job of boning the entire pig, rib by rib, bone by bone. "The cold meat is slippery," he said, "so it's dangerous work. But I'm very careful; in all these years I have never cut myself." Forty-five minutes later, he had transformed the pig into a slab of boneless meat.

"Stefano is a *porchetta* expert," said Massimo. "His seasoning is the best."

"I use my eye to mix the spices," explained Stefano. He combined salt with white wine vinegar, whole fennel seeds, and freshly ground fennel seeds (they grind their own spices). Stefano poured the liquidy spice mixture over the inside of the pork. He tossed whole garlic cloves over the pork and rubbed more salt into the flesh, saying the more salt the better. Stefano left the pork lying on the table and told me to return in a few hours. The meat needed time to absorb the flavors.

When I went to the basement later that day, Stefano was removing some of the garlic; people here don't appreciate garlic, he said. He added pepper, salt, and dried stalks of wild fennel. Marco and Stefano struggled to bring the sides of the pig together; it took a lot of effort. Then Stefano pushed a huge needle threaded with coarse twine through the skin and made a few stitches in the middle of the pig to hold it together. Despite the softening action of the salt, Stefano had a hard time piercing the tough rind.

"It's important to completely cover the meat with skin," said Stefano. "That way the pork stays moist and the skin gets crispy outside." After a lot of struggling, Stefano finished sewing the pig closed. He tied string around the pig about every eight inches; it looked like a giant rolled roast. To prevent the pig from ballooning up while roasting, he pricked the skin. He and Marco lifted the pig onto a rolling cart fitted with an enormous baking pan and rack. Stefano rubbed salt over the entire *porchetta*—the secret to a crispy skin, he said—and Marco filled the baking pan up to the level of the rack with water. "It cooks better with water," Stefano said. "By tomorrow morning, the water will be gone and the pan will be filled with fat." They pushed the pig on its gurney into the oven, and Stefano set a timer that would turn the oven on in the middle of the night. The porchetta would bake for five hours at 428°F.

The next morning at nine, Stefano and Marco carried the roasted pig upstairs to the shop on a long board; I followed behind. The *porchetta* had rested an hour; it was ready to sell. Stefano pulled the fennel stalks out while Marino put on a white lab coat. After carving several slices of *porchetta*, Marino tucked the meat with lots of brown, crispy rind inside of a fresh *panino* (bread roll), and he handed it to me. "Mmmmm," I mumbled with my mouth full. *"Buonissima* [very good]!" There is no better sandwich filling. As if he had been waiting for my approval, Stefano wrote *"Oggi Porchetta"* (*porchetta* today) in bold letters on a sheet of yellow paper. Almost as soon as he taped the sign to the window, customers began arriving. Marino sliced *la famosa porchetta* to order.

Il Maiale—Pork

In the past, almost every family kept pigs—pork is still Umbria's favorite meat. Every winter, farmers slaughtered a pig, and without refrigeration, they had to salt and dry most of the meat to preserve it. Today cured pork— salami, prosciutto, pancetta—still plays an important role in the region's cuisine. Farmers had to be frugal. They used every part of the pig, wasting nothing. Intestines hung above fireplaces to dry—eaten out of hand or simmered in sauces. Pig ears were chopped and used in stuffing. Chunks of liver, wrapped in caul fat, were sautéed with wine and bay leaves. Fresh blood was used to make sausage and a puddinglike dessert. The fat was ground, cured, or rendered. Now that most people are city dwellers, they buy what they need from supermarkets and local butchers. A short glossary of the lesser-known pork follows:

Cured Meats: In Umbria, most cuts of pork are cured—salted, peppered, and aged. At 2M Carni Centro, they use the same recipe for all of their cured meats, but the aging time varies depending on usage, the cut of meat, and personal preference. *Capocollo,* cylinder shaped, is made from the fatty shoulder; aged four to six months. Pancetta, also called *ventresca,* is Italian bacon. It comes from the belly. Pancetta comes rolled (*arrotolata*) or in a slab like bacon. Aged one month to five months. *Guanciale,* also called *barbozzo, góta,* and *gola,* is like pancetta, but it is made from the cheek of the pig—it is considered more gourmet than pancetta.

Lombo is lean, shaped like the loin roast it is made from. When aged a month or two, paper-thin slices of *lombo* are called *carpaccio di maiale.* Prosciutto: *Prosciutto crudo* (raw), air-dried ham, is simply called prosciutto in the States. *Prosciutto cotto* is what we call ham.

Pork Fat: In the recent past, pork fat was the main fat used in Umbria's kitchens. Today's cooks have the disposable income to buy olive oil that was once too expensive. And health concerns have made extra virgin olive oil more desirable. There are four kinds of pork fat sold at Umbria's butcher shops. *Lardo:* Cured fat that resembles bacon, but without the stripes of meat.

Lardo can be used in place of pancetta or served in paper-thin slices with bread as part of an antipasto plate. *Lardo macinato* or *tritato:* Ground fresh pork fat that is seasoned, sometimes with just salt, but often with garlic, spices, and pepper. *Rete:* Called caul fat in English, it is a lacy fat that separates the abdominal cavity from the rib cage. *Strutto:* Lard, rendered pork fat. In Umbria, *strutto* is sold seasoned with salt and pepper for savory dishes or unseasoned for desserts and bread recipes.

How to Make Lard: There is usually a thick layer of fat on pork roasts, so I trim it off, cut it into ⅜-inch cubes, and freeze it until I have enough to make lard. To make lard, put the frozen cubes of lard into a heavy saucepan and cover about halfway with water. Cover and bring to a boil; reduce the heat to low. Simmer uncovered, stirring frequently, until the water evaporates. Reduce the heat to low and cook, stirring frequently, until the fat turns to liquid and the bits of pork are brown and crispy, about 1½ hours (longer for large quantities of fat). Cool slightly; strain with a fine sieve. Let cool slightly; pour into a jar. Cool to room temperature. Cover and refrigerate or freeze. In Umbria, the bits of crispy meat, called *cicoli,* are used—often with pecorino cheese—to flavor bread dough.

THE PROSCIUTTO WORKOUT

Every three weeks, the crew at 2M makes prosciutto. So on the appointed date, I met Stefano, Massimo, and Marco in the basement, where they made cured meats—they donned white lab coats. "We're going to make fifty prosciutto today," Marino said. "It will take us about an hour. A big factory can make a thousand or more in that time."

Prosciutto crudo (raw), cured ham, is one of their specialties. To make the *salamoia* (brine), Stefano poured nine liter bottles of white wine vinegar into a huge tub and mixed in mountains of rock salt, pepper, and minced garlic.

"When you leave here, you will smell like garlic," said Stefano, "even if you don't touch the marinade or meat."

"The brine Stefano is making gives the meat a unique flavor," Marino said. "Marinade is not traditional—it's our touch. But our method is traditional. We make prosciutto like the farmers did in the past when they slaughtered a pig."

Stefano selected a large hind leg from the rack laden with fifty ready-to-cure *prosciutti* that Marino had just rolled into the room. After Stefano dropped the meat into the brine, he massaged it for several minutes before transferring it to the worktable. "It's important to make sure all the blood is drained out," said Stefano, "or the meat won't cure properly."

Stefano heaved another leg into the brine and Marino took over as masseur at the table. Marino rubbed salt over the entire surface and pushed lots of rock salt into the pockets around the bone at the hip joint. With the fat side against the table, he completely covered the pork flesh with salt. It was Marco's job to line the refrigerator's sloped shelves with a thick layer of rock salt, and then to arrange the salted hams on a shelf. It takes a lot of salt—about four pounds—to make one prosciutto. Each time Marco nestled another prosciutto into the bed of salt, he took a handful of brine, and slurped the vinegar and crunched on the salt.

"He's like a goat," said Stefano. "He eats everything."

"I like the salt," Marco said. Consuming brine didn't seem odd to him—it did to me.

As soon as Marco took a prosciutto off the table, Stefano heaved another ham out of the brine and put it on the table. Marino would massage and salt it and then Stefano would take another ham from the rack and drop it into the brine. The three men worked steadily and in harmony, with Marco nibbling on salt and Stefano doing the majority of the lifting—and at an average weight of thirty-five pounds per ham, he got quite a workout. The cycle continued until Marco put the fiftieth prosciutto into the refrigerator. The *salatura* phase of prosciutto making was now done.

In twenty days, they would flip over each prosciutto. A week later, the *spazzolatura* would take place—they would scrub the hams, all by hand. Then the prosciutto would rest in the refrigerator. About three months later, they would wash and dry the hams during the phase called *toelettatura*. During the *prestagionatura,* a period of about seven months, the prosciutto would slowly lose moisture. For the *sugnatura,* the legs would be cleaned and covered with fresh pig fat (*sugna*), salt, and pepper. The *sugnatura* helps prevent loss of moisture and excessive hardening where the ham is exposed to air. The final step, called the *stagionatura,* is the aging. The length of aging depends on the size of the leg, but the usual time is about a month per kilogram. At an average weight of sixteen kilograms, the *prosciutti* we made that day would be ready in sixteen months. At the end of the *stagionatura,* the ham would be ready to sell as prosciutto. Making prosciutto is very labor-intensive. According to Stefano, each prosciutto is handled ten times before it is ready to sell.

That evening when I got home, I did reek of garlic—and I had not touched the brine or meat. I was too busy taking notes.

Cantaloupe with Prosciutto

This is one of the best summertime appetizers. Cut a cantaloupe melon in half from top to bottom; scoop out the seeds. Slice the melon into ¾-inch lengthwise wedges; slice off the rind. Wrap a thin slice of *prosciutto crudo* around each slice of melon; arrange on a platter. Serve chilled.

7 ❧ Dining Out—*Mangiare fuori*

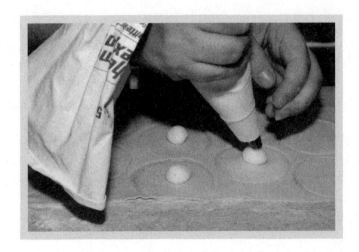

Chiamare i fichi fichi e la tazza tazza

(Call figs figs and the cup a cup—speak frankly)

IN UMBRIA, MOST RESTAURANTS OFFER TRADITIONAL CUISINE BECAUSE that's what the local clientele wants. But new chefs and young customers are changing the restaurant scene—more and more restaurants are offering contemporary dishes or classic dishes with a twist.

To find out what was hot, I went to Città di Castello to meet with Marco Bistarelli, whose Il Postale is one of Umbria's best-known restaurants. In Cannara, I spent an evening at Perbacco with the youthful Elisa, who cooked traditional dishes based on the town's famous onions. Then I drove down south to Norcia to lunch at Cantina de Norsia. And I saw my old friend Mirko at his new digs at the trendy Caffè Accademia.

COCKTAILS, DINNER, AND MUSIC IN CITTÀ DI CASTELLO

Before Mirko came to Caffè Accademia, he and his friend Patrizio owned Gildo, a restaurant in the remote hills above Umbertide. When the rent went up, they closed. Its remote location would have killed Gildo in the States (and it didn't help there), but from my country apartment it was convenient—just a five- or ten-minute drive up Monte Acuto. It had a large patio with pastoral views, a good wine list, ancient stone walls, modern furnishings, and a wood-burning pizza oven with a *pizzaiolo* who tossed pizza dough in the air. But best of all, there was Mirko. Young, fit, good-looking. Light brown hair, medium height, charming, with an engaging, ever-present smile.

Mirko waited tables and greeted guests, but he was also a chef. He had worked in prestigious European restaurants, and he had taught Italian cooking in Japan. But he enjoyed the front of the house—greeting people, chatting, explaining the menu, and speaking to tourists in nearly perfect English. On the counter at the bar, he kept a current copy of Gambero Rosso's Italian wine guide—he was always ready with an interesting wine recommendation. On his days off, he drove miles into the countryside to buy handcrafted cheese from a small artisan cheese maker or he studied and tasted wine. He made the small country restaurant a special place.

Patrizio did the cooking. One afternoon when I was in the kitchen watching Patrizio make ravioli, a salesman let himself in. Patrizio was annoyed. He didn't want to see the guy. So while he kept the salesman waiting, he cracked jokes in English at the expense of the man hanging around outside the door. The vendor wasn't discouraged—Patrizio finally gave up and met with him. Patrizio is young, lively, and friendly, with a wry sense of humor and a passion for cooking.

With the closing of Gildo, Patrizio landed a job as a chef in Sansepolcro (in nearby Tuscany). Mirko joined Caffè Accademia with the hope of luring Patrizio back. When Mirko started at Caffè Accademia, the *osteria* served aperitifs and beverages to an evening crowd. But with Mirko's arrival, there is a bigger focus on food—and there's live music. The Accademia doesn't lack for traffic—it's located in the busy historic center of Città di Castello, with easy access to a large parking lot just beyond the town's walls. The restaurant is under a bell tower behind the Duomo (cathedral), in one of the most ancient buildings in Umbria. During good weather, patrons can sit at tables and chairs out front, but eating inside is also a treat. Stone walls and ancient arched stone-and-brick ceilings surround the modern, stylish furnishings. The restaurant is divided into several rooms, each with limited seating. As you enter, there is a small seating area near a crackling fireplace. To the left is a small, chic room for tea and cocktails. Then straight ahead is the bar, with a few tables. And beyond is the main room, with about thirty seats. A narrow stairway leads to a romantic loft with four small candlelit tables.

Mirko plans the menu, orders the food, works out front, and does some of the cooking. The night I arrived to meet him, after not seeing him for a few years, he kissed me on both cheeks, gave me a tour, and told me that I had full run of the place. Then he took me to the kitchen to meet the chef, Paola. He apologized for taking leave, but he had papers to sign to become a partner in the business.

Paola had just added water to a mountain of flour on a well-worn wooden board. She was making rolls and focaccia for dinner. A pot of mushrooms simmered on the stove—their perfume filled the air. The bar had just opened, and someone turned up the volume of a jazz album—the singer's name I couldn't recall. Paola now had to juggle between making bar appetizers and prepping for dinner. When the bartender, a young man with moussed strawberry blond hair and a bright pink shirt, passed an order to Paola, she put the immersion blender down to fill it.

For the first order, she toasted thin slices of bread and spread a thick layer of herbed ricotta over the crostini. Then she cut each slice of bread into small squares and garnished each with a bit of anchovy and chopped parsley. For another, she filled tiny dinner rolls with salami and mixed baby greens. Then back to what she had started—a radicchio timbale. She had already sautéed a large head of chopped radicchio in olive oil until it was tender and had added a liter of fresh cream, a cup or so of grated Parmigiano-Reggiano, and about ten eggs. With the immersion blender, she finely processed the mixture, and then spooned it into small buttered baking cups to bake.

Next she tackled the cookies—*i fagottini,* small turnovers filled with jam. By now the bread dough had risen, so she stretched some of the dough out in a pan, dimpling the oil-drenched dough with her fingers to make *focaccia all'olio.* With the rest of the dough, she made three kinds of dinner rolls—sesame seed, poppy seed, and black olive with walnuts—oh, the heady aroma of the baking bread.

By the time the rolls were done, the dinner crowd was streaming in—and so were the food orders. Fortunately, Paola's assistant had just put on her apron and was ready to work. A few minutes later, I joined my friends in the dining room—they had already ordered and were eating the just-baked focaccia. I ordered the house antipasto with the radicchio *sformatino* that I had watched Paola make. It was rich, cheesy, and not bitter. The plate included barley salad, a couple slices of mortadella and prosciutto, and two kinds of cheese. Next I had *strangozzi* (eggless pasta) with tomatoes, sausage, and Gorgonzola cheese. Rich and yummy. Then for my *secondo piatto,* I asked for *tagliata, alpena al sangue* (sliced steak, medium-rare). And yes, I ate dessert. A tasting plate that included *fagottini,* jam tart, sponge cake with pastry cream, and crème brûlée.

While we drank our espressos, a small band of musicians was setting up. By eleven o'clock, when we said *buona notte* to Mirko and the gang, the place was packed, and the young crowd were tapping their feet and swaying to the music. But I was crashing. Feeling fatigued and drugged from overeating, I wished that Mirko still owned Gildo on Monte Acuto—I'd be home in five minutes, instead of forty-five.

DINING OUT

In Umbria, most restaurants serve pretty good food, even in the most out-of-the-way, hole-in-the-wall places. Up until somewhat recently, patrons demanded traditional dishes, but now trendy restaurants that offer *cucina nuova* are enjoying popularity. They're popping up in small villages, along country roads, and in cities. During the summer months, most restaurants have an outdoor dining room, often with magnificent views.

Hours: Bars offer the kind of breakfast most Italians eat—a *cornetto* (an Italian croissant) or sweet roll and cappuccino or caffè latte. Hotels often serve a buffet—cakes, sweet rolls, cereal, yogurt, ham, salami, bread, fruit, juice, espresso drinks—but American ham-and-egg breakfasts are rare.

Unless you are in a big city or a tourist area, where you find restaurants open at all hours, lunch is typically served from about 12:30 to 2:30 p.m. They reopen for dinner around 8:00 p.m. and stop service around 9:30. It can be difficult to find a place to eat at off hours. Many restaurants are closed (*chiuso*) one day a week—and the day can be any day from Monday to Sunday. Many close for several weeks in July or August for vacation, while others close for a month during the winter. And some hang a sign on the door at any time of the year, *chiuso per ferie* (closed for vacation).

Types of Restaurant: Dining choices range from moderately priced to expensive *ristoranti* to the less-expensive family-run *trattorie*. *Trattorie* often have fewer menu choices—and often no printed menu at all, so you'll need to listen carefully when the waiter rattles off the day's dishes. The traditional *osteria,* with a focus on wine, is usually open long after the dinner hour. In the past, *osterie* were known for being good value, but today some expensive restaurants have adopted the name. The pizzeria, another inexpensive choice, typically stays open late and offers a full menu—not just pizza. In fact, most serve pizza only at night. For snacks and drinks, stop at a bar or where you see a sign for *pizza a taglio* (by the slice). My favorite refreshment (and bathroom) stop along the highway is the Autogrill. The largest Autogrills span overhead and across all lanes of the tollway, serving travelers on both sides of the road. The restaurant/bar/store offers espresso drinks, sandwiches, pizza, pasta, and full meals. Shelves and cases display prosciutto, Parmigiano-Reggiano cheese, pasta, wine, sodas, toys, DVDs, and books, to name a few items from the amazing array of goods for sale.

Make a Reservation: It's a good idea to make a reservation, especially before driving miles out of town to a remote restaurant. *Vorrei fare una prenatazione per sei persone, per favore* (I would like to make a reservation for six people). Without a reservation, say, *Avete un tavolo* (Do you have a table)? *Siamo in sei* (There are six of us)—hold up your fingers if you don't know Italian numbers. *Vicino la finestra* (near the window). *All'alperto* (outside).

What to Order: Steer clear of *il menu turistico* (the tourist menu). Instead ask for recommendations and local and house specialties. *Qual è la specialità della casa* (What is the specialty of the house)? *Quale sono i piatti locali tipici* (What are the typical local dishes)? *Cosa ci consiglia* (What do you suggest)? Good, local wines are usually reasonably priced, so ask for *la carta dei vini* rather than ordering ho-hum house wine in a carafe. Most restaurants allow you to order just one or two courses, but in some tourist towns you might not be seated unless you agree to order a full meal—from appetizers to pasta to meat.

Paying the Bill: Unless you are in a touristy place, you probably won't be given the bill until you ask for it—they don't want to rush you. Even after asking for *il conto, per favore,* be prepared to wait a half hour or more to receive it. Be ready to pay with cash just in case the restaurant doesn't accept credit cards (although most do) or the credit card computer is out of order.

In restaurants, expect to be charged a fee for *pane e coperto* (bread and the table setting). The amount is usually stated on the menu. According to my food historian friend Adriano, this ancient custom dates back to a time when people brought their own food to the *taverne*. The restaurant charged the guests for the wine they drank, and tacked on *un coperto* to cover the bread eaten and napkin and utensils used.

The price of the meal usually includes service (indicated by *servizio incluso* or *servizio compreso* on the menu), which in theory means you don't need to leave *una mancia* (tip). Yet Adriano says many waiters expect you to leave whatever change is left after paying the bill. If you spent ninety-five euros and you paid with a hundred-euro bill, you'd leave the five on the table. The fancier the place, the more likely the wait staff will expect a tip. *La mancia* is not obligatory, but a small tip—a few euros—is always welcome.

BRESAOLA

This air-dried beef called *bresaola* is similar to prosciutto, which is air-dried pork. Bresaola comes from northern Italy, but *bresaola con rucola* (with arugula) is popular in Umbria's restaurants.

In the United States, look for *bresaola* in gourmet or Italian delis—it won't be Italian, but what I have found has been almost as good. When ordering, ask to see the first slice, specifying that you don't want it paper-thin. Ultrathin slices are too hard to handle. *Bresaola* is at its peak the day it is sliced, but it will hold several days in the refrigerator.

Air-Dried Beef with Arugula

Bresaola con rucola

Patrizio's rendition of this dish is unique. He covers the mound of arugula with thin slices of bresaola so all the greens are hidden. Although I appreciate his creativity, I always put the rucola *on top. When my brother Warren came to visit me in Umbria, he liked this salad so much that we ate it almost every night for two weeks. And I still love it!*

There are no substitutes for the ingredients—bresaola, Parmigiano-Reggiano cheese, good quality olive oil, fresh lemon juice, and arugula. It is these simple but high-quality ingredients that make this dish squisito. *Many grocery stores now sell arugula in bags or in bulk, and it is often sold at farmers' markets. When buying arugula, look for tender small leaves with jagged edges.*

This is one of those recipes where you "use your eyes" as Italian cooks do to decide how much of each ingredient to use. In restaurants, the salad usually arrives at the table with a wedge of lemon, a bottle of extra virgin olive oil, and a salt shaker—you dress the salad yourself.

Increase the ingredients according to the number of servings you need.

Yield: 1 serving

1 to 1½ ounces thinly sliced *bresaola* (not paper-thin or it will tear apart)

¾ to 1 cup lightly packed baby arugula, stems removed

Wedge of Parmigiano-Reggiano cheese (see Note, below)

Kosher salt

Freshly ground pepper

About ¼ medium lemon

½ to 1 tablespoon extra virgin olive oil

1. Loosely fold the individual *bresaola* slices into halves and curl each to form a loose "rose." Arrange the "roses" on a plate (or on a platter, if serving a crowd). At this point, you can cover and refrigerate the dish until serving time.

2. Shortly before serving, top the *bresaola* with the arugula. Use a vegetable peeler to shave thin "leaves" of cheese (the equivalent of a small handful) over the salad. Season lightly with the kosher salt and pepper; squeeze the lemon over the salad and drizzle with the oil. Do not toss—it is a composed salad.

NOTE: You need a wedge of cheese to make shavings. Allow ¼ to ½ ounce of cheese per serving. ❧

AT THE BAR

Bars are everywhere—in piazzas (town squares), gas stations, neighborhoods, parks, and on busy street corners. But unlike American bars, Italian bars are for people of all ages—the focus is not alcoholic beverages. Teens stop at the bar before school for coffee. Moms take their toddlers there for an afternoon snack. And the same group of retired men can be seen every day sitting outside the bar in the historic downtown piazza playing cards.

At all hours of the day, there is something for everyone at the bar. In the morning, it's the place for reasonably priced caffè latte (if you order a "latte," you'll get a glass of milk) or cappuccino with a *cornetto,* an Italian croissant. For kids, there's hot chocolate (as thick as syrup) or *cappuccino d'orzo* (made from barley, not coffee). Mid-morning (or afternoon) is the time for *caffè corretto*—espresso laced with liquor, usually sambuca or grappa. At lunch there are sandwiches, sodas, and *aqua frizzante*—if you want to avoid looking like a tourist, skip the cappuccino or caffè latte at lunch. And in the afternoon, there are aperitifs, beer, wine, gelato, or espresso served in a tiny cup filled half full. Drinking cappuccino is tolerated late in the day, but ordering *caffè macchiato* (espresso with a splash of milk) is more Italian. If you simply order *macchiato* (without the modifier *caffè*), you might be served a *latte macchiato* (hot milk with a bit of espresso).

At most bars, you pay first and pick up your order second, so you'll need to look around before you go to the cashier. There's pretty much no such thing as coffee-to-go. Instead people stand at the counter, hand the *barista* their receipt, gulp down what they ordered, and leave within minutes. In fact, some bars charge more if you sit, and even more if you choose a table outside. Underage? What's that? Unless you're a babe in arms, you can usually order what you want.

And when you pay or get up to go, if you leave some small change you'll make the *barista* happy (although many locals never tip).

Mini Jam Turnovers
Fagottini di ricotta
❧

At Caffè Accademia, Paola served i fagottini (the little bundles) as part of a dessert sampler that included an espresso cup filled with crème brûlée, a wedge of jam tart, and a cake filled with pastry cream.

"I don't know how old this recipe is," she told me. "Un'anziana [an elderly woman] gave it to me and I've been making it for many, many years." Whether the recipe's origins are Umbrian or not, these marvelous cookies disappear quickly. You might plan on doubling the recipe.

The recipe directions, which detail how to make perfect triangular turn-

overs, are actually simple. I use a ruler to measure the rolled dough and then make the turnovers in a production line. Before I developed this system, I haphazardly rolled and cut the dough, ending up with irregularly shaped turnovers, lots of scraps, and only a few turnovers each time I rolled out a piece of dough. Cleanup is easier if you line the baking sheets with parchment paper.

Yield: 30 to 32 (3-inch) turnovers

8 ounces ricotta cheese

2 cups (9 ounces) all-purpose flour plus more for rolling

1 teaspoon double-acting baking powder

1/2 teaspoon kosher salt (*important:* see "About Salt," page xxv)

6 ounces butter, softened (3/4 cup or 1 1/2 cubes)

1/3 to 1/2 cup seedless blackberry, raspberry, or other seedless fruit jam

1/2 cup unsifted powdered sugar

You'll also need: Parchment paper. A zigzag pastry cutter and a clean ruler are helpful.

Getting started: Put a damp towel under a lightly floured large wooden board to prevent slipping.

1. If the ricotta is soupy, drain it in a sieve for 5 minutes. Put the flour, baking powder, and kosher salt into a medium bowl; toss with a fork. Add the ricotta and butter; stir with a mixer or fork until well mixed. Shape the dough into a ball and transfer the dough to the floured board. (If mixing with a fork, before making a ball knead the dough on the board until the ingredients are well blended and the dough holds together, 30 to 60 seconds.)

2. Divide the dough into 4 equal pieces. Shape each piece into a 3/4-inch-thick rectangle; individually wrap in plastic wrap. Chill the dough until firm, 2 to 3 hours (the dough must be well chilled or it is difficult to work with).

3. Arrange a rack in the middle of the oven; preheat the oven to 375°F. Line a large baking sheet with parchment paper. Roll one piece of dough at a time

into a ⅛-inch-thick rectangle about 8 by 10 inches (if too thick, the turnovers split during baking). Use a zigzag pastry cutter or a knife to cut the rectangle into a tidy 6×9-inch rectangle. Cut the rectangle in half lengthwise, then cut crosswise every 3 inches (to make six 3-inch squares). Wrap and chill the scraps.

4. Put about ½ teaspoon of the jam in the center of each square; fold to form a triangle. Dip the back of a fork into flour and press around the edges with the tines to seal the turnovers. Put the turnovers about ¼ inch apart on the paper-lined baking sheet (bake as soon as the pan is full—see step 5). Continue rolling out the dough and shaping the cookies. Knead and re-roll the scraps of dough (chill if needed) to make the rest of the turnovers.

5. Bake the turnovers until lightly browned, about 15 minutes. Cool on a wire rack; sift the powdered sugar over the tops.

NOTE: When completely cool, the turnovers can be stored in an airtight container for several days (but I've never managed to keep any that long). ❧

PIZZA IN ITALY

On my first trip to Italy, a pizzeria's sign for wood-oven pizza ("the best and most authentic") drew me in—inside I discovered that the lunch menu didn't include pizza! For lunch (as well as dinner), the restaurant offered the usual antipasti, pasta dishes, and meat and side dishes— they fired up their oven only at night. But most pizzerias that sell *pizza al taglio* (pizza by the slice) offer it all day. Sometimes pizza by the slice has a thin crust and a round shape, but usually *pizza al taglio* has a thick crust, and it is baked in huge rectangular pans. Slices are usually sold by weight rather than the slice. Whatever kind of pizza you buy in Umbria, toppings tend to be minimal—from the traditional *margherita* to the creative *caprese,* named after the salad. *Pizza rossa* has tomato sauce, while *pizza bianca* has no sauce.

MY FAVORITE SOUVENIRS

There are many great food souvenirs to bring back from Umbria. But don't be tempted to bring back meat. An acquaintance brought a suitcase filled with forbidden Italian cured meats—*bresaola,* salami, prosciutto—through U.S. customs. Her bags were examined, the meat was confiscated, and she was fined. It was an absolutely horrible experience, she told me. Check the U.S. Customs website before leaving to see what is and isn't allowed into the States—rules can change. The lists that follow include my favorite souvenirs—for more information, refer to Resources, page 351.

FROM GROCERY OR GOURMET STORES

- *Lenticchie:* Lentils, from Castelluccio (the best) or Colfiorito.

- *Cicerchie:* Dried chickling peas.

- Farro: Also called emmer wheat. *Semiperlata* (pearl), crushed, or whole.

- *Funghi porcini:* Dried porcini mushrooms.

- *Perugina Baci:* Chocolate kisses with hazelnuts, from Perugia. The big *Baci* come with a fortune.

- *Tartufi:* Truffles. Jars of sauce, whole and dehydrated, or in jars—"precious white" (*bianco pregiato*) are the best.

- *Zafferano:* Saffron. You will probably find the best saffron at the source, in Cascia or Città della Pieve. Buy pure red whole threads, not powder.

- *Vinsanto:* Dessert "holy" wine. If you're willing to pack it tightly in your suitcase.

- *Olio di oliva extravirgine:* Extra virgin olive oil. In November or early December, just pressed *olio nuovo* is worth lugging. Again, wrap and protect it well before packing it (don't blame me if it breaks).

- *Pecorino staginato*: Aged pecorino cheese. Look for vacuum-sealed packages, or bring back a whole wheel.

- *Roveja*: A small brownish-green wild pea. Sold dried or as polenta.

- *Pasta di farro*: Dry pasta made from farro.

- *La fagiolina del Trasimeno*: A tiny dry bean from around Lake Trasimeno.

From Artisans, Kitchen Shops, and Weekly Markets

- Honey: Ask locals where to buy *miele* directly from *un apicoltore* (beekeeper).

- Hand-painted ceramics: Deruta is a city devoted to ceramics, with a history that goes back to the 1200s. Other cities known for ceramics include Gubbio, Orvieto, and Gualdo Tadino, but most Umbrian towns sell them. Shipping is available.

- Olive-wood products: Cutting boards, mortar and pestle, bread cutting boards, pepper mills, bowls, spoons, and more.

- Iron: Fireplace tools, wall sconces, bed frames. Some artisans exhibit at festivals, in Gubbio and Montone, for example.

- Linens: Beautiful woven fabrics with ancient designs. Visit Tessuto Artistico Umbro Montefalco (Piazza del Comune Palazzo Nanni, Montefalco) and Sposini Tessuti Umbri (near Perugia)

- Espresso pots: All sizes and styles, from classic to modern.

- Espresso cups: From the expensive Illy brand to cheap.

- Espresso spoons: These tiny spoons make great gifts. Or buy them by the dozen to use as tasting spoons.

- Milk frother: A stainless-steel pot with a mesh plunger that works well as long as the milk is piping hot.

LUNCH ON POLVESE ISLAND

Lake Trasimeno, in western Umbria near the Tuscan border, is the region's largest lake. There are three islands in the lake. Isola Polvese is the largest. Isola Maggiore, a centuries-old fishing village, is the second-largest, and the privately owned Isola Minore is the smallest. Isola Polvese is part of the Trasimeno Regional Park—it's a fun place to spend the day or even stay the night.

My son, Jacob, who was visiting, was eager to hike and swim, so one day in June we drove to San Feliciano near Magione to take the ferry to Isola Polvese. That morning, we hiked around the island, past the ruins of a castle, and we stopped to visit one of the island's churches and the water gardens. Around one o'clock, we returned to La Villa, a hotel with a restaurant near the ferry landing. We asked for an outside table with views of the lake. We were in grubby hiking clothes, carrying backpacks, but you'd never have guessed that we were at an outdoor recreation area by how nicely dressed the host and waitstaff were. Our waiter wore black dress pants and a starched white dress shirt with a tie—only in Italy! The tables were set with clean, crisp white tablecloths and red underskirts. The menu featured regional food—not just sandwiches and drinks as we had expected.

For an antipasto I ordered *bruschette Umbre*—toasted bread with three different toppings. Jacob had *l'insalata di luccio*—cold poached lake perch seasoned with garlic, parsley, lemon juice, and lots of olive. The side of the tiny white bean grown around Lake Trasimeno—*la fagiolina*—was plain: dress the beans with olive oil, the waiter advised. For a second course, I had *regina in porchetta* (queen carp), which I had read about, but not tasted.

In porchetta refers to any number of dishes, from rabbit to fish, prepared in the style of *porchetta,* a whole roasted pig seasoned with fennel. After a leisurely lunch with wine—and excellent service—we headed to the beach for a nap and a late swim.

Here is my rendition of the simple but tasty fish dish. Since carp isn't available, I recommend swordfish, but Pacific sea bass or halibut are good choices. Garlic lentils, roasted potatoes, and braised chard are good accompaniments. If you are lucky enough to have a bag of *la fagiolina,* these tiny little beans would be perfect (see *La fagiolina del Trasimeno,* page 222).

Fish with Fennel

Pesce in porchetta

Preheat the oven to 450°F. For 4 servings: Arrange 4 swordfish steaks (¾ to 1 inch thick, 6 ounces each) in a shallow nonreactive baking pan (such as stainless steel or glass). Grind 1 teaspoon of fennel seeds with a mortar and pestle. Pull the needles off two (5-inch) sprigs rosemary; finely chop the needles. Season the fish in the following manner (per side): (1) squeeze a half lemon over the fish, (2) season as desired with kosher salt and pepper, (3) sprinkle with half of the fennel and rosemary, (4) drizzle with 2 tablespoons of extra virgin olive oil. Rub the seasonings in with the back of a spoon. Turn the steaks over and season the other side. Marinate for 5 minutes. Bake uncovered until just done (no longer opaque in the middle), about 10 minutes. Drizzle the pan drippings over the fish and drizzle with additional olive oil, to taste. Serve with lemon wedges. ❧

LA FAGIOLINA DEL TRASIMENO

This once-popular dry bean, not much larger than a plump grain of rice, is making a comeback after almost dying out in the 1800s. Up until then the beans had been a traditional food around Lake Trasimeno, where *la fagiolina* has grown for eons—since the Etruscans! The beans are usually cream colored, but some farmers grow dark beans. To cook *la fagiolina*, simmer the beans (without soaking) in water with sautéed diced carrot, celery, onion, and garlic until tender, 45 to 60 minutes. Season the beans with salt, pepper, and plenty of extra virgin olive oil.

ALTA CUCINA—HAUTE CUISINE

Il Postale in Città di Castello is one of Umbria's hottest restaurants, and the owner, Marco Bistarelli, is one of the region's most-talked-about chefs. For more than a dozen years, he has been a member of Europe's exclusive

Jeunes (young) Restaurateurs. Marco's father used to have a pizzeria in town—that's what inspired Marco to open his own place.

"But it was my sister who found the building," said Marco. "She saw the sign go up, so she came to the restaurant where I worked. She told me to come immediately. I closed up with customers inside! Five minutes later, I told the owner I would take the place. I signed a contract the next day."

That was back in the late nineties. Since then, Marco, his wife, Barbara, and his sister and her husband have worked together to create what has become a popular restaurant.

While I waited to see Marco, I sat in Il Postale's espresso bar on a modern leather love seat, drinking caffè with my feet on a handsome Persian rug. A ceramic Japanese "beckoning cat," with one paw raised, stared at me from the counter. When Marco arrived, I followed him past a frosted glass-brick wall into the dining room. I felt as though I had been transported from Umbria to San Francisco in that nanosecond. The wooden trusses and dark wood ceiling were unlike anything I had seen in Umbria. Modern lights dangled above each table from wires that traversed the room. The mood, even at that mid-morning hour, was romantic, elegant, and contemporary. The furniture was made of glass and black lacquer—and many details had an Asian flair. The artwork that hung on peach-colored walls was abstract— except for a large painting of an antique bus.

"I named the restaurant after that bus," said Marco, referring to the painting. "In the nineteen thirties, the building was an old bus garage. The bus called *Il Postale* was the first vehicle in town to transport both people and mail."

"The building looks modern," I said. "When was it built?"

"The trusses and square-end bolts suggest the ceiling was built in the seventeen hundreds, but the building itself dates back to the nineteen thirties."

In the kitchen, Marco introduced me to the five young men prepping. The pastry chef was kneading dough.

"Today I am making five kinds of bread," he said. "Tomato, rosemary, fennel, onion, and semolina."

"You're lazy today," said Marco, laughing. "You usually make six."

While the bread dough was rising, the chef cracked a dozen eggs to make chocolate cream. Next he wrapped narrow strips of dough around tiny metal cones—when baked, these crisp pastries would hold the chocolate cream.

At another table, a cook was stuffing tiny squab legs with liver and truffles and then wrapping them in caul fat—a lacy mesh of pork fat. On a nearby counter, a chef was using tweezers to pluck feathers from a pile of small ducks. A blast of flame from a blowtorch finished the cleaning. The whole legs would be seasoned with wild fennel, rolled and tied, and cooked slowly for ten hours under extra virgin olive oil.

Marco was piping filling onto rounds of fresh pasta to make *tortelli*—a hat-shaped filled pasta. "Our pasta dough is really yellow because we use sixty percent egg yolks and forty percent egg whites," he said.

"Well, egg yolks in Umbria are bright orange, too," I said. "Ours are much less vivid."

That January day, he was making two kinds of *tortelli*—*fonduta* cheese and guinea fowl. To make the *fonduta,* Marco had heated Fontina Val d'Aosta with milk in a bain-marie for a couple of hours.

"It must be very creamy," Marco said. Then he chilled the *fonduta* so it would be easy to pipe.

The *tortelli* pasta, filled with guinea fowl, was tinted pink with beets. To make the filling, he sautéed *faraona* (guinea fowl) with garlic, thyme, carrots, onion, and celery, and he stirred in a rich wine-cognac reduction broth. Finally he ground the mixture.

Shortly after one o'clock, Marco invited me to lunch. Within minutes of sitting, I was nibbling on a warm tomato roll that I had seen being made. The basket held a sampling of rolls, homemade crackers, and bread sticks. The menu shows Marco's flair for using traditional foods—squab, pork, rabbit, duck, fennel, gnocchi, saffron, potatoes—in creative and innovative ways. Onion risotto with foie gras and chocolate, and scampi carpaccio are two examples. Everything on the menu sounded delicious.

"What do you recommend?" I asked Marco.

"Everyone comes for *piccione*," he said. "People say it's the best in Italy."

So I ordered squab, with *tortelli* for a *primo piatto.* The *tortelli,* swimming in butter and garnished with extra virgin olive oil and shaved white truffles, were divine. When I cut into the squab, and saw how rare it was, I expected not to like it. But after a few bites I was convinced it *was* the best *piccione* in Italy—maybe in the world! The roasted breast was stacked on top of a bed of crisp vegetables—carrots, asparagus, red onion, zucchini, cabbage, and broccoli. A thin slice of liver was hidden under the breast. Rich pan drippings were drizzled around the plate. It looked so simple, but the flavors were exquisite and complex.

When I met with Marco, he told me his goal in opening Il Postale had been to pursue *alta cucina* (haute cuisine) but at the same time honor tradition—and serve only the best. I wonder what he'll do next. He has already reached, if not exceeded, these goals.

Scallops with Tomato Fennel Confit

Potacchio di cappesante

∞

The name potacchio *comes from the neighboring Marche region. It refers to simmering meat or fish in tomatoes with aged* guanciale *(pancetta made from pork cheeks), garlic, black pepper, and wild fennel. I have substituted commercial fennel seeds for the wild seeds—and the dish is just as delicious. The seeds need to be coarsely ground to bring out the flavor—a mortar and pestle or a heavy glass work perfectly. Marco garnishes the scallops with sprigs of fresh fennel, but chopped parsley also makes a good garnish.*

The pancetta-wrapped scallops are rich and filling, so two scallops make an ample serving—especially when preceded by pasta or soup and served with side dishes, such as bread and roasted vegetables, potatoes, artichokes, cauliflower.

Yield: 4 servings

2 medium Roma tomatoes (about 9 ounces)

½ basket cherry tomatoes (6 ounces)

10 thin slices pancetta (see "Pancetta versus Bacon," page 9; and Note, page 226)

8 large day-boat or Eastern (USA) sea scallops (1 to 1⅓ pounds)

Kosher salt

Freshly ground pepper

2 tablespoons extra virgin olive oil plus more if needed

1 large garlic clove, lightly crushed with a knife blade, and peeled

½ teaspoon fennel seeds, hand ground

You'll also need: A mortar and pestle or a heavy glass to grind the fennel seeds.

1. Grate the Roma tomatoes (see "How to Grate Tomatoes," page 34). Cut the cherry tomatoes into quarters. Put the cherry and grated tomatoes into a

bowl; set aside. Dice 2 slices of the pancetta; set aside. If the pancetta slices are coiled, unroll the rest of them to form strips.

2. Cut off the tough muscles on the side of the scallops, if needed; pat the scallops dry with paper towels. Season the scallops lightly with the salt and pepper. Wrap a strip of pancetta around each scallop, from top to bottom and around the sides; tuck in the end of the pancetta to hold it in place.

3. Heat a large, heavy skillet over medium heat. Swirl the 2 tablespoons of oil around the skillet. When the oil is hot, put 4 of the scallops into the skillet (put the "seam" down—where the pancetta is tucked in—so the heat seals it in place). Sauté, turning as needed to brown all sides, a total of 6 to 8 minutes for medium-rare or longer, to taste (don't overcook or the scallops become rubbery).

4. Transfer the scallops to a warm plate; cover with foil. Repeat with the 4 remaining scallops; transfer to the plate when done.

5. Reduce the heat to low; add a tablespoon of oil, if needed. Sauté the garlic in the skillet about 1 minute (do not brown). Add the reserved diced pancetta; sauté, stirring frequently, until almost browned. Add all of the tomatoes; sauté over medium heat, stirring frequently, until creamy and soft, 8 to 10 minutes. Stir in the fennel; simmer 1 minute. Season with salt to taste. To serve, spoon the sauce onto a platter or plates; top with the scallops, two per serving. Garnish with freshly ground pepper (and with a sprig of fresh fennel like Marco does).

NOTE: If you substitute bacon for pancetta, you will need to drain all but a couple tablespoons of the fat in the skillet at the end of step 4 and again in step 5 after cooking the diced bacon (before adding the tomatoes). ❧

DINING IN CANNARA, WHERE THE ONION IS KING

Cannara is Umbria's onion capital, but the town's bulbs are famous throughout Italy. In these southern Umbrian flatlands, *contadini* have cultivated onions in and around the town for several centuries—some say as early as the 1300s. Farmers claim the growing conditions, the soil (sandy clay, but porous and well-draining), and the abundance of water (the Topino River borders the town) make the area ideal for onions. The round, delicate, sweet, more digestible red variety is the onion Cannara is known for, but growers also produce round yellow onions and a flat yellow onion (*la cipolla piatta*). Just after harvest, farmers sell their onions in long, beautiful braids—the traditional method for bundling them, for ease of use and to help conserve them.

Since onions are the major crop in the area, cooks feature onions prominently in dozens of dishes. I went to Perbacco, a restaurant in downtown Cannara, to learn some of the town's specialties. Ernesto, the owner, introduced me to his twenty-three-year-old chef, Elisa—I spent the afternoon and evening in the kitchen with her. In addition to five years of culinary school, she had already worked in two other restaurants before coming to Perbacco. The Italian school system jump-starts people in trade careers much earlier than our schools do.

"Have you seen the onion fields?" she asked.

I told her I hadn't.

"Well, then, we must go to my uncle's," she announced.

Her *zio*, who grows onions, shallots, and garlic, has fields just minutes outside the town. The valley—Valle Umbra—around Cannara is wide and expansive. That June day, the landscape was divided between never-ending fields of blooming waist-high onions and an endless blue sky with puffs of clouds. Near her uncle's house, Elisa uprooted a red onion. "*La cipolla rossa* from Cannara is a vivid purple inside and out," she said, showing me the dirt-covered bulb. "The onions stain your hands when you cook with them."

Although Elisa would be alone in the kitchen that evening, she was in no rush to get back to the restaurant—she was calm and confident. On weekends and other busy times, Elisa has an assistant who prepares the antipasto plates and side dishes, and she also makes fresh pasta, ravioli, and gnocchi. Ernesto's mother makes the desserts.

Once we returned from the onion field, Elisa had just a couple hours to go before the *ristorante* opened for dinner, so she picked up her pace. She still managed to chat and answer my questions while she darted around, stirring and chopping.

"Our menu is unique," she explained. "You won't find what we offer in other restaurants." Elisa serves up traditional Umbrian dishes, but the specialties of the house are based on Cannara's famed bulb—penne with onions and *guanciale, crostini di cipolla,* tagliatelle with onions and pine nuts, spaghetti with onions and anchovies, onion soup with cheese crostini.

"I'm going to make *zuppa di orzo e farro* [barley-farro soup]," said Elisa. "It's a recipe from antique times." She dumped several cups of pearl barley into a pot on the stove and covered the barley with water. About forty minutes later, she stirred in a couple cups of pearl farro. While the grains cooked, she diced several slices of pancetta, three large yellow potatoes, and three medium onions. In another pot, she sautéed the mixture in a thin layer of olive oil and then added diced carrots and celery, four of each. And finally, she poured cold water over the vegetables and added a bottle of *pomodori passati* (equal to a 28-ounce can of whole tomatoes, puréed).

"My grandmother never added tomatoes," she said, "but I like it better this way. The recipe is antique—much older than my grandmother. We've had the same cuisine in Umbria for three hundred years!" After the vegetables had simmered and turned into a flavorful broth, Elisa drained the grains and added them to the soup.

While the soup simmered, Elisa prepared potato cakes with roasted onions and a red onion timbale. To make the *sformato* (timbale), she simmered four large red onions in water with extra virgin olive oil. Water, so they don't burn, she explained. When the onions were tender, she added white wine, cooking to reduce it. Then she stirred in lots of fresh sheep's milk ricotta and grated Parmigiano-Reggiano with four egg yolks. And finally, she folded in the beaten egg whites just before baking the mixture in a hot water bath for half an hour. For the sauce, she heated heavy cream and grated Parmigiano-Reggiano, which she drizzled along with extra virgin olive oil over the top of the unmolded timbales.

"The timbale is better if you make it a day ahead—the onions are more mellow. I heat them in the microwave."

By the time the timbales were done, it was almost time for the restaurant to open.

"Elisa," called Ernesto from the dining room, "what are you making for the staff dinner?"

"*Spaghetti alla carbonara,*" she said. At that moment she dashed to the stove to toss the pancetta and onions sizzling in a huge skillet. She was just seconds away from adding the hot spaghetti, eggs, and cheese—then the *carbonara* would be ready.

Ernesto invited me to join the staff for *spaghetti alla carbonara*. *Quanto mi piace quel piatto* (How much I like that dish)! But first, Elisa plated an onion *sformato* for me. Cheesy, oniony, lovely, and delicious.

After dinner, I headed back to the kitchen to take photos and ask a few questions, but orders starting coming in. Elisa juggled—slicing salami for an antipasto dish, seasoning onions for a pasta dish, plating cookies for dessert.

"Elisa, I think I had better go," I said. "You need to concentrate."

"No, no. I never have company—it is so lonely. What else would you like to know how to make?"

So I stayed to watch her cook two more dishes—steak with herb sauce and roasted potatoes. Then I said good night and headed home. It was too dark to see the glorious onion fields, but a pleasant taste of onions still lingered in my mouth from dinner. I would look forward to buying braids of Cannara onions and going to Cannara's onion festival in September.

In Search of (the Best) Gelato

My favorite place to buy gelato is at *la gelateria*—the ice cream shop. (But bars and cafés often sell gelato, and so do grocery stores.) Unless you have an insider's tip, your best bet is to look for a sign in the shop stating the gelato is homemade—*produzione propria, nostra produzione, produzione artigianale*. Fruit gelato—*pesca, fragola, melone, limone* (peach, strawberry, cantaloupe, lemon)—should taste fresh and fruity. Chocolate, coffee, hazelnut—*cioccolato, caffè, nocciola*—and all the rest should be rich and full-flavored. If not, try another *gelateria* next time.

Before ordering, decide on *un gusto* (a flavor) or two, three, or four *gusti*, and whether to have *un cono* (a cone) or *una coppa* (a cup). Then place your order referring to the menu price—*due gusti, due euro*. For example, say, *Vorrei una coppa di gelato da due euro* (I would like a cup of gelato for two euros). Then tell what flavors you'd like—hand signs and pointing work! Pay for the gelato when you are served at the counter. Sitting at a table might cost more. But I have more fun eating gelato outside on the nearest bench or walking down a picturesque street. *Buon appetito!*

STUFFED IN NORCIA

I met Camillo, the owner of Cantina de Norsia, at the professional pizza-and-bread class I took in Perugia. He invited me to lunch at his restaurant in Norcia—one of the nine Umbrian towns included in a guidebook called *I borghi più belli d'Italia* (The Most Beautiful Villages in Italy). The *borgo* of about five thousand inhabitants isn't just about views and antiquity; Norcia is a walled town in southeastern Umbria that is renowned for food. Centuries ago the town's pig butchers became famous for their skills in pork production—from butchering to making cured pork such as prosciutto. When you walk around town, and you see the numerous butcher shops, you know you're in a place that adores pork. In Italian, the term for pork butcher—*norcino*—comes from the town's name. Norcia is also celebrated for black truffles, cheese, farro, honey, and the best lentils in all of Italy—*le lenticchie di Castelluccio*. So dining—and food shopping—in Norcia is always a pleasure (see "My Favorite Souvenirs," pages 219 to 220).

The Cantina is down a side street, rather than on the busy main drag or on the piazza. When I arrived, Camillo took me through the large outdoor dining room with heavy rustic wooden tables and chairs, past the small interior dining room, into the kitchen to meet his chef, Daniela. With one hand, she was stirring tomato sauce on the stove, and with the other hand, she was pouring lentils into a pot. Beside a smoking indoor grill stood a stack of zucchini slices ready to cook. Eggs sat next to a mound of flour on one of the two workspaces in the tiny kitchen. The calm Daniela greeted me, but quickly returned to work. In minutes she had transformed the eggs and flour into soft pasta dough. And not much later, she had rolled the dough out by hand and cut it into rustic tagliatelle. When Daniela had a breather, she began wiping the counters and cleaning up.

"Don't you have help?" I asked.

"Most days I have an assistant," she said, "but today is her day off."

Next she rinsed a colander filled with steaming farro under cold water. "If you don't rinse it, it sticks together."

Minutes later she was slicing green olives and tomatoes. "I am making farro salad for an antipasto plate," she said. "I'll serve it with roasted peppers and grilled vegetables. On a warm day like today, salad is more popular than pasta."

Next, Daniela drizzled a fragrant *torta di farro* (a buttery crust filled with farro custard) with *alchermes*, a fuchsia-colored liqueur.

"When I was young," said Daniela, "we didn't have farro, *cicerchie,* or *roveja* [emmer wheat, chickling peas, or wild legumes]." Now these ancient grains, again popular, filled Camillo's menu—and he sold bags of them to restaurant customers.

When I sat down to eat in the private patio, I discovered the portions were generous and the prices were reasonable—and Camillo was a very gracious waiter. He and a young busboy managed to keep up with the busy lunch crowd that arrived shortly after I sat down. The three-year-old restaurant's menu featured many local products and traditional dishes—bruschetta, crostini, local trout, lentil soup, farro soup, chicking pea soup, spaghetti made of farro.

To start, I ordered the salami plate—a lovely variety of flavors and textures, from mild to garlicky to spicy to moist to dry. Next, I had Daniela's antipasto plate with the farro salad, roasted peppers, and grilled zucchini with bread crumbs. When the tagliatelle with truffles—the restaurant's most popular dish—came, I didn't think I'd be able to eat it, but the earthy truffles were so irresistible that I ate the entire plate. I was really too full for dessert, but the *torta di farro* had so intrigued me that I asked for a sliver. The buttery crust was dark golden and crunchy, just how the Umbrians like it—a lovely contrast to the sweet, creamy, but chewy farro interior. Interesting. It could become addictive.

On the way out, I paid Camillo for the bags of lentils, farro, and *roveja* that I selected from the restaurant's store. By the time I reached my car, I had bought salami at one of the butchers, and a package of farro spaghetti, a jar of truffles, and some pecorino cheese at a food shop. Fortunately, I made it past the copper vendors on the piazza without buying anything. What a wonderful thing—a town focused on selling local food products (let's hope they are all local!).

Grilled Zucchini with Bread Crumbs
Zucchini alla griglia
❧

Daniela's grilled zucchini dish is one of those enticing appetizers on display throughout the summer in many of Umbria's restaurants. The dish is easy to make at home—and practical when you have a bounty of zucchini in the garden.

According to Daniela, the secret to these vegetables is to make them a day ahead so the zucchini absorb the flavors of the garlic and herbs. Cooking the squash on the grill gives it a light smoky flavor, but when the weather is bad I use a stovetop griddle with almost equal results. If you don't have homemade bread crumbs, make the dish without bread crumbs—powder-fine commercial crumbs won't do. Daniela uses the same bread crumb mixture on roasted red peppers and roasted tomatoes.

Yield: 6 servings

2 medium-small garlic cloves, peeled and halved

1 cup lightly packed fresh basil leaves

1 cup lightly packed fresh Italian parsley

⅓ cup homemade dry bread crumbs (see "How to Make Bread Crumbs," page 16)

4 medium zucchini (2 pounds total)

Extra virgin olive oil

Kosher salt

Freshly ground pepper

GETTING STARTED: Start the charcoal in a barbecue or preheat a gas grill.

1. Put the garlic in the food processor; process until minced. Add the basil and parsley; pulse until minced. Transfer the mixture to a bowl. Stir in the bread crumbs; set aside. Slice the zucchini lengthwise into thin slices, less than ¼ inch thick.

2. Just before grilling, lightly brush both sides of the squash with the oil. Grill over a medium-hot fire, turning once or twice, until nicely browned and tender when pierced with a knife, 2 to 5 minutes.

3. Arrange a layer of zucchini slices in a large baking pan; season lightly with the salt and pepper. Sprinkle the zucchini with some of the herb-

crumb mixture. Continue layering and seasoning the zucchini in the same manner. At this point, the dish can be covered and refrigerated for up to 30 hours.

4. To serve, arrange a layer of zucchini (with the bread crumbs) on a platter; drizzle with the oil. Continue layering and drizzling with oil; let stand at room temperature about 10 minutes before serving (if chilled, let stand ½ hour).

On a Griddle

Follow the recipe instructions but substitute these instructions for step 2. Preheat a griddle on the stove over high heat; reduce the heat to medium-high when hot. In a small bowl, mix 3 tablespoons olive oil with ¼ cup cold water; just before cooking, brush both sides of the zucchini with the oil-water. Cook side by side in batches on the griddle, turning twice, until nicely speckled and tender when pierced with a knife, about 5 minutes. ᴈᴑ

Farro Salad with Tomatoes and Arugula
Insalata di farro
∞

During the summer in Umbria, farro salad appears in supermarket delis alongside other prepared foods—stuffed peppers, grilled eggplant, rice salad, seafood salads, pasta salad, and a variety of spreads for crostini. Insalata di farro, in various renditions, is also a popular restaurant dish.

I have eaten a simple farro salad embellished solely with arugula and Parmigiano-Reggiano. I've had farro salad made with everything the cook found nel frigo—red peppers, artichoke hearts, ham, cheese, peas, corn, zucchini, and carrots. But I am addicted to this chewy farro salad that Daniela makes with arugula, basil, tomatoes, and green olives. I am partial to cherry tomatoes, but like Daniela, you can use a large tomato cut into ½-inch dice. I have added lemon juice to the recipe (which Daniela does not use) because I prefer salads with a slightly acidic backdrop.

To slice the basil, stack the leaves neatly one on top of another. Slice the leaves crosswise into a chiffonade of thin slivers.

Yield: 6 to 8 servings (about 6 cups)

2 cups (12 to 13 ounces) semipearl farro or pearl barley

3½ teaspoons kosher salt (*important:* see "About Salt," page xxv)

8 ounces (30 to 40) tiny cherry tomatoes, preferably the Sweet 100
   variety

2 to 3 tablespoons fresh lemon juice

¼ teaspoon freshly ground pepper

¼ cup extra virgin olive oil

1 cup lightly packed baby arugula, thinly sliced or chopped

1 cup lightly packed fresh basil leaves, thinly sliced

1 cup sliced green or black olives (optional)

1. Rinse the farro; put it into a large saucepan. Add about 8 cups of cold water and 2 teaspoons of the kosher salt. Set the timer for 25 minutes. Bring the water to a boil. Immediately reduce the heat to low. Simmer gently, stirring occasionally, until the farro is *al dente*. (Taste test at 20 minutes—the farro or barley can take 35 to 45 minutes; consult the package.)

2. Drain the farro and rinse it well under cold water so that the grains do not stick together when cooled. Let the farro drain for about 5 minutes, shaking the colander occasionally to help remove excess water. Put the farro in a large bowl. At this point, the farro can be covered and refrigerated for several hours.

3. Shortly before serving, if the cherry tomatoes are on the larger side, cut them into halves or quarters; set aside. Sprinkle the farro with the 2 tablespoons of lemon juice, the pepper, and the remaining 1½ teaspoons kosher salt; toss to combine. Drizzle with the oil; stir. Add the tomatoes, arugula, and basil (if using olives, add them now); toss gently to combine. Stir in the remaining tablespoon lemon juice, if desired. Adjust the salt to taste. Serve chilled or at room temperature. 🍃

Farro or Emmer Wheat (but Never Spelt)

Farro is the Italian name for emmer wheat, *Triticum dicoccum*. In the States, farro is sometimes mistakenly translated as spelt, but spelt is a different kind of wheat. Cultivation of farro in Umbria dates back at least a couple thousand years to the Etruscans, but it was grown elsewhere in Europe possibly as far back as nine thousand years ago. This ancient grain, which had fallen out of favor in Umbria, is popular again.

As a whole grain, called pearl or semipearl, it is simmered in soups or made into salads. An old dessert recipe calls for *farro perlato*. To make the *crostata*, the cooked grain is mixed with eggs and cream and baked in a rich crust. Farro is also sold crushed, which makes the base of a traditional soup—*zuppa di farro*. And farro is ground into flour to make pasta. Farro's chewy texture, when cooked *al dente*, is reminiscent of pearl barley. If you cannot find farro at your Italian grocer or specialty store, barley makes an acceptable substitute.

Dessert at La Locanda del Capitano

This dish is inspired by the *pere al passito* (pears poached in dessert wine) that I ate at La Locanda del Capitano, an inn and restaurant in the heart of Montone. The daily newspaper *Corriere dell'Umbria* has rated it one of Umbria's top restaurants. The *locanda* (inn) has eight rooms with private baths and a lovely restaurant that serves good, creative food at moderately high prices. And it has an extensive wine list. In the summer, there is a beautiful garden for outside dining. During the fourteenth century, the handsome villa that houses the *ristorante* and inn was home to the famous military leader Braccio Fortebraccio.

The charming, well-preserved medieval hill town is a few miles north of Umbertide. A stone wall encloses several hundred ancient houses, a few shops and restaurants, three churches, a post office, a museum, a park, a piazza, a bar, and a *gelateria* that make up the quaint village. The panoramic views looking down into the valley are stupendous. Montone can be seen in less than half an hour, but staying for dinner or attending one of its festivals makes it well worth the trip.

At the restaurant, the pears were poached in *sagrantino passito* and served with Gorgonzola and bread. *Sagrantino passito,* an Umbrian dessert wine, is expensive and difficult to find in the States, so I use a good-quality dry Italian red wine instead and add sugar for sweetness. If you're lucky enough to find *passito,* drink it with the pears.

I dedicate these pears to my friend Michela, who adores them. The first time I served them, she ate the pear—and the core—saying she couldn't bear to leave anything. She was too polite to lick the plate.

Pears Poached in Sagrantino
Pere al sagrantino
ᏮᏮᏳ

Yield: 6 servings

1 medium lemon

1 medium orange

6 firm (but not hard) pears (about 6 ounces each)

½ cup sugar

¼ teaspoon kosher salt (*important:* see "About Salt," page xxv)

⅛ teaspoon ground cinnamon

1 cup sagrantino or good-quality dry Italian red wine

5 whole cloves

1. Use a vegetable peeler or a paring knife to cut the zest in strips from the entire lemon but just half of the orange. Cut the orange and lemon into halves; set aside the zest and the fruit.

2. Select a pot broad enough to hold all 6 pears standing upright and tall enough to be covered with a lid. Peel the pears, leaving the stems intact; stand the pears in the pot and immediately squeeze the orange and lemon over them. Sprinkle the sugar, kosher salt, and cinnamon over the pears. Add the wine; toss the cloves and the reserved zest into the pot.

3. Cover and simmer over medium heat until the pears are just tender when pierced with a knife, 20 to 30 minutes (depending on size and ripeness). Use a slotted spoon to transfer the pears to a serving dish that is large enough to lay the pears on their sides.

4. Boil the cooking liquid over medium-high heat, without stirring it, until it is slightly syrupy, about 5 minutes. Pour the sauce over the pears; turn and baste them occasionally until you serve them. To serve, plate the pears and drizzle with sauce. Serve chilled or at room temperature.

VARIATION: To serve the pears as they did at La Locanda del Capitano, cut the pears into halves and core them. Per serving, slice half of a pear and fan it out on one side of a plate. Put a wedge of Gorgonzola dolce (or your favorite blue cheese) and a slice of Italian or French bread on the other side. ❧

Scaloppine with Artichokes

Scaloppine con carciofi
❧

Several friends and I were in Città di Castello on a cold fall evening, looking for a place for an inexpensive dinner. We decided on Trattoria Pizzeria Roma, a busy, very simple neighborhood restaurant with reasonable prices. I ordered this scaloppine with artichokes braised in milk. The restaurant's modest interior didn't promise much—but the dish was delicious. If you use pork cutlets rather than loin, the dish is very economical at home, too. I serve it often to guests—everyone loves it.

This is a simple dish to make—don't be intimidated by the long instructions.

Yield: 4 main-dish servings (or 6 to 8 second-course servings)

3 large or 4 medium artichokes

Juice of 1 lemon for acidulated water

1½ pounds sliced (¼ to ⅜ inch thick) boneless pork cutlets or loin (at least 8 slices)

Extra virgin olive oil

Kosher salt

2 tablespoons water

$^1/_2$ cup all-purpose flour

2 or 3 garlic cloves, peeled

Freshly ground pepper

$^3/_4$ cup dry white wine, such as pinot grigio or sauvignon blanc

$1^1/_2$ cups whole milk

You'll also need: A flat-bottom meat pounder or a heavy glass to pound the meat and a heavy gallon-size plastic bag.

Getting started: Since the thin meat cooks very quickly, you will need to have all of the ingredients ready to go before you start to cook—and you will need to work fast once cooking begins.

1. Prepare the artichokes and hold them in the lemon water (see "How to Prepare Artichokes," page 240). One at a time, lay a pork cutlet flat inside a heavy plastic bag; put the bag on a cutting board. Pound the meat until it is about $^1/_8$ inch thick; cover and refrigerate.

2. Drain the artichoke halves; put them with the flat side down on a clean cutting board. Cut the artichokes lengthwise into thin slices (less than $^1/_4$ inch). Heat a large skillet over medium-high heat. Swirl 1 tablespoon of the oil around the skillet. Add the artichokes, $^1/_2$ teaspoon kosher salt, and the 2 tablespoons water; simmer without stirring until the water evaporates.

3. As soon as the water is gone, reduce the heat to medium and stir frequently until the artichokes are lightly browned and tender, 3 to 5 minutes total. Transfer to a plate. Keep the skillet handy.

4. Spread the flour out on a dinner plate. Just before cooking, dredge the pork, lightly coating each side in flour; shake off the excess. (You will sauté the pork in 2 or 3 batches, depending on the size of the skillet.) Heat the skillet over medium-high heat.

5. To cook the first batch of pork, swirl 2 tablespoons oil around the skillet and add 1 garlic clove. Sauté until the garlic begins to sizzle (do not brown). Arrange the pork slices side by side in the skillet without crowding; season one side with salt and pepper.

6. As soon as the pork is lightly browned on both sides, 1 to 2 minutes per side, transfer it to a large platter; discard the garlic. The skillet will have lots of browned bits in it (these add flavor and color)—regulate the heat as needed to prevent burning them. Repeat to cook subsequent batches, adding 1 tablespoon oil and 1 garlic clove each time.

7. Return all of the pork to the skillet. Deglaze the skillet with the wine, scraping to loosen the browned bits. Simmer on medium high until the wine is almost gone, 3 to 4 minutes. Toss the artichoke slices over the pork; pour the milk into skillet. Simmer on medium heat, stirring frequently, until the milk has thickened and the meat is cooked through, about 3 minutes. Adjust the salt to taste. 🙠

Versatile Scaloppine

The method for preparing scaloppine—pounding and then dredging thin slices of meat in flour—makes even less-expensive cuts of meat tender and delicious. In Umbria, pork scaloppine is popular but chicken and turkey are also used. Cut breasts into ½-inch-thick fillets; pound to a thickness of about ³⁄₈ inch thick. Dredge and cook the poultry per recipe steps 4 through 6 (see "Scaloppine with Artichokes," page 237), cooking until the poultry is no longer pink in the center when cut into with a knife. Basic pork, chicken, and turkey scaloppine (without artichokes) can be finished in a variety of ways. **Truffles:** Sauté thin slices of black truffles with a little garlic in olive oil; spoon over the cooked scaloppine. **Lemon:** Squeeze lemon juice over the top of the cooked scaloppine. **Mushrooms:** Substitute sautéed sliced mushrooms for the artichokes, finish cooking with or without the milk.

How to Prepare Artichokes

Fill a medium bowl half full with water and the juice of a lemon. Trim ¼ inch off the end of the artichoke stem; remove any leaves from the stem. Bend the bottom leaves back toward the stem to break them off; discard the leaves. Continue breaking off leaves until only tender inner leaves remain. Cut across the leaves, about ½ inch above the heart; discard the leaves. Use a vegetable peeler to peel the stem and any dark, tough portions off the base of the choke. Cut the artichoke in half; use a melon baller or knife to cut out the fuzzy center. Rinse the artichoke well. Submerge the artichoke in the acidulated water— the artichokes can be held up to two hours. Before using in recipes, drain and pat the artichokes dry with paper towels. They are ready to sauté, roast, or fry.

Steak with Arugula and Cherry Tomatoes

Tagliata con rucola e pomodorini

Tagliata simply means "sliced," but on a menu it refers to sliced steak. This dish is served in restaurants all over Umbria—and it is the steak recipe I cook most often. A good-quality steak is essential, but what makes this dish irresistible is the contrast between the rich, smoky grilled beef and the tangy, slightly bitter arugula salad that tops the sliced meat. Serve tagliata *with grilled bread and a glass of sagrantino or sangiovese wine for a simple meal.*

Yield: 4 servings

STEAK INGREDIENTS

4 (6 to 8 ounce) New York (strip), coulotte, or boneless rib-eye steaks (¾ to 1 inch thick)

1 lemon, cut in half

Kosher salt

Freshly ground pepper

1½ tablespoons plus 1½ tablespoons extra virgin olive oil

SALAD INGREDIENTS
6 tablespoons extra virgin olive oil

2 tablespoons balsamic vinegar

½ teaspoon kosher salt (*important:* see "About Salt," xxv)

¼ teaspoon freshly ground pepper

8 cups packed baby arugula, stems removed

1 pint tiny cherry tomatoes such as Sweet 100s, cut into halves

Wedge of Parmigiano-Reggiano cheese (optional, see Note, page 242)

GETTING STARTED: Start the charcoal in a barbecue or preheat a gas grill.

STEAK DIRECTIONS
1. Score the steaks on both sides by making ⅛-inch-deep cuts about ¾ inch apart in a diamond pattern across the surface. Arrange the steaks side by side in a shallow nonreactive pan (such as stainless steel or glass). Squeeze one of the lemon halves over the steaks. Season as desired with the kosher salt and pepper. Drizzle with 1½ tablespoons of the oil; rub the seasonings in with the back of a spoon. Turn the steaks over and season the other side in the same manner. Cover; marinate in the refrigerator for 20 to 60 minutes.

2. Grill the steaks over a medium-hot fire until well browned and cooked medium-rare (or as desired), 3 to 4 minutes per side. (Alternatively, the steaks can be broiled or sautéed.) Transfer to a cutting board. Cover loosely with foil; let stand 5 minutes (the steaks will continue to cook).

SALAD AND ASSEMBLY DIRECTIONS
1. Combine the 6 tablespoons oil with the vinegar, the ½ teaspoon kosher salt, and ¼ teaspoon pepper in a small jar; seal and shake well to mix. Put the arugula and tomatoes into a large bowl.

2. Just before serving, pour several tablespoons of the dressing over the salad; toss to coat. Add more dressing, if needed to lightly coat the salad. Adjust the salt and pepper to taste.

3. Cut each grilled steak crosswise into ¼-inch-thick diagonal slices. Arrange the steaks (fanning out the slices) on individual plates; season lightly with kosher salt, if desired. Top each steak with salad, dividing it evenly among the plates. If using cheese, use a vegetable peeler to shave a little cheese over each serving. Pass additional dressing at the table.

NOTE: You need a wedge of cheese to make shavings. Allow ¼ to ½ ounce of cheese per serving. ❧

8 🌿 Holidays—*Le feste*

Prendere due piccioni con una fava

(Take two pigeons with one fava bean—kill two birds with one stone)

MANY OF UMBRIA'S HOLIDAYS ARE RELIGIOUS—FROM CHRISTMAS TO Easter to the Assumption of Mary. In a country where the majority of inhabitants are (or were raised) Catholic, it makes sense that public schools and businesses observe the holy days, too. In this chapter, I take you with me to an Easter Vigil, to a New Year's party in downtown Umbertide, and to Christmas and *Ferragosto* at Mario's house. You'll follow me into local kitchens to learn about the food served at these holy feasts.

CHRISTMASTIME

Natale (Christmas) is a very festive time in Umbria. Strands of glittering lights illuminate main streets and ancient stone buildings. Piazzas bustle with gift markets, children's programs, marching bands, concerts, and singing. The days are short and outside the evening air is frigid, but young and old bundle up and join in the fun.

Nativity scenes fill park lawns—in Gubbio, an entire street transforms into a living Nativity (*il presepe*), with locals playing parts in the miracle of Christ's birth. From a distance, the entire hillside that makes up the town of Gubbio is lit with colorful lights in the shape of a Christmas tree—it is a stunning view that is worth the drive. It takes a team of volunteers about two thousand hours to erect the 2,132-foot-tall-by-1,148-foot-wide tree and fill it with the three thousand colored lights (www.alberodigubbio.com).

In my town of Umbertide, a series of city-sponsored festivities kicked off the first week in December with a tree-lighting ceremony. In one shop window, a tall mechanical Babbo Natale (Father Christmas/Santa Claus) waved to shoppers. But the season's focus is not on Santa Claus or shopping and gift giving. The emphasis is on family, food, and festivities—and for some, attending Mass is important.

On the days leading up to Christmas, preparing food for the holidays consumed a lot of time. A week before Christmas, Paola cooked the meat— veal, pork, and chicken—for the cappelletti that we would make the next day. But Michela went into labor and delivered Bruno, Paola's second grandchild. Paola's focus changed from *Natale* to Bruno, so for the moment Silvia and I were on our own. We ground the meat that Paola had cooked, and seasoned it to taste with Parmigiano-Reggiano cheese and nutmeg. We took turns rolling out the dough and worked together to fill and shape the cappelletti. We were discouraged when after an hour we had made just one serving! Paola came to our rescue the next night.

"You forgot the mortadella," Paola said when she tasted the filling.

"We couldn't find it," said Silvia.

"Well, it needs mortadella—and a lot more cheese and nutmeg."

So Paola adjusted the flavors and we worked late to make fifteen servings of *cappelletti*. Next Paola taught me how to make *panpepato*—an ancient candy made with dark chocolate, pine nuts, almonds, hazelnuts, walnuts, spices, pepper, raisins, and citron.

I offered to make liver crostini, the traditional Christmas appetizer. A few days before Christmas, I went to the store to buy the chicken innards— liver, heart, gizzards. On an average day, the poultry section had an abundance of chicken *interiore*, but that day the case was empty. I rang the bell to talk to the butcher.

"Do you have chicken giblets?" I asked.

"We're sold out," he said. "Come tomorrow morning."

The next morning, I bought enough *interiore* for one recipe, but went back that afternoon to get more—worried I didn't have enough. The shelf was empty again, so I rang the bell. The same man answered.

"Do you have chicken livers?" I asked.

"I told you yesterday to come this morning."

"I did, but I need more."

"Sorry, no more until after Christmas."

In California, we never have a run on chicken livers.

Along with crostini, I planned to make Silvana's recipe for *gobbi alla Parmigiana* (Cardoons Parmesan), a traditional Christmas dish. The dish is virtually the same as eggplant Parmesan, except cardoons replace the eggplant. Silvana's version uses both tomato sauce and béchamel. On Silvana's recommendation, I took three days to make the dish. The first day, I soaked 4-inch pieces of cardoons in salted acidulated water for half an hour, then peeled the *gobbi,* and boiled it in salted water for an hour. The next day I prepared the tomato sauce and fried the *gobbi.* I dipped the vegetable in a thin batter of sparkling water, flour, and salt, and fried them until golden. I saved the rest of the work—making the *besciamela* and assembling and baking the casserole—for Christmas morning.

The first celebratory meal of the holidays was at Paola's on Christmas Eve. By tradition, the meal was meatless. When I entered Paola's kitchen, the steamy air was filled with the wonderful aroma of *brodo di carne* (meat broth) simmering on the stove—but that would be served with cappelletti on Christmas. For dinner, Paola was preparing a simple Portuguese dish made up of layers of *baccalà* (salt cod), sliced potatoes, and hard-cooked eggs. For dessert, we sipped the hot wine I brought, and nibbled on *panpepato* and panettone, a tall sweet bread that is eaten at Christmas. It was a quiet dinner with just seven of us. Mario and Michela spent the evening with friends.

Around one o'clock on Christmas day, the Ramaccioni family and I arrived at Mario and Michela's for the lunch feast. Since Michela wanted to keep her newborn Bruno at home, we went there instead of to Paola's. Two platters of assorted crostini—liver, tuna, and olives with mayonnaise—were already on the table. Michela's mother had brought the crostini, so with mine there was more than enough. When everyone was seated, Paola stood at the head of the table, ladling cappelletti into bowls. After we had eaten seconds of cappelletti, we ate the *gobbi,* and finally the chicken and potatoes that Michel's mother had made.

We hung around all afternoon, listless after eating too much, but we rallied again, showing up at Paola's for dinner and a gift exchange. It was a casual dinner—we ate leftovers from lunch. We drank *vin brulè* and ate roasted chestnuts late into the night.

A Traditional Umbrian Christmas Menu

Antipasto

Assorted crostini, such as liver (page 66), mushroom-truffle (page 318), and tuna (page 68)

Primi piatti

Cappelletti in Broth (pages 118 and 247)

Cardoons Parmesan (see Eggplant Parmesan recipe, page 24)

Secondo piatto

Roast Chicken (or duck) with Potatoes (page 12)

Contorni

Roasted Potatoes (page 146)

Mixed Salad (148), or any seasonal vegetables
(see "Umbria's Vegetable Dishes," page 161)

Dolci

Spiced Chocolate-Nut Candy (page 251)

Roasted chestnuts (see "How to Roast Chestnuts," page 250)

Panettone (a traditional Christmas cake, tall and round with nuts
and dried fruit)

Vini

Antipasto and cappelletti: Umbria's traditional whites—*grechetto,*
Orvieto Classico.

With salmon crostini, try pinot grigio.

Try the same whites or Montefalco rosso or pinot *nero* (noir) with the liver or mushroom crostini, cardoons, roast chicken, and contorni.

Dolce: *Vin brulè* (see recipe, page 254) or *sagrantino passito* with the candy, *vinsanto* with the cake, and *vino novello* (nouveau/new) with the chestnuts.

Cappelletti (Little Hats) in Broth
Cappelletti in brodo
☙

Homemade cappelletti in brodo *(broth) is traditionally served at Christmas lunch and at weddings. "When young people were traditional—and still got married," said Bruna (Michela's mom), "women would make cappelletti for the wedding dinner—rolling the dough by hand and cutting it with a glass. We worked all day and into the night—until one or two in the morning—mamma mia!"*

After spending a couple of days making cappelletti for a crowd at Christmas, it became crystal clear why these "little hats" are reserved for special occasions—it can take a couple of cooks most of a day to make them. I recommend preparing the filling a day ahead—and inviting a friend or two to join you to assemble them. With help, you might want to double the recipe, but make one batch of dough to start—and a second one when needed. Today pasta shops in Umbria sell excellent fresh cappelletti—oh, if only I had a pasta shop nearby.

Paola adds mortadella, like her mother from Bologna did, and a bit of lemon zest—nice additions but not traditional or essential.

Yield: 2 pounds (8 first-course servings
or 6 main-dish servings)

4 ounces boneless, skinless chicken breast or thigh (see Note, page 250)

5 ounces boneless pork loin (see Note, page 250)

5 ounces boneless beef, preferably flat iron or top sirloin steak (see Note, page 250)

½ medium celery stalk, cut in 2

½ small carrot, peeled and cut in 2

¼ medium onion, cut into 4 pieces

½ cup dry white wine, such as pinot grigio or sauvignon blanc

¼ cup extra virgin olive oil

1¼ teaspoons kosher salt (*important:* see "About Salt," page xxv)

1 thin slice mortadella (optional)

1 tablespoon soft butter

¾ teaspoon freshly ground nutmeg

Finely shredded zest of ¼ lemon (optional) (see "About Zest," page 37)

1¼ ounces grated Parmigiano-Reggiano cheese plus extra to pass (see "Grated Cheese," page 6)

1 pound, 10 ounces Fresh Egg Pasta (see recipe, page 84)

You'll also need: A meat grinder (or food processor), a pasta machine, and a round (1¾-inch) biscuit cutter or small glass.

DIRECTIONS FOR FILLING

1. Cut the chicken in half; refrigerate it. Cut the pork and beef into 1½-inch cubes. Put the pork and beef into a medium saucepan with the celery, carrot, onion, wine, oil, and kosher salt; stir. Cover and bring to a boil over high heat. Reduce the heat to low; cook 20 minutes, stirring occasionally. Add the chicken; simmer uncovered until the chicken is no longer pink in the middle, about 5 minutes (do not let the liquid boil away—add a little water if needed). If the cooking liquid is not thick and saucy, cook over medium heat until it is (but do not let it boil away).

2. While the meat is still hot, put a large bowl under a meat grinder fitted with small holes. Push the meat and vegetables (if using mortadella, add it now) through the grinder in batches—reserve the sauce in the saucepan. (Alternatively, use a food processor to very finely mince the meat; transfer to a large bowl.) Stir the reserved sauce, butter, and nutmeg into the warm meat mixture (if using lemon zest, add it now); mix well. Stir in the 1¼ ounces of

cheese; adjust the salt and nutmeg to taste (Bruna says she goes by aroma rather than taste!). Let cool slightly; refrigerate until thoroughly chilled. (The filling can be made a day ahead.)

DIRECTIONS FOR ASSEMBLY

Three important steps to take to keep the cappelletti at safe temperatures during assembly are (1) work with only a few tablespoons of filling at a time, (2) on hot days, refrigerate half of the pasta dough until needed, (3) do not leave the assembled cappelletti at room temperature for more than half an hour.

1. While the filling chills (or about 1 hour before assembling the cappelletti), prepare the pasta dough. Dust 2 large trays with flour or line with parchment paper. Have a clean, damp cloth handy to wipe hands. Set up the work area (see "How to Roll and Cut Fresh Pasta," page 87). Put a few tablespoons of filling into a small bowl (keep the rest refrigerated, refilling the bowl as needed). Have a small bowl of water handy (refill occasionally with fresh water). Keep in mind that you are making tiny hats, so you understand better how to shape the pasta. Roll and fill one piece of dough at a time (see instructions for machine rolling, pages 88 to 90); the correct thickness for the pasta is probably the second to the thinnest setting (8 on my Marcato Ampia 150).

2. Cut the pasta into 8 pieces; roll 1 piece at a time. Cut the sheet of pasta in half lengthwise to make 2 sheets of equal length. Arrange the sheets side by side on the wooden board. (If you are working alone, cover one sheet loosely with plastic wrap to keep it moist.) Immediately use the biscuit cutter to cut the dough into circles—cut them as close together as possible. Arrange the circles in rows. Put a small handful of filling in one hand—squeeze it so it sticks together. Take a pea-size bit (about ¼ teaspoon) of filling, using index finger and thumb of the other hand—pinching it so it holds together—and put it in the center of each circle of pasta. If there is too much filling, it will not shape or seal properly.

3. Working one at a time, fold each circle in half to cover the filling (making a half moon); press the pasta firmly around edges to seal it—if it doesn't stick together, dab a little water around the inside edges and press again. With a tip of the half moon in each hand, hold the half moon with the flat edge down and the curve facing up. Bringing the two outer points together, bend

the half moon down. Overlap the tips to form a hat shape; press firmly on the points to hold them together. The "brim" of the hat (the unfilled edges of pasta) should have turned up to make a hat—if it didn't, turn it up by hand.

4. Put the cappelletti on the floured or paper-lined trays—keeping them slightly separated so they don't stick together. Freeze cappelletti until firm; transfer to freezer bags. Freeze up to 3 months. (Even if you plan to eat the cappelletti within a few hours, it is just simpler to freeze them—no risk of them getting soggy and sticking together.)

TO COOK *CAPPELLETTI IN BRODO*

For a generous first-course serving, allow about 1 cup broth and 1 cup cappelletti (4 ounces/114 grams). Per main-course serving, allow about 1½ cups broth and 1½ cups cappelletti (about 6 ounces/175 grams). Bring the broth to a boil over high heat. Drop the frozen cappelletti into the broth; stir. Bring to a boil and immediately adjust the heat to keep the broth at a gentle boil so the cappelletti do not break. Cook until *al dente* or just tender, about 6 minutes (large batches may take longer—taste for doneness). Pass grated Parmigiano at the table.

NOTE: Five ounces of pork or beef cut into 1½-inch cubes measures about ⅞ cup. If you cut a medium-size half boneless chicken breast in half, it should weigh close to four ounces. A small boneless thigh weighs about 4 ounces. ❧

HOW TO ROAST CHESTNUTS

During the fall and early winter, *castagne* (chestnuts) are a popular treat. Old-timers gather chestnuts in the forests, but most people now buy chestnuts at the supermarket. At autumn festivals, vendors roast chestnuts over huge fires and sell paper cones filled with hot, slightly smoky chestnuts. In November, when the *nuovo vino* (new wine from the recent harvest) is released, many Umbrian wineries throw a party— they serve *nuovo vino* with roasted chestnuts.

To prepare chestnuts, use a sharp paring knife to carve an X on the side of each chestnut, cutting just through the skin. Then toast the chestnuts in the oven or in a pan over a fire until the skins pop open. Immediately wrap the chestnuts tightly in a thick towel; let stand a couple of minutes. As soon as the chestnuts are cool enough to handle (but still hot), peel off the skin. If the chestnuts cool, it is impossible to get the skins off.

Spiced Chocolate-Nut Candy

Panpepato
ಌ

At Christmas, when this centuries-old Umbrian sweet was served, I quickly became addicted to it. The name panpepato *(peppered bread) refers to the black pepper used in the dessert. But what makes this candy so utterly fantastic is how all the ingredients work together. Cinnamon and nutmeg, along with the pepper, add an intriguing complexity and spiciness. Raisins and citron add a chewy sweetness. The nuts—almonds, walnuts, hazelnuts, and pine nuts— add crunch and a rich, earthy flavor. Espresso and chocolate add a pleasant bitterness, while honey adds a floral note.*

The extensive ingredient list and long directions are deceiving—this is a very simple candy recipe that is made without using a thermometer. To save time, buy blanched almonds and toasted hazelnuts, if possible. In many cases, the darker the chocolate, the better, but not this time. The darker the chocolate, the more cakelike the product—since this candy should be somewhere between the texture of caramel and fudge, superdark chocolate doesn't work. The recipe works best with moderately dark chocolate bars—around 62 percent cocoa is ideal.

Panpepato is traditionally baked on edible wafer paper that is to be eaten along with the candy.

During the holidays, I often make a double batch of panpepato *so I have plenty to serve at festive meals—and lots to give as gifts to family and friends.*

Yield: 9 (4-inch) rounds (about 7 ounces each)

3 (8×11 inch) sheets edible wafer or rice paper (optional) (see "Wafer Paper," page 254)

8 ounces almonds (about 1½ cups), preferably blanched

8 ounces hazelnuts (about 1¾ cups), preferably toasted

⅓ cup freshly brewed espresso or strong coffee

2 tablespoons sugar

1 cup all-purpose flour

1 tablespoon freshly grated nutmeg (about ½ medium nut)

2 teaspoons freshly ground pepper

2 teaspoons ground cinnamon

6 ounces walnut halves (about 1¾ cups)

4 ounces pine nuts (about 7/8 cup)

1 cup raisins (about 5 ounces)

½ cup diced candied citron

1 pound dark chocolate (about 62% cocoa), chopped

⅓ cup honey

⅔ cup rum, brandy, or *vinsanto*

You'll also need: Parchment paper (optional, if using wafer paper).

Getting started: Preheat the oven to 325°F. Line 2 large baking sheets with parchment paper for easier cleanup. If using wafer paper (use dry hands and utensils), cut a 4-inch round template from a clean sheet of paper—a 4-inch plate makes a good pattern. Use the template as a pattern to cut (with clean kitchen scissors) three layers of wafer paper at a time to make nine 4-inch rounds. Arrange the rounds on the baking sheets side by side, spaced about 2 inches apart (put the bumpy side of the paper facing up).

1. Blanch the almonds and separately toast the almonds and hazelnuts, if needed (see "How to Blanch Almonds and Toast Nuts," page 253). While the espresso is hot, stir in and dissolve the sugar; set aside. In a large bowl, toss together the flour, nutmeg, pepper, and cinnamon. Add the almonds,

hazelnuts, walnuts, pine nuts, raisins, and citron (break up the citron and raisins if they are stuck in clumps). Set aside.

2. In a large pot (large enough to accommodate tossing ingredients), melt the chocolate and honey over very low heat, stirring frequently and watching closely, about 10 minutes. Turn off the heat; add the rum and reserved espresso, stirring until smooth. Add the nut mixture in several batches, stirring with a wooden spoon after each addition until the nuts are evenly coated.

3. Confirm that the wafer rounds are spaced about 2 inches apart on the baking sheets. Use a silicone or rubber spatula to mound the nut mixture on top of the wafers, dividing the mixture evenly. Spread the mixture evenly to the edges of each wafer round to cover (but not overflow) the wafer. (If not using wafer paper, make nine 4-inch rounds on top of the parchment paper.)

4. Bake until the candy is just set but still glossy (it should feel almost firm when pressed gently with a finger—it will still seem gooey but it will firm up and become fudgelike as it cools), about 20 minutes. Watch carefully to avoid burning. Cool in the pan until firm enough to transfer to a wire rack with a metal spatula.

5. Although the candy can be cut when completely cool, it slices best after 24 hours. To serve, cut a round candy in half and then slice each half crosswise into ⅜-inch-thick slices—slice only as much as you plan to serve. To store, when completely cool individually wrap each candy in foil and put the wrapped candy into plastic bags. *Panpepato* can be stored at room temperature for a week or in the freezer for up to 3 months. ❧

How to Blanch Almonds and Toast Nuts

Almonds with their brown skins removed are called "blanched." Blanching almonds is easy, but time-consuming. To blanch almonds, fill a small saucepan half full with water; bring to a boil. Drop the almonds into the boiling water. Simmer the almonds about 3 minutes. Drain the almonds and wrap them in a clean dishtowel. While still hot but cool enough to handle, one at a time, pinch an almond between the thumb and index finger of one hand, pointing the almond toward the other hand. Squeeze hard and the almond will pop out of the skin into your other hand. Toast the blanched almonds in a preheated 325°F oven until light golden and fragrant, 10 to 15 minutes. Toss the almonds halfway through baking time. Let cool. (Use the same method to toast raw hazelnuts.)

WAFER PAPER

If you have had the host (*l'ostia*) during communion at church, then you are familiar with this white, flavorless edible "paper" that dissolves almost instantly on the tongue. Several of Italy's ancient sweets—*torrone, panpepato, panforte*—have a layer of wafer paper on the top or bottom. In Umbria, local bakeries sell the paper in rolls. Although wafer paper is also called rice paper, the edible papers found at online baking supply stores (see Resources, page 352) are made of potato starch—plus water and vegetable oil. Most of the paper comes in 8×11-inch sheets, although a few places sell rounds.

HOT WINE—*VINO CALDO, VIN BRULÈ*!

At Christmastime, and during winter months, this hot spiced wine is a popular beverage. The recipe dates back to medieval times in Umbria, when spices were infused in the cuisine. Call it *vino caldo* or *vin brulè*. Serve it in the evening to warm up after a day out and about or serve it after dinner with dessert. For a couple of weeks around Christmastime, vendors often sell *vino caldo* by the cup at the weekly markets. And the *erbalista* (herb) shops sell convenient spice mixes, but it's easy to make on your own.

Vin brulè: Use a vegetable peeler to remove the zest (but not the white pith) from 1 large lemon. Juice the lemon. Put the juice and zest into a large pot; add 3 cups of water, 1 sliced orange, 2 small sliced apples, ½ cup honey, ½ cup sugar, ⅓ cup raisins, 3 cinnamon sticks, and 8 cloves. Cover and bring to a boil; reduce the heat to low and simmer ½ hour. Let stand 1 hour; strain and discard solids (at this point, the syrup can be held about 1 week in the refrigerator). Just before serving, add two (750 ml) bottles of dry red wine to the syrup. Heat, but do not boil. Ladle into espresso or coffee cups. Serve immediately. Refrigerate leftovers.

NEW YEAR—*CAPODANNO*

Walking through Piazza XXV Aprile (April 25) at 9:30 p.m. on New Year's Eve in historic downtown Umbertide was like entering a war zone. Loud booms vibrated through me. Rat-a-tat-tat machine-gun sounds put me on edge. Over a half century earlier, on April 25, 1944, the residents who lived in what had been a densely populated space probably just had time to register the sound of a bomber overhead before falling victim to Britain's accidental bombing, which flattened their houses and killed residents. The actual target had been the nearby bridge that spans the Tiber River—an attempt to stop the German forces. Today Piazza XXV Aprile is a parking lot and a clever memorial. On the pavement the walls of each demolished house are outlined in red brick, and the doorways are marked with white bricks engraved with the house number. A nearby plaque explains the tragic event.

A short distance away, when my friend Anna Gloria and I arrived at Piazza Matteotti, the sounds of combat intensified. Every now and then we saw a teenage boy violently thrust his arm above his head—seconds later we'd hear the blast from the firecracker he had thrown. With relief, we entered the Teatro dei Riuniti near La Rocca, the tower of an ancient fort. The free city-sponsored New Year festivities were already under way inside the theater—*tombola* started at nine. This bingolike game is the season's diversion—at some time during the holidays almost everyone participates. Anna Gloria and I bought *tombola* cards—five for ten euros—and selected two red velvet seats in the center section of the theater. Luxurious red velvet curtains, trimmed in gold braid and fringe, framed the stage. A stylish white-haired woman MC sat onstage behind a table draped in burgundy cloth. Tall stacks of colorful tins and gift-wrapped packages with huge gold bows dwarfed her. But the grand prize—a huge whole prosciutto leg—was barely disguised by its bright cellophane and pretty bows. The MC wore an elegant black-and-white sparkly suit and spike heels. Her voice was deep and powerful. She dug deep inside a printed cloth bag to retrieve a new *tombola* number. She put the number on the table and said "*Trrrrrrrrrentuno* [thirty-one]." Before I had a chance to search my card for 31, she shouted, "*Otto* [eight], *sesanta trrrrrrrre* [sixty-three]."

"Wait, wait," several people in the audience cried. Another shouted, "Did you say sixty-three or seventy-three?"

"Am I speaking too fast?" she asked.

"*Sì.*" "*Sì.*" "*Sì.*" "*Sì.*" The yeses continued around the room.

She never managed to slow down her tempo; her only concession was to repeat a number when there was mass confusion. Soon someone shouted *terno,* which meant they had three in a row.

"Are you sure?" the white-haired lady asked. "Without the *famosa buca* [famous hole]?" If someone had a *buca,* it meant the numbers were not consecutive. When the MC was satisfied there wasn't a *buca,* she said, "*Va benissimo* [it goes very well]." Her helper would pass out a prize—wine, cake, or candy. *Cinquina,* five in a row, won a prize, too, but the top prize went to the first person to shout *tombola,* signifying he or she had five consecutive numbers in ascending order.

When the last prize—the coveted prosciutto—had been awarded, the enormous gold-fringed velvet drapes swept across the stage, concealing the backstage crew. Winners and losers (I was one of the latter) were invited upstairs for snacks, while stagehands set up for the late-night concert. Two of my friends, Adriano and Silvana, poured at the bar—spumante, sodas, mineral water, red and white wine, syrupy hot chocolate. The crowd swooped down on the buffet table, emptying tray after tray of petite bite-size pizza, sausages in pastry, and tiny sandwiches. When volunteers brought out dessert—rich tarts with pastry cream and jam and Napoleon pastries—they were gone in seconds, too.

Soon flashing lights cleared the room. Onstage, an elderly man played a cello, a thin young woman accompanied on violin, another elderly man sat poised at the grand piano, and a well-dressed middle-aged man sang. Firecrackers punctuated every song like a drummer out of sync. About midway through the concert, Anna Gloria snuck out for a cigarette.

"All of the action is outside," she said when she returned.

"In the war zone?" I asked

"*Basta* [enough]. Piazza Matteotti is packed with people. There's music. Dancing."

The white-haired hostess promised us sparkling wine at midnight, but Anna Gloria and I tiptoed out a few minutes early to join the festivities on the piazza. Walking through the narrow ancient street from the *teatro,* I looked up at a noisy balcony in time to see a young man toss a glass to the ground. It landed with a huge crackle several feet in front of us. Up ahead we could see a group of boys tossing firecrackers into the air, so we took a small side street to the piazza.

At the piazza, we said *scusate* (you-all excuse me) to the hundreds of people we passed on our way into the middle. Near the enormous lighted Christmas tree, musicians played—a drummer, an electric guitar, and an electric keyboard. A young woman in a miniskirt and knee-high boots sang. A group of school-age kids hung out near the band, surrounded by dancers, lighting sparkler after sparkler. In the swaying crowd, people held tightly to bottles of sparkling wine. A young man near us passed out plastic cups until he ran out—his friend followed behind filling them with bubbly. At midnight, the violent ringing of the piazza's bells drowned out the cheering and shouting.

From La Rocca, professional fireworks tinted the ancient fort walls a rainbow of colors and streaked the dark sky with pink, blue, and red streamers. When the last sparkle faded, the stench of sulfur lingered behind. The rabble pushed Anna Gloria and me along with them toward La Rocca and the group of kids tossing firebombs and firecrackers. When the mini bombs exploded in the town's empty moat just beyond the mob, the thunderous booms reverberated against the thick stone walls. A lone police officer watched but did nothing to stop the unruly kids.

Anna Gloria and I stayed for about twenty minutes before heading home—the scene was intoxicating but also a little frightening. When I got home, the lights were still on at Michela and Mario's, next door; they stayed up until five in the morning drinking Champagne and playing cards with friends. The next day at lunch, Mario told me that he and his friends expected snow on New Year's Day.

"Really?" I said. "It has been so warm."

"Well, there was a miracle last night," he explained. "Michela cooked dinner, a miracle. With that kind of miracle, we say it might snow."

Silvia invited friends and family to lunch at her house to celebrate New Year's Day. It was a potluck. I made liver crostini for an appetizer. Silvia's sister, Paola, brought our first course, homemade broth with cappelletti. Silvia served roasted duck and potatoes.

"Silvia has become a great cook," Paola declared, nibbling on the crispy duck.

"The duck is perfect," I added. The skin was brown and delicious, and the rich meat was perfumed with rosemary and garlic. The potatoes were moist inside, but the rich duck fat they cooked in made them crunchy on the outside. Anna Gloria brought the requisite lentils, which are always eaten on New Year's Day—the tiny coin-shaped legumes are said to bring money and fortune in the new year.

For several days after the New Year festivities, firecrackers disrupted the *tranquilità* in the countryside and rattled residents in downtown Umbertide.

Lentils with Garlic
Lenticchie di Castelluccio con aglio
❦

Ring in capodanno *(New Year's Day) with lentils like the Umbrians do! This recipe is so easy, you won't need to spend the holiday in the kitchen. When Daniela told me how to make these lentils, I was skeptical. The simple recipe sounded flavorless, but I was wrong—it is delicious.*

The authentic lentils for this recipe are the tiny tan lenticchie *from Castelluccio in Umbria. Lentils from the hills of Colfiorito near Foligno—or any tiny Umbrian lentils—are also ideal. Other good alternatives—all tiny—include: "Italian verdi" or "Italian green" (both tan in color), French "green lentils" (almost black) or tiny brown Canadian lentils. Standard American lentils can be used in a pinch. Gourmet and Italian markets are a good source for these specialty lentils (also see Resources, page 352).*

Lentils are a good accompaniment to grilled sausage or roasted or grilled meats and poultry. They make a delicious crostini appetizer, spooned on top of sliced, toasted Italian bread. Served as a sauce for fresh pasta, they are exquisite (see Pasta with Lentils and Truffles, page 165). This recipe is also the base for two traditional dishes, Lentil Soup and Lentils with Rice (see pages 259 and 260).

Yield: *7 to 8 cups (about 8 servings)*

1 pound (or 500 grams) tiny lentils, preferably from Castelluccio or
   Colfiorito

6 cups cold water

1 tablespoon kosher salt (*important*: see "About Salt," page xxv)

⅓ cup extra virgin olive oil plus extra for garnish

3 or 4 large garlic cloves, sliced

1. Rinse the lentils and put them into a large saucepan. Add the 6 cups water. Turn the heat on high and set the timer for 25 minutes—you will taste for doneness at this point. (Refer to the package for cooking time, but taste for doneness early. Most lentils cook within 30 to 35 minutes.)

2. When the lentils boil, immediately reduce the heat to medium low—reduce heat as needed to keep the lentils at a gentle simmer. Simmer uncovered, stirring occasionally, until the lentils are just tender, 25 to 40 minutes. Stir in the kosher salt.

3. Meanwhile, heat the ⅓ cup oil and garlic in a small skillet over low heat, stirring occasionally, for 5 minutes (do not brown the garlic). When the lentils are done, add the oil with the garlic. Simmer over low heat, stirring occasionally, until the lentils are tender and flavorful, about 15 minutes. Adjust the salt to taste. Drizzle each serving with additional olive oil. ❧

LENTIL SOUP—*ZUPPA DI LENTICCHIE*

This soup is fast and tasty—and flexible. To vary it, add slices of cooked sausage instead of pancetta during the last 10 minutes of cooking. Or leave the meat out to make a vegetarian soup. To make the soup, prepare Lentils with Garlic (page 258), with the following changes. Add these ingredients: 3 ounces diced pancetta (optional), 2 medium stalks celery (diced), 1 medium carrot (diced), ½ onion (diced), and 1 sprig (6 inches) rosemary or sage (optional). Increase the water to 8 cups, and if using pancetta, reduce the oil to 3 tablespoons. To cook the soup, heat the oil in a large pot over medium heat; sauté the pancetta, celery, carrot, onion, and rosemary in the oil, stirring frequently, until soft, about 10 minutes. If desired, add 1 or 2 grated Roma tomatoes; simmer until slightly thickened. Add 8 cups of water and the lentils to the pot and continue cooking per the directions in recipe steps 1 and 2 (see page 259); skip step 3. Season to taste with salt and pepper. Drizzle each serving with additional olive oil and serve with toasted Italian bread or bruschetta (see recipe, page 200).

LENTILS WITH RICE—*LENTICCHIE CON RISO*

Another traditional dish. Make Lentil Soup, adding the optional grated tomatoes. Just before serving, stir in several cups of cooked (*al dente*) medium-grain rice. If needed, add hot chicken broth to make it soupy. Adjust the salt to taste. Serve immediately—the rice will continue to absorb the liquid. Drizzle servings with extra virgin olive oil.

LENTILS FROM CASTELLUCCIO

In mid-June every year, people from all over the world make the arduous drive up the narrow, steep mountain road to Castelluccio for *la fiorita* (the flowering). During *la fiorita* field after field is transformed into an explosion of colors when the wildflowers bloom.

But Castelluccio, high in the hills above Norcia in southeastern Umbria, is also famous for its tiny, flavorful lentils. They cook quickly and hold their shape and texture better than the large lentils we grow in the United States. They have a spicy, intriguing flavor that I've tasted only in lentils from Castelluccio. The petite lentils from the Umbrian hills around Spello and Colfiorito are also excellent. Some gourmet markets carry lentils from Umbria—they are costly but worth it.

THE WITCH

Shortly after *Natale* (Christmas) in Umbria, stores sell stockings filled with goodies, similar to Christmas stockings. But witches on brooms, rather than

Santa Claus and reindeer, decorate the *calze* (stockings). On the night before January 6, *la Befana* (the name of the witch) enters houses through the chimney to leave a stocking for each good child.

In her younger years, my friend Rita dressed up as a wicked witch for the Befana festival in her village—she loved scaring the kids. Her disguise was so good that even close family and friends didn't recognize her. Adhering to tradition, Rita carried a big sack filled with treats. She gave the good *bambini* (children) a small bag of candy. She told the children who had been bad to expect coal—but she gave them dark candy shaped like coal.

The name *Befana* might be a bastardization of the word Epiphany, a Christian holiday celebrating the coming of the Magi (the three wise men). *La Befana* and the Epiphany share the same date—and both date back to ancient history.

CARNEVALE

Carnevale is an ancient tradition celebrated in January or February—the actual date changes each year based on Easter. Years ago when families lived on farms, country folk held lively *carnevale* parties; they wore masks and danced to the accordion. When Rita was young, she remembers her family giving gifts, such as eggs, to singers who came to entertain. When the singing was over, they enjoyed dinner together.

The day before the *festa* at Mario and Michela's, Silvia, Paola, and I made *frappe,* a traditional cookie served during *carnevale*. To make the cookie dough, Paola mixed flour, eggs, butter, sugar, and a splash of anise liqueur. She rolled and cut the dough into small rectangles, and she twisted them in the middle so they looked like large bow-tie pasta. After frying the cookies until they were golden and crisp, she sprinkled one plate of *frappe* with sugar and the other with honey. Someone else brought *castagnole,* fried cookie balls drizzled with honey.

A little before five on the evening of the party, Paola arranged the platters of cookies on the table and Mario got out the drinks. In Umbria, sweets are usually served with *vinsanto,* a dessert wine, but Mario's bar offered Coke, mineral water, and an assortment of beer (it was a young crowd). The two kids dressed in costumes—a tiger and a patch-eyed, sword-swinging pirate. The grown-ups wore casual clothes, but no masks or costumes.

Carnevale customs vary by family and by town, but traditional *carnevale* foods are sweets. In Spoleto, *crescionda* (amaretti cake) is served for *carnevale,* and in Umbertide, *frappe* and *ceciata,* also called *cicerchiata,* are common. To make *ceciata,* my friend Silvana rolls cookie dough into ¹/₂-inch balls, fries them, and covers them with honey, sliced almonds, and cocoa. Finally, she presses the balls together, decorates them with colorful edible confetti, and slices the *ceciata* into wedges.

THE THIRTY-TWO-EGG EASTER BREAD

At Easter in Umbria, almost everyone makes *torta di Pasqua* (Easter bread). The style of bread varies from place to place. Some breads are sweet and others are savory. In the town of Umbertide, the classic *torta* is rich and cheesy. The farmhouse bread was initially made only at Easter when eggs were abundant, but today the *torta* is sold in Umbertide's supermarkets and bakeries year-round.

For several weeks before Easter, Paola and Silvia talked about making the *torta.* In the old days, the *contadini* used homemade pecorino cheese and lots of eggs—forty-eight or even more—to feed large households of twenty-plus people. Silvia and Paola's family recipe called for thirty-two eggs and three kinds of cheese—Parmigiano-Reggiano, Swiss, and pecorino.

"Making the *torta* is exhausting," Paola warned when I volunteered to help. "You have to work the dough by hand for at least one hour."

"And it's a lot of work getting the wood-burning oven hot," added Silvia.

For centuries, the bread was baked in the only kind of oven available—a wood-burning oven—but today many people bake the *torta* in a standard oven. In the days before every family had their own oven, the *contadini* baked bread in a communal wood-burning oven.

During Easter week, Silvia cleaned the oven's chimney and organized the firewood—several wheelbarrows of small logs and a dozen or so bundles of kindling that she had collected on the property the year before. The wood-burning oven that we would use is built into the side of the *capanna,* a small building just a few yards from my apartment. For centuries, the *capanna* had housed the family's farm animals—pigs, chickens, geese, and ducks. Today, during the warm weather, it is the family's party house. We would make the bread in the *capanna* and dine there on Easter Sunday.

The Wednesday before Easter, Paola bought the eggs, flour, yeast, cheese, and "mother" dough—the bread's base, sold at local bakeries. Early on Thursday, Silvia lit a fire in the *capanna*'s ancient terra-cotta stove to help warm the room's interior so the dough would rise. Paola and I arrived at eight that morning. Silvia had already arranged the ingredients on the worktable and had begun kneading the four pounds of "mother" dough from the bakery on a huge wooden board. Paola and I cracked the three dozen eggs the recipe called for. So began our day of labor, doing the kind of work women in Umbertide had done during Easter week for centuries.

"What craziness, working with so much dough," said Silvia, laughing and struggling to control the huge sticky mound. (For someone who says she doesn't like to cook, I've noticed that she is always happy in the kitchen.) Silvia gradually kneaded in the grated cheese, yeast, eggs, flour, and salt. She handed Paola a bit of dough. "Taste it," she insisted. "Last year it didn't have enough salt."

"It's fine," Paola mumbled, her mouth filled with dough.

"Add more salt," persisted Silvia, without tasting the dough herself.

Paola ignored Silvia's demands, pushing her aside to take over the job of kneading. Paola dropped half of the dough in front of me. "It's too much for one person to handle," she said.

Paola lifted the dough above her head and violently slammed it down onto the board. Remnants of soft dough scattered across the room and bits stuck to Paola's face and blouse. A large blob clung to her shoe.

"Paola! What are you doing?" asked Silvia, annoyed by the mess.

"That's how the *contadini* did it," insisted Paola, again slapping the dough onto the board. "It won't turn out right otherwise." She held up a hand covered in gooey dough. "See how the dough sticks to my hand?" I nodded. "When the dough is ready, it doesn't stick."

Paola continued whacking the dough on the board, so Silvia excused herself and left, shaking her head. She spent the next hour or so feeding bunch after bunch of kindling into the oven, later adding larger pieces of wood until the oven was really hot. Once the food was in the oven, Silvia didn't want to add more wood because the fire might flare up.

After about an hour of kneading, the dough had lost its stickiness and was manageable. At this point, Paola divided the giant blob into six portions and put each piece into a large, tall aluminum *torta* pan—an inexpensive pan that replaced the handsome (but fragile) glazed terra-cotta pots of yesteryear. Paola scraped the wooden board with a long knife to remove the bits of dough left behind. She gathered these remnants into a ball and pushed them into an empty twenty-eight-ounce tomato can.

"The can makes a good pan for *il bico*," she explained, "the small *torta di Pasqua* for the children." She covered the *bico* and the large *torta* pans with a cloth. "We'll let them rise a couple hours," she said, wiping her floury hands on her apron. "Now let's fix lunch."

Under Paola's guidance, we prepared and roasted our lunch in the wood-burning oven—a chicken and a guinea hen stuffed with garlic and rosemary, a pan of fresh pork sausage and potatoes braised in white wine, and a simple yellow caked called *il torcolo*.

We ate a delicious lunch punctuated by trips to the oven to check the baking bread. When the bread was well browned, Silvia covered the pans with foil to prevent burning. But foil or no foil, baking in a wood-burning oven is tricky because the oven's temperature fluctuates. Things burn easily or don't cook through. When Silvia pulled the pans out of the oven with huge potholder gloves, black spots on the crust were visible where the foil had torn. "The char adds character," I said to soothe Silvia, who was disappointed in the bread's appearance. When the bread had cooled enough to slice, Paola handed me an enormous wedge.

"*Ti piace la torta* [Do you like the bread]?" asked Paola.

"Yes, I like it very much," I said. It was tasty—light, cheesy, and a bit dry, like most Umbrian baked goods.

"Not enough salt," said Silvia, biting into a thick slice of the warm bread. She had a twinkle in her eyes and a smile that told me she was delighted that I had liked the bread.

A CATHOLIC EASTER

Pasqua (Easter) is an important holiday in Umbria, a time when extended family from other towns in Italy, other parts of Europe, or abroad come home to spend time together. It is also a religious time. A couple of weeks before *Pasqua,* priests in small towns and in the countryside post signs on church doors announcing when they will arrive to bless each parishioner's house during Holy Week. In the past, a couple of boys with large baskets accompanied the priest from house to house. The baskets held the fresh eggs and cheese people gave to the church as an offering for the blessing. The farmers didn't have money, so they gave what they had. Today people give cash for the *benedizione.*

On *venerdì santo* (Good Friday) in towns all across Umbria, an important religious procession—*la processione del Cristo morto*—takes place. At 8:30

p.m. on Good Friday, the Friday before Easter, Silvia, Paola, and I headed to the Piazza San Francesco to take part in the procession. We arrived just as a man carrying a tall, heavy wooden cross emerged from one of the three churches that border the tiny piazza. A group of men carrying a life-size Jesus in a glass casket fell in step behind the man with the cross. Four men conveying a life-size figure of the Madonna trailed the casket. Next came a priest, pronouncing thanks to God, Jesus, and the Madonna into a loud-speaker. A group of women draped in black veils—Le dame di San Vincenzo, an ancient organization of women who help people in need—a marching band playing funereal music, and dozens of nuns carrying torches followed.

We joined the thousands of townspeople—men and women of all ages, kids on bikes, tots in mothers' arms, fathers pushing strollers—who snaked through the streets of Umbertide. Those who didn't come along watched from candle-lined terraces above the street. The procession paused at the hospital to say prayers for the sick. An hour and a half after departing from the piazza, the statue bearers returned Jesus and the Madonna to the church. The crowd dispersed and we went home.

For many, including Paola, Silvia, and me, the religious festivities continued over the weekend. On Saturday night, we drove into the countryside between Umbertide and Città di Castello to attend the Easter Vigil at Santuario della Madonna di Canoscio, a nineteenth-century hilltop church with glorious views. At 8:30, outside the church, the priest passed out long white candles to the congregation. *Il prete* lit one candle and then neighbor turned to neighbor, offering a burning candle to light yet another candle until all the candles were glowing. Mass continued inside the frigid church for an hour and a half. When the offering basket was passed, I was more than ready to go. Being a non-Catholic, I was fascinated by the ancient rituals and the constant shifting among standing, kneeling, and sitting. But I hadn't eaten and my stomach was rumbling. And I was frozen after sitting so long on a hard bench in an ice-cold church. I decided that I would make a better Catholic on a warm, sunny day.

THE BEST PART OF THE LAMB

On Easter morning, we got up early to cook because we had gotten home from church too late the night before to prepare the lamb. Paola arranged the half lamb—a rack, a leg, other pieces of meat, and half of the liver, lung, heart, head, and intestines—on the table where we would prepare our noon meal.

"Cook the intestines," begged Silvia. "They are the best part of the lamb."

Paola ignored Silvia, holding up the bloody half lamb head. "The butcher told me the head is exquisite. But I can't cook it—it's too ugly."

Paola prepared the rack of lamb for the children, seasoning it simply with a bit of lard, pepper, and salt. "Use *sale grosso* [coarse salt]," she advised, "because it dissolves more slowly." She made slits in the rest of the lamb, and pushed a garlic clove, some rosemary needles, and salt into each hole. She sealed the slits with seasoned lard and dropped the lamb into large pots to marinate in white wine. We had planned to marinate it overnight, but after last night's Mass we were too tired to do it. So today the lamb would marinate only a couple hours.

While the lamb and potatoes roasted in the wood-burning oven, we ate Paola's homemade *passatelli in brodo*. This nutmeg-scented bread crumb pasta served in broth is a delicious Easter tradition. After the soup, we exchanged beautifully gift-wrapped, giant chocolate Easter eggs—a custom all over Italy. The large eggs, packaged in colorful paper, foil, or netting, and tied with fancy ribbons and bows, vary in height from about eight inches to several feet tall. Each egg has a surprise inside—a toy car, a stuffed animal, a key chain, a silver pendant.

While we nibbled on bits of chocolate egg and waited for Easter lunch to finish cooking in the wood-burning oven, we talked about *Pasquetta*, the Monday after Easter. *Pasquetta* is a day in Umbria when families traditionally take an outing together. We talked about having a picnic on the top of Monte Tezio, tasting wine in Montefalco, or having lunch at the castle near Sansepolcro. But when Silvia brought the steaming, fragrant lamb and potatoes to the table, our planning abruptly ended and our feasting began. The lamb was *buonissimo* (very good). It had a subtle smoky flavor from the wood oven, a crisp, salty crust, and a moist, garlic-scented interior. The head, liver, lung, heart, and "the best part of the lamb"—the intestines—never appeared on the table.

Grilled Lamb
Agnello alla griglia
∝

Remove the needles from 4 (4-inch) sprigs of rosemary. Cut 3 large garlic cloves lengthwise into 4 slices. Trim the fat off of a 3½- to 4-pound butterflied boneless leg of lamb. Make 12 deep (½-inch-wide) slits in one side of the lamb. Push a slice of garlic, 3 rosemary needles, and a pinch of coarse sea salt into each slit. Seal each slit with a little home-rendered lard (see "How to Make Lard," page 206) or minced/ground pancetta. Put the lamb into a large non-reactive pan (such as stainless steel or glass). Prepare one side of the lamb at a time in the following manner. Drizzle the lamb with dry white wine. Sprinkle the lamb to taste with kosher or coarse sea salt and pepper. Toss half of the remaining rose-mary needles over the lamb. Drizzle generously with extra virgin olive oil. Cover and marinate in the refrigerator at least 2 hours and up to 48 hours.

Let the lamb stand at room temperature ½ hour before cooking. Start a charcoal or gas grill. Grill the lamb over a moderate charcoal or gas fire with the lid closed, turning as often as needed to prevent burning, about every 5 minutes. Total time 30 to 35 minutes (medium to medium rare)—adjust time to suit your personal taste. To help judge doneness, insert an instant-reading ther-mometer into the thickest parts—125°F for rare; 130°F for medium rare; 145°F medium—this is the safe temperature recommended by the FDA. Transfer the lamb to a clean platter; let stand 15 to 20 minutes—the lamb will cook a little more as it sits. To serve, cut into thin slices and adjust the salt to taste. ❧

A TRADITIONAL UMBRIAN EASTER MENU

Antipasto

Assorted crostini, such as liver (page 66), cauliflower, egg, and smoked salmon (see "Crostini—Anything Goes!," page 68)

Primi piatti

Parmesan Egg-Drop Soup, Chard-Ricotta Ravioli (pages 117 and 268), or bread crumb pasta in broth (*passatelli*)

Secondo piatto

Grilled Lamb (see recipe, page 266)

Contorni

Cheese Bread (*torta di Pasqua*)

Roasted Potatoes (page 146)

Mixed Salad (page 148)

Peas with Prosciutto (page 163)

Dolci

Vanilla Cream with Strawberry Sauce and Almond-Orange Biscotti
(pages 289 and 55) or any of the other desserts in the book
(except the strudel—apples are not in season).

Vini

Antipasto and *primi piatti*—traditional Umbrian dry whites such as
grechetto or Orvieto Classico, or sauvignon blanc. With liver crostini and
the *ravioloni* with red sauce (with butter, go with white), try pinot *nera*
(noir) or a young sangiovese. *Secondo piatto*—traditional Umbrian reds
such as sagrantino or Sangiovese, or Syrah. *Dolci*—*limoncello* (see recipe,
page 325), *vinsanto* (page 345), or *passito* (page 315).

Chard-Ricotta Ravioli
Ravioloni di ricotta
❧

Attached to the end of a word, -oni means big, -ini means small. Thus ravioloni
means big ravioli. Although ravioloni *are quicker to make than small ravioli,
making filled pasta is more fun when friends help. But even with assistance, it
is helpful to make* ravioloni *over the course of two days. Day one, make the filling and pasta. Day two, assemble the* ravioloni *and make the sauce. Classic
Tomato Sauce and Sage Butter (see pages 26 and 272) are delicious with this
filled pasta. Or simply simmer cream with a little butter until slightly thickened; remove from the heat and whisk in some Parmigiano-Reggiano cheese.*

*This special occasion recipe is from Silvia and Paola's mother, who came from
Italy's Emilia-Romagna region. The* ravioloni's *creamy filling is enriched with
mortadella, a popular ingredient in Emilia-Romagna (but less common in Umbria). High-quality ingredients are important. The best mortadella is freshly sliced
at the deli counter, and the creamiest ricotta is fresh, made from whole milk.*

Silvia and Paola use a combination of sheep's and cow's milk ricotta, but sheep's milk ricotta is hard to find here. They cut the ravioloni *into round shapes. To speed up the process, use a pastry wheel to cut them into squares.*

Yield: 65 to 70 ravioloni (*allow 3 or 4 per first-course serving; 6 or 7 per main-course serving*)

24 ounces whole milk ricotta cheese, preferably fresh

3 large bunches chard (10 to 12 ounces each)

1/2 cup water

4 ounces Parmigiano-Reggiano cheese (see "Grated Cheese," page 6)

5 ounces sliced mortadella, coarsely chopped

2 1/2 teaspoons kosher salt (*important:* see "About Salt," page xxv) plus more for cooking ravioloni

1 1/2 teaspoons freshly grated nutmeg

1/2 teaspoon freshly ground pepper

1 large egg, beaten

1 pound, 10 ounces Filled Pasta Dough (see recipe, page 86)

All-purpose flour for dusting

Grated Parmigiano-Reggiano cheese for garnish

You'll also need: A pasta machine, a 3-inch round biscuit cutter or glass, kitchen shears, and parchment paper. A clean ruler is helpful.

Tip: Make the filling first, then make the pasta dough.

DIRECTIONS FOR FILLING
1. If the ricotta is soupy, drain it in a fine sieve for 10 minutes; set aside. Use kitchen shears to cut the greens off the chard stalks. (Save the stalks for another use—braise, batter and fry, or simmer in soup—or discard.) Coarsely chop the chard; wash thoroughly.

2. Transfer the chard to a large pot. Add the ½ cup water. Cook on medium high, stirring frequently, until tender, about 10 minutes. Dump the chard into a large sieve. Use a wooden spoon to force out the excess water; let cool.

3. Meanwhile, cut the Parmigiano into ½-inch cubes. Process in a food processor until very fine; transfer to a large bowl. Mince the mortadella in the food processor; transfer to the large bowl of Parmigiano. Spoon the ricotta into the food processor; pulse quickly 25 times to make the cheese fluffy and less grainy but not completely smooth.

4. Transfer the ricotta to the large bowl of Parmigiano. (Set aside the food processor to use again later.) Sprinkle the mixture with the 2½ teaspoons kosher salt, the nutmeg, and pepper; mix well. Set aside.

5. When cool enough to handle, take one handful of chard at a time and squeeze out the excess water. Repeat as many times as needed until the chard is quite dry. Pulse the chard in the food processor until minced.

6. Add the chard to the ricotta mixture; mix well. Adjust the salt and pepper to taste. Stir in the egg; mix well. Cover and refrigerate ½ hour (at this point, the mixture can be held up to 24 hours, refrigerated).

DIRECTIONS FOR ASSEMBLY

Three important steps to keep the *ravioloni* at safe temperatures during assembly are (1) work with a small bowl of filling, (2) on hot days, wrap and refrigerate half of the pasta dough until needed, (3) do not leave the assembled ravioli at room temperature more than one hour (less on hot days).

1. While the filling chills (or about 1 hour before assembling the *ravioloni*), prepare the pasta dough. Line two large trays with parchment paper; dust lightly with flour. Have a clean, damp cloth handy to wipe hands. Set up the work area (see "How to Roll and Cut Fresh Pasta: Setting Up," page 87). Fill a small bowl with filling (keep the rest refrigerated, refilling the small bowl as needed).

2. Roll and fill one piece of dough at a time (see instructions, pages 88 to 90); the correct thickness for the pasta is probably the second to thinnest setting on the machine (8 on my Marcato Ampia 150). If the rolled pasta sheet is

wider than 3½ inches, trim it to 3½ inches; cut the sheet in half to make two 3½-inch-wide sheets of equal length. While working, keep any scraps of dough well covered for use later.

3. Arrange the two pieces of dough side by side on the wooden board. (You will put filling on one sheet and use the other as a cover.) Working quickly so the pasta stays moist, dollop about 1 tablespoon filling about 1 inch from the end of one pasta sheet. Continue putting dollops 2 inches apart down the center of the pasta. Arrange the other sheet of pasta over the filling; lightly press over the filling to flatten and spread it out (be sure to leave about 1 inch between the dollops of filling). Gently stretch the top dough over the filling so the top aligns with the bottom sheet.

4. Starting at the first mound of filling at one end, use fingertips to press around the edges of the filling. Work from the filling to the outer edges, stretching the dough as needed to seal it. (If the dough is too dry to seal, dab it with a small amount of water.) When all of the mounds of filling are sealed, center the 3-inch biscuit cutter over one mound of filling; press and turn slightly until the dough is cut through.

5. As each *raviolono* is cut, put it on a paper-lined tray, spacing about ¼ inch apart (do not stack). As soon as a tray is full, cover it with plastic wrap; freeze until firm. (Alternatively, cover with parchment paper and refrigerate up to 2 hours, checking occasionally to make sure the *ravioloni* bottoms are not soggy—if soggy, freeze on parchment.) After the 8 original pieces of dough are used, knead a handful (at one time) of scrap dough until smooth; roll to make more *ravioloni*. Transfer the slightly frozen *ravioloni* to freezer bags; freeze up to 3 months.

HOW TO COOK AND SERVE *RAVIOLONI*
You can serve all of the *ravioloni* at one time or serve them in small batches. Warm a serving platter and have the sauce heated and ready (see recipe for Classic Tomato Sauce, page 26, or Sage Butter, page 272). Spread a clean, damp nonterry dishtowel over a board. Bring about 3 quarts of cold water to a boil in a large pot to cook the pasta (page 28); add 2 tablespoons kosher salt to the boiling water. Carefully drop fresh or frozen *ravioloni* into the boiling water, cooking in batches without crowding. Cook at a gentle boil, stirring occasionally, until they are *al dente*. Once they rise to the top, they

need to cook 1 to 2 minutes more. Fresh *ravioloni* take about 3 minutes, frozen take 4 to 5 minutes. When done, use a large skimmer or slotted spoon to drain 2 or 3 *ravioloni* at a time; transfer them to the damp dishtowel to drain a few seconds. Spread a little sauce over the platter and arrange the *ravioloni* on top. Spoon sauce over the *ravioloni* and sprinkle with the grated cheese; hold in a warm oven (150 to 200°F) while the rest of the *ravioloni* cook. Repeat the process of cooking, draining, and layering the *ravioloni* with sauce and cheese until you have cooked as many *ravioloni* as desired. ❧

SAGE BUTTER

Salvia e burro is one of the most delicious sauces for *ravioloni*, cheese ravioli, or dumpling-style spinach ravioli (see recipe, page 151). If you grow your own sage, the sauce is inexpensive, and it can be made at a moment's notice.

To make the sauce, melt ½ cup butter in a small skillet over low heat. Tear 20 large sage leaves into thirds. As soon as the butter begins to melt, add the sage leaves. Adjust the heat as needed so the butter does not burn. The sauce is ready when the butter is lightly browned and the sage is crispy—remove the pan from the heat immediately so the sauce does not continue to brown. Makes enough sauce for about 35 *ravioloni*. (For other quantities of *ravioloni*, allow about 1½ tablespoons of butter and 3 sage leaves per serving.)

FERRAGOSTO

At the end of the Virgin Mary's life, she was taken directly to heaven. The event is called the *Assunzione della Madonna;* the holiday is called *Ferragosto*. Although today the Assumption of Mary is an important Catholic holiday, the celebration and its name have Roman pagan roots that date back over two thousand years. Over time, the Latin name *Feriae Augusti* (Emperor Augustus's holidays) has become *Ferragosto*. As with other Catholic holidays, the entire country takes the day off.

This holy feast is observed on August 15. In Umbria, days before the celebration, supermarkets and butcher shops feature fresh *oca* (goose), now a rarity at other times of the year. The tradition of eating goose on *Ferragosto* is Umbrian, not Italian.

At Mario and Michela's, we celebrated *Ferragosto* with a traditional lunch. Paola made an assortment of crostini for the antipasto. I simmered a quarter of a goose with pork, tomatoes, onion, celery, and carrot for a couple of hours, until it was rich and flavorful. Then I made homemade pasta for our first course, *tagliatelle con sugo d'oca*. Paola roasted potatoes and a goose—it came with its feet and innards attached. Before baking, she filled slits in the goose with fresh pork fat seasoned with sage, rosemary, garlic, salt, and pepper. When the roast came out of the wood-burning oven, it had deep brown crispy skin and moist aromatic meat. And the potatoes were amazing—simmered in the rich, tasty goose fat, they became crunchy and delicious.

9 ❧ Festivals and Events—
Le sagre e gli eventi

Sono pieno come un uovo!

(I am as full as an egg!)

THERE ARE HUNDREDS, MAYBE THOUSANDS, OF FESTIVALS AND CELEBRATIONS in Umbria every year. The festivities are one of the ways that past traditions, lifestyles, crafts, and culture are transferred from generation to generation. Many of the celebrations such as harvest festivals are linked to work, while others rejoice in the bounty of the earth—Montone's Festival of the Forest and Cannara's Onion Festival. Many have religious roots—Spello's *Le Infiorate del Corpus Domini*. Others are commercial—Perugia's Eurochocolate. Some focus on entertainment—Umbria Jazz.

During the main festival season, May through December, I spent many of my Sundays at *sagre* and *feste* (festivals and parties). My friend Silvia often came along. Highlights of this chapter include a summer solstice party at a villa in Perugia; a culinary competition; Gubbio's famous *Ceri* race; Umbertide's celebration of the 1800s; Foligno's marvelous Quintana, where for a week people dress and eat as their ancestors did during the Renaissance. There are too many festivals to talk about them all.

FESTA DELLA CIPOLLA

Umbrians love Cannara's ten-day Onion Festival in September, where every dish features the town's beloved bulb. In the evening, the food stands, exhibits, and festival restaurants open. Menus feature onions: steak with arugula and onions, roasted onions, onion soup, onion pizza, onion lasagne, to name a few. There's live entertainment. The only night we could go, it rained nonstop, so we ate, dashed back to the car, and drove home to dry out.

LA FESTA DEI CERI DI GUBBIO

My son Jacob and I arrived in Gubbio mid-morning on May 15 for the Festival of the *Ceri,* an annual celebration that dates back to at least the fourteenth century. That morning around 5:30, drummers marched through town to wake up the event's participants. Mass was held at eight o'clock, and we hoped to be at the Piazza Grande in time for *la alzata* (the rising) of the *Ceri.*

Long ago, the *Ceri* (which means candles) might actually have been lighted wax tapers carried in a procession to honor Sant' Ubaldo, but since the late 1800s the *Ceri* have been what you see today—three sixteen-foot-tall structures each topped with a miniature carved wooden statue of a saint, San Giorgio, Sant' Antonio, or Sant' Ubaldo, the town's patron. All the wooden saints wear flowing cloth vestments. The structures—made up of two bulky prisms, one stacked on top of the other—each weigh around six hundred pounds. That is a lot of weight for teams of men to carry on a 2.75-mile footrace through town and up a steep, winding road to the basilica above Gubbio. The *ceraioli* (men who bear the *Ceri*) wear white pants, and red sashes and neck scarves. Their shirt color depends on the saint they run with—gold for Sant' Ubaldo, blue for San Giorgio, and black for Sant' Antonio.

When we got to the Piazza Grande around 10:30, it was almost empty, but we could hear drummers and trumpeters below, where the procession had already started. We waited and waited, wondering if we were in the wrong place, but finally thousands of people squeezed into the piazza and *Eugubani* (citizens of Gubbio) filled second- and third-story balconies and windows facing the square. Shortly before noon, a group of drummers entered the piazza, followed by a man on horseback and people dressed in medieval costumes. The crowd sang; trumpets and drums played. People shouted, cheered, and clapped. From the steps on the piazza, people waved a half dozen flags. The *Ceri* had arrived.

Then things got a little scary. The three six-hundred-pound *Ceri* swayed and jerked unsteadily on the shoulders of the *ceraioli,* who raced around the flagpole in the tightly packed piazza. Somehow the crowd seemed to anticipate the *Ceri's* movements—the mob scurried to get out of the way. Suddenly the bells in the tower began ringing at a frenetic pace. The saints came to a halt and the *ceraioli* lowered the huge prisms to a horizontal position. The three captains each climbed their *Ceri's* H-frame (used to bear the *Ceri*). From the top of the frame, they each tossed a ceramic jug into the exuberant crowd. Then the teams of *ceraioli* struggled to lift the prisms upright again, to put the saints away so the *cittadini* (citizens) and *ceraioli* could attend the *banquette* at the Palazzo dei Consoli.

We ate lunch at a nearby restaurant and later wandered back to the Piazza Grande, so we missed the bishop giving his blessing at the start of the race, down below us near the town's entry. But we heard the trumpeters lead the procession of *Ceri*. We had been told that the first stretch of the race is particularly dangerous because the downhill is difficult to maneuver, but the *Ceri* finally arrived at the Piazza Grande. Soon after, the mayor waved a handkerchief from a second-story window—the cue for the bells to ring and the *Ceri* to speed around the flagpole again. Then the three saints, heads bobbing stories above the ground, raced up the ancient street. We followed the throng, walking behind the heavy carved statues, which wobbled and swayed—having near misses with balconies and the corners of buildings that lined the tight streets. Wherever the saints went, the crowd parted, letting them through, then closing up tight as soon as the trio passed. We stayed behind the *Ceri* all the way to the top of the mountain, huffing up the last mile, a steep, twisting road that ends at the Basilica di Sant' Ubaldo. The *ceraioli* ran the entire way.

Finally, Sant' Ubaldo reached the basilica, winning the race. With all the hooting and hollering, it was hard to believe that Sant' Ubaldo has won every race since the first one centuries ago. That Sant' Ubaldo always wins is one of the festival's unwritten rules—San Giorgio comes in second, and Sant' Antonio takes third place.

THE FESTIVAL CIRCUIT

Local festivals are a fun way to learn about the region's culture, cuisine, and history. To find out about events, the best sources are the town's tourist office or website and local residents. If you speak Italian or can get help with the language, check out the region's newspaper *Corriere dell' Umbria* culture section under *Appuntamenti—feste, mercati, e sagre* (Appointments—celebrations, markets, and festivals). Getting accurate, clear information can be a challenge. Oddly enough, newspaper articles and event advertisements often leave out crucial information, such as the time and date of the event! Most festivals do not charge an admission fee, and the crafts and food sold are generally reasonably priced. The food is usually rustic but delicious.

LE INFIORATE DEL CORPUS DOMINI

Several towns in Umbria have an *infiorata* (flower-art festival). Those of Città della Pieve and Cannara are supposed to be among the most beautiful, but people go to Spello's *le Infiorate del Corpus Domini* (Corpus Christi) by the busload, so I went to find out why. The *infiorate*, where ancient narrow streets were covered by intricate artwork made from flower petals and seeds, were noteworthy, but the religious procession celebrating Corpus Christi is what I found really fascinating. Since this daytime affair is tied to the holy feast, the *infiorate* falls in either May or June. After the festival, we lunched on La Bastiglia's elegant dining terrace, which has some of the best views—and most refined food—in the region. The herb-scented fried rabbit was exquisite.

SUMMER SOLSTICE AT VILLA COVONE

Friends invited me to join them for a summer solstice party at Villa Covone, about nine miles north of Perugia. Two decades ago, the family turned their private mansion into an inn and restaurant. The house was too large for the family, said Francesca, who grew up on the 124-acre estate. There are fourteen rooms and a large dining room on the second story, with floor to ceiling windows. During summer, meals are served on the patio. Today Francesca runs the kitchen and her mother works at the inn.

The evening of the party, the old stately villa, a black silhouette against the summer sky, windows aglow, made a romantic backdrop to the party that was held in the lush garden behind it. It was a cool June evening, but comfortable enough to sit outside bundled in a sweater.

The grounds are filled with surprises. A small herb garden waits to be discovered, hiding behind tall bushes. A meandering grass carpet, covered by a canopy of trees and decorated with statues, entices strollers to follow the Tiber River, which borders the property.

The family held the *festa* to celebrate the arrival of summer—as well as Umbrian cuisine and music. A young woman with a rich voice sang old Umbrian songs, accompanied by a guitar, an accordion, a mandolin, a bass, and bagpipes. After filling our plates and bellies from the splendid Umbrian buffet prepared by Francesca, we danced under the stars until midnight.

I returned to Villa Covone a month later to learn how to make some of the dishes Francesca had served at the party.

VILLA COVONE'S SUMMER SOLSTICE BUFFET MENU

Verdure fritte
Battered fried onions, zucchini, and eggplant

Pizze
Two-inch-diameter pizzas with tomato sauce, cheese, and bits of sausage

Patate sotto cenere
Potatoes cooked under ash (page 282)

Imbrecciata

Bean, farro, barley, and lentil salad (page 283)

Formaggio, noci e miele

Fresh and aged pecorino and *caciotta* cheese with assorted
nuts and honey

Cipolline in agrodolce

Sweet-and-sour onions—small, flat onions cooked in vinegar,
sugar, and oil.

Arvòltolo

Fried flat bread topped with salami and prosciutto (page 280)

Carne con salsa alle erbe

Thinly sliced roast beef and pork served with fresh
herb sauce (page 287)

Pollo all'arrabbiata

Chicken simmered in tomatoes with sage and
rosemary (page 286)

Salsiccie alla griglia

Grilled sausage

Torta al testo

Griddle bread (page 296)

Bietole

Chard (page 162)

Trofie con pancetta e pomodori

Pasta with lots of pancetta and bits of tomatoes

Panna cotta
Vanilla cream with strawberry sauce (page 289)

Torta di mele
Apple cake with fresh strawberry sauce

Fried Flat Bread
Arvòltolo
∞

I like to serve this light, chewy bread—hot out of the fryer—with a glass of wine to guests hanging out in the kitchen. But it is equally good served at the table as an appetizer, which is more in the Umbrian style of dining. Like many recipes from Umbria's rural areas, arvòltolo has become a trendy dish in the region's restaurants. Large wedges or sometimes pizza-size arvòltoli come to the table topped with goodies—sautéed spinach, prosciutto, salami, pecorino.

In Umbrian dialect, arvòltolo means "to turn again," probably referring to turning the bread while frying, or to the fact that farmers filled it with thin slices of meat and rolled the bread into a cylinder. The ingredients vary and the name changes, but fried bread similar to this one is common to most of Umbria.

This version of arvòltolo is the style of fried bread made in and around Perugia. This preparation is so regional that Umbrians outside of Perugia may have never heard of it. Francesca makes arvòltolo with yeast, but other cooks simply use flour and water.

Yield: 8 to 12 servings (you can cut the dough into as many pieces as you like)

Flour for rolling

1¾ pounds Quick Dough (see recipe—made with all-purpose flour, page 281)

Vegetable oil, for frying

A variety of thinly sliced cold cuts and cheese, such as mortadella, prosciutto, salami, and pecorino cheese

GETTING STARTED: Line several trays or plates with paper towels. Put a damp towel under a lightly floured large wooden board.

1. Cut the dough into quarters. Roll one piece of dough at a time on the floured board to a thickness of about ¼ inch. Use a zigzag pastry wheel, biscuit cutter, or knife to cut the dough into 2- or 3-inch pieces—squares, rectangles, trapezoids, circles, triangles. For flatter bread, prick the dough in several places with a fork.

2. Heat 1 to 2 inches of the oil in a large wok or skillet over medium-high heat until the oil is hot (375 to 385°F); adjust the heat as needed throughout frying to maintain the temperature. Briefly remove the wok from the heat if the oil becomes too hot or begins to smoke.

3. Carefully drop 3 or 4 pieces of dough (depending on size—do not crowd) into the oil. Fry until both sides are light golden, 1 to 2 minutes, turning once or twice. Use a skimmer or slotted spoon to transfer the bread to the trays lined with paper towels and then immediately to a platter with the cold cuts and cheese, or top the hot bread with the cold cuts and cheese. Serve immediately—the bread is best when it is fresh and hot.

Salted arvòltolo

As soon as the bread is fried, sprinkle it lightly with kosher salt. Salted arvòltolo can be served with wine as an appetizer or as a bread to accompany a meal. ❧

Quick Dough
Impasto rapido

This quick dough is ideal for arvòltolo (see recipe, page 280). It also makes acceptable pizza dough, but the flavor is not as good and the texture is not as chewy as the slow rising Pizza "On the Plate" (see recipe, page 130). It makes four individual pizzas (1¾ pounds dough). Refer to "Making Pizza" and "Pizza Toppings" (pages 132 and 135) to make pizza with the dough. For pizza, you can use either all-purpose flour or bread flour. To make Fried Flat Bread, use all-purpose flour. The recipe works in a bread machine on the dough cycle.

Toss together with a fork in a large bowl: 4 cups of all-purpose flour, 1 packet (2¼ teaspoons) instant yeast such as RapidRise (see "About Yeast," page 20), 1 teaspoon kosher salt (*important*: see "About Salt," page xxv), and 1 teaspoon sugar. Immediately mix in 1⅓ cups hot water (between 120 to 130°F) and 2 tablespoons extra virgin olive oil; mix well. Form a ball; let stand 10 minutes. Knead the dough until it is smooth and elastic, 10 to 15 minutes. Put the dough in an oiled bowl; cover with a clean nonterry towel. Let rise in a warm draft-free place until doubled, about 1 hour. (Alternatively, cover the bowl of dough with plastic wrap and let it rise overnight in the refrigerator.) The dough is now ready to use. ❧

POTATOES UNDER ASH

Patate sotto cenere is an old recipe dating back to the days when the *contadini* did much of their cooking in the *camino* (fireplace). Per serving, scrub one medium yellow potato and wrap it in foil. Several hours ahead, build a fire with untreated firewood. Put the potatoes on top of a layer of hot ash near the logs; cover with ash and bits of glowing embers, adding more once or twice during cooking. Bake until tender, about 45 minutes. To test for doneness, remove a potato with tongs; hold it in a clean towel, and squeeze gently. The potato yields to pressure when done. When done, discard the foil. Cut the potatoes lengthwise into quarters. Season with kosher salt and pepper; drizzle generously with extra virgin olive oil.

ONIONS UNDER ASH

To make *cipolle sotto cenere*, allow one medium red or yellow onion per person. Prepare the onions (without removing the skin) using the method for Potatoes Under Ash (above); wrap the onions in foil. Bake until tender, about 40 minutes. Discard the foil; peel the onions and cut them lengthwise into quarters. Season with salt and pepper; drizzle generously with extra virgin olive and add a few drops of balsamic vinegar.

Bean, Farro, Barley, and Lentil Salad
Insalata imbrecciata
☯

Once the legumes and grains are cooked, this exceptional salad is easy to put together. Francesca's method of cooking each item separately and precisely takes time, but it is worth the effort. This approach ensures that the legumes and grains retain their distinctive flavor, shape, and texture. Borlotti beans are the exception; they often split.

Corn, usually canned, is popular in Umbrian salads and even on pizza. For a brief period during the summer, dozens of packages of corn—two cobs each—in plastic-wrapped Styrofoam trays appear in produce sections, but I have never seen the gigantic displays of corn on the cob that we have in our stores.

You can vary the salad ingredients—add red onion, cucumbers, or fresh basil. I sometimes substitute fresh lemon juice for vinegar. Francesca used large tomatoes, but I prefer tiny cherry tomatoes such as Sweet 100s.

Francesca's recipe, a mix of five grains and beans, makes an abundant salad—perfect for a summer party. But if you'd prefer fewer portions (or cannot find farro), omit the farro (or barley), reduce the dry garbanzo beans to ½ cup, and slightly reduce the amount of tomatoes, corn, and parsley. Add the dressing to taste.

For a quick salad, substitute canned beans for dry beans—a 14-ounce can of garbanzo beans and a 14-ounce can of pinto beans (drain and rinse before using them). Adjust the dressing as needed.

This salad is often served as un contorno *(a side dish) with grilled meats or poultry, and on occasion it is served as an antipasto.*

Yield: 8 to 12 servings (about 8 cups)

¾ cup dry garbanzo beans, sorted and rinsed

½ cup dry *borlotti* or pinto beans, sorted and rinsed

Kosher salt (*important:* see "About Salt," page xxv)

½ cup semipearl or pearl farro

½ cup tiny dry brown or green lentils, sorted and rinsed (preferably from Umbria's Castelluccio or Colfiorito; see page 260)

½ cup pearl barley

3 to 5 tablespoons white wine vinegar or fresh lemon juice

1 large garlic clove, pressed through a garlic press

½ cup extra virgin olive oil or more to taste

12 ounces cherry tomatoes, preferably Sweet 100s

1 cup packed Italian parsley, chopped

1 to 1½ cups cooked corn kernels, about 2 ears fresh corn (optional)

Freshly ground pepper

1. Put the garbanzo beans in a medium saucepan and the *borlotti* beans in a small saucepan. Add water until it reaches several inches above the surface of the beans. Cover and bring to a boil over high heat; simmer 4 minutes. Turn off heat; let stand about 1 hour. (Alternatively, soak beans separately in cold water, refrigerated, for 8 hours.)

2. Drain and rinse the beans well under cold water. Return the beans to their respective saucepans; add 4 cups cold water to the garbanzo beans, 3 cups to the *borlotti*, and 1 teaspoon kosher salt to each saucepan. Bring to a boil; cover and simmer gently, stirring occasionally, until the beans are just tender (garbanzo beans take 2½ to 3 hours; *borlotti*, 40 to 45 minutes; pinto beans or old beans may take longer—refer to packages). If necessary, add water to keep the beans covered.

3. Drain the beans; let cool. When cool to the touch (do not leave at room temperature longer than 1 hour) put the beans together in a large bowl; cover and refrigerate.

4. While the beans cook, rinse the farro; put it into a small saucepan. Add 2½ to 3 cups cold water and 1 teaspoon kosher salt. Turn the heat on high and set the timer for 25 minutes—you will taste for doneness at this point. (Refer to the package for cooking time.) When the farro boils, immediately reduce the heat to medium low—adjust the heat as needed to keep the farro at a gentle simmer. Simmer uncovered, stirring occasionally, until the farro is *al dente,* 25 to 30 minutes.

5. Drain the farro and rinse it well under cold water so the grains do not stick together when cooled. (Set aside the saucepan to use later.) Let the farro drain for 5 minutes, shaking the strainer occasionally to help remove excess water. Put the farro into the large bowl with the beans.

6. Use the same saucepan and steps to separately cook, drain, and rinse the lentils and the barley (lentils take 25 to 40 minutes; barley 30 to 45 minutes—taste early so you don't overcook them). When the lentils and barley are cool, add them to the bowl with the beans.

7. Meanwhile, mix together in a small bowl 3 tablespoons of the vinegar, the garlic, and 1½ teaspoons kosher salt. Whisk in the oil. By now, the beans, farro, lentils, and barley should be together in the large bowl. Pour just enough of the dressing over the legume mixture to lightly coat; toss. At this point, the salad can be covered and refrigerated for several hours.

8. About 40 minutes before serving, cut the cherry tomatoes into halves (or quarters if they are large). Add the tomatoes and parsley to the bowl of beans (if using corn, add it now); toss gently. Add more dressing to taste. Adjust the vinegar and salt; season to taste with pepper. Let stand ½ hour so the flavors marry. Serve chilled or at a cool room temperature. ❧

ROCKY ROAD—*L'IMBRECCIATA*

The Umbrians have a sense of humor when it comes to naming recipes. Take *imbrecciata*, for example—the name of two wonderful traditional Umbrian dishes. One is a soup and the other a salad, both made from legumes and grains.

In Umbrian dialect, *imbrecciata* refers to a rock-strewn road—not exactly a mouth-watering term. "Turn right when you come to the first *strada imbrecciata* [gravel road]." The soup and salad get their name from the rocky appearance of the beans, lentils, barley, and other legumes and grains that Umbrian cooks use to make these classic dishes—not a pebble, stone, or bit of gravel in the ingredient list.

Chicken Braised in Tomatoes

Pollo all'arrabbiata

This rustic dish is an old favorite from the countryside. Bread, the scarpetta *(little shoe), is served with the chicken to scoop up the rich sauce. If you like dark meat, chicken drumsticks and thighs are ideal—during the long simmering they stay moist. A mix of chicken parts is fine, too. In Umbria, all'arrabbiata is made with all kinds of poultry, and even rabbit. Stores sell an array of poultry—* faraona, anatra, pollo, gallina, piccione, grangallo, *and* ruspante *(guinea hen, duck, chicken, old hen, squab, and two kinds of free-range chicken). Most poultry is sold with the head and feet intact and the* interiora *(innards) attached inside the belly—cook the giblets with the chicken if you want to. The first time I cooked a* grangallo, *I was a bit unnerved by cutting off its head and feet—and startled when a foot moved as I tried to cut it off with poultry shears! The bones seemed harder and more difficult to cut than those of an American chicken.*

Yield: 4 main-dish servings (or 6 to 8 second-course servings)

1 can (14 ounces) whole tomatoes with juice

3½ pounds chicken pieces

2½ teaspoons kosher salt (*important*: see "About Salt," page xxv)

⅛ to ¼ teaspoon red pepper flakes (use ¼ teaspoon for a spicier dish)

¼ cup extra virgin olive oil

2 (6-inch) sprigs rosemary

2 sprigs fresh sage (about 6 leaves each)

5 large garlic cloves, lightly crushed with a knife blade, and peeled

2 bay leaves

1¾ cups dry white wine, such as pinot grigio or sauvignon blanc

1. Purée the tomatoes using an immersion blender or food processor; set aside. Season the chicken on both sides with the kosher salt and red pepper.

Heat the oil with 1 rosemary sprig, 1 sage sprig, 3 garlic cloves, and 1 bay leaf in a large skillet over medium heat, but do not let the garlic brown.

2. Add half of the chicken to the skillet (do not crowd); sauté until well browned on both sides, 15 to 20 minutes. With a slotted spoon, transfer the chicken, herbs, and garlic to a large bowl. Brown the rest of the chicken with the remaining rosemary, sage, garlic, and bay in the same manner. Dump the chicken (and aromatics) from the bowl into the skillet. Pour the wine over the chicken.

3. Reduce the heat to medium low. Simmer the chicken uncovered, turning once or twice, until the wine is almost gone, about 15 minutes. Stir in the reserved tomatoes; cover and simmer, stirring occasionally, until the sauce is thickened and flavorful and the chicken is tender and no longer pink at the bone, 20 to 30 minutes. Remove the rosemary sprigs and bay leaves. Season to taste with salt.

NOTE: If the sauce is soupy rather than saucy when the chicken is done, remove the chicken and simmer the sauce until thickened. For moist white meat, remove white pieces as soon as done; finish cooking the dark meat. Return the white pieces to the skillet during the last few minutes of cooking to reheat. ❧

Herb Sauce

Salsa alle erbe
∞

When Francesca and I made this salsa together, we picked a selection of herbs from her garden, so the sauce was inexpensive. If you buy the herbs, the farmers' market will probably offer better prices than the grocery store. The recipe is flexible, so use whatever mix of herbs you like or have on hand. Basil and thyme are not in the ingredient list, but they are both good additions. Thyme is potent, so if you use it, a teaspoon is enough, but basil is similar to parsley—you can use lots of it. Before mincing the herbs, remove and discard any woody stems.

This fragrant herb sauce transforms the plainest roast into an elegant dish. To serve the salsa with roast beef, pork, or turkey breast, slice the meat very thin (for easy slicing, slightly cool or chill the meat ahead). The sauce is also wonderful with grilled steak, chicken, fish, lamb, or pork tenderloin (see "How to Grill Pork

Tenderloin," below). These long one-pound roasts cook quickly—and make just two servings each, but you can cook as many as you need to serve a crowd.

Yield: About ¾ cup (allow 2 tablespoons per serving)

⅓ cup packed parsley, minced

¼ cup thinly sliced chives

12 large mint leaves, minced (about 2 teaspoons)

2 (3-inch) sprigs oregano, minced (about 2 teaspoons)

2 (3-inch) sprigs marjoram, minced (about 1 teaspoon)

1 (4-inch) sprig rosemary, stem discarded, minced (about ½ teaspoon)

2 large sage leaves, minced (about ½ teaspoon)

⅔ cup extra virgin olive oil

2 teaspoons balsamic vinegar

½ teaspoon kosher salt (*important:* see "About Salt," page xxv)

1. Put the parsley, chives, mint, oregano, marjoram, rosemary, and sage into a jar or small bowl; pour the oil over the herbs. Stir in the vinegar and kosher salt; mix well.

2. Let stand about ½ hour to develop the flavor. (Do not leave at room temperature longer than 1 hour—can be made ahead and stored in the refrigerator up to 2 days. If refrigerated, bring out ½ hour before serving to melt the oil.) Serve the sauce with fish, thinly sliced roasts, or grilled pork, beef, lamb, turkey, or chicken.

NOTE: Seasoned oils such as this *salsa* must be refrigerated to prevent the risk of botulism. ❧

How to Grill Pork Tenderloin

Rub a tablespoon of oil over a pork tenderloin to coat all sides—allow ½ tenderloin per serving. Season on all sides with kosher salt and freshly ground pepper. Grill the tenderloins on a covered grill over medium heat until the internal temperature reaches between 145 to 150°F, 20 to 30 minutes. Transfer to a cutting board; tent with foil. Let stand 15 to 30 minutes. Use a long, sharp knife to cut the meat crosswise into ⅛- to ¼-inch slices. Spoon a thin layer of *salsa alle erbe* (see recipe, page 287) on a platter. Arrange the sliced meat over the sauce. Spoon more *salsa* over the meat.

Vanilla Cream with Strawberry Sauce
Panna cotta con salsa di fragole
∞

Panna cotta, which means "cooked cream," is a heavenly dessert—a cross between custard and whipped cream. Restaurants all over Umbria serve panna cotta with a variety of sauces, from berry to caramel to chocolate. Francesca served it at Villa Covone's summer party with this fresh strawberry sauce. Her recipe uses clear, paper-thin sheets of gelatin, which I think make a more delicate panna cotta. Unfortunately, this type of gelatin is not readily available to home cooks in the States, so I have adapted the recipe for granulated gelatin.

Panna cotta is the perfect dinner party dessert—it takes minutes to make and needs to be made ahead to set the gelatin. This method of heating just the milk and then adding cold cream to the hot milk helps set the panna cotta more quickly. For even faster setting, you can use small containers—shot glasses, espresso cups, or small bowls (all perfect sizes for a dessert sampler plate).

For the recipe to work properly, the milk and cream must be homogenized—not the cream-on-the-top style. (See "About Homogenized Milk," page 167.)

Yield: 8 to 10 servings

2¾ cups cold homogenized whole milk

2 envelopes unflavored gelatin (7 grams each)

1 vanilla bean, split lengthwise, or 1 teaspoon vanilla extract

⅔ cup sugar plus more to sweeten the sauce

1 quart cold homogenized heavy cream

2 pint baskets strawberries, quartered (about 4 cups)

Strawberries for garnish, small or sliced (optional)

YOU'LL ALSO NEED: 8 to 10 wineglasses (to use a mold or other containers, see Note, below). A funnel is helpful.

1. Off the stove, pour the cold milk into a heavy, medium saucepan; sprinkle the gelatin over the milk. Whisk to mix well; let stand 5 minutes to soften the gelatin. Split the vanilla bean lengthwise with a paring knife; scrape the open pod to remove the seeds inside. Add the seeds and bean pod to the milk (if using vanilla extract, add it later).

2. Heat the milk over medium-high heat, stirring constantly, until the milk is steaming hot but not boiling, 4 to 5 minutes; remove from the heat. Use a slotted spoon to remove and discard the vanilla bean pod. Add the ⅔ cup sugar; stir until dissolved. Stir in the cream (if using vanilla extract, add it now).

3. To ladle the cream mixture into the wineglasses, rest a funnel in the glass to keep the glass clean—allow at least 1 inch of headspace for the sauce. Cover each glass with plastic wrap; carefully transport the glasses to the refrigerator. Chill until set (allow several hours).

4. For the sauce, purée the 2 pint baskets of strawberries in a food processor. Strain the sauce; discard the seeds. Add 3 tablespoons sugar; stir to dissolve. Adjust the sugar to taste. Cover; refrigerate until serving time.

5. Just before serving, spoon sauce on top of each glass of *panna cotta* (if using, garnish with the small or sliced strawberries). If there is extra sauce, pass it at the table.

NOTE: To use molds instead of glasses, divide the mixture between 2 medium-size metal molds or stainless-steel bowls, each with about a 4-cup capacity. Cover; refrigerate until set (allow about 8 hours). Shortly before serving, fill a large bowl three quarters full of warm water. Dip one mold at a time into the water up to the cream; remove after about 10 seconds. When the *panna cotta* pulls away from the bowl's edge when pressed with a finger, it is ready to unmold (dip into the water again as needed to unmold). Run cold water over 2 serving plates; drain excess water. Put a plate upside down on top of each mold. One mold at a time, hold the plate and mold firmly together and turn the mold upside down. When the *panna cotta* has transferred to the plate, lift off the mold. If the *panna cotta* isn't perfectly plated, shake and jiggle the plate until it is centered. ❧

THREE IDEAS FOR *PANNA COTTA*

Make the recipe for Vanilla Cream (see recipe, page 289), using one of the variations that follow.

1. **Berry Sauce:** Substitute the equivalent of 2 pint baskets—or an equal amount of frozen—mixed berries for the strawberries: blackberries, blueberries, raspberries, strawberries.

2. **Quick Berry Sauce:** Rather than puréeing the strawberries for the sauce, finely dice them or use a mix of diced berries. Sweeten the fruit with sugar to taste. Cover and refrigerate at least ½ hour and up to 2 hours ahead.

3. **Saffron Cream:** To make *panna cotta con zafferano,* follow the recipe for Vanilla Cream with the following changes: Lightly grind 1 teaspoon of saffron threads with a mortar and pestle or between your fingers. Steep the saffron in 2 tablespoons of hot water for at least ½ hour but preferably 2 hours. Substitute ⅔ cup honey for the sugar. Stir in the saffron water (and any bits of saffron) with the cream. Serve with berry sauce.

THE WEEKLY MARKET—*IL MERCATO*

Almost every town, village, and city in Umbria has a weekly outdoor *mercato* (market). While I lived in Umbertide, I went to the Wednesday *mercato* in the historic downtown almost every week, and sometimes

I visited markets in other towns. In addition to the weekly markets that focus on produce, clothes, and household goods, a lot of towns have regular flea/antiques markets. Many of the vendors at the market in Umbertide are local farmers, so the produce is really fresh. But the market is also the place to shop for cheese, cured meats, dried fish and mushrooms, cheap-but-chic clothes, purses, shoes, boots, cosmetics, scissors, bedspreads, blankets, towels, aprons, linens, jewelry, sunglasses, flowers, plants, and kitchen utensils—skillets, bowls, espresso pots. The *mercato* is where locals go for bargains—and to have *caffè* with a friend.

Another reason locals flock to the market is to buy *porchetta* (whole roast pig). From a catering truck, the butchers slice the fennel-scented pork to order. Some customers buy slices of meat, wrapped to go, but most people order a sandwich and eat it on the spot. The sandwiches are divine—the pork is warm and flavorful, and the bread rolls are fresh. Before closing the sandwich, the vendor tops the meat with a handful of crispy pork rind and sprinkles it with salt.

FESTA DEL BOSCO

The Festival of the Forest is held in late October in Montone, a charming hill town in the Upper Tiber River valley. The mood is merry—the sound of live music can be heard throughout the village. Several neighborhoods run *taverne* (casual restaurants) staffed by locals wearing medieval costumes. The menus offer traditional dishes—bruschetta with truffles, griddle bread stuffed with sausages, garbanzo bean soup. The village's winding streets are lined with vendors selling handmade crafts—baskets, tablecloths, jewelry—and local food products: fresh truffles, olive oil, dried porcini, polenta with truffles, garbanzo beans, salami, cheese, chestnuts, cookies.

One year, there was a fascinating exhibit of wild mushrooms. Three long tables displayed dozens of varieties of the *funghi*. Some were *commestibile* (edible), many were *velenoso* (poisonous), and a few were *tossico* (toxic). At one table, strange brown flowerlike mushrooms sent a steady stream of vapor into the air—they were not edible. Were the fumes *tossico*? Jars of preserved local snakes were scattered among the mushrooms—a reminder of another danger lurking in the woods. All the snakes had the distinctive triangular head of the deadly viper.

AND THE WINNER IS . . .

I drove to meet the cookbook author Rita Boini for a traditional dinner in Colombella, a tiny village in the hills north of Perugia. Rival culinary teams from all over Umbria would prepare the dinner at this culinary competition, which attracts the best home cooks. Rita would be one of the judges—and she promised to introduce me to Silvana, one of the cooks.

Driving to *la cena* (the dinner) with my stomach growling, I thought about what might be served. *Crostini con fegato* (bread with liver pâté), the quintessential Umbrian antipasto. Certainly homemade pasta or polenta and grilled meat. I had been to dinners like this before, and I remembered the sights and smells with pleasure. *Nonne* kneading mounds of dough and rolling it into tablecloth-size sheets of pasta. A kitchen fragrant with garlic, tomato, and onion rising from a bubbling pot of meat sauce. A woman in a floral apron stirring the sauce with a spoon the size of an oar. An old man engulfed by smoke, hunched over an outdoor hearth grilling homemade sausages and chops over glowing coals.

When I arrived at the dinner, rows of cafeteria tables and hundreds of folding chairs had turned the community auditorium into an enormous dining hall. The smell of bread baked in a wood oven filled the air, and steam clung to the windows as it did when I cooked spaghetti at home. Bottles of homemade *vino* and *acqua naturale* decked the tables along with a copy of last year's winning recipe, Salt Cod with Prunes. Six judges, including Rita, sat at a VIP table, ready to begin the critique. Waiters passed by carrying trays suspended above their shoulders, their arms like pedestals. As they headed toward the table of judges, whiffs of grilled sausage lingered behind.

"Umbrian sausages are *semplice* [simple]," announced the head judge, reading from a script into a microphone. "Ground pork, garlic, salt, pepper, *basta* [that's it]." In Umbria, *salsiccia* (sausage) is often cooked with grapes or *lenticchie* (lentils). For the contest, the cooks served the sausages with wild greens between slices of *torta al testo,* an ancient Umbrian flat bread. "Our *nonne* used to cook the *torta* on a very hot *testo* [griddle] on a stand over the coals in the fireplace." The judge returned to his seat to begin the job of tasting.

As the judges chewed and swallowed bites from each sample, the crowd quieted, turning their eyes to the head table. The judges silently took notes, quaffing water between tastes, with a seriousness I had seen only at wine tastings. The cadre of waiters returned to the head table with *il secondo piatto*.

We in the audience sat with eyes on the judges, anxiously waiting for our plates to arrive. On the judges' plates, I could see green vegetables and chunks of dark meat, but no pasta or polenta with meat sauce, no grilled pork chops.

"What do you think they're eating?" I whispered to my neighbor.

"I think it's some kind of stew, maybe *agnello* [lamb]," she replied.

The sights and aromas surprised me. They didn't fit the traditional dinner I had imagined. I watched a judge put a dark morsel into his mouth. He chewed and swallowed methodically. The head judge stood again, wiping his mouth with a paper napkin, "The side dish, *verza e patate* [cabbage and potatoes], is a very traditional recipe from Umbria's *contadini*. Everyone grew potatoes and cabbage." He told us the chopped cabbage and bits of potatoes were sautéed in olive oil when times were good or in lard when times were tough.

"In the past, whenever a farmer slaughtered a pig, the neighbors would come to help," he continued. "Farmers were isolated. They lived far from their neighbors, so the event became an important social occasion. When the work was done, they ate dinner together—*fegato, polmone e cuore* of the pig."

"Liver, lung, and heart," I echoed when the judge finished speaking.

When my plate appeared, I looked down at the pork *interiora* and ate the liver, which I was acquiring a taste for. I took hunks of the heart and swallowed them like aspirin with swigs of red wine. I pushed bits of the spongy lung around my paper plate, trying to make it look as though I'd eaten more than I had. I ate every last crumb of the *torta* and the *verza e patate* on my plate.

At the end of dinner, a judge announced the winners and presented the cooks to the audience. In turn, Rita introduced me to Silvana. I got Silvana's phone number and the promise of a cooking lesson at her house.

As I drove home, I thought about how lucky I had been to partake in the dinner—even though the menu wasn't what I had expected. I had spent the evening with neighbors and friends, celebrating the bounty of the pig as Umbrian farmers had done for centuries. I could eat pasta anytime.

Fennel Salad

Insalata di finocchio
∞

I eat this salad more often than almost any other salad, including tossed greens. With only a couple of ingredients, I can make this special salad in just a few minutes.

When making insalata di finocchio *for a crowd, it is tempting to use a mandoline to slice the fennel into ultrathin slices in seconds. But unless you have a mandoline that allows you to adjust the thickness, it is better to slice the fennel by hand—and the unevenness of hand-sliced fennel adds texture and interest to the salad. If the fennel is too thin, the salad quickly turns limp and watery.*

Silvana's fennel salad is simple—sliced fennel, white wine vinegar, olive oil, salt, and pepper. Using fresh lemon juice rather than vinegar and adding shaved Parmigiano-Reggiano, as many restaurants do, is a contemporary version—and one that I adore. These simple changes transform a rustic salad into an elegant dish—perfect for company.

Yield: 4 to 6 servings

2 medium fresh fennel bulbs

Wedge of Parmigiano-Reggiano cheese (see Note, page 296)

2 to 3 tablespoons fresh lemon juice

¾ teaspoon kosher salt (*important:* see "About Salt," page xxv)

Dash of freshly ground pepper

3 tablespoons extra virgin olive oil

1. Use a vegetable peeler to trim off the tough portions of the fennel bulb. Do not cut off the bulbs' stalks—they make a useful handle for slicing. Cut about ¼ inch off the bottom of each bulb; slice the bulbs lengthwise into halves.

2. Holding on to the stalk, slice each bulb crosswise (starting at the bottom of the bulb) into very thin slices until you reach the stalk (you should

have about 8 cups of fennel). Put the fennel into a bowl large enough to accommodate tossing. At this point, you can cover and refrigerate the fennel for several hours.

3. Use a vegetable peeler to shave thin "leaves" of cheese into a bowl (you will need about ¾ cup of shavings, about 1½ ounces); cover and refrigerate.

4. Shortly before serving, drizzle 2 tablespoons of the lemon juice over the fennel. Sprinkle the fennel with the kosher salt and pepper; toss well. Drizzle with the oil; toss until the fennel is well coated. Adjust the lemon juice to taste. Add the cheese; toss gently. Adjust the salt and pepper to taste. Serve immediately.

NOTE: You need a wedge of cheese to make shavings even though you will use less than 2 ounces of cheese.

Substitution
Use 3 or 4 teaspoons white wine vinegar for the lemon juice. ❧

Griddle Bread
Torta al testo
❦

This ancient bread predates home ovens. In Umbrian farmhouses, a testo *(griddle) near the fireplace was always handy. The earliest style of* testo *was made of clay and marble dust and chips that were shaped into a large disk and fired in an oven used for making bricks. Today people often cook the bread on the stove using a heavy metal griddle, but a Mexican* comal *or a cast-iron skillet also works well. An electric griddle is another option.*

The original cooking method involved covering the top of the bread (after browning one side and turning it over) with embers and ash. The traditional recipe calls for flour, water, and a pinch of salt and baking soda. When wheat flour was scarce, cooks made the bread with corn flour. With today's prosperity, recipes sometimes include milk, eggs, cheese, and olive oil or lard—ingredients that make the torta *tender and more flavorful. And baking power often replaces the soda. Silvana has adopted many of these changes—her recipe makes a dense, moist bread that is soft inside, with a slightly crunchy, chewy crust.*

Torta al testo *is affectionately called* la scarpetta *(the little shoe) when it is used to mop sauce off a plate. But the bread is more than a scoop. It can be split open and stuffed to make a meal or a snack. Traditional fillings include fresh mozzarella or pecorino cheese; grilled sausage and sautéed wild greens or spinach; fresh mozzarella and sautéed greens; prosciutto, salami, and other cured meats with or without cheese.*

You'll find this bread all over Umbria under a variety of names, depending on the locale. In Umbertide, where I lived, it was originally called torta bianca *(white bread) but now it is usually called* torta al testo, *named after the* testo *it is cooked on. About forty minutes away in Gubbio, the bread is called* crescia sul panàro. Panàro *is another name for the griddle. In Città di Castello, just south of the Tuscan border, the* torta *goes by* ciaccia sul panàro.

Yield: 4 servings

3 cups (13½ ounces) all-purpose flour plus more for rolling

2½ teaspoons double-acting baking powder

1 teaspoon kosher salt (*important:* see "About Salt," page xxv)

⅔ cup cold sparkling water (preferred) or tap water

3 tablespoons milk

2 tablespoons extra virgin olive oil

1 large egg yolk

YOU'LL ALSO NEED: A rolling pin and a heavy griddle or *comal* (large enough to accommodate a 10½- to 11-inch circle of dough). Alternatively, use a heavy skillet—make two breads if the skillet is too small for one.

GETTING STARTED: Put a damp towel under a large floured wooden board to keep the board from slipping.

1. Put the flour, baking powder, and kosher salt into a large bowl; mix with a fork. Make a well in the center; add the water, milk, oil, and egg yolk. Use a fork to mix, slowly incorporating the dry ingredients. Work the dough briefly by hand to form the dough—there will be lots of crumbs.

2. Transfer the dough and crumbs to the floured board; work by hand to make a ball. (Set the bowl aside to use later.) Knead the dough, working in the crumbs, by using the heel of your hand to push the dough away from you, slightly flattening the ball. Then fold it in half and turn it halfway around. If the dough is sticky, dust it with a little flour. Knead until the dough is smooth and elastic, 7 to 8 minutes.

3. Flatten and shape the dough into a 6-inch disk. Scrape the surface of the board clean, if needed. Lightly flour the board. Put the dough on the board, and cover it with the mixing bowl. Let rest ½ hour.

4. Lightly rub flour over the board, rolling pin, and surface of the dough. Flatten the dough into a fat disk. Starting in the center of the disk, roll out toward the edge of the dough; reduce pressure near the edge so it doesn't become too thin. Continue rolling from the center out, going clockwise around the dough to create a 10½- to 11-inch circle, about ⅜ inch thick.

5. Heat a heavy griddle over medium heat. After 5 minutes, sprinkle a little flour on the griddle. When it feels hot a couple of inches above the griddle and the flour turns golden, the griddle is ready—about 10 minutes total. Carefully wipe the griddle clean with a paper towel.

6. Transfer the dough to the hot griddle and carefully adjust it to fit on the griddle. Set a timer for 20 minutes. As soon as the dough begins to rise, push the backside of fork tines into the dough, lowering the fork to about a 25-degree angle to make a ¾-inch-long pattern in the dough. Repeat every inch or so over the entire surface. When the bottom is brown (about 3 minutes), turn the bread over; reduce the heat to medium low.

7. When both sides are brown (after 2 or 3 minutes), reduce the heat to low and turn the dough four more times, for a total of 20 minutes. Transfer to a clean board. When cool enough to handle, cut the bread with kitchen shears or a knife into 6 to 8 wedges. Serve the bread with braised meats or poultry, or stuff as desired. To stuff the bread, slice open the wedges. Serve immediately. (Alternatively, store bread for a day or two in a plastic bag—reheat in a 400°F oven for a few minutes. Or store in a freezer bag in the freezer for up to 2 months.) 🐾

Mostra Mercato Nazionale del Tartufo Bianco

Gubbio's four-day National White Truffle Exhibition and Market is a good place to buy truffles and to taste them in traditional dishes. When I went, there were three large exhibition halls. Several stands sold fresh white and black truffles and truffle products, including sauces, liqueur, pecorino, salami, bread, honey, butter, and polenta and rice mixes—all flavored with truffles. There were vendors selling cookies, pastries, candy, and cheese from Sardinia, olives from Puglia, and spicy jars of sauce from Calabria. One hall featured artisans and their products—embroidery, ceramics, clothes, oil paintings, carved wood, marble and stone sculptures, and iron fireplace screens and tools. One ironworker made authentic-looking reproductions of the medieval iron pieces seen in the palaces and buildings around town. The fair's program included entertainment and dining in an elegant makeshift restaurant where nine of the menu items featured white or black truffles, including salt cod, carpaccio, pasta, risotto, and frittata. Prices were moderate to high, but the food was good.

Feste di Settembre di Fine '800

During four evenings every year in September, the twenty-first century collides with the nineteenth in Umbertide, formerly called Fratta. Clerks in shops, wait staff in restaurants, and many of the *cittadini* (citizens) dress in period clothing from two hundred years ago. Men sport military uniforms and carry rifles or wear suits, vests, and skinny bow ties—and, of course, a straw or top hat. Women dress in frilly floor-length dresses, cinched in tightly at the waist, and cover their heads in broad-brimmed hats decorated with ribbons, lace, and flowers. Craftsmen and peasants wear plain, long skirts or pants and blousy white tops, covered with a utilitarian apron. During the *feste,* the downtown becomes a living theater with tall red curtains hanging from the walls of adjacent buildings framing the main stage, the Piazza Matteotti. The *festa* program changes nightly, but always includes food, music, and lectures on style, culture, and traditions of the 1800s.

The Historical Association of Fratta '800 organizes this four-day affair. The festival is a history lesson and a celebration of the 1800s, an important period that ushered in many social and cultural changes due to industrialization. One new industry at the time in Fratta was the manufacture of silk.

The year I attended, men dressed in military attire told stories to an ever-changing audience at La Rocca (the tower of an ancient fort), and at a nearby piazza, someone recited poetry. Later there was a puppet show and a comedy act. The next day there would be balloon rides near La Rocca. Every night, an old-fashioned merry-go-round tempted *bambini* (children), and ten *osterie, taverne,* and *locande* (casual dining places) served authentic 1800s fare. At the end of the *feste,* these dining spots would disappear, reverting to their current use—a church courtyard, a bar patio, a basement, a room in a private home, a park lawn.

Most of the restaurants had a theme—and a menu to match. One served simple convent food; polenta was one of the frugal dishes. Another promised food of the country *osteria*—sautéed pork and griddle bread with wild greens. Others featured flavors from antiquity, such as salt cod with potatoes, or hearty food such as polenta with pork rind and beans, simmered lamb innards, tagliatelle with chicken giblets or goose ragù, pork liver with herbs, and braised "angry" chicken.

People strolled from menu board to menu board, nibbling on corn on the cob, sold by a woman who grilled it on a distant corner. By 8:30 that evening, the town was packed and almost every restaurant had a long line. My visiting American friend Ann and I chose an *osteria* in an open church courtyard on Piazza San Francesco. The setting was pleasant and the queue was short. Candles in the upper church windows and on tables brightened the dark courtyard. A few minutes after we sat down, Umbertide's city band, men dressed in white pants and blue tops with white sailor collars, swaggered around the dining tables. Then each musician took up a post in one of the archways and raised an instrument—trumpet, trombone, saxophone. But minutes after they started to play, a group of young men in red shirts and blue pants—the Garibaldini—arrived, toting rifles and waving Italian flags. The crowd went nuts. In the mid-1800s, the popular hero Giuseppe Garibaldi led these volunteer soldiers in a fight to unite Italy. The Red Shirts and the men in blue sang joyous victory songs.

Our waitress, wearing a coarse ankle-length tan skirt and white peasant blouse, delivered our food on long wooden trays. Ann and I shared an antipasto plate—sliced salami and *capocolo* (cured pork), liver crostini, fresh pecorino, bruschetta with olive oil, and *panzanella* (bread salad). For a second course, I ordered pork sautéed with rosemary and Ann ate *torta al testo* (griddle bread) filled with grilled sausage and wild greens.

After dinner, in our search for dessert, we came upon the bustling Via Bovicelli. For the *feste,* residents of the narrow street transformed garages and entryways into centuries-old shops and businesses—an ironworker's shop, a woodworker's studio, a card reader, and a fortune-teller. A garage in an old stone house was converted into a nineteenth-century house. A hostess, wearing an apron over a long skirt and blouse, greeted us in the main room— used for living, dining, and cooking. The furnishings were rustic and simple, but stone walls and a beamed ceiling made it feel cozy. A worn *battilarda* (wooden cutting board) sat inside a top-opening cabinet—the forerunner of a kitchen cupboard. A long-handled basket (used to scoop up pasta) hung near a blackened pot at the fireplace. A long rolling pin and a wooden pasta board peeked out from under the dining table. A trunk held a bin of flour and loaves of bread. A wooden saltbox (used to keep salt dry) and two gadgets, one for toasting *orzo* (barley) and another for grinding it, were stored on a nearby shelf. People drank *caffè d'orzo* when coffee was too expensive or unavailable. Near the fireplace, baby chicks chirped inside a handmade wooden crate. The small bedroom had a bed with an iron frame, a ceramic washstand, and a few simple garments hanging from hooks on the wall.

By the time we traversed the city, from Via Bovicelli to our car, we had seen soldiers firing rifles in a mock war, militiamen marching and singing victory songs, fragments of a comedy act, and part of magic and puppet shows. We had visited the house of a nineteenth-century city dweller, and eaten a peasant meal. The *Feste di Settembre di Fine '800* is an event too good to be missed.

La Quintana

If you want to step back in time and see how Italians lived, ate, and dressed during the Renaissance, go to Foligno in September during the Quintana. This two-week event in the central Umbrian city will keep you busy and amused. The festival opens with the *Fiera dei Soprastanti,* a fair based on a Renaissance marketplace. The event planners insist that everything be authentic—from the crafts sold to the costumes worn to the food served. The euro is worthless—merchants accept only the *quattrino,* the coin used centuries ago. Artisans—weavers, spinners, bakers, ceramicists, artists, woodworkers, ironworkers, coppersmiths, lace makers—sell their wares. Craftsmen offer how-to demonstrations. The *fiera* has the bustling atmosphere of an ancient marketplace. It is packed with people and enlivened with entertainers—flag jugglers, dancers on stilts, musicians.

Throughout the two weeks, ten of the city's districts operate *taverne* (casual restaurants), serving traditional dishes from the seventeenth century. When I went, a group of us ate at the Rione Giotti (Giotti district) *taverna*. The food was simple but good—we shared plates. An antipasto of mixed *bruschette*—with tomatoes, anchovies, and olive oil. Beans with pork rind, polenta with sausage, grilled pork chops, roast lamb, fried potatoes, and salad. We passed on the snails, tripe, salt cod, and braised lamb innards. But we drank our fill of cheap red house wine and enjoyed apple strudel, biscotti, and *vinsanto* for dessert.

When we came out of the *taverna*, a parade was at the restaurant's door. Row after row of onlookers made it hard to see the marching drummers and trumpeters, but we could hear them loud and clear. When we inched our way into the crowd, we saw a group of elegant knights prancing on horseback, wearing helmets with two-foot-tall colorful feather headpieces. Their horses' backs were draped in satin and velvet blankets decorated with gold braid and tassels. From where we stood, the parade looked endless. Couples—ladies and gentlemen—strode by arm in arm, dressed in Spanish-inspired Renaissance costumes. The women wore brocade, satin, and velvet dresses with long, sweeping trains and V-shaped waists. Bodices were decorated with embroidery, jewels, and pearls. Sleeves were long and puffed, pleated, or slashed and trimmed with gold braid and ruffled, lacy white cuffs. Hair, woven with gold ribbons, was worn piled high on top of the head. Stiff, white, upright and pleated or frilly collars framed their faces. The gents wore clothes as feminine and ostentatious as the women's. Elegant knee- to ankle-length capes and jackets were made of the same fabrics, trimmed with the same braid and jewels. Sleeves were slashed; slashes were outlined in gold braid. Tights covered their legs and dainty shoes adorned their feet. Collars and cuffs were lacy and showy. Some of the men wore knee-length pants with knee-high boots, snug V-waisted vests, and velvet beret caps.

The next day on the way to the *Giostra della Quintana* (jousting tournament), we saw many of these same regal folks lounging about at the park near the stadium. Later, when the stands were full, they promenaded across the field to take their seats at center field. The modern-day jousting at Foligno takes tremendous skill and concentration, but it isn't a lethal battle like medieval jousting was—back then knights were often injured, some were killed. Today the knights on horseback—one representing each of the ten districts— carry eleven-foot-long metal lances. One knight at a time gallops around a two-thousand-foot-long figure-eight course. The Quintana (a wooden soldier) stands at the intersection of the figure eight, an outstretched arm bearing a three-inch metal ring. The knight must spear the ring with his lance while racing by at full speed and then sprint back to the finish with it. Each knight must do nine rounds—for the last two rounds, the ring is replaced with one only two inches in diameter! The fastest knight with the fewest penalties wins the joust and the Palio, a banner painted by a famous artist.

The knights' dexterity and skill is something to see, but half of the show takes place in the stands. Every district has its own colors and flags. Loyal fans sported hats and shirts in their district's colors and sat together in their district's bleachers. While the ten knights on horseback were introduced one by one, the fans went nuts, shouting, cheering, whooping. The district across from us set off colorful, stinky smoke bombs and clapped with huge cardboard hands. Above the commotion, a voice boomed over the loud-speaker to announce that the first *giostra* was about to begin.

"It is important to be completely quiet," said the announcer.

The crowd quieted but many were restless—and coughing could be heard.

"The game takes a lot of concentration and requires silence."

As soon as the announcer said the word *silence,* you could literally hear birds chirping and the breeze blow. The fans were absolutely quiet. At the end of each joust, the mob went into a frenzy of excitement, but at the an-nouncement of the next knight, there was complete silence again. At inter-mission two horses and their riders entered the field. The horses danced and tapped their feet to the music—I've never seen anything like it. They were beautiful and elegant to watch.

The giostra was the grand finale to the two-week festival. The next day, life would return to the twenty-first century in Foligno.

10 🍂 The Wineries—*Le cantine*

Tu vuoi la botte piena e la moglie ubriaca

(You want your wine barrel full and your wife drunk—
but you can't have both)

SINCE ANCIENT TIMES, WINE HAS PLAYED AN IMPORTANT PART IN THE culture, traditions, and diet of Umbrians. For centuries, it has been an everyday beverage, often served at both lunch and dinner. Until recently, winemaking was mostly a domestic affair. Fathers, sons, uncles, and grandfathers worked together to make enough for the family's needs—using basically the same methods the Romans did millennia ago. Today winemaking is big business.

Umbria's wines are gaining renown in the United States as the noteworthy sagrantino from Montefalco and the white wines from Orvieto reach markets in the States. This chapter introduces you to a few families and winery owners who are passionate about making good wine. You'll meet

Adele and Eugenio, a husband-and-wife team, who make *vinsanto* (holy wine) in their attic. And you'll come with me to pick grapes in the vineyards outside my country apartment, and then on we go to Cantina Chiorri near Perugia for a harvest party. Then I introduce you to the owners of the Antonelli, Lungarotti, and Barberani wineries in Umbria's most important wine zones—Montefalco, Torgiano, and Orvieto.

WINE IN UMBRIA

The history of wine in Umbria is much like the story of the region's cuisine— winemaking dates back thousands of years, to the Etruscans. During Roman times, Umbria's southwestern town of Orvieto was famous for its sweet white wines. Since ancient times, farmers have known that Umbria's hilly, mountainous landscape is good for cultivating grapes. The hillsides provide good drainage and poor soils—ideal conditions for grapevines. Soil compositions vary greatly, sometimes from vineyard to vineyard—rocky to sandy to clayey to volcanic to calcareous (limestone). The local mountains and the Apennine range, rolling hills, rivers, and lakes create a multitude of microclimates where certain clones do better than others and where grapes produce wines with a sense of place. A network of lakes (the largest, Trasimeno) and major rivers (the Tiber, Nera, and Topino) provides good humidity. And the region's plentiful rainfall is important, since government wine codes usually forbid irrigation. Warm to hot and humid summer days provide ample sunshine to ripen and mature the grapes. Winters can be frigid with occasional snow flurries, but for the most part Umbria has a moderate climate.

Grapevine cultivation that stretches back to antiquity has delivered to present-day Italy at least two thousand wine grape varietals—more than any other country in the world. Over the centuries, Umbrian growers have settled into growing the grapes that make the best wine in the various (and many) microclimates. Sangiovese is the region's traditional red grape, except in Montefalco, where sagrantino is king. The most Umbrian of white grape varietals is grechetto, but trebbiano, malvasia, verdello, drupeggio (canaiolo *bianco*), and other local grapes are all important. International varietals such as cabernet sauvignon, pinot *bianco* and *nero,* merlot, and chardonnay have become more common over the last few decades.

For years, wineries focused on making as much wine as possible—wine quality wasn't that important. Fast-forward to Umbria, early 1960s. The Italian government invited wineries to apply for DOC status—a new wine category (see "The ABC's of Italy's DOC . . . ," page 308). To use DOC on the label, wineries had to abide by national production standards. The government was flooded with applications. Over the next twenty years, there was a marked improvement in wine quality. After years of conscientious stewardship, modern vineyards are in good shape. Their owners have adopted new styles of trellising and learned to manage crop yields by pruning and cutting crop. They now plant vines more densely.

"In ancient times, they planted two or three thousand vines per hectare [2.47 acres]," said Bernardo Barberani, Cantina Barberani, Orvieto. "Today we plant about nine thousand per hectare—but each vine produces only a few clusters. Small crops make wine aromas more intense and give wine more character."

Many of Umbria's wine estates are still family-owned and -operated. They often handpick the entire crop and transport the grapes to the winery in small bins so the fruit won't get crushed. Winery facilities are often located within minutes of the vineyards, so the grapes arrive in good condition.

While big changes in vineyard management have boosted wine quality, modernization of the wineries has been just as important. Gravity pulls grapes and juice to the next stage of winemaking, so forceful pumping can be avoided. Temperature-controlled stainless-steel fermentation tanks are the norm. Cold fermentation and barrel fermentation are used for some wines. Many winemakers use *barriques* (small wood barrels) for aging wine—and they replace the barrels after three years. In traditional winemaking, *botti* (huge wooden casks) were used for decades. Humidity and temperature are regulated in barrel-aging cellars. Bottling lines are sterilized, and lab tests are conducted during the bottling run. Not all wineries have implemented these changes, but Umbrian winemaking is definitely on the right track.

UNDERSTANDING AN ITALIAN WINE LABEL

Italian wine labels can be very confusing to Americans, who are used to seeing the name of the grape(s)—chardonnay, merlot, zinfandel—on the label. Instead, in Umbria, labels often use the descriptors *rosso, bianco, rosato* (red, white, rosé) plus the appellation, or a fantasy name such as Lungarotti's Rubesco. The kind of grape isn't important to local quaffers, who already know what style of wine to expect and what grapes are grown in the region. In addition, government regulations dictate grape varietals for DOC and DOCG wines (see "The ABC's of Italy's DOC . . . ," page 308).

The sample label below explains the information that is required on labels. For definitions of other terms used on labels, such as *secco*, refer to "A Guide to Umbria's Wine Words" on page 346.

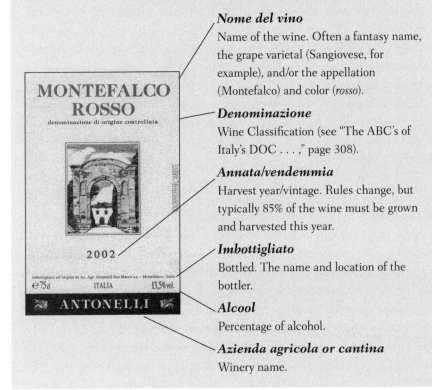

Nome del vino
Name of the wine. Often a fantasy name, the grape varietal (Sangiovese, for example), and/or the appellation (Montefalco) and color (*rosso*).

Denominazione
Wine Classification (see "The ABC's of Italy's DOC . . . ," page 308).

Annata/vendemmia
Harvest year/vintage. Rules change, but typically 85% of the wine must be grown and harvested this year.

Imbottigliato
Bottled. The name and location of the bottler.

Alcool
Percentage of alcohol.

Azienda agricola or cantina
Winery name.

[Label text:]
MONTEFALCO ROSSO
denominazione di origine controllata
2002
Imbottigliato all'origine da Az. Agr. Antonelli San Marco s.a. - Montefalco - Italia
℮ 75 cl   ITALIA   13,5% vol.
ANTONELLI

WINE CULTURE

In Umbria, since ancient times *vino* has been considered a part of the diet and part of the ritual of eating and dining. Wine is often served at lunch and dinner, but it is rarely a cocktail. At dinner parties in the California wine country, where I live, people stand around sipping wine with abandon before dinner. In Umbria, there is more restraint—the first glass of wine is typically poured at the table. On special occasions an aperitif might be served.

Americans want alcohol out of the reach of minors. In Umbria children grow up around wine—they see it as a natural part of life, not forbidden fruit. Schoolchildren take field trips to wineries to learn about winemaking. Parents might add a drop of wine to a child's water at the table. Wine is a part of the culture with a long history and culture. *Vino* is something to be enjoyed.

To understand Umbrian red wines better, you need to know that winemakers make wines to go with food. Wines are aged longer than most American wines, so they are less fruity and more mature. And most wines do not have smoky, oaky flavors, although now nontraditional wines are often aged in small wood barrels.

THE ABC's OF ITALY's DOC, DOCG, AND IGT

In the United States, consumers are used to seeing the wine's appellation, such as Napa Valley or Santa Barbara County, listed on the label. After sampling chardonnay from Napa and the same varietal from Santa Barbara, you might decide you prefer the tropical flavors from the southern appellation's wine. The fact that the flavor of wine depends upon where the grapes are grown is one reason wine regions around the world have set up appellation systems—a way to name and delineate a grape-growing zone. In 1963 the Italian government established appellations and codes to regulate viticulture and winemaking practices within geographic areas. The codes, called the *Denominazione di Origine Controllata* or DOC, were followed by a more rigid set in 1980, the *Denominazione di Origine Controllata Garantita,* or DOCG. The newest category of wines is the *Indicazione Geografica Tipica,* or IGT, established in 1992.

DOC (*Denominazione di Origine Controllata*): This mark on a wine label certifies the origin of the grapes and indicates that specific viticulture and winemaking standards established by the Italian government have been met. Production codes regulate vineyard practices and winemaking methods—grape varieties, crop yields, alcohol percentage, aging (duration and type of container), and wine character. Over time some of the codes have been updated to allow modern winemaking practices—many of the original codes made traditional methods mandatory. In Umbria there are eleven DOC appellations—there are more than three hundred DOC zones in the country.

DOCG (*Denominazione di Origine Controllata Garantita*): In addition to certification of grape origin and production standards, wines in this category have passed laboratory analysis and been approved by tasting panels. Throughout the twenty regions of Italy, there are only two dozen DOCG wines, but the list is still growing. Umbria has two of them—Sagrantino di Montefalco (both dry and *passito*—sweet) and Torgiano Rosso Riserva.

IGT (*Indicazione Geografica Tipica*): Before this category came into being, wines that did not fit into the rigid DOC or DOCG categories were labeled *vino da tavola* (table wine), the lowliest class of wine. IGT wines are linked to a geographic area—but the zones tend to be broader than DOC and DOCG appellations. IGT codes also dictate production standards and grape varietals. In Umbria an IGT varietal wine (i.e., Sangiovese) typically must have at least 85 percent of the primary grape.

Vino da Tavola: Wines in this category—table wine—do not have production codes or grape-origin requirements. Since well-made nontraditional wines, such as those aged in small barrels or made from nontraditional varietals, now fit into the IGT category, fewer wines use this label.

WINE, DINE, AND VISIT TWO MUSEUMS

Sometimes when I hear Torgiano mentioned, I have to stop and think, is that the name of the winery or the town?—the two names are so intertwined. The prestigious Giorgio Lungarotti winery is located on the outskirts of the town of Torgiano—less than ten miles southeast of Perugia. The Lungarotti Foundation's wine and olive oil museums, run by Maria Grazia Lungarotti, are downtown in the small medieval village. The family's five-star Hotel Le Tre Vaselle and the hotel's Ristorante Le Melagrane are nearby.

Since Giorgio Lungarotti opened the winery in 1962, the Lungarotti family has played an important role in shaping Torgiano—and in bringing the world's attention to Umbrian wine. Today Giorgio's two daughters, Teresa Severini and Chiara Lungarotti, run the winery.

The day I visited Lungarotti, I met with Teresa, the older of the two. She is one of Umbria's dynamic women in wine. At a time when very few women held degrees in wine, Teresa graduated in enology from the University of Perugia. She was also one of the founders of the national organization Le

Donne del Vino (Women of Wine). This attractive mother of three is polished, stylish, and well spoken—and her English is perfect. It's been over thirty years since Teresa finished her studies in winemaking and started her career at the family's winery, working originally with her stepfather, Giorgio. About eight years after Teresa joined the business, her mother (Giorgio's wife), Maria Grazia, who has a degree in literature and art history, started the Lungarotti Foundation. "My mother made us appreciate art," said Teresa, "and my father made us appreciate good wine."

The family has an eye for beauty. The winery, with its red tiled roof, brick trim, and vine-covered walls, is modern and handsome. Many Umbrian wineries have been slow to welcome customers and to open tasting rooms— Lungarotti leads the pack. On the ground floor of the winery, under the offices, is a spacious and comfortable tasting room—with lots of seating. From the tasting room, they sell their wine and olive oil, canvas bags, aprons, T-shirts, and an Umbrian dual-language (Italian/English) cookbook. When I visited, Teresa was in the process of updating the book. Lungarotti's flagship wine, Rubesco Vigna Monticchio DOCG (Torgiano rosso riserva—70% Sangiovese, 30% canaiolo) is delicious; other notable wines: San Giorgio Rosso dell' Umbria IGT (50% cabernet sauvignon, 40% Sangiovese, 10% canaiolo) and Torre di Giano "Vigna il Pino" DOC (*bianco di* Torgiano—70% trebbiano, 30% grechetto).

The foundation's museums are impressive. The wine museum features thousands of items—jugs and bottles dating back thousands of years, centuries-old hand-painted, doughnut-shaped jugs from Deruta, and antique texts and tools. The olive oil museum tells the long, important history of olive oil—covering its role in cooking, medicine, cosmetics, religion, lighting, and heating.

If you want to take in all that the Lungarotti properties have to offer— from the self-guided museum tours (allow one to two hours for each) to lunch or dinner at Ristorante Le Melagrane to wine tasting—you'll need the whole day.

IDEAL TEMPERATURES FOR THE BEST FLAVOR

Maybe you've noticed that some wine labels suggest a serving temperature—that's because wine tastes best at the right temperature.

The proper temperature depends on the wine's varietal and whether it is sparkling, dry, or sweet. To help maintain the temperature in the glass (and to avoid smudging the glass), hold on to the wineglass stem, rather than the bowl. The stem isn't just for looks!

White Wine: To bring white wine to serving temperature, chill the (750 ml) bottle in the refrigerator for at least two hours. To speed-chill the wine, submerge the bottle for just half an hour in a bucket filled about halfway with water and ice—once chilled, keep the wine refrigerated until needed. In the summer, bring white wines out of the refrigerator just before serving. In the winter, allow the wine to stand at room temperature for about fifteen minutes before serving.

Red Wine: If the red wine bottle feels cool, it's probably ready to serve. Around 64°F is usually ideal—between cellar and moderate room temperature. Bring red out of the cellar about half an hour before serving. If the wine has been stored at room temperature, refrigerate it for about half an hour before serving.

Wine Storage: Wine is fussy about how it is stored and where it is kept. Store wine bottles horizontally so the cork stays moist and maintains a tight seal. Choose a spot for cellaring wine where temperatures are constant, preferably around 55°F with about 70 percent humidity—a basement, under the house, in a closet in the interior of the house. A kitchen refrigerator is too cold (and room temperature is too warm) for long-term storage. Never leave wine in a hot car, in a sunny window, or near the stove or oven—even for a short time.

How to Serve Wine

Typically, you open wine just before serving it, but if you are having a big bash you might want to get a head start. Up to an hour ahead, open the number of bottles you expect to serve. Don't open too many bottles—once wine is opened, it begins to deteriorate. Reseal the white wines and refrigerate them. Leave the red wines uncorked at room temperature.

To serve wine, fill the glass one quarter to one third full—that allows for swirling the wine to aerate it and release aromas. Red wines that taste harsh at first often improve by "breathing" in the glass. Brief exposure to air may open up the wine and improve its flavor. At dinner, if you'll use the same glass for a variety of wines, have a dump bucket and a pitcher of water available to swish the glass clean with water in between wines.

TORGIANO ROSSO RISERVA DOCG

Wine is alive—reserve wines need time to dream in the cellar.
—Teresa Severini, winemaker and marketer,
Cantine Giorgio Lungarotti

This *riserva* is an important wine in Umbria. It is one among the elite two dozen wines in Italy that belong to the highest-ranking DOCG category—and one of only two Umbrian DOCG wines. Torgiano, both *rosso* and *bianco* (red and white), was the first wine in Umbria to earn DOC status—that was in 1968. In 1990, Torgiano Rosso Riserva was upgraded to a DOCG wine.

Winemaking: The primary grape in the riserva is Sangiovese; canaiolo is the secondary grape. As dictated by DOCG codes, the wine must be aged at least three years. The Lungarotti Torgiano Rosso Riserva, called Rubesco, is aged in large wood casks for about one year and then in the bottle for about three years. The wine has a long aging potential—ten or more years.

How to Serve: Slightly above cellar temperature—60 to 64°F—is ideal.

Tasting Notes: Deep ruby-red color. Full-bodied and sumptuous, with a lingering finish. Flavors and aromas range from dark berries and cherries to chocolate to spicy notes.

Food Pairing: Aged cheese. Grilled steaks or roast beef. Hearty stews and pasta with rich Umbrian Ragù (page 7). Polenta with Ragù (page 4). Steak with Arugula and Cherry Tomatoes (page 240). Squab in Red Wine and Vinegar (page 59). Creamy Risotto with Mushrooms (page 185). Pork Chops with Rosemary and Sage (page 31). Lasagne with Ragù (page 75).

PEACHES IN *VINO ROSSO*

During the summer, Paola and Silvia's aunt, *la* Zia Maria, loved to peel and slice a fresh peach and drop it into her glass of red wine after dinner. She'd let the peach sit for a few moments and then scoop out each slice with a spoon—savoring first the luscious *pesca,* and finally drinking the peach-scented *vino.*

WINEGLASSES

In some of Umbria's most humble restaurants, if you order a bottle of wine—good but not necessarily expensive—the waiter might make a show of pouring the wine into big, expensive wineglasses. A savvy restaurateur knows that a good wineglass makes wine taste better. If you choose *vino della casa* (house wine), you will probably have to drink the wine in cheap stemware. Or your water glass (without a stem) might double as a wineglass—you get to drink either wine or water, unless you are given two glasses.

If I have the option, I use an untinted, high-quality wineglass with a stem. Wine simply tastes better in a well-designed glass—one with a roomy oval bowl that curves in at the top and a long stem that is easy to hold. Not only does a generous bowl capture aromas and let flavors expand, it also allows for robust swirling without splashing. Ideally, you'd have a set of twenty- to thirty-ounce glasses for red wine and a set of twelve-ounce glasses for white wine, but a set of twelve- to twenty-ounce glasses can be used for both red and white. A nine- to twelve-ounce glass is good for dessert wine—although *vinsanto* is often served in smaller glasses. Grappa and *digestivi* ("digestive" liqueurs) that are very high in alcohol are served in three- to six-ounce glassware.

SAGRANTINO DI MONTEFALCO DOCG

Some thirty-plus years ago, sagrantino almost disappeared. Today there is a boom period for Sagrantino di Montefalco.
—Filippo Antonelli, Azienda Agricola Antonelli San Marco

Before my stay in Umbria, a Tuscan winemaker told me that Umbrian wineries were really making some big changes. He thought the region's wines would be the next big wine discovery. In fact, one wine in particular had already been discovered, he said. That was the first time I had heard of Sagrantino di Montefalco, a big, bold red wine made from sagrantino grapes.

According to Filippo Antonelli, Arnaldo Caprai's is the most famous winery in Montefalco—and Signor Caprai has been Montefalco's ambassador. But Antonelli must be one of Montefalco's most charming spokespeople. He is quietly eloquent, and his English is beautiful. He dresses and carries himself like a modern-day *principo* (prince).

In 1881 Francesco, Filippo's *bisnonno* (great-grandfather), bought a 420-acre property from the bishop of Spoleto in what is now the heart of Montefalco's DOCG winemaking area. According to Filippo, the sale so angered the pope that he vowed to excommunicate anyone who bought property from the church. Francesco built a house and planted vineyards on the land he bought—that was the start of the Azienda Agricola Antonelli San Marco (Antonelli San Marco Wine Estate). About a century later, Filippo, who studied agriculture at the University of Perugia, started running the winery. Filippo recently oversaw the winery expansion—the addition of an underground barrel cellar and fermentation area that uses gravity rather than pumps to move the fruit.

Sagrantino is the winery's main focus—it is the grape that has recently made Montefalco famous. The grape has been around for centuries—from as early as the sixteenth century. Some historians think it is native to Montefalco; others do not. "A Franciscan friar probably brought the grape to Montefalco via the Middle East," Filippo said. "But sagrantino is exclusively in Montefalco." The traditional Sagrantino di Montefalco was sweet. In the 1970s, winemakers in Montefalco began making a dry sagrantino.

Dry Sagrantino di Montefalco is the winery's most important product, but Antonelli also produces an excellent Sagrantino di Montefalco Passito (dessert wine). In 1992 Sagrantino di Montefalco became the second Umbrian wine to gain DOCG status.

Winemaking: This DOCG wine is made with 100 percent sagrantino grapes. Aged at least thirty months—and twelve must be in wood barrels.

DOCG Production Area: The sagrantino grapes must be grown in the area of Montefalco, Castel Ritaldi, Giano dell' Umbria, Gualdo Cattaneo, and Bevagna—all in the province of Perugia.

How to Serve and Store: The ideal serving temperature is around 64°F—slightly above cellar temperature. Sagrantino is at its best five or more years from the vintage date—properly stored, a good vintage can age ten years or more.

Tasting Notes: Deep garnet red. A big-bodied wine that is fruity in the nose and mouth—jammy, blackberries, dark cherries, and spice. Balanced but bold tannins. Long finish.

Food Pairing: This is not a sipping wine—it is meant to be drunk with food. Aged pecorino cheese. Pasta with rich meat sauce—rabbit, duck, beef, wild boar. Grilled or roasted beef, wild boar. Grilled Lamb (page 266). Squab in Red Wine and Vinegar (page 59).

Sagrantino di Montefalco Passito DOCG: This dessert wine is made from the concentrated juice of semidried sagrantino grapes. Aged thirty months, at least twelve in wood barrels. The grapes—100 percent sagrantino—dry on trellises or mats for at least two months and sometimes up to three. Rich, full-bodied, ruby-red dessert wine. Sweet but not cloying. Dark berry jam, blackberries, and dark cherries. Serve at cellar temperature—between 57 and 60°F—with Umbria's traditional desserts. Strudel (page 320). Jam Tart (with berry or fig jam, page 52). Biscotti (page 55). Anise Wine Cookies (page 174).

Pears Poached in Sagrantino (page 236). Vanilla Cream (with mixed berries, page 289). Spiced Chocolate-Nut Candy (page 251). Aged pecorino or Parmigiano served with honey. The small yield from the shriveled sagrantino grapes makes *passito* expensive, but it is worth the occasional indulgence.

SETTING THE TABLE

The Italian table is so important that the language has a verb that means "to set the table" (*apparecchiare*). The dining table is usually covered with a crisply ironed tablecloth. The plates are put on the table, since meals are usually served family style. A pasta bowl is set on top of the dinner plate. On the left of the plate is a fork and to its left, a folded napkin (cloth, if you please!). The dinner knife (serrated is best), blade facing the plate, goes to the right of the plate. At a family meal, sliced bread is put on the tablecloth, but for a fancy meal a small bread plate goes above the fork. A dessert fork, spoon, and/or knife are placed horizontally above the plate.

To set the table with the glasses in the proper order, put the water glass on the right side of the place setting, directly above the knife. The wineglasses—one is essential, but one for each wine is even better—line up to the left of the water glass above the dinner plate. Serve the heartiest wine (usually red) in the glass next to the water, and pour each successively lighter wine down the line, ending with the lightest white wine in the last glass on the left side. Taste from left to right—light and dry wines first, followed by sweet or bold wines.

A GREAT FEAST

Signor Filippo Antonelli, who runs the Antonelli winery, invited me to attend the annual party that the winery throws for the olive and grape harvest workers. I arrived early at Antonelli's Casale Satriano *agriturismo* (farm rental-apartments) on the afternoon of the party to see what was cooking. The day before, one of Filippo's cousins had prepared several huge trays of fresh pappardelle pasta—the preferred style of homemade pasta in the area. Two winery employees, Maria Teresa and Leonella, were cutting slits in goose and butterflied lamb, pushing lard, sage, and rosemary into the holes to flavor the meat before roasting. Someone else was feeding kindling into the huge wood-burning oven outside the kitchen. While the lamb and goose marinated, a team of cooks rolled the strudel dough until it was very thin— it almost covered the table. Then they doused the sheet of dough with extra virgin olive oil and sprinkled it with sugar. They spread a mixture of chopped apples, pears, walnuts, raisins, cocoa powder, and dried figs over the dough. It took two pairs of hands to manage the enormous dough—they rolled it into a cylinder and shaped it into a coil.

Several hours later, the forty guests arrived for the feast. We stayed late into the evening, eating, drinking, and dancing to an accordion. It was a grand evening and a great feast with excellent Antonelli extra virgin olive oil and wines. The menu follows.

Antipasto
Crostini with Mushroom-Truffle Pâté (page 318)
Crostini with Liver Pâté (page 66)
Crostini with Tomatoes (page 318)

Primo Piatto
Pappardelle with goose ragù

Secondi Piatti
Roasted lamb (see Grilled Lamb, page 266)
Roasted goose
Grilled sausage

Contorni
Roast Potatoes (page 146)
Mixed Salad (page 148)

Dolce
Apple Strudel (page 320)

Dalla Cantina (from the cellar)

Antonelli Grechetto (with antipasto)

Antonelli Montefalco Rosso DOC (with dinner)

Antonelli Sagrantino di Montefalco DOCG (with dinner)

CROSTINI WITH TOMATOES

To make the *crostini con pomodori* served at Antonelli's harvest party, dice ripe tomatoes. Let stand in a colander to drain off the juice. Toss the tomatoes in a bowl with whole, peeled, lightly crushed garlic cloves and a chiffonade (thin slices) of fresh basil. Season to taste with extra virgin olive oil, kosher salt, and red pepper flakes. Let stand half an hour to marry flavors. Adjust seasoning. Spoon over sliced Italian bread or baguettes (not sourdough)—toasted, if you want (see "To Toast Crostini," page 67). Drizzle with additional extra virgin olive oil, if desired. Serve open-faced.

Crostini with Mushroom-Truffle Pâté

Crostini con funghi e tartufi

༺✲༻

For the harvest party at the Antonelli winery in Montefalco, the cooks made this delicious spread with three parts white mushrooms to one part fresh black truffles. I have reduced the quantity of truffles because the prices of tartufi *are exorbitant in the United States.*

You can choose from a variety of truffle products to make this recipe (see Resources, page 351, for information on where to buy truffles). Fresh, fragrant tartufi, *sometimes sold at upscale markets in the States, are ideal. Whole truffles or dehydrated sliced truffles (see Note, page 320), both sold in jars, are also good choices. If truffles are out of your budget or impossible to find, make Mushroom Pâté (page 320) instead.*

In Umbria, the bread for crostini is usually not toasted, but with funghi e tartufi, *I like to toast it.*

Yield: About 1⅓ cups (enough to top 35 to 40 baguette slices)

1 baguette (not sourdough), cut into ¼-inch-thick slices

3 tablespoons plus 1 tablespoon extra virgin olive oil

3 large garlic cloves, peeled, and halved

1 pound mushrooms, quartered or sliced

1 teaspoon plus ¼ teaspoon kosher salt (*important:* see "About Salt, page xxv)

Freshly ground pepper

⅓ cup packed Italian parsley

1 to 2 ounces fresh summer black truffles (see Note, page 320)

1. If you are toasting the bread, preheat the oven to 350°F. Arrange the bread slices side by side on a large baking sheet; bake until lightly toasted, 10 to 12 minutes. Set aside. (If you prefer not to toast the bread, set it aside until step 5).

2. In a skillet large enough to hold all of the mushrooms, heat 3 tablespoons of the oil with 4 halves of garlic over medium-low heat for about ½ minute. Add the mushrooms, the 1 teaspoon kosher salt, and a dash of pepper; sauté 1 minute, tossing to coat the mushrooms with the oil. Cover and simmer for 20 minutes, stirring occasionally. Uncover and cook over medium-high heat, stirring frequently, until the liquid evaporates and the mushrooms are lightly browned, about 8 minutes. Stir in the parsley and cook ½ minute; remove from the heat.

3. Meanwhile, gently scrub the fresh truffles with a vegetable brush under running water to remove dirt. Grate or thinly slice the truffles. Heat the remaining tablespoon of oil with the remaining 2 garlic halves in a small pan over low heat for 1 to 2 minutes. Remove the pan from the heat; stir in the truffles and remaining ¼ teaspoon kosher salt. Let stand 10 minutes; discard the garlic.

4. Put the truffle-oil mixture and mushrooms into a food processor; process, scraping the sides with a rubber spatula as needed, until very finely minced, almost puréed. If necessary, add a teaspoon of water or additional oil to moisten the spread. Adjust the salt and pepper to taste.

5. Just before serving, spread the warm or chilled pâté on the bread or toast. Serve open-faced on a platter.

Mushroom Pâté

Make Mushroom-Truffle Pâté (page 318) with these changes: Add all of the kosher salt (1¼ teaspoons—*important:* see "About Salt, page xxv) to the mushrooms, and skip step 3. At the end, add up to 1 more tablespoon oil, if desired.

NOTE: To substitute dehydrated summer truffles for fresh truffles, use a 10-gram jar, which equals about 1 ounce of rehydrated truffles (soaked in warm water for 1 hour to rehydrate). After soaking and draining, the truffles are ready to use as you would use fresh, sliced truffles (save the soaking water; use 1 to 2 teaspoons in step 4 if the spread is too dry). To use jarred truffle sauce or truffle oil (do a taste test, as some oils taste bad) instead of fresh truffles, make Mushroom Pâté (above) and add truffle oil or truffle sauce at the end to taste. ❧

Apple Strudel

La rocciata
∞

Several centuries ago, many Dutch families lived in the area around Montefalco. They brought with them their adored dessert, strudel. The Umbrian rendition of strudel, called la rocciata, *is filled with apples, pears, raisins, nuts, and dried figs.*

In the past, cooks in Montefalco made the crust with lard and extra virgin olive oil because butter, the traditional fat, was unavailable. The ladies at Cantina Antonelli prefer to use only oil. Although the strudel's crust is easier to make than piecrust, a two-part recipe like this does take time to make—but it is worth the effort. Alchermes, a fuchsia-colored liqueur used in Umbrian desserts, adds an intriguing, spicy flavor to the filling and gives the crust a pale pink cast. You can make your own alchermes (see recipe, page 323) or substitute another liqueur.

La rocciata *is traditionally served at Christmastime and* Tutti i Santi *(All Saints' Day), on the first of November. At those times, fresh apples and walnuts are plentiful and the recently harvested figs and raisins are shriveled. Although it isn't the custom to serve* la rocciata *with vanilla ice cream, it is delicious—and dessert wine such as* Sagrantino di Montefalco Passito *or* vinsanto *is highly recommended.*

Yield: 12 servings

FILLING INGREDIENTS

3 apples (about 7 ounces each)

1 pear (about 7 ounces)

10 dried figs

1/2 cup walnuts, chopped

1/3 cup pine nuts

1/3 cup raisins

2 tablespoons cocoa powder, preferably 100% cocoa

1¼ teaspoons ground cinnamon

Finely shredded zest of 1 lemon (see "About Zest," page 37)

1/2 teaspoon kosher salt (*important:* see "About Salt," page xxv)

1 cup granulated sugar

1 tablespoon all-purpose flour

1 tablespoon extra virgin olive oil

1 tablespoon *alchermes,* almond, orange, or hazelnut liqueur, or white wine

DOUGH INGREDIENTS

2⅓ cups all-purpose flour (10½ ounces) plus more for kneading

1/2 cup warm milk

1 large egg at room temperature

2 tablespoons warm *alchermes* liqueur, or white wine

Extra virgin olive oil

1 tablespoon plus 1 tablespoon granulated sugar

TOPPING

4 tablespoons *alchermes* (optional), and/or 3 tablespoons unsifted
powered sugar

YOU'LL ALSO NEED: A large wooden board (15×20 inches is ideal), parchment paper, and a rolling pin. A pastry blade is helpful.

GETTING STARTED: Put a damp towel under a lightly floured large wooden
board to help prevent slipping.

FILLING

1. Peel and core the apples and pear. Cut the apples, pear, and figs into ⅜-
inch cubes. In a large bowl, combine the apples, pear, figs, walnuts, pine nuts,
raisins, cocoa, cinnamon, lemon zest, and kosher salt. Sprinkle the granulated
sugar, flour, oil, and *alchermes* over the fruit mixture; toss well to coat. Let
stand about 45 minutes.

DOUGH AND ASSEMBLY

2. Put the flour into a large bowl; make a well in the flour. Add the milk,
egg, and *alchermes;* gradually mix in the flour with a fork until a dough is
formed. Use hands to mix in the crumbs and to form a ball. Transfer the ball
to the lightly floured board; knead 5 minutes to hydrate the flour.

3. Flatten the dough into a thick rectangle with your hands; drizzle a teaspoon of the oil over the dough. Fold the dough to enclose the oil; knead
until the oil is absorbed, about 1 minute. Continue kneading in the same
manner, adding a total of 4 teaspoons of oil; knead until the dough is very
smooth, about 5 more minutes (10 minutes total). The dough will be soft
and slightly sticky.

4. Shape the dough into a ball; rub 1 teaspoon of oil over the ball. Cover
with plastic wrap; let the dough rest 30 to 45 minutes. Use a pastry blade or
knife to scrape the board clean.

5. Preheat the oven to 400°F. Line two large baking sheets with parchment paper. Divide the dough into two equal pieces; keep one piece covered. Press the uncovered dough with your hands into a rectangle about ½ inch thick. Lightly dust both sides of the dough with flour (and repeat frequently while rolling to prevent sticking).

6. Starting in the center of the rectangle, roll out toward the edge of the dough. Continue rolling, clockwise, to form a very thin 12×18-inch rectangle. Brush 1 tablespoon oil over the dough; sprinkle with 1 tablespoon of the granulated sugar.

7. Toss the reserved fruit filling to mix well; spread half of the filling evenly over the dough, leaving about 1¼ inches free around the edges. Starting at a wide end, roll the dough into a long cylinder to enclose the filling. Pinch the ends closed and fold them under. Carefully transfer the roll, with the seam side facing up, to a baking sheet lined with parchment. Shape the cylinder into a coil. Brush the coil with about 1 tablespoon oil. (Bake this strudel now; make the second strudel while this one bakes.)

8. Bake until the crust is browned, about 35 minutes (the apples should be very tender at this point). During baking, "syrup" from the apple mixture will leak out of the coil—that is to be expected.

TOPPING
If using, drizzle 2 tablespoons *alchermes* over the top of each *rocciata* while the strudel is warm. If using powdered sugar, sift half of the sugar over each coil (if using both *alchermes* and powdered sugar, drizzle with the liqueur first). Let cool slightly before cutting. To serve, cut the coils crosswise into wedges. 🍂

ALCHERMES LIQUEUR

This ancient fuchsia-colored liqueur is a popular flavoring—and coloring—in Umbrian desserts, such as the Apple Strudel (page 320). The liqueur is easy to make—but hard to find—so I have included this recipe.

To make 1¾ cups of *alchermes*: Use a vegetable peeler to peel the zest off 1 orange; put the zest in a 2- or 3-cup jar. Grind the following spices with a mortar and pestle: 1 tablespoon cloves, 1 tablespoon coriander seeds, 1 tablespoon cardamom pods, 1 teaspoon anise seeds, and 1 cinnamon stick (3-inch piece, broken in half). Add the spices, 1 chopped vanilla bean, 1 teaspoon freshly grated nutmeg, and 1½ cups vodka to the jar. Seal the jar tightly; shake well. Refrigerate for 1 week; shake daily. Strain the vodka mixture over a fine sieve; discard the solids. Strain the liquid through a coffee filter—it will fall drop by drop. Add ½ cup Thin Simple Syrup (below); add red or bright pink food coloring until the liquid turns fuchsia. Pour boiling water into a clean jar; let stand 5 minutes. Drain and cool the jar. Fill the jar with the *alchermes*; refrigerate up to 1 year.

SIMPLE SYRUP

Simple syrup takes minutes to make. It goes into many American cocktails, but it's also an essential ingredient in two liqueurs—*limoncello* and *alchermes* (see recipes, pages 325 and 323). The syrup is also used to make glazes and sorbet. And it is ideal for sweetening iced tea and lemonade.

Thin Simple Syrup: To make 1¾ cups syrup, bring 1 cup water to a boil in a small saucepan—but do not let it boil down. As soon as the water boils, add 2 cups sugar; stir to dissolve. When the mixture has started to boil again, reduce the heat to low; simmer and stir over low heat for 5 minutes. Let stand at room temperature until cool. Pour into a clean jar; seal tightly and refrigerate up to 3 weeks.

Thick Simple Syrup: To make about 2⅓ cups syrup for *limoncello* or *arancello* (orange liqueur), follow the instructions for Thin Simple Syrup but use a medium saucepan and increase the sugar to 3 cups. Because of the large amount of sugar, the cooling syrup will start to crystallize and cloud, so continue whisking the syrup as it cools. Stir the syrup into the lemon vodka (or orange vodka) after the syrup has cooled about 40 minutes. Adjust the flavor, if desired, by adding sugar, water, or vodka.

AFTER-DINNER DRINKS

In Umbria, at the end of a special meal, hosts bring bottles of liqueur, grappa (spirits), and *digestivi* ("digestive" liqueurs) to the table. They pour these strong drinks into small wineglasses—or glasses as small as a thimble. If you turn down the proffered drink, you'll be encouraged to have at least *un goccio* (a drop) to aid your digestion.

Some families make their own liqueurs such as *visner* (sour-cherry red wine), *nocino* (green walnuts and spices), or *limoncello* (lemon). To me, most *digestivi* taste bitter and medicinal, so a drop is all I can swallow. But I love syrupy, lemony *limoncello*. My friend Ugo, who divides his time between Milan and Gubbio, gave me his recipe. He was horrified when I told him I substituted vodka (which is aromatic) for *alcol puro* because pure alcohol (Everclear is one such brand) is banned in many parts of the United States. I have made *limoncello* with pure alcohol, but I am happier with the tamer vodka version (if you dare to use *alcol puro*, make a simple syrup using 6 to 8 cups of water and 7 to 8 cups of sugar).

Limoncello is as easy to make as it is to drink. It is flavored with the zest of lemons, so you'll have a lot of "naked" lemons—make lemonade! Do not use Meyer lemons, because the *limoncello* will taste medicinal rather than lemony. To make *arancello* (orange liqueur), substitute 8 oranges for the lemons (or use a combination of oranges and lemons). To give *limoncello* as a gift, look for small, pretty bottles with corks or caps.

Lemon Liqueur

Limoncello

To make about three (750 ml) bottles: Use a vegetable brush or clean dishcloth to gently scrub (under running water) 10 organic lemons (not Meyer). Use a vegetable peeler to peel the lemon zest off in strips (avoiding the white pith). Put the zest into a 2½-quart jar; add 2 quarts/liters vodka. Seal the jar tightly; shake. Let steep in the refrigerator or a cool place for 1 to 3 weeks; shake daily.

Strain the vodka; discard the zest. Mix in the 2⅔ cups Thick Simple Syrup (see recipe, page 324) with the lemon-vodka after the syrup has cooled slightly. Stir well—if there are sugar crystals, continue stirring to dissolve.

Pour boiling water into three clean (750 ml) bottles (empty wine bottles with screw caps are ideal); let stand 5 minutes. Drain and cool the bottles. Put a funnel into a bottle to fill it with limoncello. Seal the bottles tightly; refrigerate up to 1 year. Serve well chilled or over ice. ❧

SAGRANTINO WINE FESTIVAL

For over thirty years, *Settimana Enologica* (wine week) has been held in the heart of the medieval town of Montefalco during September. The couple of times that I attended the four-day affair, prices were reasonable. Entry to the tasting, with dozens of wineries pouring, was under ten dollars. A guided competitive tasting of Montefalco and Montalcino wines was priced at twenty dollars. A four-course dinner with three wines prepared by one of Umbria's top chefs was under sixty-five dollars. Over the years, the program has expanded to include a variety of activities for wine enthusiasts—workshops, visits to wineries, food pairings. If wine isn't your thing, there are usually other activities scheduled for the week—films, parades, concerts, or other entertainment.

In its twenty-seventh year, the event was dubbed Sagrantino Wine Festival (yes, the name is in English). The name change reflects the importance of the grape—sagrantino—that put the small village of Montefalco on the world map. Sagrantino flowed freely at the tasting, but the event also provided an opportunity for tasting other wines. Grechetto, chardonnay, cabernet sauvignon, rosso di Montefalco—all from the Montefalco region, which includes Bevagna, Castel Ritaldi, Giano dell'Umbria, and Gualdo Cattaneo. The area's most important wineries poured at the grand tasting—Arnaldo Caprai, Colpetrone, Lungarotti, Antonelli, Adanti, Perticaia, Ruggeri, Scacciadiavoli, Fattoria Colleallondole. The tasting salon was serene and elegant. The winery personnel who poured were professional and friendly—and attendees were sober and serious!

If you have any interest in wine, a detour to Montefalco during the Sagrantino Wine Festival is worthwhile. But festival or not, Montefalco is a fun town to visit—there are good restaurants and nice shops.

Pear, Arugula, and Prosciutto Salad
Insalata di pere, rucola e prosciutto
ᴕᴚ

This salad, inspired by one I ate at Villa Pambuffetti in Montefalco, makes a good antipasto, a light lunch, or a second course on a hot summer day. At the restaurant, the salad was made with a delicious carpaccio di lonza—*pork loin that is cured for a brief time. I use prosciutto, which is a good substitute, because it is readily available in the States. It is easy to make a single serving or enough for a party—simply increase the ingredients to suit your needs. You'll need a good-size chunk of cheese, no matter the number of servings, to shave off "leaves" of cheese.*

Yield: 1 serving

2 or 3 thin slices prosciutto di Norcia or Parma

¾ to 1 cup lightly packed tender, baby arugula, long stems removed

Balsamic Vinaigrette (see recipe, page 328)

Kosher salt

½ medium-size ripe pear (preferably red Bartlett), cored and sliced

1 fresh fig (preferably black mission), quartered

Wedge of aged Umbrian or Tuscan pecorino or Parmigiano-Reggiano cheese (see Note, page 328)

Freshly ground black pepper

1. Loosely fold the individual prosciutto slices and curl each to form a "rose." Arrange the "roses" on a plate (or on a platter, if serving a crowd). At this point, you can cover and refrigerate the dish until serving time.

2. Shortly before serving, put the arugula into a bowl large enough to accommodate tossing. Add enough of the vinaigrette to coat the salad; toss gently. Adjust the salt to taste. Put the arugula salad on top of the prosciutto "roses."

3. Fan the pear over the arugula; top the salad with the fig. Drizzle with additional vinaigrette, to taste. Use a vegetable peeler to shave thin "leaves" of cheese (the equivalent of a small handful) over the salad. Season with the pepper. Do not toss—it is a composed salad.

NOTE: You need a wedge of cheese to make shavings. Allow ¼ to ½ ounce of cheese per serving. ❧

Balsamic Vinaigrette
Vinaigrette balsamico

In Umbria, olive oil, salt, and a whiff of vinegar are usually added separately to salad, rather than being combined as a dressing. For Insalata di pere, rucola e prosciutto, it's better to make a vinaigrette.

Yield: about ¾ cup

2 tablespoons fresh lemon juice (about ½ large lemon)

2 tablespoons balsamic vinegar

½ teaspoon kosher salt (*important:* see "About Salt," page xxv)

½ cup plus 2 tablespoons extra virgin olive oil

In a small bowl, combine the juice, vinegar, and salt; mix well. Whisk in the oil. Adjust the salt to taste. Refrigerate until needed. Bring to room temperature and whisk again before using to dress salads. ❧

EST! EST!! EST!!!

According to an ancient legend, a man named Johannes, who was traveling with King Henry V in the early twelfth century, sent his servant ahead to look for the best wines en route. When the servant found an exceptional wine, he was instructed to identify the inn with the word *est*—"it is" (Latin). When the servant tasted a wine in Montefiascone, in the Lazio (Latium) region just south of the Umbrian town of Orvieto, he wrote *Est! Est!! Est!!!* He loved the wine—and so did Johannes, who supposedly never left Montefiascone after tasting the wine.

At least two Umbrian wineries—Falesco and Bigi—make Est! Est!! Est!!! DOC, a crisp (when dry), light, floral white wine made from trebbiano, rossetto, and malvasia grapes grown in Montefiascone. The DOC codes allow for the production of dry, sweet, and sparkling wine.

LET'S MAKE A TOAST—*FACCIAMO UN BRINDISI!*

- *Auguri!* (ah-uu-GOO-ree): Best wishes. Used for birthdays, holidays, and celebrations.

- *Cento di questi giorni* (CHEN-toh-dee-KWES-tee-JORH-nee): One hundred of these days.

- *Cin cin* (cheen-CHEEN): Cheers.

- *Lunga vita* (LOON-gah-VEE-tah): To a long life.

- *Salute* or *alla salute* (AHL-lah-sah-LOU-teh): To your health.

A FAMILY'S HARVEST DAY—*LA VENDEMMIA*

In late September, my friend Silvia and Silvano, the farmer who grew up in the Ramaccioni farmhouse, began tasting grapes in the vineyards to determine a picking date. By early October, the grapes were ready. It had been a difficult growing season—too little sunshine and too much rain. The tightly clustered grapes stayed moist and turned moldy—not good for making wine.

"We're picking tomorrow," Silvia told me when she came for espresso. "Do you want to help?" I told her I did, so we agreed to meet at the vineyard.

The next morning a veil of fog covered the valley and crept into the hills, draping the vines like a sheer tablecloth. But by two o'clock, when we met in the vineyard, it was warm and sunny. With all of us assembled—Paola, Mario, Silvano, some friends, and me—Silvia handed out serrated kitchen knives and told us to cut the stems just above the grapes and toss the bunches into a bucket.

I started picking at the bottom of the hill. The work was a bit crazy at first. I nearly carved a slit in Silvia's hand when we both reached in for the same bunch of grapes, so I moved away to work alone. As hard as it was to find good grapes, I managed to quickly fill my bucket, dropping the good ones into the bin and tossing the bad bunches on the ground. Silvia the Workhorse had been watching. As soon as the bucket was full, she grabbed it.

Standing with nothing to do until I got my bucket back, I admired the Ramaccioni country house, parts of which had been built more than four hundred years ago from local fieldstone. Below the house, gently sloping vineyards led to fields that had been bursting with yellow sunflowers the previous summer. Densely forested hills, dotted with an occasional farmhouse, rimmed the far edge of the now-empty fields on the valley floor. Above us stood a twelfth-century tower, its castle hidden from view. Looking toward town, I could see another medieval tower and an old circular church in historic downtown. A solitary skyscraper jutted up, soaring above the other buildings. I thought it was ugly, but some people liked it.

The sky, which had earlier been foggy and then an intense blue color, was filled with billowy white clouds. Down in the valley, dogs barked, as they often did. An occasional car or motorcycle sped by and insects buzzed, but besides that, the only other sounds came from us talking as we picked grapes. By late afternoon, the heat and the smell of ripe grapes had attracted swarms of pesky honeybees.

When Paola and Silvia were children, the family cultivated several hectares of wine grapes—a little more than seven acres produced more than enough wine for their big extended family. In those days, their father made wine in the large *cantina* next to the old family house where the two sisters still live. The remodeled *cantina*, now Silvia's son's house, was large even by the standards of the time when it was built. Silvia and Silvano would be making today's wine in a bedroom-size room on the ground floor of Casa Caldese.

Silvano, just back after taking a load of grapes to the winery, noticed my pile of rejected grapes on the ground. *"Tutto,"* he said, bending to pick up my castoffs. He scolded me gently in the local dialect, which I barely understood.

"Mario, he doesn't want me to save the moldy grapes, does he?" I asked when Silvano had gone.

"We lose money on the wine," he said, "so yes, keep all of them." I gave in and added the bad grapes to the good. I knew the wine we would make from those poor-quality grapes would be undrinkable to me. But Italians who had grown up drinking their family's wine didn't seem to mind the flavors that I found unpleasant—some preferred them. Paola was one of them.

"Our wine is the only wine I drink," Paola said at dinner later that evening. "I don't like store-bought wine."

The Ramaccionis, while not wine aficionados, are passionate about carrying on their family's winemaking traditions, which date back centuries. Today, no one remembers what varietals grow in the vineyards—and it doesn't matter. White grapes make white wine. The red grapes make red wine.

Back at the winery, Silvano and Silvia lifted the heavy bins of grapes above their shoulders and dumped them into the thumping, roaring destemmer. The machine spat out the stems, sending some airborne and hurling others to the ground. It spewed the grapes out into a wooden vat below. From the destemmer, the grapes went into a wooden tank called *la tina*. In a few days, Silvia and Silvano would crush the grapes in a wooden-slatted press called *il torchio*.

"The *torchio* looks old," said Silvia, "but it's younger than I am. When I was a child, I remember men stomping the grapes with their bare feet to crush them, but nobody does that anymore."

The pressed red juice would age in a large wooden barrel called *la botte,* and the white would go into the new tank Silvia bought at her cousin Tomaso's prompting. The wine would be topped with a layer of olive oil to help prevent contact with the air. It was a very simple, rustic process. The wines fermented as nature would have them ferment, without added yeast or temperature control.

It was close to seven in the evening when we finished cleaning up the *cantina* and Paola called us to dinner—mortadella, salami, bread, and last year's homemade wine. We may not have made exceptional wine that day with those moldy grapes, but we had passed an extraordinary day together under the brilliant Umbrian sun.

GRECHETTO DOC

*The grechetto vine was brought from Greece to Umbria—
now grechetto is the classic white grape in Umbria.*
—Remo Sportoletti, owner, Azienda Agricola Sportoletti,
Spello (Perugia)

Grechetto DOC is a varietal wine—the majority of the juice comes from one kind of white grape, grechetto. But throughout Umbria, this traditional varietal is often used in white blends. Some *bianco* DOC wines have a high percentage of grechetto; Montefalco Bianco DOC is one example, made with at least 50 percent of the grape. Some of Umbria's *spumante* (sparkling wine) has a high percentage of grechetto, such as those from Colli Perugini DOC, Colli del Trasimeno DOC, and Colli Altotiberini. Grechetto is an important grape in Umbria—but it isn't the wine that put Umbria on the world's wine map.

Winemaking: Grechetto DOC wines must be at least 85 percent grechetto.

DOC Production Areas: Colli del Trasimeno (area surrounding Lake Trasimeno), Colli Martani (near Torgiano, Montefalco, Todi, and Spoleto), Colli Perugini (south of Perugia), Colli Altotiberini (straddles the highway from Perugia to Città di Castello), Assisi (area surrounding Assisi).

How to Serve: Chilled but not ice-cold—46 to 53°F, slightly below cellar temperature. Drink young.

Tasting Notes: Golden straw color. Typically a full-bodied, dry crisp white wine. Aromatic—floral and tropical fruit on the nose. Flavors lean toward citrus, apples, pears, almonds, and vanilla.

Food Pairing: Cheese—Gorgonzola dolce, fresh or aged pecorino. Fish and seafood. Prosciutto, carpaccio. Pasta—Spaghetti Carbonara (page 22). Creamy Risotto (page 185). Soups—Farro Soup with Saffron and Garbanzo Bean Soup with Pasta (pages 179 and 170). Spring Garlic Frittata (page 157). Focaccia with Onions and Rosemary (page 17).

Cantina Chiorri—A Small Family Winery

On my first visit to Cantina Chiorri, I met with Monica Mariotti—the bright, well-educated (she studied business and law) great-granddaughter of the man who started the family winery. She has a very engaging manner—a big, beautiful smile and long, bouncy dark hair. When Monica espouses her family's philosophy of making good, distinctive wines, you can feel her passion and dedication, both to quality and tradition. The winery got its start when Monica's *bisnonno* (great-grandfather) made more *vino* than the family needed—he sold the extra wine to local restaurants.

The winery was still on the ground floor of the estate's *casa padronale* (owner's house) on that visit. Monica's mother, Franca, had grown up in the stone house with her sister, parents, and two unmarried aunts. The character of the house hasn't changed much in the more than one hundred years since it was built. On the second floor, the old kitchen has the original fireplace with a large hearth for cooking. A shelf above the fireplace displays antique kitchen vessels—terra-cotta jugs used to carry water, terra-cotta pots wrapped in wire used to simmer legumes over the fire. Two tall identical iron stands, each with a plate rack, are positioned on either side of the hearth. On cold days, the family put dinner plates on the stands and sat on the benches at the fireplace to eat, Franca explained.

During harvest several years later, Monica gave me a tour of the new winery that had been built across from the *casa padronale,* under the offices and the new entertainment terrace. She and I wandered around the shiny new temperature-controlled stainless tanks carrying a wineglass, tasting fermenting wines in the immaculate *cantina.* The four-day-old grechetto juice tasted crisp but sweet and fruity. The garnet-red cabernet sauvignon had been in the tank for twenty days, so it had almost finished fermentation—its sweetness had been replaced by a delicious fruitiness. Last we sipped a salmony pink *rosato* (rosé). "Yum, the *rosato* is really grapy—sweet," I said. "What's the varietal?"

"Sangiovese—picked late yesterday, so it still tastes like grape juice. We'll blend it with cabernet sauvignon," said Monica. "We use red grapes but make *rosato* like white wine. The grapes stay six to eight hours on the skins. When the color looks right, we remove the skins."

Next Monica and I drove out to the vineyards. What a picturesque scene! An ancient village crowned a distant hill. In the foreground, *ragazzi* (young men and women) walked among the grapevines in groups of four, laughing, talking, and picking grapes—carefully dropping the near-purple bunches into red plastic baskets. A couple of guys gently emptied the full baskets into a bin on a red tractor. There was one older worker, a lively middle-aged woman, her eyelids carefully brushed with baby-blue shadow, lips tinted red. The spry *signora* was working as hard—and having as much fun—as her younger counterparts.

"You remember my mother?" Monica said, introducing me to the woman who held a bucketful of Sangiovese grapes in one hand and shears in the other.

"Of course. *Buongiorno,* Franca."

"My mother likes to help at harvest," said Monica. "The *ragazzi* are fast, huh, Mamma? They can fill the tractor bin in thirty to forty minutes. Then we rush the grapes to the winery. The grapes are unloaded within forty-five to sixty minutes after harvest."

"Sounds like a record!" I said.

"The berries arrive at the winery whole, in good condition. And bacteria and microorganisms don't have time to get started." That's the advantage of having the estate's fifty acres of vineyards within minutes of the winery.

At another location, we bumped into Monica's father. He was walking up and down the vineyards, picking one berry every fifteen to twenty steps. Back at the winery, he would run a test to determine the sugar level. With that information, and his own judgment, he would decide when the grapes were ready to harvest. Monica handed me a grape to taste.

"When the seeds are green," she said, "the grapes are not mature. The seeds turn *neri* [black] when they are ready." The grape I bit into had dark seeds.

"Yes, these grapes are mature," her father said. "We'll probably pick this vineyard next."

The Chiorri family and workers spend a lot of time in the vineyards. When harvest is done, they will be back to work the land so it will hold winter's rain. "We never irrigate, even this year with all the new plants," Monica explained. "If you remove the surface roots, the roots are forced to grow deeper to get water—and down deep the soil is always moist."

To manage crop load, they do shoot pruning—by hand—and later, sometime between the middle and end of August, they send workers into the vineyards to "drop crop," reducing the number of bunches on each vine if necessary to balance the crop and improve fruit quality. At the same time, workers remove some of the leaves to reduce humidity and to give the grapes more sun exposure. "You have to work in the vineyards all year, without interruption, to grow good grapes," explained Monica. "Wine is a living thing. The grapes must be healthy and in good condition—all winemaking depends on the quality of the fruit."

On our last stop, each vine had only one bunch of purple grapes left on each cane (mature shoot)—and no leaves. I'd seen grapes drying on the vine before. The withered, sugary grapes were used to make sweet wine.

"I didn't know you made *passito* [dessert wine]," I said.

"It's our first vintage! We plan to pick in November, but it depends on the weather. Rain is best avoided—it encourages mold."

"The grapes must be really sweet by November."

"Not sweet enough—after picking, we dry them longer at the winery. The traditional method we're using requires patience. The grapes have their own schedule, you cannot force it."

A few nights later on a cool autumn evening, I sat with over forty other people in the cellar at Cantina Chiorri waiting for dinner to be served. Round tables and chairs had been set up among the cellar's wine-filled casks. The crowd was lively and young—the majority were university students who had spent the last several weeks harvesting grapes on the wine estate.

Suddenly everyone stood up to toast Monica's father, who had just joined us. The sound of clinking glasses and cheers, amplified by the cement, drowned out the toaster's words. Minutes later, when the *ragazzi* sitting near the doors saw Franca and Monica approaching with steaming platters, everyone jumped up and cheered and clapped louder than the last time. Mother and daughter carried the platters from table to table, serving each guest a bowl of hot penne with Franca's *sugo di carne* (meat sauce). Franca had enriched the *sugo* with beef marrowbones and lots of Chiorri grechetto (it's important to cook with good wine, she had said)—and then she layered the pasta with grated Parmigiano-Reggiano and Romano cheese. Monica's father kept the wine flowing—when he saw an empty pitcher, he filled it from the spout of a wooden cask.

Like Umbrian women had done for centuries, mother and daughter waited to eat until everyone had been served seconds. And of course, the women refused help—so just the two of them dashed back to the old farmhouse to get the next course—*torta al testo con salsiccia alla griglia* (griddle bread with grilled sausage). For dessert Franca and Monica served homemade *ciaramicola*—one of Umbria's traditional desserts, a dry white tube cake with an egg-white glaze decorated with tiny rainbow-colored sprinkles. Monica's father passed around *vinsanto*—Chiorri, of course.

Harvest parties like this one have probably happened every year since wine-making began on the property in the 1880s. The faces have changed, wine quality has increased, and production is far beyond what Monica's great-grandfather ever dreamed of when he sold wine to restaurants in Perugia.

ORVIETO CLASSICO DOC

The [dry] wine is sincere—complex but at the same time, it is light.
—Bernardo Barberani, Cantina Barberani, Orvieto

The roads that connect Orvieto, Todi, and Perugia today were main roads during Roman times. Even in antiquity, Roman kings and popes traveled to Orvieto seeking its famous white wines. Back then, Orvieto winemakers specialized in sweet wines. Although wineries still produce Orvieto Classico *amabile* (semisweet) or *dolce* (sweet), modern quaffers tend to prefer the *vino secco* (dry wine).

Orvieto wines have come a long way since Roman times—and have made great strides in the last twenty years. "We produce more elegant wines than before," said Bernardo Barberani. "Wineries in Umbria used to focus on quantity, but sometime in the 1980s quality became more important in Orvieto. Now each plant produces fewer grapes. As a result, the wines' aromas are more intense and the wines have more character." The Cantina Barberani—one of Orvieto's top producers—sits above the *superstrada* with views of Lake Corbara and the rolling hills, but you can also buy Orvieto wines at Enoteca Luigi Antonio Barberani near the duomo in historic Orvieto.

Winemaking: A blend of traditional grapes—procanico (trebbiano) and verdello, plus grechetto, malvasia, and/or drupeggio (canaiolo *bianco*).

How to Serve: Bring *secco* (dry) wine out of refrigerator 15 to 30 minutes before serving; 50 to 54°F temperatures are ideal. Serve *amabile* (semisweet) and late harvest (sweet/dessert) at about 46°F, just out of the refrigerator.

Tasting Notes: Dry: Light straw color. At its best—an elegant, silky mouthfeel and long finish. Aromatic, fruity, and floral in the nose. Crisp, tart apples and grapefruit flavors. *Amabile*: Sweet and fruity.

Must-Try Late Harvest: Barberani Calcaia Orvieto Classico Superiore DOC "Muffa Nobile" (botrytis). "The Romans loved this *dolce* [sweet] style of wine," said Bernardo. The grapes are picked in late November or early December. "The presence of the lake—the fog—helps this wine develop botrytis, noble rot [a fungus]." The botrytis intensifies the sweetness of the grapes to make this elegant, delicious wine, which is honey-sweet but not cloying. The wine is deep golden, almost orange in color.

Food Pairing: "Every dish has its favorite wine," Bernardo Barberani. *Secco*: Aperitif and sipping. Good with appetizers—crostini with tuna or cauliflower ("Crostini—Anything Goes!," page 68). Seafood, Fish with Fennel, and Roast Chicken (pages 222 and 14). Creamy Risotto (page 185). *Amabile*: aperitif, cheese, Liver Pâté (page 66). Late-harvest wines, such as Calcaia, pair with aged cheese and desserts— Vanilla Cream, Biscotti, Anise Wine Cookies, Umbrian Yellow Cake (pages 289, 55, 174 and 341).

HANGING IN THE ATTIC

If you have ever dunked biscotti into an amber-colored wine when dining in Umbria or Tuscany, you have probably quaffed *vinsanto* (holy wine)—it is offered at the end of most special meals.

"*Vinsanto* is the wine of friendship and hospitality," said Eugenio Bistarelli. Eugenio is probably one of the Upper Tiber River valley's most ardent (but small) *vinsanto* producers.

"In Umbria, hospitality is very important," he added.

"Isn't hospitality a big part of being Italian?" I asked.

"No, hospitality isn't as important everywhere in Italy."

Eugenio learned to make this holy wine from his father, who was taught by his father. In the past, families made their own *vinsanto* to serve at Christmas, Easter, harvest, *carnevale,* and other special occasions. "*Vinsanto* is more than a dessert wine," said Eugenio. "The wine has particular significance for friendship and generosity—and it is a wine of meditation."

Eugenio and his wife, Adele, make *vinsanto* in *la soffitta* (the attic) of their stone farmhouse called La Consuma, outside Pistrino near the Tuscan border. About a quarter of the third-floor attic is devoted to the *vinsantaia* (*vinsanto* winery). As part of their bed-and-breakfast, they rent out the bedrooms that share the same floor. The second floor has more B&B rooms, plus Eugenio and Adele's living quarters. The *piano terra* used to have stalls for the many farm animals that worked the land, but part of the space was used to dry tobacco and make wine. Today Eugenio and Adele use the *piano terra* for entertaining and for drying grapes to make *vinsanto*. Although much of the house is original, the couple had to do extensive restoration and remodeling. When they bought the house in 1981, it had been abandoned for twenty years.

"The house was crumbling," said Adele.

"The farmhouse is *molto antica* [very ancient]," added Eugenio. "It appears on a local map from the sixteen hundreds."

They left the original wood ladder-style stairs to the attic—but added a modern handrail. They left untouched the old stone fireplace, black from centuries of smoky fires.

"When we bought the house," said Eugenio, "it didn't have heat, electric lights, or running water."

"*Che fatica* [how exhausting]!" said Adele, "carrying water upstairs to the house. We kept the original kitchen sink but added a faucet for running water."

Back when the last *contadina* family lived at La Consuma, the Italian sharecropping system (*mezzadria*) was still in effect. The sharecroppers worked the land and split the crops with the landowner.

"Originally the majority of the crops went to the *padrone* [landowner]—the *contadini* got a smaller share," explained Eugenio. "The relationship between the *contadini* and the *padrone* was very strict. The first question the *padrone* asked a prospective tenant farmer was 'How many in your family?' He wanted strong grown children." Peasant farming required many hands, so families tended to be large. "There were twenty-two people living here," said Eugenio. "Perhaps the house was called La Consuma because there were so many of them. They must have consumed a lot."

Back then there was a lot of poverty. The farmers worked hard but had just enough to survive. Finally the crop split changed to fifty-fifty, and by the

1960s, the sharecropping system ended. At that time, many farmers ended up with the land, but a lot of families moved on.

When I drove up to La Consuma in late September to help with the grape harvest, Adele and Eugenio had just returned home after picking up their grandson Michele. That morning he had begged them to pick him up early from preschool to help harvest grapes. The four of us immediately left La Consuma to drive to the vineyards, about ten minutes away in nearby Tuscany. When we met the other helpers on the hilltop vineyard, Eugenio gave us instructions—for my benefit, I am sure. The rest of them knew what to do, including four-year-old Michele.

"The berries must be dry and healthy," said Eugenio. "No withered or moldy fruit. Ripe, but not too ripe. Pick only the best grapes."

We watched as Eugenio cut off a juicy bunch and handled it like fragile crystal, carefully placing it in his basket.

"When your basket is full," he said, "gently transfer one bunch at a time to a bin. But be careful not to rupture the grapes or let the bunches get tangled together."

We each grabbed a basket and headed down the steep vineyard to start work. Michele trotted alongside his grandfather. He never whined or complained about being too hot or about having to carry his own basket. He was an enthusiastic, even-tempered worker. And he was productive! "*Guarda* [look]," he shouted joyfully whenever he found a particularly large bunch of grapes.

Michele wasn't the only one having fun. "Families and friends have always gotten together to help, so picking has never seemed like work," said Eugenio.

"But when we were young," said Adele, "picking grapes used to be a lot harder. The grapevines were trained to grow up *oppio* trees [field maples]. We carried a heavy ladder around and then hooked a basket to a rung on the ladder to hold the grapes we collected."

"But even with a ladder, it was hard to reach the grapes," added Eugenio. "The vines spread way out and grew high up in the trees."

"And remember the wooden bins?" said Adele. "They were big and heavy— they held about a hundred pounds of grapes." The modern plastic bins we used that day were light by comparison—they held just thirty-six pounds of grapes.

In about one hour, the six of us had filled fifteen bins with grapes. While we waited for the vineyard owner to weigh the harvest, we sat under a large shade tree. From Eugenio's tailgate, Adele passed out slices of homemade *torcolo* (yellow cake) and plastic glasses of *vinsanto*.

"*Torcolo* and *vinsanto*," said Eugenio, "have always been the reward for hard work. In the past, when the workers gathered a hundred *chilogrammi* [2,200 pounds] of grain, they took a break to drink *vinsanto* and eat *torcolo*."

Back at La Consuma, Adele and I squatted over the bins on the ground, hooking one at a time onto an electric pulley. From the third-floor window in the attic, Eugenio and Michele guided the bins on their precarious journey up to the *vinsantaia*. When all fifteen bins had been brought through the attic window, Eugenio asked me to put two bunches of grapes on each of the *cappie* (loops of string used to hang grapes). He told me it was important to hang one bunch lower than the other so the air could circulate around the grapes. When I had balanced two bunches on the loop, I handed it to Eugenio to hang from a nail in the ceiling. It was my job to make sure the grapes were clean and undamaged. I set aside any bunches with visible damage—Eugenio would hand-pluck the bad grapes and dry the rest on the *cannucci* (mats), where he would be able to easily check the grapes for mold or rot. It took us several hours to hang the grapes. And what a sight—a ceiling covered with rose-tinged green bunches of grapes!

"The attic is a good place to dry grapes," explained Eugenio. "To wilt, the grapes need an airy, dry place—above a kitchen with a fireplace, and a window is also ideal. The grapes need to be accessible so you can check them frequently."

After we finished in the *vinsantaia*, Adele and Michele showed me how to make *il torcolo* while Eugenio prepared the antipasto—slices of the home-made sausage (dried and preserved in olive oil), sliced fresh figs, slices of pecorino cheese, and skewers of cherry tomatoes with tiny mozzarella balls. After we ate the antipasto, Adele served homemade nutmeg-scented cappelletti in a rich beef broth. The second course was delicious—sliced veal roast and sausage accompanied by chard sautéed in olive oil with garlic. After dinner, Adele cut the *torcolo* into thick slices. "Typically, *torcolo* is a dry cake," Adele explained.

"I like it dry," said Eugenio.

"Because it's better for dunking in *vinsanto*?" I asked.

"That might be so," said Adele, "but the cake lasts longer if it doesn't start out so dry."

"*Mmmm,* but your *torcolo* is moist," I said. "I like it this way." I dipped a piece of *torcolo* into the glass of amber holy wine. "And it's great dunked in *vinsanto*."

Before I left La Consuma, we made plans for me to return in three months.

During this period, called the *appassimento dell'uva* (the wilting of the grape), Eugenio would keep a close eye on the grapes, picking out any that didn't look good. And in January, he would teach me the Umbrian art of making *vinsanto*, as Eugenio's father had taught him, and his grandfather before him.

Umbrian Yellow Cake
Torcolo
∞

Torcolo is one of Umbria's most traditional desserts. Like most Umbrian baked goods, it is on the dry side—dry for dunking in vinsanto *dessert wine! The cake is reminiscent of American pound cake, but it is not as rich or as fine-textured. A hint of lemon zest and* vinsanto *gives it character. "In the past, we didn't have tube pans," said Adele, "so we floured and buttered a glass and put it in the center of a round baking pan—that's how we got a hole in the middle of the cake." Adele bakes the cake in the traditional way, in a wood-burning oven.*

For variety, my friend Gabriella adds 1/2 cup of raisins and 3/4 cup of chopped walnuts to the dry ingredients.

Yield: *10 to 12 servings*

2 tablespoons melted butter for the pan

3 cups plus 3 tablespoons (14 ounces) all-purpose flour plus more for the pan

2 teaspoons double-acting baking powder

Finely shredded zest of 1 lemon (see "About Zest," page 37)

4 large eggs

1 large egg yolk

1 1/2 cups (10 1/2 ounces) sugar plus 1 1/2 tablespoons for the top

1/3 cup very soft butter

1/2 cup milk

1/3 cup *vinsanto* or Marsala wine

You'll also need: A Bundt or tube pan (about 15-cup volume/10×4 inches).

Getting started: Preheat the oven to 350°C. Brush the inside of the Bundt pan with the melted butter; sprinkle flour inside the pan to cover it well. Tap the upside-down pan on a board to get rid of excess flour.

1. Toss together the flour, baking powder, and lemon zest in a medium bowl; set aside. Separate the eggs—put the 4 yolks plus the additional yolk into a large mixer bowl; set aside. Put the 4 whites into a medium mixer bowl; beat to form stiff peaks. Set aside.

2. Add the 1½ cups sugar to the reserved egg yolks; beat with an electric mixer on medium low until fluffy and pale yellow, about 2 minutes—scraping the sides of the bowl as needed. (Alternatively, beat by hand with a wooden spoon.)

3. Add the soft butter. Beat until smooth, about 2 minutes—scraping the bowl once or twice. Add half of the dry ingredients, half of the milk, and half of the wine. Mix a few seconds on the lowest speed; beat on medium low for 5 seconds. Scrape the sides of the bowl; add the remaining dry ingredients, milk, and *vinsanto*. Beat on the lowest speed for 5 seconds. Scrape the sides of the bowl; beat on medium low for about 30 seconds.

4. Add the reserved egg whites; stir with a wooden spoon until the whites are just mixed in. Spoon the batter into the prepared Bundt pan; sprinkle the remaining 1½ tablespoons sugar over the top. Tap the pan on the counter 5 or 6 times to help remove air bubbles.

5. Bake until a toothpick inserted in the center comes out clean, about 40 minutes. Turn off the oven; leave the cake in the oven for an additional 15 minutes (20 minutes for a drier cake). Transfer the pan to a wire rack; cool 15 minutes. Run a silicone spatula around the edges of the pan. Put the wire rack on top of the pan; invert the pan to transfer the cake to the rack. Let cool. ❧

Making Holy Wine

The year I went to the Bistarellis' to learn about *vinsanto,* the grapes finished their *appassimento* (wilting) in a little more than two months, instead of the usual three. So I returned to La Consuma the first week in December. Just as he did the day we picked grapes, Eugenio took his post on the ladder. This time he lifted the grape bunches off the nails in the ceiling and handed them down to Adele, his grandson Michele, or me. The three of us put the grapes into bins. We had them down in no time—they were lighter and less bulky now. During harvest, the Bistarellis had hung twelve bins of grapes in the ground-floor room. After the *appassimento*, there were less than five bins.

"When the grapes are withered and sweet, they are ready to press," said Eugenio, handing me a grape to taste. "If they look like raisins, they have gone too far."

We carried the bins to *la soffitta* (the attic), on the third floor. The first step would be to feed the grapes into the machine to crush and destem the bunches.

"Our old machine only crushed the grapes," said Adele. "We had to remove the stems by hand."

"And years before the *macchina*," said Eugenio, "we crushed the grapes with our feet in large wooden tubs."

Eugenio and Adele dumped one bin of grapes into the crusher at a time. Adele pushed the grapes toward the chute that led to the two ribbed wheels that crushed the grapes and moved them to the bin below. Eugenio turned the hand crank that worked the crusher's wheels. When the machine was filled with grapes, he had a difficult time turning the crank. Michele wanted Eugenio's job, but he couldn't budge the crank.

"I put the *grappoli* [bunches] through the crusher twice," said Eugenio, "because if the berries don't get broken, the *torchio* [press] will not extract the juice. Pressing dried grapes requires patience because they are not really juicy like fresh grapes are."

Eugenio carried the twice-crushed bin of grapes across the room to the press, and Adele put a bucket under the *torchio* to collect the juice. She used a big plastic pitcher to scoop the grapes into the *torchio*. When Eugenio and Adele went back to crush another bin of grapes, Michele dragged a chair to the side of the *torchio*. Eugenio had given him a large wooden paddle and had instructed him to press the grapes with it. Michele stayed at the *torchio*, smashing grapes with the paddle, until his grandparents had crushed all five bins of grapes.

When Eugenio finished at the destemmer, he joined his grandson at the press. Michele watched his grandfather's every move. But suddenly the four-year-old changed his focus—he ran to the front of the *torchio*. He stood with his eyes glued to the empty bucket underneath. The moment he saw a few drops of milky brown grape juice rolling toward the bucket, he dashed off. When he returned, he collected the now steady flow of juice in a plastic cup. He drank the must (grape juice) with gusto. When he was done, his eyes twinkled, and he wore a big smile. He filled another cup and offered it to me.

"Wow, that is really sweet and concentrated," I said.

"After the *appassimento*," Eugenio said, "the juice should be more than thirty percent sugar."

Eugenio used the wooden paddle to encourage the flow of juice, and then he put weights on the *torchio* to press down on the grapes. At first it took very little effort to swing the *torchio*'s long handle to compress the grapes, but soon it was almost impossible to turn.

"This forty-year-old *torchio* requires time and patience," said Eugenio, "but it is better than the new machines—they are too fast. If I let it rest, the juice will start to flow again and it will be easier to turn. My father used to press the grapes after dinner. We would play cards. Every now and then he would get up to work the *torchio*."

Later that night, Eugenio would put the must directly into *caratelli* (eight- to twenty-gallon wood barrels) with the *madre* wine, and seal the opening in the top of the barrel with putty. The wine would ferment and age untouched over the next three years.

"The *madre* is the sediment left in the bottom of the *caratello* after the wine is siphoned off," said Eugenio. "You must have *madre* wine—also called the *morchia*—to make *vinsanto*. The mother wine ensures consistency in flavor from year to year."

New wood is never used to make *vinsanto*—it would add too much flavor. Instead, winemakers use old barrels that do not impart wood flavor. The type of wood is also important. Oak and chestnut are common because they are relatively neutral in flavor and these woods also have the ideal porosity for air exchange, which is important in making *vinsanto*.

The *caratelli* are filled no more than 80 percent full to allow room for fermentation. Usually controlled temperatures are critical in winemaking, but for *vinsanto*, fluctuating temperatures are an essential.

"The room's temperature is important in making *vinsanto*," said Eugenio. "At first, in autumn, fermentation is slow, but in the spring when the weather warms up, it is tumultuous. By summer, the *caratello* is filled with carbon dioxide—and fermentation stops. In the fall, fermentation starts up again but it slows when winter comes. The cycle of fermentation continues, but each time it is slower until it stops completely. Slowly the sediments fall to the bottom, and the wine clarifies itself, naturally. We don't need to filter it."

The last step in making *vinsanto* is called *la spillatura*—the opening of the wooden barrels after a three-year wait. Eugenio and Adele usually have a big party in March to celebrate the new release. They invited me to come back for *la spillatura*. *Magari* (I wish)! With luck, I told them, I would make it.

VINSANTO—UMBRIA'S HOLY WINE

It takes a lot of time, a lot of passion—and nothing added. That's what it takes to make good vinsanto.
—Eugenio Bistarelli, *vinsanto* winemaker, La Soffitta

Vinsanto is Umbria's celebratory dessert wine. There are many stories about the origin of the wine's name. Some suggest that monks may have used the wine to heal the sick—those cured would have declared the wine a miracle, *un santo* (saint). Others suspect that because various winemaking processes take place during religious holidays, the wine became known as holy wine. No one knows for sure.

Winemaking: *Vinsanto* is usually made from Umbria's local white grapes—trebbiano toscano, canaiolo *bianco,* malvasia, grechetto, and vernaccia. Some winemakers add a small percentage of red grapes, too. *Vinsanto* is sometimes (rarely) made exclusively from red grapes— then the wine is called *occhio di pernice*. After harvest, the grapes dry for about three months before pressing. The wine ferments and ages for several years in small wood barrels called *caratelli*. Umbrian, *vinsanto* tends to be sweeter than the *vinsanto* made in Tuscany.

How to Serve: Cellar temperature—57°F—is ideal. Colder temperatures mask its flavor. Store open bottles in the cellar for up to one month.

Tasting Notes: Deep golden to amber color. Flavors and aromas range from honey to caramel to apricots to dried fruit to nuts. From semisweet to sweet, rich to almost syrupy.

Food Pairing: This dessert wine is for sipping and dunking—perfect with any of Umbria's traditional dry desserts. Umbrian Yellow Cake (page 341), Jam Tart (page 53), Almond-Orange Biscotti or Anise Wine Cookies (pages 55 and 174). Apple Strudel or Amaretti Cake (pages 320 or 165). *Vinsanto* is also good at the end of the meal with moderately aged pecorino cheese.

Castello della Sala's Italian-style Chardonnay

Antinori's award-winning winery Castello della Sala, not far from Orvieto near the Tuscan border, has turned many American and Italian wine critics' attention toward Umbria. The winery's IGT barrel-fermented darling, Cervaro della Sala, is considered one of Italy's best white wines. The primary grape, chardonnay, is blended with Umbria's most classic white grape, grechetto, to make a complex, aromatic wine with long-aging potential. A lovely crisp wine with citrus, apples, pineapple, and a hint of mineral. A floral nuance in the nose.

A Guide to Umbria's Wine Words

This short glossary includes some of the basic words you might need to know during your travels—armchair or actual—in Umbria.

abboccato (ahb-boh-KAH-toh): Slightly sweet.

amabile (ah-MAH-bee-leh): Semisweet, on the sweet side. Sometimes appears on the label.

amaro (ah-MAH-roh): Bitter.

annata (ahn-NAH-tah): Vintage date.

appassimento (ahp-pahs-see-MEHN-toh): Wilting of grapes to intensify sweetness before pressing. A technique used for making dessert wine such as *vinsanto* and *passito*.

assaggio (ahs-SAHJ-joh): Tasting.

azienda agricola (ah-ZYEHN-dah-ah-gree-KOH-lah): Wine estate.

barrique (bahr-REE-keh): A small 50- to 60-gallon oak barrel. In Umbria, small barrels have not been used in traditional winemaking. Many IGT (nontraditional) wines are aged in barrels.

bianco (bee-YAHN-koh): White. Generic name used on labels for a white blend.

bicchiere (bee-KYEA-reh): Glass. The influential Italian wine publication *Gabbero Rosso* rates wines using a wineglass icon. *Tre bicchieri* (three glasses) is the highest rating.

botte (BOHT-teh): A huge wooden cask, in the five-hundred-gallon range. Used for aging traditional Italian wines. Unlike small barrels, *botti* impart little or no wood flavor.

bottìglia (boht-TEE-lyah): Bottle.

bottiglierìa (boht-tee-lyeh-REE-ah): Wine shop.

caratello (kahr-ah-TEHL-loh): A small wood barrel. *Vinsanto* is aged in *caratelli* that range in size from eight to twenty gallons.

cavatappi (kah-vah-TAHP-pee): Corkscrew.

degustazione (deh-goos-tah-ZEEOH-neh): Tasting. *Degustazine di vino*: wine tasting.

digestivo (dee-gehs-TEE-voh): Liqueur served after meals—reputed to aid digestion. Often medicinal and bitter tasting.

dolce (DOHL-cheh): Sweet.

enoteca (eh-noh-TEH-kah): Wine shop.

etichetta (eh-tee-KEHT-tah): Label.

fattorìa (faht-toh-REE-ah): Farm.

frizzante (freet-ZAHN-teh): Sparkling.

fruttato (fruut-TAH-toh): Fruity.

grappa (GRAHP-pah): A distilled high-alcohol drink made from grape skins, seeds, and stems leftover from winemaking.

invecchiamento (een-vehk-keeah-MEHN-toh): Aging.

limoncello (lee-mohn-CHEHL-loh): Lemon-flavored liqueur.

mosto (MOHS-toh): Must—the juice from wine grapes—used to make wine. Sometimes must includes grape skins, pulp, and seeds.

nero (NEH-roh): Literally "black," but also used to refer to red wine.

novello (noh-VEHL-loh): Young wine that is consumed shortly after harvest. Also called *vino nuovo* (VEE-noh-nuu-OH-voh).

passito (pahs-SEE-toh): A sweet wine made from grapes dried on mats or hung until semidry.

podere (poh-DEHR-eh): Farm.

riserva (ree-SEHR-vah): A reserve wine that exceeds DOC or DOCG requirements, often by aging the wine longer.

rosato (roh-SAH-toh): Rosé.

rosso (ROHS-soh): Red. Generic name used on labels for a red blend.

secco (SEHK-koh): Dry.

sollucchero (sohl-luuk-KHE-roh): An Umbrian cherry-flavored liqueur. Sour *visciole* cherries ferment with red wine, or sour cherries steep in pure alcohol and red wine, and then are mixed with simple syrup.

spumante (spuu-MAHN-teh): Sparkling wine.

tappo (TAHP-poh): Cork.

tenuta (teh-NU-tah): Farm, estate.

vendemmia (vehn-DEHM-myah): Harvest, vintage date.

vigna (VEE-nyah): Vineyard.

vino (VEE-noh): The Italian word for wine.

vinsanto (veen-SAHN-toh): Holy wine, also *vino santo*. An aromatic, amber-colored semisweet to sweet dessert wine made from semidried local white grapes.

visner (VEES-ner): See *sollucchero*.

RESOURCES

This section is to assist you in finding Umbrian products and information about the region. Restaurants, lodging, wineries, festivals, and some of the artisans mentioned in the book are also listed. There are many other wonderful restaurants, inns, and places to visit in Umbria, but those are outside the scope of this cookbook.

Please note that because I have not purchased goods from all of the websites listed, nor stayed at all of the hotels, inns, and bed-and-breakfasts included, I cannot endorse them.

Note: When calling from the USA to Italy, add 011-39 before the number and # after dialing the entire number (# speeds up the call).

SHOPPING IN UMBRIA

- **Fresh pasta:** Rasgnolo. Excellent cappelletti (buy the tiny ones), ravioli, fresh sheets of pasta for cannelloni and lasagne—and more. Via Martiri della Libertà, Umbertide (near the modern church).

- **Artisan butcher shop:** 2M Centro Carni (Chapter 6). Fresh meat, house-cured meats, and house-made sausages. Via Martiri della Libertà, 5, Umbertide.

- **Truffles:** Tartufi Bianconi, Loc. Santo Stefano del Piano, 21, Badiali, Città di Castello. Phone: 075.851.1591. www.tartufibianconi.it.

- **Linens:** Sposini, Tessuti Umbri. Tablecloths, runners, napkins in rustic old-world Umbrian designs. Strada Marscianese, S. Valentino della Collina (near Perugia). Phone: 075.878.4134. www.tessutiumbri.it. Sposini is near Chiorri Winery, so if you go to one, visit the other.

- **Linens:** Tessuti di Montefalco. Beautiful linens in ancient patterns. Via Ringhiera Umbra, 25, Montefalco (in front of the Museo di San Francesco). Phone: 0742.378.119. Also locations in Perugia (075.572.6565), Spello (0742.301.870), and Todi (075.894.3785).

- **Olive oil:** Marfuga. Modern olive press and showroom/sales. Viale Firenze, Campello sul Clitunno. Phone: 0743.521.338. www.marfuga.it.

- **Olive oil:** Azienda Agraria Clarici. Ring the bell to buy oil. Via Garibaldi, 144, Foligno. Phone: 0742.340.788. www.olioclarici.it.

- **Jewelry:** Burzigotti. Via Garibaldi, 70, Umbertide.

- **Ceramics:** Deruta Placens. Owned by Novella Nicolini (Chapter 6). Centro storico (historic downtown), Via Biordo Michelotti, 25, Deruta. Phone: 075.972.4027.

- **Ceramics:** Antonio Margaritelli. Via Tiberina, Deruta. Phone: 075.971.1572.

- **Ironwork:** Artigianato Ferro Artistico di Tonino Scavizzi. Via Baldassini, 22, Gubbio. Phone: 075.927.5461.

Shopping Online

- **Perugina Chocolate Baci:** www.tasteitaly.com (click Our Store>Grocery Store>cookies).

- **Squab:** www.squab.com.

- **Wafer paper:** www.cakeartsupplies.com. Phone: 415.456.7773; www.wineandcake.com (search for wafer paper).

- **Italian food products:** www.agferrari.com; www.buonitalia.com (truffles, Italian rice, pecorino toscano, ricotta salata); www.ansonmills.com (polenta, farro); www.dibruno.com. (truffle products, lentils, pecorino, and cured meats); www.urbanitrufflesonline.com (truffles).

- **Saffron:** www.saffron.com.

- **Green garlic:** www.veggiegardeningtips.com/baby-garlic.

- **Seeds from Italy:** www.growitalian.com.

- **Wine:** www.snooth.com; www.wineaccess.com (search Umbria).

Food Information and Recipes

- **www.suzannecarreiro.com** (travel tips, custom tours, recipes, classes, photos).

- **www.zafferanodicascia.com** (saffron).

- **www.italianmade.com** (Italian Trade Commission).

- **www.gamberorosso.it/en** (food, wine, and travel magazine).

- **www.lacucinaitalianamagazine.com.**

- **www.alice.tv** (Italian television site).

- **www.montereybayaquarium.org/cr/seafoodwatch.aspx** (best seafood choices).

About Umbria

- **www.english.regioneumbria.eu** (in Italian, www.regioneumbria.eu).

- **www.umbriatourism.com.**

- **www.borghitalia.it** (guide to the most beautiful Italian villages).

- **http://english.umbriadoc.com** (in Italian, www.umbriadoc.com).

- **www.parks.it/parco.trasimeno/Eindex.html** (Lake Trasimeno).

- **www.tipicamenteumbria.it** (in Italian).

Festivals

- **Region by region:** www.sagreinitalia.it (in Italian).

- **Foligno's Quintana:** www.quintana.it.

- **Gubbio's *Ceri*:** www.ceri.it.

- **Cannara's Onion Festival:** www.festadellacipolla.com (in Italian).

- ***Infiorate* (flower art festivals):** www.infioratespello.it (Spello) and www.infioritalia.org (in Italian); info@iat.cascia.pg.it or 0743.71147 (Castelluccio).

- **Umbertide's Feste di Settembre:** www.comune.umbertide.pg.it (click Eventi e Cultura>"Fratta di fine Ottocento") (in Italian).

- **Montefalco's Wine Week:** www.english.montefalcodoc.it.

PLACES TO STAY

- **Umbertide:** (Romeggio): This property, next door to where I stayed to write my book, is owned by Fabrizio Ramaccioni, a cousin of my "adopted" Umbrian family. Beautiful grounds and pool with views of Umbertide. www.casaledegliolmi.com.

- **Montefalco** (outside): Casale Satriano (owned by Antonelli winery). www.satriano.it.

- **Località Acqua Santo Stefano** (above Foligno): Agriturismo Borgo La Torre (owned by Rita, Chapter 6). www.borgolatorre.com.

- **Localita' Cerreto** (Baschi, near Orvieto): Agriturismo Barberani. www.barberani.it.

- **Umbria:** www.umbriahomes.com, www.umbriasi.com.

PLACES TO EAT AND STAY

- **Perugia** (outside): Il Covone (Francesca, Chapter 9). www.covone.com.

- **Montesperello di Magione:** Relais Il Cantico della Natura (Monia, Chapter 3). www.ilcanticodellanatura.it.

- **Montefalco:** Villa Pambuffetti. www.villapambuffetti.com.

- **Montone:** Locanda del Capitano. www.ilcapitano.com.

- **Torgiano:** Le Tre Vaselle (hotel) and Le Melograne (restaurant). Owned by Lungarotti Winery. www.3vaselle.it.

- **Spello:** La Bastiglia: Piazza Valle Gloria, 7, Spello. www.labastiglia.com.

PLACES TO EAT

- **Città di Castello** (in Italian): Caffè Accademia (Mirko, Paola, Patrizio, Chapter 7). Phone: 075.852.3120. www.caffeaccademia.com.

- **Perugia** (outside): Castello di Monterone and *ristorante* Il Postale (Marco, Chapter 7, moved from Città di Castello in February 2010 to this beautiful castle). www.castellomonterone.com. Restaurant phone: 075.852.1356; general phone: 075.572.4214.

- **Norcia:** La Cantina de Norsia (Camillo and Daniella, Chapter 7). Via Dante, 25. Phone: 0743.816.395.

- **Città di Castello:** Trattoria Pizzeria Roma: Via Mario Angeloni, 2. Phone: 075.855.3560.

WINERIES AND WINE

- **Adanti (Bevagna):** www.cantineadanti.com.

- **Antonelli–San Marco** (Montefalco): www.antonellisanmarco.it.

- **Arnaldo Caprai** (Montefalco): www.arnaldocaprai.it.

- **Barberani-Vallesanta** (Baschi): www.barberani.it.

- **Bigi** (Orvieto): www.cantinebigi.it.

- **Castello della Sala** (Ficulle): www.antinori.it.

- **Chiorri** (Sant'Enea): www.chiorri.it (see Linens: Sposini, page 352).

- **Còlpetrone** (Gualdo Cattaneo): www.colpetrone.it.

- **Falesco** (Montecchio): www.falesco.it.

- **La Carraia** (Orvieto): www.lacarraia.it.

- **La Soffitta** (Pistrino): www.vinsantolasoffitta.it.

- **Lungarotti** (Torgiano): www.lungarotti.it.

- **Palazzone** (Orvieto): www.palazzone.com.

- **Sportoletti** (Spello): www.sportoletti.com.

- **Wineglass guide:** www.wineglassguide.com.

- **Wine tourism:** www.stradadelsagrantino.it.

ONLINE REFERENCES

- **Time in Italy:** www.worldtimeserver.com (click Current Times>Italy).

- **Food glossary** (in Italian): www.alimentipedia.it/Alimenti_Glossario.html.

- **Money conversion:** www.xe.com/ucc.

- **Translations:** http://babelfish.yahoo.com.

- **Measurement conversions:** www.onlineconversion.com.

- **Wine dictionary** (in Italian): www.agricamping.it/agricamping-vino/dizionario-enologico-a.htm.

- **Italian/English dictionary:** www.wordreference.com.

- **Useful phrases for dining out:** www.talktalk.co.uk/reference/phrases/italian/data/eatingout.html.

PHOTO CAPTIONS

Jacket   Vincenzo, the truffle hunter, and his dogs return to the car after hunting for truffles.

Title page   Vincenzo's dogs digging for truffles.

Page xvii   Coming into the town of Umbertide from my apartment in the countryside of Romeggio.

Page 1   Paola with her granddaughter Giulia at age six months.

Page 40   Michela, Giulia, Mario, and my son, Jacob, hanging out in the Tuscan town of Sansepolcro.

Page 62   Michela's mother, Bruna, cracks eggs onto a mound of flour to make fresh pasta.

Page 106   Melchiorre rices steaming hot potatoes to make gnocchi.

Page 143   Eleven-year-old-cook Alberto presents the ravioli he just prepared for me.

Page 168   Marco and Stefano from 2M Carne in Umbertide stand with the just-out-of-the-oven *porchetta* (roasted pork).

Page 209   Chef/owner of *ristorante* Il Postale pipes a rich *fonduta* (cheese) filling onto pasta to make *tortelli*.

Page 243   Handmade *ravioloni* (large ravioli), ready to cook or freeze.

Page 274   A close-up of the statue of Gubbio's patron saint, Ubaldo, taken during the famous *Ceri* race.

Page 304   Four-year-old Michele mixes batter to make *il torcolo*, a traditional Umbrian cake.